WALKING NEW YORK

WALKING NEW YORK

MANHATTAN HISTORY ON FOOT

WRITTEN BY

KEITH TAILLON

Quadrille

CONTENTS

WALKING THE WALK

This is not a conventional New York City guidebook. There are endless options out there for those readers looking for a list of the city's most popular tourist destinations or this season's hottest new bars and restaurants. Instead, over the course of a dozen walking routes, this book aims to imbue readers with the ability to peel back the layers of the New York City streetscape and see Manhattan not just as it is, but as it once was. It is a study and celebration of the people and places which make New York so important and incomparable. In essence, this book is my attempt to let you view the cityscape through my eyes.

My name is Keith Taillon, and I am a New York City historian and walking tour guide. With university degrees in History and Urban Planning, I have been studying this city for many years, poring over old maps, census records, newspapers, and library archives trying to piece together the fragments of its story. I share my findings on Instagram as *@KeithYorkCity* and have led thousands of guests on hundreds of walking tours, sharing my knowledge and understanding with anyone willing to listen. When I began leading walking tours in 2021, I went out of my way to tell the stories of New York in a way that felt fresh. I didn't want to add more of the same to the din of the New York City tourism industry. My tours are more like moving seminars, delving into the complexities of urban social, architectural, infrastructural, and cultural history.

Over time, my work has attracted a loyal following, for which I am endlessly grateful. But what has been most surprising and gratifying is that most of my tour customers today are locals, whether born-and-bred New Yorkers or longtime transplants who have earned the right to call themselves such. I recognize that it is not easy to convince New Yorkers to spend hours of their day walking around listening to someone tell them about their own city. That they do in such ample numbers tells me that I have tapped into something unique and valuable in my research and storytelling, something that even the most confident, jaded New Yorker can benefit from and enjoy.

Manhattan is an island built for walking. From the narrow canyons of the Financial District to the hilly expanses of Inwood, its sidewalks crisscross innumerable invisible barriers of language, culture, tradition, and fortune. The benign drama of countless lives has played out on its blocks, behind its walls, in its parks, and beneath its streets. Perhaps no city in human history has grown quite so quickly, in quite such breathtaking fashion, as New York. Its rise has rather neatly coincided with the emergence of modernity itself: from the industrial revolution and the global economy to the rise of rail, electricity, and skyscrapers, New York has always stood at the forefront of humanity's progress.

From its establishment as a colonial outpost in the 17th century through 400 years of madcap growth, New York's history is laid bare in its streetscape and architecture. Founded at the very southern tip of Manhattan Island, New York's footprint pushed northward over time as its fortunes improved and its population expanded. Throughout its history, every inch of Manhattan has been built up and rebuilt again and again as need dictates and technology allows. Understanding the complexities of this growth and change allows the well-informed pedestrian to see through the modern streetscape and catch glimpses of the past.

Though I began writing this book in 2023, it is the culmination of a lifetime of research. I have logged countless hours walking an untold number of miles trying to better see and understand this city. This is a guidebook for sightseers hoping to better contextualize the city's built environment, for locals curious about the nuts and bolts of their hometown, and for anyone who may never even visit New York, but who longs to make sense of one of the greatest cities in the world.

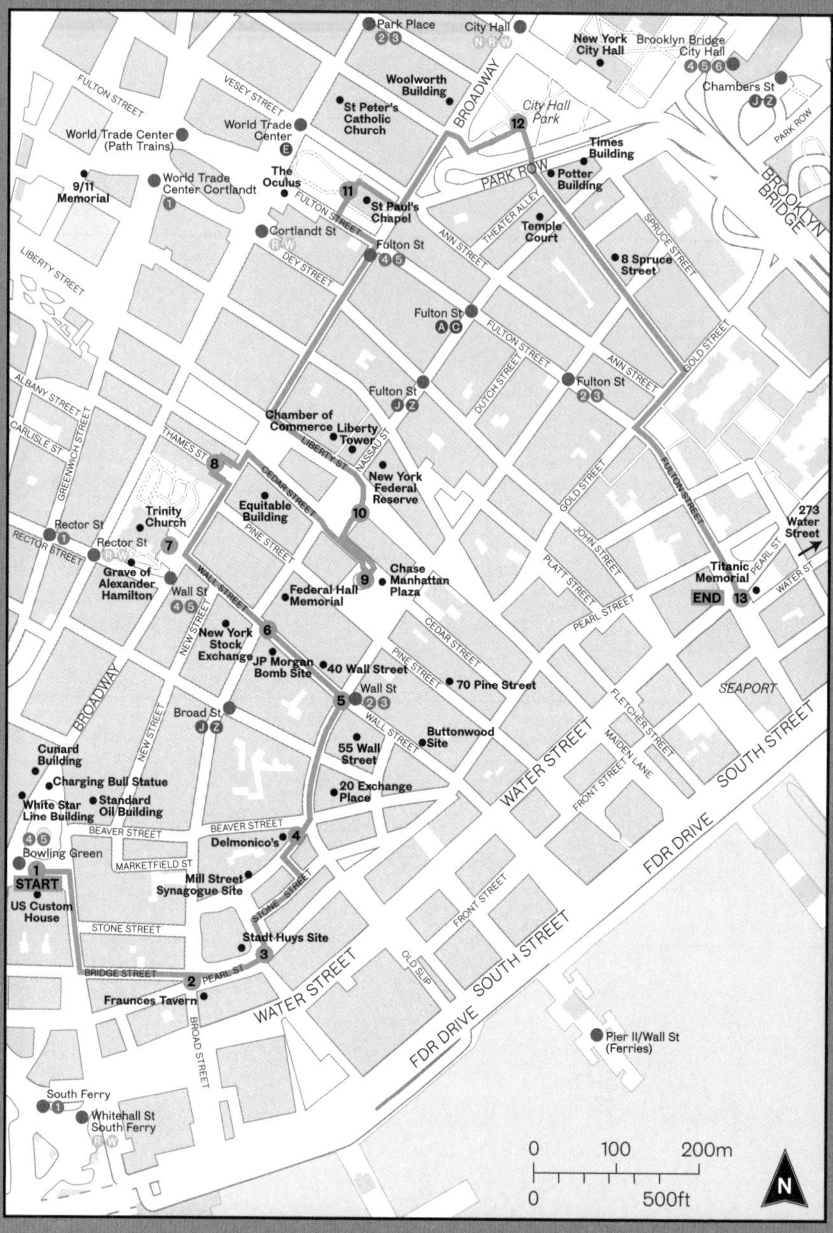

Park Place
City Hall
New York City Hall
Brooklyn Bridge City Hall
Chambers St
Woolworth Building
St Peter's Catholic Church
World Trade Center
World Trade Center (Path Trains)
City Hall Park
Times Building
Potter Building
9/11 Memorial
World Trade Center Cortlandt
The Oculus
St Paul's Chapel
Cortlandt St
Fulton St
Temple Court
8 Spruce Street
Chamber of Commerce
Liberty Tower
New York Federal Reserve
Equitable Building
Trinity Church
Rector St
Grave of Alexander Hamilton
Wall St
Chase Manhattan Plaza
Federal Hall Memorial
New York Stock Exchange
JP Morgan Bomb Site
40 Wall Street
70 Pine Street
Broad St
Buttonwood Site
55 Wall Street
20 Exchange Place
Cunard Building
Charging Bull Statue
White Star Line Building
Standard Oil Building
Delmonico's
Bowling Green
START
US Custom House
Mill Street Synagogue Site
Stadt Huys Site
Fraunces Tavern
Titanic Memorial
END
273 Water Street
SEAPORT
Pier II/Wall St (Ferries)
South Ferry
Whitehall St South Ferry
FULTON STREET
VESEY STREET
BROADWAY
PARK ROW
BROOKLYN BRIDGE
PARK ROW
ANN STREET
THEATER ALLEY
SPRUCE STREET
DEY STREET
LIBERTY STREET
GOLD STREET
DUTCH STREET
ALBANY STREET
CARLISLE ST
GREENWICH STREET
THAMES ST
CEDAR STREET
LIBERTY ST
NASSAU ST
PINE STREET
JOHN STREET
PLATT STREET
PEARL STREET
RECTOR STREET
WALL STREET
NEW STREET
FLETCHER STREET
MAIDEN LANE
WATER STREET
FRONT STREET
SOUTH STREET
FDR DRIVE
BEAVER STREET
MARKETFIELD ST
STONE STREET
BRIDGE STREET
PEARL ST
BROAD STREET
OLD SLIP
WATER ST
0 100 200m
0 500ft
N

THE FINANCIAL DISTRICT AND SEAPORT

The Financial District occupies the narrow southern tip of Manhattan Island, encompassing four centuries of growth and development. It was here that the city was founded by Dutch settlers in the 1620s, it was here that George Washington was sworn in as the nation's first President in 1789, and it was here that some of the nation's first skyscrapers began rising from the pavement. This area's tight, narrow streets host an embarrassment of historical riches, some of which survive from New York's colonial days, when the world's bounty began pouring through its harbor.

ROUTE STOPS

1. Bowling Green
2. Fraunces Tavern
3. Colonial Ruins
4. Delmonico's
5. Wall Street
6. Federal Hall and the NY Stock Exchange
7. Trinity Church
8. Thames Street and the Equitable Building
9. 28 Liberty Street
10. Federal Reserve Bank of New York
11. St Paul's Chapel
12. City Hall Park
13. South Street Seaport

DISTANCE
2 miles (3 km)

TIME ALLOWED
2–3 hours

ROUTE No. 01

WHERE IT ALL BEGAN

New York is a city that's been made and remade countless times over its 400-year history. In those four centuries, its population has ballooned along with its economy. A growing city needs to expand, but New York (specifically Manhattan) was always hemmed in by water on all sides, forcing it to grow in one direction: up. Both uptown and up into the sky, New York grew through the 19th century, a time of drastic change for the city: the imposition of the street grid in 1811; the opening of the Erie Canal in 1825; the arrival of the Croton Aqueduct in 1842; the opening of Central Park in the 1860s. Manhattan's population exploded, from 60,489 in 1800 to 1,850,093 in 1900. With that growth came a deluge of commerce and industry. The original city below Chambers Street was remade as a commercial center to serve the teeming port. Wealthy New Yorkers, members of the so-called Knickerbocracy (page 139), sold their homes, often at great profit, and moved north to the suburbs of Greenwich, Washington Square, and Lafayette Place. But wherever they went, commerce followed, seeking their dollars. Wherever commerce went, so went industry to produce goods for the shops. And wherever industry went, so went a poor, often immigrant, labor class to work in the factories. Within perhaps 20 years, those wealthy New Yorkers who'd fled to the edge of town found themselves surrounded by the very urbanity they hoped to escape. So they'd move uptown again, beginning a pattern which would fill Manhattan by the turn of the 20th century: to Houston Street in the 1820s, 14th Street by the 1840s, 42nd Street by the 1860s, and north of 59th Street by the 1880s and 90s. The areas they left behind, once bucolic and exclusive, were given over to lesser uses: mansions were carved into boarding houses or were demolished outright to be replaced by something larger and more lucrative to feed the ceaseless growth of the city. Neighborhood by neighborhood, this churning growth filled Manhattan from tip to tip by the 1910s. By then, New York was emerging as a world-class cultural and economic juggernaut. But it all began here at the edge of the Battery, where the city was first established in the 1620s as a far-flung outpost of the Dutch Republic.

Start 1 → At **Bowling Green**

US CUSTOM HOUSE

To stand in the plaza in front of the US Custom House on Bowling Green is to stand where New York City began. The Custom House, a deliciously overwrought beaux arts pile designed by Cass Gilbert and completed in 1907, sits on the site of old Fort

Amsterdam. Around the fort, which was constructed in 1624, grew a Dutch colonial village called New Amsterdam. That village, and the surrounding colony known as New Netherland, was captured by the British in 1664 and renamed New York. Other than a brief period in 1673–74 when the Dutch took the city back (and renamed it New Orange), it has been New York ever since.

After more than a century of British rule, in 1775, New York joined its fellow American colonies in revolution against the Crown. The main flashpoint was taxation, with colonists bristling at the imposition of ever-increasing fees on everyday items to help King George III pay for the French and Indian War (the American theater of the European Seven Years' War, which raged between Britain and France from 1756–63). That war had been fought largely on the frontier between the coastal English colonies and French Canada, impacting cities like New York only tangentially. Colonists, including New Yorkers, did not feel this was their war and therefore did not feel the King was justified in forcing them to pay for it. Anti-monarchy fervor grew through the 1760s, with the rise of rebel groups such as the Sons of Liberty, who regularly protested not just the taxes but the entire colonial and monarchical system of rule.

An obvious target for anti-monarchy passion was the leaden statue of King George which had been erected in the middle of Bowling Green in 1770 to celebrate Britain's victory in the war. It was regularly pelted with paint and assorted refuse. In response, colonial authorities outlawed graffiti and in 1773 erected an iron fence around Bowling Green, the city's oldest public greenspace. That fence remains in place today, thought to be the oldest fence in New York City, but the statue of King George is gone. What happened to it?

In 1775, the American Revolutionary War began with the Battle of Lexington in Massachusetts. A formal Declaration of Independence was drafted in Philadelphia on July 4, 1776, and was ratified the following day. On July 9, a copy of the Declaration made its way to New York and into the hands of General George Washington, who was at that time encamped with his army on the town Common (today's City Hall Park). He ordered the document read aloud to the assembled populace, which whipped New Yorkers into such a patriotic fervor that they marched from the Common down Broadway to Bowling Green. There, they pulled down the two-ton statue of King George and set upon it with axes and scythes, loading it in pieces onto an oxcart to be carried off to a foundry in Connecticut. It would be melted down to make musket balls which were later used against British forces.

While George and his horse were being hacked to bits, some New Yorkers walked the encircling fence of Bowling Green and lopped off the tops of the iron fence posts (thought to have originally held crowns) which were likewise thrown onto the cart for melting. As the fence is still in place, visitors can see and feel the rough, uneven tops of the fence posts, just as they were left on July 9, 1776. It is one of diminishingly few places in New York where a piece of revolutionary history can actually be touched.

Despite the events of July 9, New York was captured by the British the following September following Washington's decisive loss at the Battle of Long Island in modern-day Brooklyn. He fled up to Harlem and onward out of Manhattan to win the war elsewhere, but his departure meant the end of New York's freedom for the duration of the hostilities. The half-abandoned city burned shortly after Washington's departure (possibly set alight by American troops to deprive the British of a comfortable perch) and was held until November 25, 1783. On that day, the British departed and George Washington triumphantly re-entered the newly independent city.

For a century thereafter, November 25 was celebrated as Evacuation Day, New York's own version of Independence Day. Though this holiday would later be overshadowed by Thanksgiving as the more popular November holiday, and by July 4 as the more popular Independence Day, Evacuation Day was for many generations the great patriotic celebration of the year in this city. Most notable among the festivities was the annual climbing of a greased flagpole on the Battery. This commemorated the fact that the British, on leaving New York in 1783, had nailed a Union Jack to the pole at Fort George (the re-named Fort Amsterdam) and greased the pole on their way out. A soldier by the name of John Jacob Van Arsdale scaled the pole and replaced the flag with one bearing the stars and stripes of the United States. The feat would be re-enacted to great fanfare every subsequent Evacuation Day.

With the war ended, New York set about rebuilding. It served briefly as the national capital, from 1785–90, during which time the Constitution was ratified and George Washington was elected the nation's first President. It was also during this time that old Fort Amsterdam was disassembled and in its place was built a grand executive mansion called the Government House. But no President would ever live in it since New York lost its status as the capital in 1790 in favor of a newly built city on the Potomac River which would become Washington DC. The mansion at Bowling Green was next used as the home of the New York state governor until the city lost its status as state capital to Albany in 1797. The Government House then began its new life as the city's Custom House, which it would remain until being demolished in 1815, having stood for just 25 years.

With the Government House gone, this block where Fort Amsterdam once stood was carved into narrow building lots and filled with rows of fine brick and marble homes. Their location was exceedingly attractive, with fresh sea breezes off the harbor and sweeping views of ships sailing in and out of the Narrows beyond. But as the city's population and economy began to grow by leaps and bounds in the middle decades of the 19th century, the neighborhood became increasingly undesirable as a residential enclave. Ever more wealthy families abandoned formerly tony Bowling Green in favor of newly developing suburban districts uptown near Greenwich Village and Union Square. The townhouses on Bowling Green were one by one converted into the headquarters of major shipping firms, a sign of the neighborhood's changing character.

By the turn of the 20th century, the old houses on Bowling Green were increasingly insufficient to meet the needs of such behemoth shipping companies as the White Star and Cunard Lines. Many of them moved into newly built highrises, some of which still line the west side of Bowling Green today, abandoning the former site of Fort Amsterdam to be reimagined yet again. The land was cleared by 1902 when construction began on a new Custom House, this one designed by Cass Gilbert in keeping with the high-minded architectural elaboration of the City Beautiful Movement made popular by the 1893 Chicago World's Fair. But the Custom House was built not just to be beautiful. It was designed to make a statement about New York and about the United States, and how they viewed themselves at the dawn of the new century.

The United States was still in its infancy as a world power and player in the early 20th century. Understanding that, it is doubly fascinating to look up at the 12 larger-than-life statues flanking the windows on the facade's top floor. These figures represent 12 historic seafaring nations from history, from oldest on the left to most modern on the right: Greece, Rome, Phoenicia, Genoa (represented by Christopher Columbus), Venice, Spain, Holland, Portugal, Belgium (originally sculpted as Germany, it was altered during World War I), France, and Britain. At the center and above these dozen statues is an heroic grouping of two women, representing war and peace, flanking a stars-and-stripes shield surmounted by an eagle. The United States has quite literally inserted itself into the historic lineage of great seafaring powers, expressing its optimism and belief that its placement would be secured by the flood of prosperity passing through this very building.

The Custom House was where tariffs were collected on goods carried into and out of New York's bustling harbor. Prior to World War I, this was the main method of funding the national government, and since New York was far and away the nation's most prosperous port, its Custom House was single-handedly responsible for an outsized percentage of the nation's budget. Daniel Chester French was the artist tasked with executing the building's sculptural embellishments (working alongside the Bronx-based Italian Piccirilli brothers, who translated French's designs into stone), and his allegorical prowess is on full display in the four immense statue groupings which sit just above eye level astride the building's grand staircase. These represent the four peopled continents of the world as viewed through the often-problematic lens of the early 20th century.

At center, flanking the main staircase, the statue groupings represent Europe and the Americas. Europe is embodied by a regal woman, crowned and resplendent in a warrior's breastplate. Her throne is made of Roman spolia and a pile of flagstaffs rest over her right shoulder. Her left hand sits atop an open book atop a globe, representing Europe's domination of the world. But her body language speaks volumes. Though impressively adorned, she sits at the back of her throne, relaxed and resigned, her gaze unfocused somewhere on the horizon. She is static, meant to represent a job completed but increasingly past tense.

Compare the European figure to that of the Americas. Dynamic and engaged, her dress is blown back against her torso, her eyes fixed and alert. She leans forward out of her throne made of blocks covered in Mayan hieroglyphs, while a helmet representing Quetzalcoatl rests beneath her right foot. She holds the torch of the future in her right hand, quite literally symbolizing the "passing of the torch" from Europe to the Americas. On her lap lies a sheaf of corn representing abundance and a man crouched to her left pushes a winged wheel representing progress. To her right, standing above an eagle and cactus, is a Native American man wearing a feathered headdress, who is whispering into her ear.

To the far left and right of the building stand statue groupings meant to represent Asia and Africa, the lands from which Europe and the Americas gleaned their enormous wealth and power. The Asian statue depicts a serene woman with a small statue of the Buddha on her lap, though a Christian cross looms over her right shoulder. She holds an opium poppy in her right hand while her feet rest atop a ring of human skulls. Three figures, in various states of prostration and bondage, stand or kneel to her left while a tiger sits to her right, a symbol of the continent's power and potential.

The African figure is depicted so deeply asleep that her dress has fallen away from her torso. Her right arm rests atop the head of the mysterious Sphinx, a symbol of Africa's past glories and history, while a cloaked figure hides just behind her, a representation of the still-unexplored reaches of the Sahara and the Congo. Similar to *Asia's* tiger, a lion rests next to *Africa*, a symbol of its potential power and greatness.

These statues represent the American world view at the turn of the 20th century. Through them, the artist has placed the United States (and specifically New York City) at the center of the emerging global economy as the natural successor to long-dominant Europe. The Custom House was completed in 1907 but these statues, including the figures along the top floor, do not quite represent the global realities of 1907. Rather, they represent the way New York wished the world to be in the near future, as the city flourished and emerged as part of the global conversation.

That said, the Custom House and nearby Bowling Green represent the first three centuries of New York's existence, from its 1624 establishment at Fort Amsterdam to its role in the Revolution beginning in 1776 to its rise as an economic powerhouse and pivotal link in the world's rapidly expanding sea trade. This is where New York began, and it is where New Yorkers began to shape their narrative in iron and stone.

From **Bowling Green**, walk south along **Broadway** and turn left onto **Bridge Street**

THE STREETS OF LOWER MANHATTAN

Manhattan's Financial District is riddled with literal street names. Bridge Street is one such name, applied to this unassuming little cut-through which runs for just two blocks east of the Battery. Back in the days of Dutch New Amsterdam, a canal sliced through the area, from roughly Beaver Street out to the East River. The canal had originally been a marshy creek that drained the tip of the island, but the Dutch settlers (being Dutch after all) dredged it out into a navigable waterway, called the *Heere Gracht*, which would allow boats to travel directly into the heart of the city.

When the British arrived in 1664, the canal was still in use but was in disrepair and was increasingly used as an open garbage receptacle. It was buried to become a sewer and the resulting street above was found to be unusually broad when compared to the otherwise narrow, twisting streets of old Manhattan. And so the old *Heere Gracht* became the aptly named Broad Street.

America statue at US Custom House

Fraunces Tavern

New York Stock Exchange, Broad Street

Delmonico's

Equitable Building

Red Cube by Isamu Noguchi

Other literal street names in the area include Water Street (because it ran along the waterline), Pearl Street (because it used to be the oyster-shell-covered riverfront), Marketfield Street (because it connected Broad Street to the market at what is now Bowling Green), Stone Street (because it was the first street in the city to be paved with stones), Maiden Lane (due to the popularity of this street for washing clothes by young maidens), and Whitehall Street (after the mansion which once stood at its southern foot, built for Peter Stuyvesant in 1655).

Stop 2 → At the corner of **Bridge** and **Broad Streets**, across from **Fraunces Tavern**

FRAUNCES TAVERN

At the corner of Broad Street and Pearl Street stands one of the neighborhood's most popular landmarks, Fraunces Tavern. While it is occasionally claximed that the tavern is the oldest building in Manhattan, this is not entirely accurate. There has been a building on the site since 1719, when Stephen de Lancey built a home there on land he had acquired from his father-in-law, Stephanus Van Cortlandt, and the de Lanceys kept it until at least 1761. That year they sold it to Haitian-born innkeeper Samuel Fraunces, who repurposed it as a tavern called the Queen's Head. As one of the most substantial public buildings in New York, it was an obvious and popular meeting spot for locals who were growing increasingly angry with the Crown and its colonial authorities.

The Queen's Head tavern survived the American Revolution, including seven years of brutal British occupation, during which time nearly half of the city's buildings burned down. With the war over in 1783, the tavern became a vital meeting place anew. On December 4, 1783, just nine days after the British troops left the city, George Washington hosted a dinner party at the tavern to thank his officers for their service, marking a dramatic and ceremonial end to the many years of hostilities. "With a heart full of love and gratitude, I now take leave of you," toasted the General, "I most devoutly wish that your latter days may be as prosperous and happy as your former ones have been glorious and honorable."[1]

During New York City's brief stint as the nation's capital, the tavern's rooms were used by the newly forming government to house various departments, including those of war, finance, and foreign affairs. When, in 1790, it was decided to relocate the capital to a new city on the Potomac River and New York was stripped of its status, the old tavern on Pearl Street reverted to its previous function as an inn and popular watering hole.

Though Fraunces Tavern escaped damage during New York's Great Fire of 1835, it was partially gutted by fire in 1837 and again in 1852. After the latter conflagration, a flat roof and two additional stories were added to the building, and much of its original detailing was stripped or altered, obscuring most surviving sense of what it might have looked like in its original use as the de Lancey family home. By the end of the 19th century, any "architecture, interior and exterior walls, windows, entrance, roof, woodwork and finishes were largely gone" according to the legendary architecture critic Ada Louise Huxtable. "What remained were foundations and a partial structural shell overlaid and obscured by irremediable 19th-century remodeling."[2]

By 1900, Fraunces Tavern was "vulgarized beyond recognition"[3] and was in danger of being demolished to make way for some modern and exponentially more lucrative highrise. The idea of preserving historical landmarks was barely in its infancy then, and convincing the city to set aside profit margins in favor of patriotic nostalgia was a hard sell. But the tavern was saved, purchased by Sons of the American Revolution in 1904 and reopened in 1907 following an extensive rebuilding and "restoration"[4] project, which sought to return it to its original colonial glory.

To return the tavern to its 1783 appearance, it was almost entirely deconstructed and pieced back together. The main problem with the restoration project was that no one actually knows what the building looked like. There are no images of it from its original construction or through any iteration thereafter. Instead, its appearance was modeled after that of Philipse Manor in Yonkers. While it is an objectively lovely building, a country manor house would likely have looked substantially different from the sort of town house the de Lanceys built here. Regardless, that is the version of Fraunces Tavern that exists today, and indeed has existed for more than a century. Most passersby take for granted that it is an authentic relic from 1719, but it is truly much more of a 1907 reinvention of the old tavern, using some of the original bricks and beams, than whatever it was in Washington's time.

From **Fraunces Tavern**, walk north along **Pearl Street** toward **Coenties Alley** Look for the glass-covered openings in the sidewalk

Stop 3 → At the corner of **Pearl Street** and **Coenties Alley**

STADT HUYS

Across Pearl Street from Fraunces Tavern looms the hulking brown slab that is No. 85 Broad Street. While the tower itself isn't anything terribly exciting, its construction in the late 1970s led to some major advances in the field of landmark preservation and urban archeology. To build the new tower, two entire blocks of what had long ago been New Amsterdam's vibrant commercial waterfront (everything from Pearl Street to South William Street between Broad Street and Coenties Alley) would be destroyed and a block of Stone Street would be de-mapped. This threat came on the tail end of more than a century of demolition and redevelopment in the city's oldest and most historically important neighborhood.

In an attempt to save what could be saved, archeologists were sent to the site in late 1979 and stayed through early 1980. Not only did they discover the foundational outlines of nearly a dozen 17th-century buildings hidden beneath the ground, they also pulled hundreds of artifacts and fragments from the site, all of which would have been obliterated during the tower's construction. Glass, bricks, nails, pottery, bottles, and clay pipes helped paint a picture of everyday life in New York's earliest years.

Most notably, the blocks being excavated once housed the old Dutch colony's original city hall, or *Stadt Huys*. When it was built as a tavern and inn in 1641, it was prominently sited on the waterfront overlooking the bustling East River (everything beyond Pearl Street today is built atop landfill) and was one of the largest and tallest structures in the city. It was converted into a *Stadt Huys* circa 1651 by Peter Stuyvesant, who was installed as the colony's director-general in 1647, in part to help clean up the bloody mess caused by his predecessor, Willem Kieft. In 1670, just six years after the British takeover of the colony, a new tavern was built directly adjacent to the old *Stadt Huys*. Officially named the King's House, it was more commonly known as the Lovelace Tavern in honor of Francis Lovelace, the British colonial governor who had overseen its construction.

Sections of the foundations and basements of both the *Stadt Huys* and Lovelace Tavern were discovered during the 1979–80 excavations and are now visible under glass under the sidewalk atrium of No. 85 Broad Street. Also preserved nearby is a brick cistern, which would have caught rainwater for daily use by local residents. It all feels so quaint and insignificant: some stones and bricks lost in the shadow of the surrounding skyscrapers. But these fragments are some of the only surviving pieces of colonial New York, and their survival was only made possible by that farsighted archeological excavation done before the new tower rose atop them.

Partly in response to the success of the archeological dig and the erasure of a block of Stone Street within the new tower, in 1983 the city's Landmarks Preservation Commission successfully landmarked the "Street Plan of New Amsterdam and Colonial New York."[5] All of the curving, narrow streets which defined the original city and which make lower Manhattan such a shadowy, interesting place to walk, are now landmarks in and of themselves. From Wall Street to the Battery, streets may not be widened, removed, or otherwise altered without permission. Lacking any other evidence of the city's original streetscape, the streets themselves now serve as the most potent reminder of what it might have felt like to walk the same paths once trod by everyone from Stuyvesant to Washington.

Before leaving, take note of the brick and stone pavers which make up the plaza on the Pearl Street side of No. 85 Broad Street. Embedded in the red brick is a large rectangle of yellow brick which outlines the original footprint of the *Stadt Huys*. Next to it is the smaller granite-block outline of the Lovelace Tavern.

From these outlines, walk around **No. 85 Broad Street** onto **Coenties Alley**

As you go, notice that Stone Street actually runs through the lobby of the skyscraper, from Coenties to Broad Street, with a bronze map of colonial New Amsterdam embedded in the sidewalk outside its entrance.

Follow **Stone Street** north, then turn left onto **Mill Lane** and right onto **South William Street**

You will pass between rows of attractive 19th- and 20th-century buildings, many of them designed to look far older than they actually are (no, the stones in the street are not original to Stuyvesant's time). Today, Stone Street is a popular spot for eating and drinking. Mill Lane is so named because it used to lead down to the town mill, which is now one of the shortest streets in Manhattan.

Stop 4 → On **South William Street** in front of the legendary **Delmonico's** restaurant

DELMONICO'S

Delmonico's traces its origins back to 1827, when two Swiss immigrants, the brothers John and Peter Delmonico, opened a shop at No. 23 William Street selling "cakes, ices, and fine wines."[6] They expanded their offerings and eventually opened one of the nation's first European-style restaurants next door at No. 25 William Street, but the entire operation was destroyed in the Great Fire of 1835. The Delmonicos rebuilt on a grand scale, opening their so-called Citadel in the wedge-shaped lot at Beaver and William Streets in 1837. That is not the building which stands on the site today, however, as it was torn down and replaced by the Delmonicos in 1890–91.

As the Delmonicos' business thrived and grew, they expanded to multiple locations across the city, following their wealthy customer base up 5th Avenue and establishing new and ever more prominent locations as they went (they operated on 5th Avenue at 14th Street from 1862–76, at 26th Street from 1876–99, and at 44th Street from 1897–1923). Additionally, as the Gilded Age raged in New York, Delmonico's established itself as the preferred caterer to most of the city's most glittering events. Most high-society families lacked the kitchen space or staff to feed hundreds of guests at one time, so Delmonico's (and later, their rival, Sherry's) hired themselves out to handle the messy details.

Though it has changed hands, closed and reopened numerous times over the past two centuries, Delmonico's has endured as a landmark presence in lower Manhattan. Before leaving the plaza in front of Delmonico's, be sure to look up: it sits unusually at a five-way intersection, the likes of which were all but forbidden elsewhere in Manhattan by the 1811 street grid plan, which gave the city its numbered streets and avenues uptown.

Follow **William Street** north to **Wall Street** and the heart of the global financial industry

Stop 5 → Anywhere near the intersection of **Wall** and **William Streets**

WALL STREET

Wall Street has perhaps the most famous of Manhattan's literal place names, earned by dint of its origins as a literal wall which once, briefly, separated New Amsterdam to the south from the open and increasingly hostile lands to the north. Following the so-called Kieft's War of 1643–47 (not so much an actual war as a brutal slaughter of local Native American populations by Dutch troops followed by retaliatory murders of European settlers throughout the New Netherland colony), Willem Kieft was replaced as head of the colony by Peter Stuyvesant. Despite his attempts at shoring up Dutch sovereignty in the region, relations with both the Native Americans and surrounding British colonial powers had never been worse.

In 1653, Stuyvesant ordered a defensive wall built along the northern edge of the city to help protect against attack. But a wall can only protect against a land invasion, and when the British finally did make a move to capture New Amsterdam in 1664, they came by sea. The town became New York without a single shot being fired, and the wall was removed by 1690. The path it once took across the island was appropriately called Wall Street, which would in time be transformed into one of the most famous streets in the world.

Wall Street's emergence as a financial center began during the British colonial period in the 18th century, when the likes of cotton, corn, and even enslaved people were traded along the East River waterfront. After the American Revolution, the city's first stock traders often met informally beneath a buttonwood tree (otherwise known as a sycamore) at No. 68 Wall Street, in part to avoid trading via a middleman who would be entitled to a commission on the transaction. On May 17, 1792, two dozen such stock traders signed a document known as "the Buttonwood Agreement"[7] which formalized the practice of purchasing and selling "Public Stock" for the first time. This agreement is considered the founding document of the New York Stock Exchange, which met in various locations around lower Manhattan until finally building a proper Stock Exchange building on Broad Street in 1865. That Stock Exchange was demolished in 1901 and replaced by the current white marble building, which has become a symbol of Wall Street's financial prowess. And it all began under a buttonwood tree just a short walk around the corner.

Walk west along **Wall Street**

Stop 6 → At **Wall Street** and **Broad Street** at the **Federal Hall National Monument**

JP MORGAN BUILDING

At No. 23 Wall Street, at the southeast corner of Wall and Broad Streets, stands the imposing lowrise marble edifice that once served as the headquarters for JP Morgan, Jr's Morgan Guaranty Trust Company of New York. Prominently situated directly across Broad Street from the New York Stock Exchange, the old Morgan Building was erected in 1913 to replace the older Drexel Building, which had long been the office for Morgan's father, the formidable Pierpont Morgan who died that same year. The new building marked a departure from the traditional, heavy and brooding architecture which defined lower Manhattan's streetscape. It also signaled a generational shift for the Morgan company, with the younger Morgan beginning to make his mark.

But New York in the 1910s was a city undergoing unprecedented growth and change. Hundreds of thousands of immigrants poured through New York Harbor at the dawn of the 20th century, meaning that an extraordinary three-quarters of New York City's population in 1910 was made up of either immigrants or children of immigrants.[8] An increasing number of these new arrivals came to New York fleeing political and economic upheaval in southern and eastern Europe. Drawn by fantastical stories about the prosperity they'd find in the United States, many were disillusioned by the abject poverty and often grotesque displays of wealth disparity in the city.

Poverty and despair stalked the crowded tenement streets of Manhattan's slum districts, often just a few minutes' walk from the gilded mansions of 5th and Madison Avenues.

Out of these immigrant populations emerged a number of anarchist and anti-capitalist groups, some of which sought to express their anger with the status quo through direct action. This included protests and union drives, but it also included occasional violence, particularly the use of bombs mailed to prominent people and locations. This violence reached a fever pitch in 1919, a year in which dozens of bombs were mailed to politicians and industrialists across the nation, including John D Rockefeller, New York City Police Commissioner Richard Enright, and Mayor John Francis Hylan. Though none of the intended targets was killed, the bombs sent a chill through American society.

The deadliest anarchist attack of the era came just after noon on September 16, 1920, when a wagon parked just across from the Morgan Building at No. 23 Wall Street exploded. Unbeknownst to the thousands of people milling about on their lunch break at the time, the wagon was loaded with 100 pounds (45.4 kg) of dynamite and 500 pounds (227 kg) of iron weights all tied to a timer set to 12:01 p.m. When it detonated, the bomb sent the iron weights flying through the crowd, killing at least 30 people instantly, and perhaps a dozen more in the following days. The target is thought to have been the Morgan Building and likely JP Morgan, Jr, himself, though he was not in his office at the time. The building was badly damaged but remained standing, and Morgan ordered it restored immediately. The one element that wasn't repaired was the building's exterior wall, which retains a constellation of deep divots and pockmarks where it was struck more than a century ago. These marks remain today, a sobering reminder not only of that deadly day but also of Wall Street's emergence as something more than merely a street, but as a symbol of an increasingly global system of money and power.

FEDERAL HALL

Across from the old Morgan building stands an impressive, relatively low-slung Greek temple with a statue of George Washington prominently placed on its entry stairs. This is the Federal Hall National Memorial, overseen by the National Park Service as a permanent celebration of George Washington's inauguration as the nation's first President in 1789. Though it is often assumed that Washington was inaugurated at the exact spot where his statue now stands, this is not quite accurate. Washington was actually inaugurated on the second floor balcony of the old Colonial Hall, built in 1699 to replace the older Dutch *Stadt Huys* as a larger, more modern seat of government for the city. During the short period when New York served as the capital of the newly independent United States, the old Colonial Hall became Federal Hall, hosting the first meeting of the Senate and House of Representatives as well as the first meeting of the Supreme Court. Additionally, the Society Library (page 225), housed in the building since its founding in 1754, was used as the first (unofficial) Library of Congress.

New York lost its status as national capital in 1790, and a new City Hall was built on the Common near Chambers Street in 1812, meaning the old Colonial-turned-Federal Hall no longer served a purpose. Worse still, it sat directly in the middle of the busy intersection of Wall, Broad, and Nassau Streets. It was demolished and the streets were run through its former location. In 1842, a new US Custom House building was completed at the northeast corner of the intersection, and that is the Greek temple-style building currently in place. The Custom House moved down the block to No. 55 Wall Street in 1862 before moving again, in 1907, to the beaux-arts building on Bowling Green where we began our journey.

Following the Custom House's removal in 1862, the old building on Wall Street served as the US Subtreasury until 1920. During that time, in 1883, a statue of George Washington was installed on its front steps, honoring the former President's inauguration, but causing never-ending confusion among later tourists who believe he was sworn in at a building which wasn't actually constructed until he'd been dead for half a century. After years of demolition threats, the building was saved and repurposed as a museum in 1939.

Before leaving the area, take a moment to admire the New York Stock Exchange building on Broad Street. It was designed by the architect George B Post and completed in 1903 on the site of the original 1865 Stock Exchange. The pediment is beautifully adorned with statues designed by artists John Quincy Adams Ward and Paul Wayland Bartlett, though they were executed in stone by the Italian-born and Bronx-based Piccirilli brothers (the same men who executed the statues adorning the US Custom House on Bowling Green (page 10) as well as the lions in front of the New York Public Library (page 175)). The symbolism in the pediment statuary is extraordinary.

At the center stands a woman with arms outstretched, representing integrity, ruling all else. To her right (left from the viewer's perspective) stands a man holding a gear and shaft, representing industry. Next to him is a man holding a ship's wheel representing international trade. Crouching next to him are two men reading books who represent intelligence and science. To the left of integrity (viewer's right) hunches a nude man weighed down by a heavy bag next to a kerchiefed woman holding baskets, together representing agriculture. Next to her are two crouched men studying rocks, representing mining and mineralogy. In the very corner of both sides of the pediment are small up-curled waves, signifying the stock exchange's reach from sea to sea. The entire notion of a newly emerging global economy is thus embodied in stone, high above Broad Street.

Follow **Wall Street** west to **Broadway**

Stop 7 → At **Broadway** in front of **Trinity Church**

TRINITY CHURCH

For more than 300 years, Trinity Church has presided over Wall Street and lower Manhattan, watching New York transform from a colonial backwater into the economic and cultural engine of the world. Chartered in 1697 under King William III, Trinity was the first Anglican congregation to form in this formerly Dutch city. At that time, it was given a generous tract of land on which to build a house of worship, the first of which was completed in 1698. Interestingly, that initial church building faced west toward the Hudson River rather than toward Broadway. Trinity burned in 1776 along with much of the city and wasn't rebuilt until 1790. The second Trinity was structurally deficient and had to be torn down after a particularly heavy snowfall in 1839 opened cracks in its walls.

The current church, designed by Richard Upjohn, was completed in 1846. Its 281-foot

Trinity Church

(86-meter) steeple was the tallest structure in the city until 1890 and remained a notable feature of the skyline until well into the 20th century when the skyscraper age at last swallowed it up. Trinity remains an active church and a major tourist draw, with notables like Alexander Hamilton buried in its yard. But less well known is the fact that Trinity is one of the city's largest landholders, with some 14 acres (5.6 hectares) of lower Manhattan under its control. The origins of Trinity's real estate empire date back to 1705, during the reign of Queen Anne, when the fledgling parish received a 215-acre (87-hectare) tract of land known as the Queen's Farm on Manhattan's Lower West Side. Following an irregular path, the "farm" granted by the Crown to the church extended from Fulton Street west of Broadway all the way up to Christopher Street in Greenwich Village.

The land was meant to support Trinity's good works, which it did for centuries. Among the recipients of Trinity's largesse over the years was King's College, now Columbia University, which was founded on Trinity-owned land in 1754. At the turn of the 19th century, Trinity also laid out a posh neighborhood near Canal Street called St John's Square. They also laid out much of what's now the southwest quadrant of Greenwich Village. Over time, the value of Trinity's land holdings grew exponentially, making the church one of the wealthiest landlords in New York by the mid-20th century. As of 2019, their real estate portfolio was estimated to be worth several billion dollars, including a recent $650 million deal with the Walt Disney Corporation, which has built their new New York headquarters at No. 137 Varick Street on Trinity land.

Back down on Wall Street, Trinity's wealth is conveyed through the church's impeccably well-kept grounds, its blemish-free brownstone facade, and a new stained-glass window designed by British artist Thomas Denny and installed in 2022.[9] In a city of such constant change, Trinity, undergirded by its substantial real estate holdings, remains a constant, providing a tangible link to the city's earliest days. Additionally, Trinity acts as an architectural and spiritual counterbalance to Wall Street's ongoing love affair with the almighty dollar. Trinity Church is, in so many ways, the beating heart of Manhattan's oldest and coldest district.

From **Trinity**, walk north along **Broadway** to **Thames Street**

Stop 8 → On **Thames Street,** just west of Broadway

THAMES STREET

Thames is one of the shortest, narrowest, and darkest streets in all of Manhattan. On both sides it is hemmed in by highrises so tall and so close together as to cast the street in darkness all year round. These towers, the Trinity Building and the United States Realty Building, were completed in 1905 and 1907 respectively, in an era before zoning laws were able to catch up to the rapid advances of technology which made such tall buildings possible. There was a real fear in the early years of the 20th century that highrise buildings, if allowed to proliferate, would eventually block out the sun across the entire city. Worse yet, they were viewed as potential hazards in the event of a fire or other disaster. Skyscrapers also increased population density across the city to the extent that no one was sure whether transit or utilities could keep up.

"In the last year the construction of these huge structures has been carried on so rapidly that what might be termed a 'skyscraper war' has resulted," lamented the *New-York Tribune* in 1903. "As long as these buildings stood isolated, surrounded by low buildings and exposed on all sides to the sun and air, their rooms were bright and healthful in winter and cooled by every available breeze in summer. With their increase in number, however, the light and air have been crowded out of some and threaten to be crowded out of many more. Wall towers up against wall; skyscraper adjoins skyscraper; rooms that were once open and commanding mile-wide views are being plastered up, as it were, by huge structures erected alongside. And with the return of darkness and dampness in some cases has come not only lesser rents to the landlord, but poorer sanitary surroundings for the occupant."[10]

THE EQUITABLE BUILDING

The city failed to act against skyscraper overdevelopment until the 1915 completion of a tower of such monstrous proportions that something simply had to be done. The Equitable Life Insurance Company had been housed in a lovely nine-story mansard-roofed pile at No. 120 Broadway since 1870. But a fire in 1912 destroyed that building, an event made all the more dramatic by the frigid temperatures that day, which froze the firefighters' hoses and turned the Equitable Building into a glistening, ice-encrusted wonder. A total loss, the old ruin was cleared away and a new tower rose in its place. At 550 feet (168 meters) tall, the new Equitable Building loomed over shadowy Thames Street, rising straight up from the sidewalk over an entire city block, from Broadway to Nassau Street between Cedar and Pine. It was the largest tower by volume ever built, enclosing more than one million square feet (93,000 square meters) of space, and cast a shadow of several acres across lower Manhattan at certain times of day.

Barely a year after the Equitable Building's completion, New York City passed its first-ever comprehensive package of zoning and land use laws. These not only delineated residential, commercial, and industrial usage zones across the city, but they required that any future highrise buildings be set back above a certain height in order to allow light to reach the streets below. Towers were to be set back again and again, like modern ziggurats, until they reached 25% of their total footprint. Only then could they rise unimpeded into the sky.

Many of New York's most famous skyscrapers were forced to adhere to the 1916 zoning laws: the Chrysler Building, the Empire State Building, and No. 70 Pine Street to name but a few. The Equitable Building, now but a blip on the skyline of lower Manhattan, did more to alter the future city's appearance than just about any other. "Although not the only building responsible for the establishment of zoning, the Equitable became the prime example cited of the evils of unregulated skyscraper construction."[11]

Leave **Thames Street**, walk north on **Broadway to Cedar Street**. Turn right and walk past the broad side of the **Equitable Building** to **Nassau Street**, crossing it to enter the Fosun Plaza

Stop 9 → At the base of **No. 28 Liberty Street** (formerly One Chase Manhattan Plaza)

Thames Street

70 Pine Street

Wall Street skyline

City Hall Park, Jacob Wrey Mould Fountain

28 LIBERTY STREET

For years following the end of World War II, the United States basked in the economic glow of victory. Its middle class was rapidly expanding, and technological advances were making the lives of everyday citizens infinitely better, faster, and more comfortable. Similarly, banks and corporations in Manhattan's financial district increasingly sought to modernize, but the 1916 zoning laws placed strict limits on what was possible in the area's tangled warren of colonial-era streets. By the laws' strictures, the highest floors—which fetched the highest rents—were also necessarily the smallest floorplates. There was a very real possibility that lower Manhattan, the heart of New York's financial sector for centuries, might be facing obsolescence in favor of the roomier blocks of Midtown.

Enter David Rockefeller. In 1955, the Bank of Manhattan Company merged with Chase Bank, where David was, at that time, executive vice president for planning and development. The combined companies hoped to build a new tower headquarters in New York to house their 8,700 employees, and it was David who convinced them to stay in lower Manhattan. To adhere to the 1916 zoning law, the newly formed Chase Manhattan Bank would need to get creative in order to build the sort of modern skyscraper they desired.

Under Rockefeller's leadership, they purchased nearly two entire city blocks between Pine and Liberty Streets, from Nassau Street to William Street. They then got permission from Robert Moses, then chairman of the City Planning Commission, to de-map the block of Cedar Street which bisected the plot. The land acquired and the street removed, the architectural firm of Skidmore, Owings & Merrill designed for Chase Manhattan Bank a monolithic glass and aluminum tower which soared more than 800 feet (244 meters) into the air. The creative catch was that the tower would occupy just 25% of the lot. The rest would be transformed into a public plaza, meaning the project technically adhered to the 1916 zoning laws, thus proving the continued viability of the financial district as a skyscraper district in a modern age.

Construction began on the Chase Manhattan Bank tower in 1958, and by the time it was completed in 1961, New York City had adopted an entirely updated slate of zoning laws inspired in part by the bank's creative plaza design. The new guidelines discouraged the so-called "wedding-cake" type of building and provided bonuses for developers who provided "public plazas, arcades, or other open spaces at ground level."[12] These laws remain in effect to this day, allowing for the construction of a whole array of modernist towers and plazas which have come to dominate whole swaths of Manhattan's business districts, landmarks like the Seagram Building, and the original World Trade Center complex.

The Equitable Building was one of the leading causes of the city's passage of the 1916 zoning laws, and the former One Chase Manhattan Plaza (now No. 28 Liberty Street) was one of the leading inspirations for the city's passage of the 1961 zoning laws. In short, two buildings sitting directly across from each other at the intersection of Nassau and Cedar Streets helped define the future of the New York City skyline.

Walk around to the west side of the **plaza** at the base of **No. 28 Liberty Street**

Stop 10 → Outside the imposing limestone fortress that is the **Federal Reserve Bank of New York**

THE FEDERAL RESERVE BANK

Rising like a great Florentine palazzo from the cold canyons of lower Manhattan, the New York branch of the Federal Reserve Bank is one of the more unusual buildings in the city. It occupies an irregular y-shaped block bound by William and Nassau Streets between Liberty Street and Maiden Lane, and despite being far shorter than many of its skyscraping neighbors, it is remarkably visible from a distance at all angles.

The Federal Reserve was created in 1913 as part of an early attempt to regulate the nation's banking system and, it was hoped, to stave off future financial calamities and bank-runs.

As the leading economic center of the nation, New York's branch of the Federal Reserve Bank was naturally built to reflect its status as the most prominent of the Fed's 12 regional districts. Called "the greatest banking house in the world,"[13] it was designed by the architectural firm of York & Sawyer and constructed mainly between 1924 and 1935. The exterior of the building is made up of yellowish Indiana limestone and lighter, more porous Ohio sandstone. Both materials age and patina differently, giving the bank an almost checkerboard appearance by the 1960s (though it has been cleaned since, the subtle color variation of the stones is still apparent to knowing eyes). The main body of the building's interior is mostly office space, with executive offices and recreational space on its upper floors. But the most fascinating part of the building is hidden deep underground.

The vaults of New York's Federal Reserve Bank are buried at least 80 feet (24 meters) below street level, partially embedded in the solid granite bedrock of Manhattan. Its walls are 8–10 feet (2.4–3 meters) thick with doors weighing 230 tons.[14] The reason for such security? There is more gold stored in this vault than in any other single location on earth: an estimated 507,000 bars weighing almost 7,000 tons.[15] Much of the gold is the reserve of sovereign foreign nations whose paper currency is backed by the metals stored at the Fed. Largely thanks to its intense security measures, the Fed's vaults have never been the victim of a heist. It survived the attacks of September 11, 2001 unscathed and has only closed its security doors once, during Superstorm Sandy in 2012. And that wasn't to protect the gold, but rather to protect the massive and expensive machinery located in the vaults, which is needed to move the gold around.

Walk west along Liberty Street to **Broadway**

On Broadway, take note of the dark stone banners embedded in the sidewalk. There are more than 200 such plaques, and each commemorates the date of a ticker-tape parade held on lower Broadway. The first occurred in 1886 to celebrate the dedication of the Statue of Liberty, and they have continued to the present day, honoring everyone from Queen Elizabeth II in 1957 to the moonwalking astronauts of Apollo 11 in 1969 to frontline healthcare professionals during the COVID-19 pandemic in 2021. The New York Yankees have received nine ticker-tape parades over the years for their World Series championships.

Follow **Broadway** north to **Fulton Street**. There, turn left and walk along the high iron fence of the **St Paul's Chapel** churchyard. Enter the church grounds via the gate midway down the block.

Stop 11 → Inside the churchyard of **St Paul's Chapel**

ST PAUL'S CHAPEL

St Paul's Chapel is the oldest church building in Manhattan, begun in 1764 and largely completed by 1766. Its two and a half centuries are rife with historic superlatives and impressive anecdotes: one of its communion chalices was gifted to the chapel by King George III in 1766; it survived the Great Fires of 1776 and 1835; George Washington worshiped at St Paul's during New York's stint as the national capital between 1785 and 1790; and more recently, it survived the cataclysmic events of September 11, 2001, when the towers of the World Trade Center crashed to the ground just across Church Street. St Paul's became a refuge in the aftermath of that dark day, its pews used by "firefighters and police officers and construction workers [...] desperate for a few hours' respite from ground zero."[16]

In a city so addicted to everything newer, bigger, more lucrative, it seems no minor miracle that St Paul's has survived at all. It is a relic from New York's quaint colonial days, when the built-up city petered out just a few blocks up Broadway from the chapel. Though it sits almost laughably close to Trinity Church down near Wall Street, St Paul's was actually built as an outlying chapel for Trinity, meant to serve the needs of the city's northern reaches. It remains affiliated with Trinity to this day, its churchyard on Fulton Street marking the southern boundary of the former Church Farm gifted to Trinity by Queen Anne in 1705, which originally stretched all the way to Christopher Street.

Architecturally, St Paul's is remarkable for its charming colonial dimensions, which exude an almost New England flair. Also remarkable is the fact that the chapel technically faces west toward Church Street and the Hudson River. Its steeple and original entrance inside the churchyard are one of the sole surviving reminders of a time when the river, and the rows of long-lost mansions which would have lined the streets leading down to its piers, was considered a more desirable orientation than even Broadway. Standing before its diminutive portico, especially in summertime when the trees are leafed out, it's almost possible to imagine what colonial New York might have once been like.

All around St Paul's, New York has evolved into something unrecognizable to its colonial residents. The rows of fine houses which once stood within sight of the chapel's fine steeple were abandoned by their wealthy residents in the late 19th century as they made their way to greener pastures uptown. The houses became stores and apartments, dominated by shops selling and repairing sewing machines, radios and, later, televisions. This neighborhood, nicknamed Radio Row, was taken by the Port Authority of New York & New Jersey in the 1960s, demolished, and replaced by the original World Trade Center. With it went any remaining vestige of what lower west Manhattan might have once been. Except, of course, for St Paul's Chapel; its presence and survival provides a rare and welcome peek inside the city's earlier, more rustic days.

Cross through the churchyard to **Vesey Street** and turn right toward **Broadway**. Follow **Broadway** north to the **Woolworth Building**, then cross to the east side of the street

Stop 12 → Inside **City Hall Park**

CITY HALL

Incredibly, New York City has only ever had three buildings serve as its city hall in its 400-year history. The first was the old Dutch *Stadt Huys* on Pearl Street (page 17). The second was the stately Colonial Hall on Wall Street (page 21), which was built in 1699 as a symbol of British rule. The third, and current, City Hall was begun in 1803 and completed in 1812, making it one of the oldest city halls in the nation still serving its original purpose.

City Hall stands in what was originally called the Common, a wedge of public land at the junction of Broadway and the Bowery Road (now Park Row). This was where, in the city's earliest days, farmers could come to graze their cattle and sell their products to city folk and travelers. The Common was also host to General George Washington's troops in the summer of 1776 prior to their devastating loss at the Battle of Long Island that September. But importantly, Washington was encamped at the Common on July 9, 1776, when a copy of the newly ratified Declaration of Independence made its way to him from Philadelphia. He ordered it read aloud to the assembled population who were thus spurred to hack apart the statue of King George at Bowling Green (page 11).

By the end of the Revolutionary War, the old Colonial Hall was in a ruinous state and had to be refurbished in 1784 for use as Federal Hall, the seat of the new national government. It was there that George Washington was sworn in as President in 1789. But New York lost its status as capital in 1790, and by 1800 it was decided to remove the old and outdated Federal Hall from Wall Street. A design competition was held in 1802, and out of the 26 proposals submitted, the $350 prize was awarded to John McComb, Jr, (designer of St Mark's Church in-the-Bowery in the East Village (page 79) and Alexander Hamilton's home, The Grange, in Harlem (page 288)), and Joseph François Mangin (designer of St Patrick's Old Cathedral on Mulberry Street (page 57)).

The cornerstone for the new City Hall was laid in May of 1803, but construction dragged on for nearly a decade. The biggest issue was financing, as such a large marble-faced building was considered a shocking extravagance for a city still rebuilding from the ashes of the Revolution. To save money, and because it sat at the very northern edge of town in 1803, cheaper sandstone was used for the building's northern facade, following the logic that it wouldn't be seen as often from that angle. The south-facing facade was allowed far more elaboration, with a grand staircase and portico, French-inflected windows and trim (a sharp departure from the simple red-brick streetscape otherwise dominant in the city at the time), all capped by a handsome cupola and a statue of *Justice*. The building was dedicated in 1811 and finally completed in 1812.

Skyline view over City Hall Park

Schermerhorn Row, Fulton Slip

TWEED COURTHOUSE

Immediately behind City Hall to the north is the Tweed Courthouse, constructed between 1861 and 1881, which remains a splendid symbol of the city's 19th-century corruption and graft. Political machine boss William Magear Tweed and his cronies used the courthouse's construction as their own personal slush fund, pocketing millions by overcharging for everyday items ($250,000 for brooms, for example) or invoicing work by companies that never actually existed. In the end, the courthouse cost taxpayers an estimated $12 million, many times the original budget[17] (see Walk 2, page 35).

MUNICIPAL BUILDING

At the northeast corner of City Hall Park stands the massive Municipal Building, constructed between 1909 and 1914, which stands sentinel 580 feet (177 meters) over the east end of Chambers Street. On January 1, 1898, more than a dozen formerly independent cities and towns officially consolidated as the five boroughs of New York City. Formerly limited to the bounds of Manhattan Island (later adding parts of Westchester County, which became the Bronx), New York suddenly included Brooklyn, Long Island City, Flushing, Jamaica, Elmhurst, and nearly half a dozen towns on Staten Island, ballooning the city's overall population from barely two million to nearly three and a half million overnight.

This expansion of municipal responsibility necessitated the construction of a new, consolidated government center which reflected the city's new scale and scope. The Municipal Building was designed by William M Kendall, a partner at the firm of McKim, Mead & White, and encompasses a staggering one million square feet (93,000 square meters) of office space. The verticality of the granite-and-terracotta facade culminates in a Corinthian-columned cupola topped by the gilded 25-foot (7.5-meter) statue entitled *Civic Fame*, designed by the sculptor Adolph Alexander Weinman. The statue is the tallest on Manhattan Island.

Exit **City Hall Park** onto **Park Row**, which is the southern leg of the **Bowery Road**

NEWSPAPER ROW

Many of the buildings along Park Row and immediately east of it were constructed in the 19th century as part of what was called Newspaper Row. All the city's major newspapers kept their offices and presses along this strip in order to be as close to City Hall and all the goings-on of city government as possible. Reporters could get their scoop and run right across Park Row to type up the story for immediate release.

This began to change in the 1890s as technological advances meant reporters didn't need to be physically present to get their story recorded. In 1893, the *New York Herald* was the first to decamp, moving to a newer, more modern headquarters on 35th Street. The plaza in front of their new building was then named for the paper: Herald Square. Following the *Herald*'s example, *The New York Times* moved uptown to 42nd Street in 1904. Like the *Herald*, *The Times* got the plaza in front of their new headquarters named for them: Times Square.

Follow **Beekman Street** to **Gold Street**. Turn right, then turn left onto **Fulton Street** and follow it all the way to **Fulton Slip**

Stop 13 → At the little lighthouse on the east side of **Water Street**

TITANIC MEMORIAL

Standing at the corner of Fulton and Pearl Streets is one of the most fascinating reminders of the city's maritime past: the Titanic Memorial, built as a small concrete lighthouse topped by a metal-wire sphere. The memorial was installed in 1913 atop the now-demolished Christian Seamen's Institute building at No. 25 South Street. The Institute provided respectable housing for retired sailors, and the little lighthouse was added to its roof to memorialize the workers who died aboard the *Titanic* at a time when much of the public outpour focused on the lost passengers. The sphere on top of the lighthouse is a "time ball," a now largely forgotten piece of maritime history.

Prior to 1883, time zones did not exist. Every city or region kept time in its own way, meaning ships arriving from across the sea had no way of knowing local time as they pulled into port. To account for this, port towns kept "time balls" on the waterfront, visible from the harbor, which were lowered at precisely noon local time, allowing sailors to reset their clocks to local time. This tradition most famously endures to this day in Times Square, where a ball is dropped at midnight every December 31, allowing everyone to ring in the new year in unison. Less famous is the metal ball atop the *Titanic* memorial on Fulton Street, a sober reminder not only of the sailors' lives lost aboard that great ocean liner, but of New York's proud seafaring history.

FULTON SLIP

Fulton Street is one of a number of so-called slips in lower Manhattan. Peck Slip, Catherine Slip, Coenties Slip, Old Slip: these were all once actual slips where ships could pull in from the river to on- or off-load goods. As waterborne commerce shifted, moved, and evolved, the old slips were filled in, leaving behind these unusually wide, often wedge-shaped plazas all along the harborfront.

Fulton Street is named for Robert Fulton, whose steam-powered ferries plied the waters between New York and Fulton Street across the river in Brooklyn for more than a century, beginning in 1814. Today, Fulton Street forms the spine of the South Street Seaport, an historic and formerly bustling district of wharves and warehouses redeveloped as a shopping and tourism mecca in the 1980s.

Calling this area the Seaport does a bit of a disservice to the much broader maritime history of lower Manhattan's storied waterfront. The whole city was developed as a seaport throughout most of its first three centuries of existence. Docks, piers, counting houses, market stalls, and sailors' hotels once dominated the whole riverfront from the East River around the Battery to the Hudson. Not to diminish its importance, but what we now call the Seaport is merely the last remaining slice of what was once a ubiquitous streetscape found all across the island.

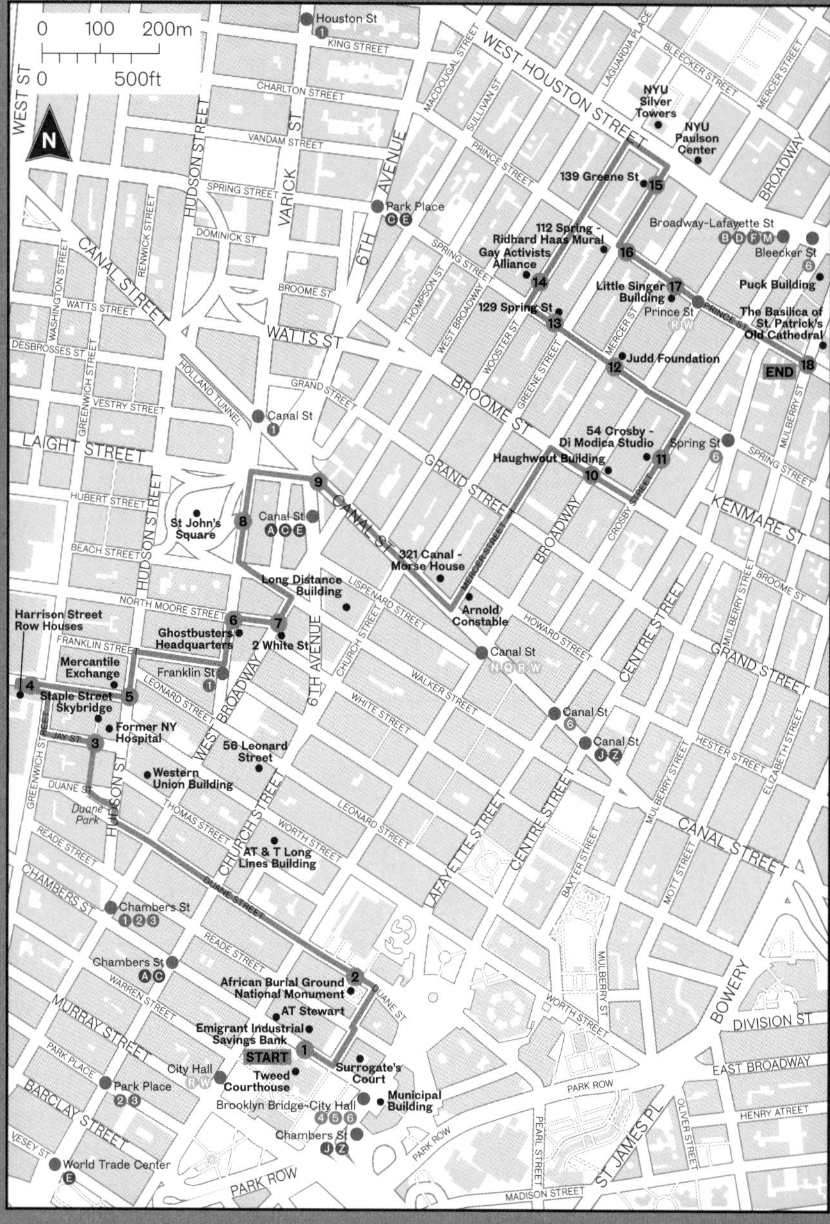

START
END
African Burial Ground National Monument
AT Stewart
Emigrant Industrial Savings Bank
Tweed Courthouse
Surrogate's Court
Municipal Building
Harrison Street Row Houses
Mercantile Exchange
Staple Street Skybridge
Former NY Hospital
Western Union Building
Ghostbusters Headquarters
2 White St
56 Leonard Street
AT & T Long Lines Building
Long Distance Building
St John's Square
321 Canal - Morse House
Arnold Constable
Haughwout Building
54 Crosby - Di Modica Studio
Judd Foundation
129 Spring St
Gay Activists Alliance
112 Spring - Ridhard Haas Mural
139 Greene St
Little Singer Building
NYU Silver Towers
NYU Paulson Center
Puck Building
The Basilica of St. Patrick's Old Cathedral

TRIBECA AND SOHO

Tribeca and SoHo: their names conjure images of rusty fire escapes clinging to cast-iron facades above evocatively narrow streets paved with granite blocks. Built in the 19th century as hives of commerce and industry, their conversion over the past half-century into wealthy enclaves of galleries, cafes, and multi-million-dollar residential lofts helped inspire the creation of similar districts in cities around the world. These areas are among the most precious and unique collections of 19th-century architecture in the world, and the story of their emergence and evolution is in many ways the story of New York itself.

ROUTE STOPS

1. Tweed Courthouse
2. African Burial Ground National Monument
3. Staple Street Sky Bridge
4. Harrison Street Houses
5. Mercantile Exchange
6. Ghostbusters Firehouse
7. 2 White Street
8. St John's Square
9. Canal Street
10. EV Haughwout Building
11. Arturo Di Modica Studio
12. Judd Foundation
13. No. 129 Spring Street
14. Gay Activisits' Alliance Firehouse
15. No. 139 Greene Street
16. Richard Haas Mural
17. The Little Singer Building
18. St Patrick's Old Cathedral

DISTANCE
2½ miles (4 km)

TIME ALLOWED
2–3 hours

ROUTE No. **02**

ARTS, INDUSTRY, AND OSTENTATION

For the first two centuries of New York City's existence, Chambers Street marked the very northern edge of town. Beyond Chambers sat a large, deep body of spring-fed fresh water known as the Collect Pond, centered near modern Chinatown (page 64). To the east and west, water oozed from the pond in wide, marshy deltas, blocking the city from expanding into the vast northern reaches of Manhattan Island. Because the East and Hudson Rivers are brackish and non-potable, the pond's springs were long the city's primary source of drinking water. The pond was drained and filled by 1811, opening the rest of Manhattan to rapid development just in time for the city's post-Revolution and Erie Canal population boom.

The canal used to drain the pond is now buried beneath Canal Street. The surrounding marshlands, once known as Lispenard Meadows, are now part of today's Tribeca and SoHo. It was here that New Yorkers took their first tentative steps north of Chambers Street, setting the stage for the development of a vast and modern metropolis which would fill the island by the turn of the next century.

Start 1 → At 52 **Chambers Street** in front of the Tweed Courthouse

THE TWEED COURTHOUSE

The Tweed Courthouse is one of the great civic landmarks of New York's 19th-century boom years. With its high marble staircase and Corinthian columns, it exudes a sense of governmental power and order. But its name betrays its shadier origins, as William "Boss" Tweed was quite likely the most corrupt politician in the nation's history. Tweed was born in 1823, part of a respectable family of Scottish extraction on nearby Cherry Street. His youth would have been defined by the city's explosive growth following the 1825 completion of the Erie Canal. Manhattan, home to barely 100,000 people at Tweed's birth, boasted a population of half a million by the time he entered politics at age 26 in 1850.

In 1858, Tweed was named leader of Tammany Hall, the political organization which ruled New York politics for much of the 19th century. Under Tammany, New York was run like a criminal enterprise, with Tweed and his ring of associates skimming vast sums of money from civic projects. By far the most egregious and infamous example of this graft was Manhattan's new county courthouse. When construction began in 1861, the building was slated to cost an estimated one million dollars. But the project dragged on for 20 years, during which time its price tag ballooned more than tenfold. Much of that expense found its way into the pockets of corrupt Tammany affiliates who submitted bogus invoices, sometimes in the name of contractors who didn't even exist.

The courthouse graft was finally exposed in 1871, when *The New York Times* received copies of the project's itemized expenses and payroll data. As the numbers were published, public opinion turned sharply against Tweed, who was arrested within days. Perhaps fittingly, his trial was held in a courtroom inside the very building which had precipitated his downfall. He was convicted on 204 counts and sentenced to 12 years in prison, though he escaped in 1875 and fled to Spain. There, he was recaptured by Spanish officials who recognized him from the masterful political cartoons of Thomas Nast. He died in his New York prison cell in 1878. Today, the New York County Courthouse unofficially bears his name, forever linking his legacy to tales of brazen corruption.

EMIGRANT INDUSTRIAL SAVINGS BANK BUILDING AND THE STEWART BUILDING

Just across Chambers Street from the Tweed Courthouse stands the 1912 Emigrant Industrial Savings Bank Building, recently converted into apartments.

To the left of that, on the corner of Broadway, is the seven-story Stewart Building, built in 1846 as one of the nation's first true department stores. Alexander Turney Stewart came to New York from Ireland in 1818 and made his way initially by selling some high-quality lace he'd brought with him. With his profits, he continually expanded his offerings until he was able to open his first dry-goods shop in 1823. As his business grew, he recognized that customers were having a difficult time finding what they were looking for amidst the crush of merchandise, and so Stewart thereafter organized his store into departments. His 1846 store, still standing today at No. 280 Broadway, was a marble marvel of its age, rivaling any store in Paris or London.

SURROGATE'S COURTHOUSE AND THE MUNICIPAL BUILDING

Before leaving, be sure to stop and admire the 1907 Surrogate's Courthouse at No. 31 Chambers Street, which looks like it was airlifted in from Paris. Beyond it, at the far eastern end of Chambers, is the 1914 Municipal Building, which was constructed to accommodate the needs of the massively enlarged city government following the consolidation of the five boroughs in 1898.

From the **Tweed Courthouse**, cross **Chambers Street** and follow **Elk Street** two blocks north

Stop 2 → At the African Burial Ground National Monument at the corner of **Duane and Elk Streets**

AFRICAN BURIAL GROUND NATIONAL MONUMENT

Slavery was introduced to Manhattan by the Dutch, with evidence of enslaved African people present in the colony as early as 1626. In 1644, a dozen or so enslaved African residents of New Amsterdam petitioned the Dutch West India Company, which controlled the New Netherland colony, for freedom from their bondage. They were thereafter granted so-called *half-freedom*, which was essentially conditional manumission. They were allowed to move out onto their own farm grants, but their children, even those yet to be born, remained enslaved. Against this backdrop, these *half-free* residents of New Amsterdam settled on farms north of the freshwater pond in the area now known as Tribeca and SoHo. This distinguishes the neighborhood as the first known free Black settlement on Manhattan Island.

Much changed following the British takeover in 1664. Under British rule, Black people were barred from owning land and were not allowed to be buried in city churchyards. Just north of Chambers Street, nestled between the Common (modern City Hall Park) and the Black-owned farmland beyond (modern Tribeca and SoHo) lay the city's Negros' Burying Ground, first labeled as such on a 1755 map of the island by surveyor Francis Maerschalck.[18] Here, hundreds of Black New Yorkers were committed to the earth, often in ceremonies involving African traditions which had been carried across the Atlantic and safeguarded through generations. It is possible that the graveyard existed since at least the 1630s and remained in use until 1795, at which point streets began to be run through the area in preparation for redevelopment.

The land was graded, gridded, and built upon, knitting it into the surrounding urban fabric. What saved the graves from obliteration was the backfilled soil which was piled 20 feet (6 meters) thick atop the burial grounds to raise it flush with the surrounding streetscape. For nearly two centuries, these graves lay hidden deep beneath streets, sewers, and building foundations, slipping from collective memory, until 1991, when excavation for a new government office tower revealed hundreds of colonial-era skeletons. It was heralded as one of the most significant archeological finds in generations.

Beneath the ground, researchers uncovered a wealth of previously undocumented information regarding the lives, customs, and funerary traditions of the Africans who lived and died in colonial New York. Some bodies had coins pressed into their hands or laid over their eyes; one had a shell next to its head and another was dressed in a British marine officer's uniform; rings, beads, pipes, and other personal effects were found in several of the graves. In all, 419 graves were exhumed from the excavation site, which encompassed a tiny fraction of the whole graveyard. It is thought that perhaps 15,000 more individuals lie hidden beneath nearby buildings, including the former Stewart department store at No. 280 Broadway (page 37).

The exhumed bodies were examined and cataloged for future research before being reinterred in 2003. For this, each body was placed inside a hand-carved wooden box. The boxes were then placed inside seven larger burial vaults, 60 per vault, which are now marked by seven earthen mounds visible within the memorial site. The burial ground was proclaimed a National Monument in 2006.

From the **African Burial Ground**, walk west along **Duane Street**.

As you walk west along Duane, look right to catch a glimpse of the monolithic 550-foot

(168-meter) AT&T Long Lines Building. It was built with no windows in 1974 to protect the sensitive telephone equipment stored inside. Crossing Church Street, take note of the high quality of the commercial loft buildings on this block. Unusual for their age and intended use, these Duane Street lofts feature fashionable cast-iron storefronts at street level but above that boast expensive marble facades. Most of these were built in the 1860s, at the same time cast-iron storefronts were proliferating across what's now SoHo to the north. The use of marble here highlights the area's enduring prominence as a center for high-end business dealings.

STAPLE STREET BRIDGE

Continue west along **Duane Street**, crossing **West Broadway** and **Hudson Street** before cutting through the small, triangular **Duane Park**. From the north side of the park, turn onto **Staple Street** and walk one block north

Stop 3 → At the corner of **Jay Street**

Among the most photographed and picturesque structures in Tribeca today is the small iron footbridge which spans Staple Street, connecting the third stories of No. 67 Hudson Street and No. 9 Jay Street. These two buildings were once part of New York Hospital, which was established in 1771. The main hospital moved uptown in the 1870s and today operates as Weill-Cornell Medical Center and New York-Presbyterian Hospital. No. 67 Hudson Street was built in 1894 as a "House of Relief" for the hospital and was supplemented in 1908 by the construction of stables and a laundry facility next door at No. 9 Jay Street. (Be sure to notice the small stone medallion which reads "NYH" on the Staple Street side of the building.) The bridge which today spans Staple Street was meant to ease the flow of foot traffic between the two facilities.

Today, like much of formerly commercial Tribeca, these old hospital buildings have been converted for residential use. The two apartments connected by the skybridge were offered for sale together in 2015 for $50 million, though the property languished on the market for eight years. It finally sold in 2023 for roughly half that amount. Still, the bridge remains a charming vestige of the area's less affluent past.

Turn left on **Jay Street** then turn right on **Greenwich Street**

Stop 4 → At the corner of **Greenwich** and **Harrison Streets**

HARRISON STREET HOUSES

Like an architectural mirage, a cluster of nine little red-brick houses sit at the corner of Greenwich and Harrison, almost lost in the shadow of the 40-story apartment towers behind them. The houses were all built roughly two centuries ago, the oldest in 1797 and the newest in 1828, and they exist as rare reminders of Tribeca's earliest history, when it was a quieter, more residential and bucolic community on the northern fringes of the city. This particular corner of Tribeca sits on land which was once part of the 215-acre (87-hectare) farm given to Trinity Church by Queen Anne in 1705 (page 24).

Staple Street Skybridge

It was filled with rows of fine Federal-style townhouses at the turn of the 19th century, offering convenience to the city alongside the grand views and fresh breezes of the nearby Hudson.

WASHINGTON MARKET

Washington Market, long New York's primary source for produce, meat, and dairy products, was established in 1813 just south of this area, on land now occupied by the World Trade Center. This brought crowds and commercial traffic to the neighborhood, in time pushing its well-heeled residents uptown. Block by block, the waterfront areas between Fulton and Houston Streets became increasingly commercialized. Old houses, such as these on Harrison Street, had shopfronts cut into their parlor floors. Some were bumped up to four or more stories, losing their peaked, dormered rooftops in the process. Many more were simply demolished to make way for more lucrative office, shop, and warehouse space.

In the 1960s, the Washington Market was shuttered as much of the surrounding area was taken by the city in the name of urban renewal. Hundreds of structures, many dating to the turn of the 19th century, were earmarked for demolition to make way for the World Trade Center and a highrise residential complex known as Independence Plaza. As the doomsday approached for the area, the Landmarks Preservation Commission identified nine historic townhouses for designation, saving them from the rubble heap. In a sort of irony, the Commission did not view the district's 19th-century brick-and-iron commercial buildings as worthy of saving in the 1960s, but in 1991 would go on to designate the area just east of Greenwich Street, which boasts a nearly identical streetscape to the one demolished west of it, as the Tribeca West Historic District.

Of the nine houses earmarked for salvation, six remain in their original locations today: the Sarah R Lambert home at No. 29 Harrison, the Jacob Ruckle home at No. 31 Harrison, and the Ebenezer Miller home at No. 33 Harrison were all built together in 1827. Around the corner on Washington Walk, a surviving leg of Washington Street here, stand the Wilson Hunt home at No. 37 Harrison (originally No. 327 Washington), the Joseph Randolph home at No. 39 Harrison (originally No. 329 Washington), and the William B Nichols home at No. 41 Harrison (originally No. 331 Washington). These were built in 1828, and together with the three 1827 houses facing Harrison Street, form a rare and picturesque corner assemblage unlike anything else found in the area.

The last three houses landmarked from the doomed neighborhood were Nos. 314, 315, and 317 Washington Street. These sat a block south of the Harrison houses, surrounded by later commercial buildings deemed unworthy of salvation. No. 314 Washington was built in 1804 as the Jonas Wood house. Across the street sat Nos. 315 and 317 Washington, built in 1819 and 1797 respectively, by the architect John McComb, Jr, who actually lived in No. 317. McComb was arguably New York's first great native-born architect, designing such landmarks as Alexander Hamilton's Harlem home, The Grange, completed in 1802, and New York City Hall, completed in 1811 (page 288). He was also prolific in designing townhouses at the turn of the 19th century, though the two Washington Street houses were the last known to survive.

In 1971, Nos. 314, 315, and 317 Washington Street were gingerly loaded onto flatbed trucks and hauled one block north to join the six other landmarked houses. There, they became Nos. 25, 27A, and 27 Harrison Street, and completed this unexpected and delightful little pocket of history amid the wreckage of modernity. Once the nine houses were in place, their ahistorical storefronts were removed and replaced with period-appropriate brick-and-stone infill, inviting criticism that the row was little more than a Disneyland facsimile. Author Paul Goldberger, in his 1979 book *The City Observed: New York*,[19] proclaimed: "all that these houses make you want to do is run back across Greenwich Street where old buildings are still real and not kept alive by artificial respirator."[20] Regardless, when the city offered the houses for sale in 1976, even with gutted interiors, they were quickly snapped up for between $35,000 and $75,000. Today, they fetch millions.

From the **townhouses**, walk east along **Harrison Street** to **Hudson Street**

Stop 5 → At the corner of **Harrison** and **Hudson Streets**

THE MERCANTILE EXCHANGE

Here you'll find the Mercantile Exchange, a beautiful red-brick pile with granite and cast-iron embellishment. The Mercantile Exchange was formed in 1872 as the Butter and Cheese Exchange, but changed its name a decade later as it expanded "to include dealers in groceries, dried fruits, poultry, and canned goods."[21] The building stands as a reflection of the commercial vitality of this area, which sat so close to the waterfront and the Washington Market.

Turn left on **Hudson Street** and then right onto **Franklin Street**. Follow **Franklin** to **Varick Street**, then turn left

Stop 6 → At the diminutive firehouse at the corner of **Moore** and **Varick Streets**

GHOSTBUSTERS FIREHOUSE

Though now best known for its role in the 1984 film *Ghostbusters*, there is more to this building than meets the eye. Completed in 1903, the firehouse of Hook & Ladder 8 was built in the immediate aftermath of the 1898 consolidation of New York's five boroughs as part of a wave of civic construction undertaken in an attempt to meet the demands of the newly formed metropolis. In 1904, one year after the Hook & Ladder building opened, the city's first subway line opened, and by 1910, city leaders were calling for the transit system's expansion down the Lower West Side, directly through this area. To make room for the new subway line, Varick Street was widened to 100 feet (30 meters), forcing the destruction or alteration of dozens of buildings along its path.

When Hook & Ladder 8 was built, it was fully 55 feet (17 meters) wide, with two garage bays for fire engines. Demolition for the widening of Varick Street began in 1914, barely a decade after the firehouse was completed. The building's western half was removed, its Italianate architectural details carefully preserved and reinstalled on the new Varick facade. The two-bay firehouse became a one-bay firehouse and, a century later, it is almost impossible to tell by looking at it that any such destruction was ever wrought. Today, Hook & Ladder 8 remains an active company of the FDNY, despite being only

Ghostbusters Firehouse

Canal Street looking east

Canal Street

half of its original size. But discerning historians and passersby know that, beyond its cinematic fame, this little firehouse tells a story of the chaos of New York's heady 20th-century modernization.

Walk east past the firehouse to **West Broadway**

Stop 7 → At No. 2 **White Street**, where you will see one of the oldest surviving houses in lower Manhattan

NO. 2 WHITE STREET, THE TUCKER HOUSE

The little white house at No. 2 White Street was built around 1809 for Gideon Tucker, a prominent local leader who served as a school commissioner, commissioner of estimates and assessments, and as the neighborhood's assistant alderman. The home is one of the most intact residential structures from this era at the turn of the 19th century. Its low profile and human scale are at jarring odds with the larger buildings which now surround it. Even the six-story loft building next door, though rather short by Manhattan standards, looms over the old Tucker house.

No. 2 White Street is startlingly well preserved, considering how much change the home has witnessed in the area. When it was constructed, Manhattan was home to fewer than 100,000 residents, and White Street stood on the very northern edges of the built-up city. The window lintels, with their decorative keystones, are original, as are the home's steep gambrel roof and dormer windows. It is difficult to imagine that this was once representative of the majority of New York's built environment, when the city was a minor port town still rebuilding from the travails of revolution.

From the **Tucker house**, walk one block north on **West Broadway** to **Beach Street**. Turn left on **Beach**, walk to **Varick Street**, and there turn right.

Stop 8 → At **St John's Square**

ST JOHN'S SQUARE

It is difficult to imagine that this pocket of Tribeca was ever anything other than the massive, traffic-snarled void you will see on your left. But the giant traffic circle here, an exit roundabout for the Holland Tunnel, was once the site of St John's Square, one of the loveliest of New York's early parks. St John's was established in 1803 as a leafy oasis anchoring the surrounding well-heeled neighborhood. Similar to Gramercy Park (page 145), established three decades later, access to St John's Park was limited to key-holding residents of the area, including such notables as the Hamilton, Schuyler, and Gibbes families. On the east side of the park, midblock on Varick Street, stood St John's Chapel, built in 1807 as a rural outpost of Trinity Church (page 22). Its high, thin steeple was one of the tallest structures in New York and the pride of the neighborhood.

St John's Park, along with its surrounding blocks of fine houses, was developed on land granted to it by Queen Anne in 1705. In its heyday of the 1820s and 1830s, its resident families were counted among society's most elite and well connected. But by the 1840s, it had begun to decline, partly due to its increasingly remote location downtown as the city marched ever northward, and partly due to its proximity to the increasingly chaotic Hudson riverfront. By 1866, the end was nigh for St John's as Trinity partnered with local landowners to sell the park itself to Cornelius Vanderbilt's Hudson River Railroad. The following year, the fence was removed, the trees were felled, and a mighty freight terminal rose on the site. Where New York's elite once attended parties and promenaded beneath a canopy of elms, smoke-spewing trains now clattered to and fro.

By the 1890s, old St John's was considered a slum, "and for those who retained any recollection of what the neighborhood had once been, the comparisons between then and now were painful."[22] In 1918, thanks to the rise of the automobile, old St John's Chapel, once the pride of lower west Manhattan, was razed for the widening of Varick Street. Any hint at the neighborhood's former glory was now gone. In 1927, the Holland Tunnel opened to automobile traffic, and in 1936, the old Vanderbilt freight terminal was torn down to make way for the current roundabout for cars exiting the tunnel from New Jersey. The completeness of St John's disappearance from the streetscape and from New York's collective memory is a wonder and a tragedy.

Walk north along **Varick Street** and turn right onto **Laight Street**. Follow **Laight** to **Canal Street**

Stop 9 → Turn right and make your way east along **Canal Street**

CANAL STREET

Canal gets its name from the actual canal which was dug along this path at the turn of the 19th century. Now buried as a sewer, it was intended to drain off the ponds and marshes which once defined the landscape of modern Tribeca and SoHo. Canal Street is a busy commercial thoroughfare, and the chaos of pedestrian traffic is exacerbated by the ceaseless flow of automobiles making their way to and from the west side highway and tunnels. It also acts as the boundary between Tribeca (Triangle Below Canal) and SoHo (South of Houston), giving it a bit of a borderland vibe, simultaneously part of both and neither neighborhood. But Canal Street's enduring vitality is a testament to its importance as the main artery of lower west Manhattan.

Walking east along Canal Street, the streetscape is a hodgepodge of all building types, materials, heights, and uses. Modern glass hotels abut cast-iron buildings from the 1870s which loom over twee dormered brick houses from the 1820s. Some of the best surviving examples of the latter can be spotted on the north side of the street between Greene and Mercer Streets. Eight adjoining buildings, Nos. 313–327 Canal Street, all date to the 1810s and 1820s when this area first developed as a wealthy suburban enclave atop the recently drained marshland along the canal. Three of them—Nos. 321, 323, and 327—retain their original peaked roofs and dormers, offering a glimpse of the sort of domestic comforts enjoyed by these early residents. Of note: Samuel F B Morse, of Morse Code fame, lived for a time at No. 321.

Turn left onto **Mercer Street**, heading north into **SoHo**

Entering SoHo, be sure to admire the marble, iron, and red-brick building on the east side of Mercer, stretching the full block between Canal and Howard Streets. This was built in 1856 as the new flagship for Arnold Constable & Co., a department store founded in 1825 by Aaron Arnold who was joined by his son-in-law, James Constable, in 1842. Long considered one of New York's most "magnificent and tempting"[23] stores, Arnold Constable relocated several times over the years in an attempt to chase its customer base uptown. In addition to this lovely marble building on Canal Street, former Arnold Constable stores can also be seen on 19th Street between Broadway and 5th Avenue as well as at the southeast corner of 5th Avenue and 40th Street, the current Stavros Niarchos Foundation branch of the NYPL, where the company finally shuttered in 1975 after 150 years in business.

Walk north along **Mercer Street**, one of the loveliest canyons of cast-iron loft buildings in Manhattan, before turning right onto **Broome Street**

Stop 10 → At the corner of **Broome Street** and **Broadway**

SOHO

SoHo is among the most beloved, most visited, and most expensive tracts of land on Manhattan Island, thanks in large part to its long stretches of cast-iron lofts and stores from the mid-19th century. But these buildings were not always as respected as they are today, and in the 1960s, much of what is now the SoHo-Cast Iron Historic District was slated for demolition to make way for a massive elevated highway, part of a tangle of automobile infrastructure cooked up by city planning czar Robert Moses. Essentially, he wanted to build the Lower Manhattan Expressway, a 10-lane, elevated road through the neighborhood, largely along the path of Broome Street, to connect the Holland Tunnel to the Manhattan and Williamsburg Bridges, destroying this neighborhood, which was widely considered a blight as its industrial tenants shuttered in droves after World War II.

HAUGHWOUT BUILDING

Credit for SoHo's endurance is owed in part to the stunning blue-gray facade of the EV Haughwout (pronounced HOW-itt) Building at the northeast corner of the intersection of Broome and Broadway. As its industrial vitality waned, the neighborhood now known as SoHo began to attract artists, drawn to the area's cheap rent, and its buildings which featured vast expanses of raw, well-lit space conducive to creating on a large scale. Against a backdrop of so-called "freeway revolts", in which urban residents nationwide pushed back against the wanton destruction wrought by highway construction, New Yorkers, including the legendary Jane Jacobs, went toe-to-toe with the proposed Lower Manhattan Expressway's "well-funded and politically connected"[24] backers. Jacobs' seminal 1961 book, *The Death and Life of Great American Cities*, helped turn public opinion against such misguided urban renewal projects.

In 1965, the newly formed Landmarks Preservation Commission designated Nos. 488–492 Broadway, the former EV Haughwout store, a New York City landmark. Calling it the best of New York's "cast

Arnold Constable Building

Mercer Street between Broome and Grand

Haughwout Building

Broome Street near Crosby Street

Crosby Street between Spring and Broome

iron palaces, and indeed one of the most interesting and important buildings in the whole city,"[25] the Commission's designation report noted how such cast-iron construction anticipated the later development of steel-frame skyscrapers. The report also referred to "the magnificent architectural heritage"[26] of New York's cast-iron palaces, noting that they are "a very New York thing, not equaled anywhere else."[27] Situated "directly in the right of way of the Lower Manhattan Expressway,"[28] the Haughwout building became an obstacle and a literal roadblock to the Lower Manhattan Expressway's implementation. The project was scrapped by 1970 and SoHo gained historic district designation in 1973.

Beyond its role in the defeat of Robert Moses's highway plan, the Haughwout Building is a splendid piece of architecture with a rich and rather incredible history. Built in 1857, it was originally home to the luxe glass and china emporium of Eder Vreeland Haughwout. The building was a marvel, not just for its imposing and ultra-modern cast-iron facade, but also for its inclusion of a passenger elevator, the first in New York to include Elisha Otis' innovative new safety cables which prevented the cab from plummeting in the event of breakage. Otis had only just unveiled his invention to the public at New York's 1853 World's Fair in Bryant Park (page 175). Haughwout's store drew customers from around the country, including most notably First Lady Mary Todd Lincoln who purchased a set of dishes for the White House here in 1861.

After more than a century of various uses and abuse, the "rusty, brooding"[29] Haughwout Building was fully cleaned, repainted, and restored in the 1990s. Today, it is one of the great highlights of SoHo's magnificent cast-iron landscape. More than that, it is arguably the main reason that landscape exists today at all.

Walk east along **Broome**, passing the **Haughwout Building**, and turn left onto **Crosby Street**

Stop 11 → In front of the two-story brick building at **No. 54 Crosby Street**

ARTURO DI MODICA STUDIO

As the sun rose over Wall Street on Friday, December 15, 1989, bankers and brokers hustling their way to work encountered something most unusual: a 3.5-ton, 18-foot (5.5-meter) bronze statue of a charging bull. It had been left there, beneath the Christmas tree in front of the New York Stock Exchange, under cover of darkness by Sicilian-born artist Arturo Di Modica. He hauled it downtown on a flatbed truck from his SoHo studio, here at No. 54 Crosby Street, which he built by hand after buying the vacant lot in 1978. It took him two years to sculpt and forge the giant animal. "He wanted to encourage everybody to realize America's power,"[30] following the stock market crash of 1987, said his assistant, Kim Stippa.

The concept of markets being Bulls or Bears can be traced to an English play, published in 1715, called *The Country Lasses* by Charles Johnson. In it, an old man criticizes modern London and its "lewdness," going on to say, "...and instead of changing honest Staple for Gold and Silver, you deal in Bears and Bulls only." Though the bull statue was an instant hit with pedestrians, the police said the statue had no permit and was obstructing traffic. It was quickly and unceremoniously carted off to a warehouse in Queens, much to the disappointment of nearby workers (and the market, which closed down 14.08 points that day). Days later, the bull was put on display near Bowling Green, where it remains.

Today, the bull statue has become one of New York's most popular and widely recognized tourist attractions. The plaza where it sits is often thronged by crowds of tourists eager to get a photo, either with its face or nether regions—the shiny testicles testament to the supposition that rubbing them will bring you good luck. But less well known is the artist behind the statue.

Arturo Di Modica was born in Sicily in 1941 and moved to New York in 1970, soon gaining a bit of a reputation for leaving giant sculptures around New York. He did it in Rockefeller Center in 1977, and again at Lincoln Center in 1985. But it was his bull statue which cemented his legacy.

Di Modica remained here on Crosby Street, part of the vibrant tapestry of residents who defined SoHo's emergence as the world's greatest artistic live-work district, until he sold the building in 2004. He died in his hometown in Sicily in 2021. His bull statue and, less obviously, his hand-built Crosby Street studio, remain as physical reminders of his impact on New York.

From **Di Modica's studio**, walk north along **Crosby Street** to **Spring Street**, then turn left

Stop 12 → At the corner of **Mercer Street**

ART IN SOHO

No. 101 Spring Street, at the northeast corner of Mercer, is an exceptionally delicate example of the possibilities of cast-iron architecture. Its windows are so large that the facade is visibly more glass than metal, giving it a light and airy appearance at odds with many of the heavier, more obviously industrial buildings elsewhere in the district. As noted as part of its inclusion in the neighborhood's 1973 historic designation report: "In this building, form, as it is used to create lightness, is the most important element; everything else merely enhances this dominant intention."[31]

Typical of such buildings in modern SoHo, No. 101 Spring Street was built as an industrial and commercial loft structure in 1871 during the heady boom years following the end of the American Civil War. By the 1960s, industry had largely abandoned Manhattan in favor of larger, more up-to-date manufacturing districts elsewhere, such as New Jersey, Brooklyn, and the American South. A 1962 study produced by the City Club of New York called the neighborhood a "true wasteland" which was "so inefficient and unsanitary that industry avoids it even at extremely low rents."[32] The plan was to demolish almost the entire area now known as SoHo, along with vast swaths of Greenwich Village, and replace it all with new roads (like the aforementioned highway along Broome Street) and housing projects.

Ultimately, this devastating plan never went through, thanks in large part to the efforts of advocates such as Jane Jacobs. A similar urban renewal project which destroyed an area known as Washington Square Southeast was met with such vociferous community

Donald Judd Foundation

backlash from its approval in 1954 through its completion in 1966 that city leaders were reluctant to invite further ire. And so this cast-iron district, now known as SoHo, though denigrated as a slum unworthy of salvation, survived just long enough to reinvent itself.

Abandoned by industry, the neighborhood's grungy lofts became home and studio space for the city's artists, many of whom had been priced out of every other corner of Manhattan. Artists were soon joined by the gallerists who represented them, lured downtown from their traditional Madison Avenue addresses by the low rents and easy proximity to clients. By 1970 this area, once known as Lispenard Meadows, then as the Cast Iron District, and even "The Valley" on account of its low-slung skyline, was rebranded as SoHo, short for the city planning department's onetime designation for it: the South Houston Industrial District. It was officially designated a historic district in 1973, preserving it as one of the most cherished architectural time capsules on earth.

JUDD FOUNDATION

Amidst SoHo's emergence as a post-industrial creative district, Donald Judd purchased No. 101 Spring Street in 1968. Born in Missouri and educated at Columbia and the Art Students League, Judd would help to redefine the very meaning of Minimalism. Color, texture, shape, and surface were all intrinsic to his work, much of it executed at the sort of monumental scale made possible by the vastness of his SoHo loft. He believed in "the autonomy of the art object, namely that the object's purpose was not to serve as a metaphor for human life, but to have a strong formal life of its own."[33] In addition to his emergence as one of SoHo's most prominent, successful, and vocal artistic residents, Judd established a contemporary art museum called The Chinati Foundation on a 340-acre (138-hectare) former military base in Marfa, Texas. It opened to the public in 1986.

Donald Judd died in 1994 at age 65, but his legacy endures through the Judd Foundation, whose stated mission is to preserve the artist's permanently installed living and working spaces, libraries, and archives in New York and Marfa. The Foundation now operates out of his former loft building at No. 101 Spring Street, which opened to the public in 2013 with many of his original works installed exactly as he left them. Likewise, Judd's Chinati Foundation transformed the sleepy town of Marfa into a world-class art destination, a sort of SoHo of the West Texas desert.

Over the past half-century, SoHo has evolved from being a byword for industrial degradation to one for artistic innovation. Today, it is better known as a district of intense tourism and gentrification. Prada, Bloomingdale's, and Louis Vuitton cater to the throngs of tourists who come to admire the architecture and gawk at one of the world's most famous arts districts. Today, SoHo is among the most expensive neighborhoods in the world, forcing out most of the artists who made it desirable in the first place. As artists move out, many galleries have followed, transforming SoHo from "the hub of the New York art world"[34] to a mere satellite. Despite this, its architecture survives thanks in no small measure to those artists like Donald Judd who saw value and potential in a neighborhood once cast off as a mere wasteland.

Continue walking west along **Spring Street**
Stop 13 → At **No. 129**, on the north side of **Spring** just past **Greene Street**

THE MURDER AT NO. 129 SPRING STREET

The little brick house at No. 129 Spring Street, with its charming dormer windows and Flemish-bond brick facade, was constructed in 1817, making it one of the oldest surviving structures in SoHo. It was built a few years before the Erie Canal opened, heralding unprecedented economic and population growth in the city. Within a decade of the house's completion, most of the surrounding blocks were filled with similarly handsome structures, transforming the area into one of the city's choicest residential districts.

But hidden beneath No. 129 Spring Street, in the basement of what is currently a COS clothing store, lies a mysterious brick structure, cylindrical and roughly formed, which is often purported to be linked to a 1799 murder mystery. (It goes without saying that it is regularly claimed to be haunted.) These claims are, unfortunately, dubious at best. The structure beneath No. 129 Spring Street is, in all likelihood, not a well but a cistern built contemporaneously with the house in 1817. Regardless of its provenance, a murder mystery did play out nearby, and its story is worth telling.

George Washington died on December 14, 1799, plunging the United States into mourning. One week after his death, on December 21, a pretty young girl named Elma Sands (some reports say her full name was Juliana or Gulielma, but all agree she went by Elma) left the boarding house on upper Greenwich Street where she'd lived with her cousins and some other boarders, planning to marry her longtime sweetheart, Levi Weeks. Elma was never to return. Her body was discovered on January 2, 1800, at the bottom of a brick well near Spring Street west of Broadway, dug only recently by the Manhattan Company for the purpose of providing drinking water to the area.

Elma's body was examined and left for public viewing before being buried in the nearby potter's field, which would later become Washington Square Park. Her fiancé, Levi Weeks, was soon arrested on suspicion of murder and put on trial that March. Thanks in part to Levi's wealthy brother Ezra, his defense was mounted by three of the nation's most prominent lawyers: Brockholst Livingston, Aaron Burr, and Alexander Hamilton. Livingston went on to serve on the United States Supreme Court from 1807 until his death in 1823. Hamilton had already served as Secretary of the Treasury under Washington, and Burr was on the verge of his dramatically unsuccessful bid for the presidency. In 1804, Burr would kill Hamilton in a duel which took place in Weehawken, New Jersey.

But in 1800, the acrimony between Burr and Hamilton had not yet spilled into public view, and the pair, along with Livingston, won acquittal for Levi Weeks. Elma's landlady, Catherine Ring, was reportedly so outraged by the verdict that she shook her fist in Hamilton's face, declaring "If thee dies a natural death, I shall think there is no justice in Heaven!"[35]

The well in which the body of Elma Sands was discovered has been lost to history, though it ought to have stood a bit north of No. 129

Spring Street, on the west side of Greene Street. It was sold off by the Manhattan Company in 1808 as it pivoted to banking, a scheme executed by none other than Aaron Burr, and it exists today as part of the financial behemoth JP Morgan Chase. The city's drinking water was ultimately provided instead by the Croton Water System, which began flowing in 1842. In time, the old mysterious murder well disappeared beneath the pavers and basements of an increasingly densely built city.

Interest in Elma Sands' murder was revived in 1974, after the neighborhood had been transformed into the modern arts district of SoHo, when the owner of a nearby shop on Greene Street claimed to be haunted by the ghost of the girl. Then, in 1980, the owners of No. 129 Spring Street discovered the remains of the 1817 cistern in their basement. Stories got conflated, fictions were repeated, and the story was given wings by major publications which repeated the tale of the rediscovered murder well.

Today, the cistern beneath No. 129 Spring Street has been stabilized and incorporated into the selling floor of the COS store, allowing visitors to get up close and personal. Unfortunately, there is no solid evidence tying it to Elma Sands' tragic demise. It is merely a cistern, built two centuries ago, and an astounding piece of SoHo's earliest residential development. The fact that the house and its brick water tank have survived so much upheaval is a minor miracle. The fact that it has all been erroneously wrapped up in an earlier murder mystery, one which involved multiple Founding Fathers, is one of those quirks of urban lore. But if it gets people interested in history and architecture, how can one complain?

Walk west one block along **Spring Street**, then turn right onto **Wooster**

Stop 14 → At No. 99 Wooster Street

GAY ACTIVISTS ALLIANCE FIREHOUSE

Greenwich Village, home to Julius' and Stonewall, often gets the lion's share of attention for being the cradle of the Queer Liberation Movement. But much happened elsewhere, too, especially in the decade after the 1969 Stonewall Riots, when New York's LGBTQ+ community began to move out of the shadows and into a more public-facing position from which they could more directly and effectively fight for equality. Between Stonewall and the beginning of the HIV/AIDS crisis in the 1980s, the 1970s heralded a drastically altered cultural and political landscape of radical activism which forms a lynchpin of Queer history. It was a decade when anything seemed possible and a malleable future was up for grabs.

The former firehouse at No. 99 Wooster Street is a vital piece of that era, having served as the headquarters for the Gay Activists Alliance (GAA) during their most active period, from 1971–74. The GAA was formed in December of 1969, just six months after the Stonewall Riots, aiming "to secure basic human rights, dignity, and freedom for all gay people."[36] Building on the success of earlier organizations, such as the Mattachine Society, whose 1966 *Sip-in* at Julius' Bar shed light on the unfairness of New York State's anti-gay liquor laws, the GAA sought to achieve change through media attention and public scrutiny. They "disrupted many events, organized well-attended marches and demonstrations, and held protests and sit-ins to shape public opinion and government policy."[37]

In April 1971, the GAA leased the old firehouse at No. 99 Wooster Street, moving to SoHo just as the neighborhood was approaching its apex as an artistic and creative enclave. The firehouse, which was built in 1881 to designs by Napoleon LeBrun, attracted the GAA in part because of its small size compared to nearby factory lofts. The group could take the whole building, operating without interference from other tenants, thus creating "a place that we could really call a home," according to their monthly newsletter, *The Activist*. "A home in which we could be gay and proud, a home for love, peace, and homosexuality."[38] The firehouse hosted meetings, film screenings, and dances, quickly cementing No. 99 Wooster Street as a major social and political hub for New York's LGBTQ+ community. More than a dozen later organizations, such as ACT UP, trace their origins to the firehouse, outgrowths of the building's many summits, happenings, and committees.

In October of 1974, arson destroyed roughly half of the building's interior, forcing the eviction of the GAA. It is unclear whether this was a homophobic attack or a result of increasing factionalism within the GAA. The organization disbanded in 1981, by which time the old firehouse on Wooster Street had been renovated for more mainstream commercial tenants, part of the overall transformation of SoHo into a more investor-friendly enclave of shops and galleries. But during its years spent in the building, the GAA made an indelible impression on the fight for LGBTQ+ equality, part of the proverbial long arc toward justice.

Walk north along **Wooster** to **Houston Street**

Here, the north side of Houston Street provides a stark example of what might have befallen the rest of SoHo had earlier urban renewal proposals been allowed to go through. Houston (pronounced HOW-ston) is more than twice the width of nearby streets, a result of its widening in the 1920s to allow for construction of a new subway line beneath it. The street's northern side is a bleak jumble of brutalist towers (Silver Towers by IM Pei, 1964–67) and misguided modern additions wrought in tiresome blue glass (NYU's Paulson Center, 2023), all part of the legacy of the aforementioned "Washington Square Southeast" project which destroyed nearly a dozen Greenwich Village blocks in the name of modernity.

Walk east along **Houston Street** and turn right onto **Greene Street**

Stop 15 → In front of the unexpected little brick house at **No. 139 Greene Street**

GREENE STREET RED LIGHT DISTRICT

By the 1850s, most of the original wealthy residents of this area had moved on and most of their fine homes were sold off and demolished to make way for new commercial and loft spaces. But this transition did not happen all at once, and for a time, much of the area housed an uneasy mixture of building types and uses. Flashy department stores lined Broadway, intermixed with theaters and large hotels, but narrower stone-paved side streets often met less rarified demands: industry, drinking, gambling and, as was the case along Greene Street, prostitution.

No. 139 Greene Street was built in 1825 for the wealthy merchant-tailor Anthony Arnoux and his family. It is a remarkable survivor, one of the last Federal-style brick houses from this era left standing in the heart of loft-filled SoHo, and like numerous similar survivor houses visited on this walk, it offers a glimpse of what the area might have looked like in its early days, when the city was booming thanks to the completion of the Erie Canal. The Arnoux family stayed until about 1860, by which time the increase of local commercialism pushed them uptown to newly fashionable Murray Hill (specifically, they lived at No. 20 East 32nd Street[39], just around the corner from the Astors).

By 1862, the former Arnoux home was being used as a brothel, one of more than a dozen such establishments on this one block of Greene Street. By 1870, a gentleman's guide noted that Greene Street had become "a complete sink of iniquity. In the short space of six squares, included between Canal and Bleecker Streets there are 41 barrooms, 8 houses of assignation, 22 houses in which furnished rooms are let to girls, and 11 segar stores."[40]

Prostitution in New York tended to follow the city's hotels and theaters, which provided much of their business, and so by the 1890s, most brothels had moved uptown to the area west of Madison Square known as the Tenderloin. Most of the old houses along Greene Street which had survived up to this point were torn down and replaced by larger, more profitable loft buildings. Somehow, No. 139 Greene Street hung on, though it was woefully abused by the addition of shop windows and a freight dock. In 1973, the same year SoHo was designated a historic district, the little house was purchased by Peter Ballantine, a local gallerist and fabricator for Donald Judd, who planned to restore it as his home.

Half a century later, the work continues, albeit so slowly that many passersby are justified in wondering if it has been abandoned. But it is not abandoned, and Peter Ballantine remains active in the local art scene. His little red-brick house stands as a welcome counterpoint to the neighborhood's profusion of luxury boutiques and swanky cafes, a reminder of the area's earliest days and more tawdry chapters.

Walk south along **Greene** to **Prince Street**

Stop 16 → At the corner of **Greene** and **Prince Streets**

RICHARD HAAS MURAL

The large-scale mural at No. 112 Prince Street at the southwest corner of Greene Street has recently been restored. The work, which covers the entire eastern facade, was begun in 1974 by the artist Richard Haas, who specializes in such monumental *trompe l'oeil* paintings. Legendary *Times* architecture critic Ada Louise Huxtable called it a triumph, extending the building's cast-iron facade as "both a tribute to the building's architectural quality and a visual punch line for the original, unintentional joke of its one-sided excellence."[41]

By the 2010s, Haas's mural was "dying a slow and painfully public death,"[42] marred by graffiti and worn away by decades of weather

Broadway & Spring Street

Corner of Spring & Wooster

129 Spring Street

Richard Haas Mural

Little Singer Building

exposure. Happily, it was restored in 2023, with the addition of a dog and two cats, pets of current building residents. The mural will continue to enliven this corner for another half-century, to the delight of any passersby savvy enough to look up.

Turn left on **Prince Street** and walk east across **Mercer**

Stop 17 → Just before **Broadway** to gaze at the spectacular Singer Manufacturing Building at **No. 88 Prince Street**

LITTLE SINGER BUILDING

Known as the Little Singer Building, this outstanding example of decorative iron in highrise design was built in 1903 for the Singer Manufacturing Company, legendary inventors and purveyors of sewing machines. It was designed by renowned architect Ernest Flagg, who'd only just finished another office building for the company downtown at Broadway and Liberty Street in 1897. That older building would be greatly expanded by the addition of a soaring tower in 1908, which at 674 feet (205 meters) was the tallest building on earth until 1909. Its destruction in the 1960s is often heralded as one of the great crimes against architecture executed in this city, which helped launch the landmarks preservation movement of later decades. But thanks to the Singer Tower's fame, SoHo's Little Singer Building is often overlooked, despite boasting one of the loveliest and most unique facades in New York.

What might have been an ordinary cast-iron loft building was instead elaborated into a glorious riot of painted metal tracery against windows so large as to almost foreshadow later glass-curtain construction in skyscrapers. All of this is set off to great effect by earthy red terracotta tiles, the likes of which were very much in vogue at the time thanks to their light weight, low cost, and fireproof qualities. Flagg embellished the building with grand tracery arches near ground level and at the roof line, giving form to its crowded verticality. And in a nod to traditional architectural design, Flagg also included false Ionic columns, rendered in almost deconstructivist iron bars to frame the third-story windows. It is a masterful building well worth a moment's gaze amid the bustle of busy Prince Street.

As a sort of reward for appreciative onlookers, Ernest Flagg and the Singer Company built this facade twice: once here on Prince Street and again around the corner at Nos. 561–563 Broadway. The Little Singer Building is actually L-shaped, wrapping around the older corner building (itself a splendid example of Italianate masonry, built in 1860 to house the jewelers and silversmiths of Ball, Black & Co.) with matching facades on both ends. The Little Singer: a building so nice they built it twice.

Continue walking east along **Prince Street** to the corner of **Mulberry Street**

Stop 18 → At **St Patrick's Old Cathedral**

ST PATRICK'S OLD CATHEDRAL

St Patrick's Old Cathedral is one of the city's oldest and most storied churches and has lain "tucked away in an undistinguished corner of lower Manhattan"[43] since its completion in 1815, more than two centuries ago.

Greene Street between Spring and Prince

Basilica of St Patrick's Old Cathedral

Despite its name, it is not the oldest Catholic congregation in New York. That superlative belongs to St Peter's, which currently occupies an imposing granite temple downtown on Barclay Street. Built in 1838, it houses a congregation which was established in 1785, just one year after the repeal of New York's colonial anti-Catholic laws, which prevented priests from even entering the state. In 1801, rapidly growing St Peter's purchased land far north of the established city for use as a burial ground. That cemetery—bound by modern Prince, Mott, and Mulberry Streets—would soon be repurposed as the location of the city's first cathedral.

The cornerstone for this new Holy See was laid in 1809, one year after the Catholic Diocese of New York was formally established by Pope Pius VII. The new cathedral would be named in honor of Ireland's patron, Saint Patrick, a reflection of the outsize influence of Irish immigrants within the community. New York's Catholic population had grown from fewer than 1,000 at the end of the American Revolution to more than 10,000 by 1806, thanks to the large number of Irish forced to flee their homeland's 1798 Rebellion. Hibernian influence would soon grow exponentially larger, thanks to an influx of Irish migrants fleeing the Great Famine of 1845–52.

From its opening in 1815, St Patrick's has served a roiling mixture of the city's neediest immigrant residents. It also initially served as a flashpoint for New York's Nativist organizations who saw these newly arrived Catholics as Papist usurpers whose very presence threatened the city's identity. As anti-Catholic violence reached a fever pitch, a substantial brick wall was erected around the grounds of St Patrick's in 1834, a wall which remains in place today. In October of 1866, much of the cathedral's interior was destroyed in a mighty conflagration sparked by embers blown over from another fire on nearby Crosby Street. Its highly flammable wooden roof and plaster-and-lath ceiling were quickly consumed and collapsed into the building's interior, destroying all. Its stone exterior walls survived, however, and St Patrick's was rebuilt and rededicated less than two years later.

By the time of the 1866 fire, however, work had already begun on St Patrick's uptown replacement. New York's Catholic population had continued to grow at a rapid clip, eclipsing 400,000 adherents by 1860. To meet the present and future needs of such a flock, Archbishop John Hughes approved the construction of a vast new St Patrick's Cathedral on 5th Avenue between 50th and 51st Streets. Its cornerstone was laid in 1858 and it was consecrated in 1879, replacing the old cathedral downtown, as the seat of New York's Catholic Archdiocese.

Now more than 200 years old, St Patrick's Old Cathedral remains one of the great pillars of lower Manhattan's social, cultural, religious, and architectural identity. Its stone facade, brick defensive walls, and time-worn gravestones speak to the depth of history in this neighborhood. Before leaving, be sure to peek through the little peepholes in the graveyard's doors to see the hidden world beyond. Preferably, if viewed in late August or September, there will be a sheep or three, part of an annual tradition which invites a flock to munch on the yard's grasses and vines.

The joy of Tribeca, SoHo, and all of lower Manhattan is the ease of wandering, people-watching, and getting lost in the endless blocks of shopping, food, and architectural history. Pick a direction and go.

From St Patrick's Old Cathedral, choices for further exploration abound: walk east into the **Lower East Side**, north into **NoHo and the East Village**, or south into **Little Italy and Chinatown**

- Visit **Jen**, the fourth-generation butcher at Albanese (No. 238 Elizabeth) for Italian meats and specialties
- Grab fluffy pork buns from **Golden Steamer** (No. 143A Mott or No. 210 Grand)
- Pick up some freshly made ravioli or tortellini from **Piemonte** (No. 190 Grand)
- Find cold cuts and cheeses at **DiPalo's** (No. 200 Grand)
- Or search out all manner of souvenirs from **E Rossi & Co.** (No. 193 Grand)
- For more cheap eats, try the sponge cake from **Spongie's** (No. 121 Baxter)
- Try a pork plate from **Wah Fung** (7 No. 9 Chrystie) but expect a line
- Choose dumplings from any number of places like **Jin Mei** (No. 25B Henry), **Super Taste** (No. 26 Eldridge), **North** (No. 27A Essex), or **King** (No. 74 Hester)

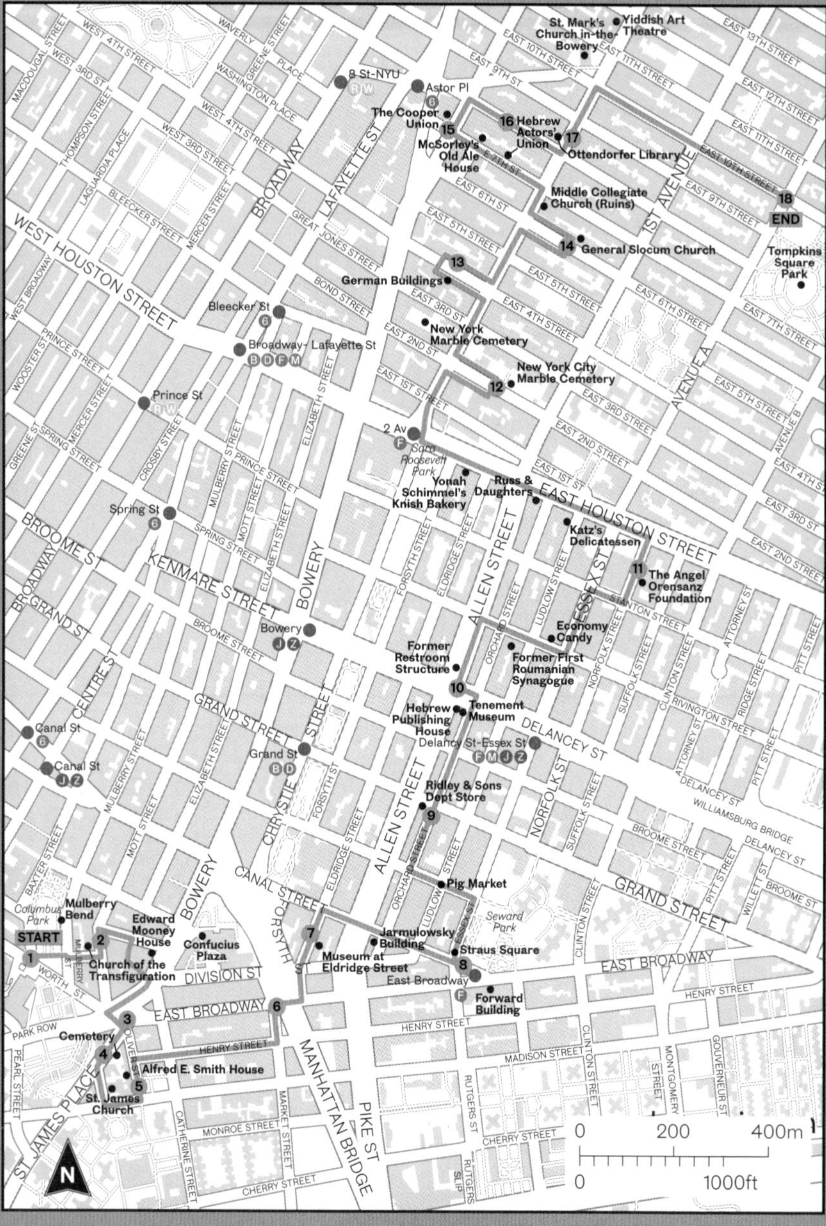

START
1
2
Mulberry Bend
Columbus Park
Church of the Transfiguration
Edward Mooney House
Confucius Plaza
3
Cemetery
4
Alfred E. Smith House
5
St. James Church
6
7
Museum at Eldridge Street
Jarmulowsky Building
Straus Square
8
East Broadway
Forward Building
Pig Market
9
Ridley & Sons Dept Store
Seward Park
10
Hebrew Publishing House
Tenement Museum
Former Restroom Structure
Former First Roumanian Synagogue
Economy Candy
11
The Angel Orensanz Foundation
Katz's Delicatessen
Russ & Daughters
Yonah Schimmel's Knish Bakery
Sara Roosevelt Park
2 Av
12
New York City Marble Cemetery
New York Marble Cemetery
13
German Buildings
14
General Slocum Church
Middle Collegiate Church (Ruins)
15
The Cooper Union
McSorley's Old Ale House
16
Hebrew Actors' Union
17
Ottendorfer Library
St. Mark's Church in-the-Bowery
Yiddish Art Theatre
18
END
Tompkins Square Park
Astor Pl
8 St-NYU
Bleecker St
Broadway- Lafayette St
Prince St
Spring St
Bowery
Grand St
Canal St
Delancy St-Essex St
West Houston Street
East Houston Street
Broadway
Lafayette St
Bowery
Kenmare Street
Grand Street
Canal Street
Division St
East Broadway
Henry Street
Madison Street
Monroe Street
Cherry Street
Manhattan Bridge
Williamsburg Bridge
Delancey St
Allen Street
Essex St
1st Avenue
Avenue A
Avenue B
St James Place
Park Row
0
200
400m
0
1000ft
N

CHINATOWN, LOWER EAST SIDE AND EAST VILLAGE

These densely built neighborhoods were the starting point for countless American dreams. On block after block, behind their tenement walls, newly arrived immigrants pieced together new lives for themselves which would fundamentally transform the city and the nation. Today, the area still pulses with the energy of half a million residents, workers, commuters, and tourists all buzzing about its endless supply of restaurants and specialty shops. Though the demographics have shifted in recent years, the streets retain a heady and vibrant mix of sights, smells, and languages.

ROUTE STOPS

1. Five Points
2. Chinatown
3. Chatham Square
4. First Jewish Cemetery
5. Al Smith House
6. Manhattan Bridge
7. Eldridge Street Synagogue
8. Straus Square
9. Ridley & Sons Department Store
10. Allen Street Malls
11. Lenin Statue
12. Marble Cemetery
13. German East 4th Street
14. St Mark's Lutheran Church
15. The Cooper Union
16. St Mark's Place
17. Ottendorfer Library
18. Tompkins Square Park

DISTANCE
3½ miles (5.8 km)

TIME ALLOWED
2–3 hours

ROUTE No.

03

CRADLE OF AMERICAN IMMIGRATION

Stand at the intersection of Worth and Baxter Streets. To the south and west are the imposing courthouses of New York's judicial system. To the northeast lies Columbus Park, beloved lungs of the Chinatown district which extends beyond it. More than a century ago, this was the heart of the Five Points, one of the most infamous pockets of New York's teeming immigrant underworld.

Much of what is now Manhattan's Chinatown was originally part of a five-acre spring-fed body of water called the Collect Pond. Its name was likely a clumsy anglicization of the Dutch word *kolk*, which refers to a stretch of water on a canal or to a small pond or lake. The Collect Pond was reportedly quite deep and teemed with fish. The marshy flatlands north and west of it were rich with game for hunting (these were called Lispenard Meadow, encompassing modern-day SoHo and Tribeca). Pumps tapped into the pond's spring provided fresh water for decades. Despite all this, the pond and its marshes were seen as an impediment to the city's growth, effectively separating the city from valuable uplands to the north.

As early as 1733, attempts were made to drain the pond, but nearby business owners (tanners and brewers, mostly) needed the water; they sued and the drain was plugged in 1734. Plans were floated in the 1760s to convert the pond into a ship basin connected to the East and Hudson Rivers by canal, giving the colony's navy a safe inland mooring. This never came to fruition, and the American Revolution stymied most other plans for the land. By 1800, the Collect Pond had become horribly polluted. Years of abuse by local citizens and businesses meant the waters were contaminated with chemicals and filled with garbage, debris, and animal carcasses.

In 1807, the city began construction on a canal which would drain the polluted swamp and its marshes into the Hudson River. Work was completed in 1811, and the pond was emptied. It was then backfilled with earth and gridded with streets. But there were several problems: first, the pond was spring-fed, meaning water continued to flow even after the canal was built; second, the canal didn't flow as readily as expected, meaning a ravine of fetid, stinking water cut across the width of Manhattan Island; third, the buildings erected atop the old pond rapidly sank into the unstable, wet soil. In 1821, the canal was buried beneath a new road, fittingly named Canal Street. As for the neighborhood built atop the former pond, it subsided into the putrid muck below, rapidly degrading into the city's most notorious slum.

These were the inauspicious beginnings of this area of lower Manhattan Island.

Chinatown (Pell Street from the Bowery)

Start 1 → At **Five Points**

FIVE POINTS

By the mid-19th century, this area was known as the Five Points in honor of its most notoriously chaotic intersection, a five-way clash of Cross (later Park, now Mosco), Anthony (now Worth), and Orange (now Baxter) Streets. The neighborhood's plight was made infamous by the photojournalism of Jacob Riis, whose 1890 book *How the Other Half Lives* made clearing the slums a top civic priority by the turn of the 20th century. By 1900, much of the Five Points had been wiped from the map, with only the intersection of Worth and Baxter Streets left as a reminder of its existence.

From the corner of **Worth** and **Baxter Streets**, walk through **Columbus Park** to **Mosco Street**. Follow it uphill to **Mott Street**

Stop 2 → In the heart of historic **Chinatown** on **Mott Street** between **Mosco** and **Pell Streets**

CHINATOWN

By the 1880s, the population of Chinese immigrants in this area had swelled to an estimated 2,000 people. Centered around Mott, Pell, and Doyers Streets, this community grew in part due to the discrimination Chinese people faced in California in the late 19th century. Some immigrated to work building the nation's western railroad networks; others came to pan for gold in the metals rushes there. But by the 1870s, anti-Chinese aggression pushed many to the relative safety of the east coast. By the 1890s, this neighborhood boasted several Chinese restaurants, introducing New Yorkers to what was then considered novel cuisine, along with dozens of shops, tea parlors, and social clubs. For tourists and locals alike, a visit to Chinatown became something of a requirement, considered a necessary excursion if one were to truly claim to have experienced New York.

But that outsiders' view of Chinatown does a bit of a disservice to the fact that, for more than a century and a half, this neighborhood has served as home and safe haven to a population whose presence in the city was long considered a problem to be tolerated only conditionally. Immigration quotas, police raids, and racist depictions of Chinese-Americans in theater, film, and the press, made the insularity of these densely built streets a necessity beyond mere convenience. It wasn't until the passage of the Immigration and Nationality Act of 1965 that Chinese immigrants were allowed legal entry into the country and those already here became eligible for full citizenship.

Today, the New York metropolitan area is home to nearly a million residents of Chinese descent, with Chinatowns established in all five boroughs and numerous peripheral cities. The majority of this growth since 1965 is the result of immigrants from China's mainland, with Mandarin now vastly outnumbering Cantonese as the primary language in these newer districts. Flushing in Queens, Sunset Park in Brooklyn, and East Broadway on Manhattan's Lower East Side are among the largest and fastest-growing Chinese neighborhoods, providing 21st-century New York with the sort of culinary, cultural, and linguistic vibrancy first developed on Mott, Pell, and Doyers Streets in the 19th century.

From the corner of **Mott** and **Mosco Streets**, walk north to **Pell Street** and turn right. Follow **Pell** to **Doyers Street** and again turn right. Follow **Doyers** out to the **Bowery**, turn right, and cross to the east side of the street at **Chatham Square**, the small pigeon-filled plaza which features a statue of Lin Zexu, a Chinese politician famous for his staunch opposition to drug use during the opium wars

Stop 3 → At **Chatham Square**

CHATHAM SQUARE

Chatham Square may not seem like much to modern eyes. Sitting at the confluence of the Bowery and half a dozen side streets, it is a relatively nondescript plaza, often filled with hundreds of pigeons and the here-there flow of shoppers, tourists, and Chinatown residents. The architectural landscape around it is a hodgepodge of heights, styles, and eras. You may be forgiven for not having heard of Chatham Square before. But in its heyday, this was to 19th-century New Yorkers what Times Square would become in the 20th. It was the beating heart of the city at a time when population growth was exploding. It was the birthplace of the concept of New York as a "city that never sleeps," a place filled with all manner of all-night entertainments, and one of the first places in the world where shop signs were lit to allow for after-dark shopping.

Chatham Square has for centuries served as the starting point of the Bowery, that ancient highway laid out by Manhattan's original residents to connect the southern and northern tips of the island. The colonizing Dutch renamed the road for the fact that it connected their city, New Amsterdam, to the farmland up the island (*Bouwerij*, anglicized as Bowery, is an old Dutch word for farm), and it was the most important thoroughfare on the island for at least two centuries. Not only is the Bowery the oldest street on Manhattan, but as explained by Eric Ferrara, founder and director of the Lower East Side Project, in his 2011 book *The Bowery: A History of Grit, Graft and Grandeur*, it is "the most architecturally and historically diverse street in the city," serving as "an indispensable resource of two centuries of American architectural design, as well as a repository of social, economic, political, immigrant, labor, underground, criminal, deviant, marginal, counter-cultural, literary, musical, dramatic and artistic history."[44]

Situated at the bustling intersection of the Bowery, East Broadway, and Worth Street, Chatham Square is a melting pot of melting pots. Walking a quarter-mile from it in any direction will land a person in a dozen different neighborhoods: Civic Center, the Seaport, and the Financial District to the southwest; Two Bridges and the East Broadway branch of Chinatown to the south and east; Tribeca, SoHo, and the older Cantonese heart of Chinatown to the north; and the sprawling, tenement-filled Lower East Side to the northeast. There are few better jumping-off points for exploring lower Manhattan and its vibrant history than this. Four centuries of growth and urban evolution litter the gritty blocks surrounding Chatham Square, New York's most important under-appreciated plaza.

From **Chatham Square**, cross **Oliver Street** along **St James Place**

Stop 4 → At the **First Cemetery of the Spanish and Portuguese Synagogue**

JEWISH CEMETERY

The Lower East Side of Manhattan holds an almost mythical place in the history of the global Jewish diaspora. Millions of Jewish people from around the world, fleeing various pogroms and evictions, found refuge in these tenement-packed blocks along the East River, toiling and struggling to enable their descendants to escape to the comfort and stability of the American middle class elsewhere. The rise of a majority-Jewish Lower East Side didn't really begin until the 1870s and 80s, when enormous waves of immigrants fled war and hostile laws in Germany and the Russian Empire. Despite this relatively recent timeline, there is one unexpectedly ancient piece of Jewish history hidden away, just east of the Bowery, which predates the Lower East Side's rise as a Jewish enclave by some two centuries: the Spanish and Portuguese Cemetery on St James Place.

This cemetery, one of three such burial grounds scattered across lower Manhattan, belonged to the first Jewish congregation established in what would later become New York. These were Sephardic Jews, forced to flee first the Iberian Peninsula and later Brazil as a result of the Spanish and Portuguese Inquisitions, who landed here in 1654. Though Director-General Peter Stuyvesant tried to prevent them from settling, Dutch law called for religious freedom, and they were ultimately allowed to stay and worship. More than three and a half centuries later, that original Sephardic group remains active as the Congregation Shearith Israel on Central Park West, making it the oldest continuously active Jewish congregation in the Western Hemisphere.

The British took over the colony in 1664, and in 1682 a plot of land was purchased by Jewish congregant Joseph Bueno de Mesquita on the Bowery Road near the outskirts of town for a burial ground. The first burial took place here the following year, in 1683, for Benjamin Bueno de Mesquita, and the land would remain in active use until 1831. Through more than three centuries, the cemetery has borne witness to the whole of New York's evolution from a colonial blip to a global cultural and economic juggernaut. In 1783, General George Washington would have ridden past the cemetery, then already a century old, as he rode down the Bowery Road to retake New York from the British at the end of the Revolutionary War. It has stood sentinel through endless waves of immigration, changes in the neighborhood's language and religion, its architectural makeup, and the ceaseless evolution of technology. In short, the little cemetery on St James Place has been a silent witness to history. As a designated city landmark, it will in all likelihood continue to do so for many centuries more.

From the **cemetery**, continue south to **James Street**, then turn left to find **St James' Church**

Henry Street Tenements

East Broadway from the Manhattan Bridge

The Museum at Eldridge Street

Hester Street near Ludlow

Canal Street

ST JAMES' ROMAN CATHOLIC CHURCH

This brownstone temple is St James' Roman Catholic Church, which was built in 1836 at a time when Catholic immigrants were arriving in the city in ever larger numbers and their churches were regularly being attacked by angry mobs of mostly Protestant nativists. The church is a stalwart survivor, a piece of the Lower East Side's earliest Irish Catholic past, which is so often overshadowed by its better-remembered Chinese, German, and Jewish histories. It was here that the Ancient Order of Hibernians was first established as an Irish fraternal organization in May of 1836.

Turn left onto **Madison Street** and then left again

Stop 5 → At **No. 25 Oliver Street**

AL SMITH'S HOUSE

From 1907–23, a Lower East Side native by the name of Alfred Emanuel Smith lived at No. 25 Oliver Street. Al Smith, "one of the greatest Americans of his generation,"[45] would go on to be elected Governor of New York State from 1919–20 and again from 1923–28. He was also the first Catholic candidate for the United States presidency, losing to Herbert Hoover in 1928. But to his friends, family, and neighbors, Al Smith would forever be remembered as "a friend who stayed with them in the spirit long after the exigencies of a great career had taken him away" from the Lower East Side. "Here his character was formed, his mind given direction, his sympathies deepened."[46]

Pass **Al Smith's house** and turn right onto **Henry Street**

MARINERS' TEMPLE BAPTIST CHURCH

As you turn onto Henry Street, notice at the corner of Oliver and Henry Streets the fine brownstone Mariners' Temple Baptist Church. Its name reflects the congregation's origins as a refuge for sailors docked along the nearby East River waterfront. First organized in 1795, the current temple was built in 1844 and has served successive cohorts of local Baptists: Swedish, Italian, Russian, Chinese, as well as recent generations of Black and Hispanic residents.

Follow **Henry Street** east

Stop 6 → At the corner of **Market Street** at the base of the **Manhattan Bridge**

FIRST CHINESE PRESBYTERIAN CHURCH

On Market Street, you will walk past the lovely stone edifice of the First Chinese Presbyterian Church. Built in 1819 as a Dutch Reformed Church, it was sold to a Presbyterian congregation in 1866. A Chinese Presbyterian congregation moved into the space in 1951 and owned the building outright by 1974.

MANHATTAN BRIDGE

The Manhattan Bridge opened to traffic on December 31, 1909, as part of an attempt to better connect Manhattan to Brooklyn, which had just been absorbed as part of the city in 1898. The bridge also helped alleviate traffic congestion on the nearby Brooklyn Bridge. Like the Williamsburg Bridge, the Manhattan Bridge carries subway train lines in addition to automobile, pedestrian, and bicycle traffic.

From **Henry Street**, turn left onto **Market Street** and walk up to **East Broadway**. Turn right to cross beneath the **Manhattan Bridge**

On the far side of the bridge, turn left and follow **Eldridge Street,** north across **Division Street**

Stop 7 → In front of the grand synagogue at No. 12 **Eldridge Street**

ELDRIDGE STREET SYNAGOGUE

Though the Lower East Side has long been closely associated with the American immigrant experience writ large, it has emerged over the past century as an almost mythical point of origin for one group in particular: the Eastern European Jewish migrants who arrived in New York by the tens of thousands in the late 19th and early 20th centuries. The American Jewish experience is rooted in the lore surrounding this neighborhood, its noises and smells, and its picturesque decrepitude. Photos of pushcarts lining Hester Street have come to represent all that the Lower East Side means to a people who arrived with nothing and built themselves into something.

The retrospective myth of the Lower East Side is as much nostalgia as it is rote history. The Jews of the Lower East Side were never a homogenous, monolithic group, nor were their reasons for immigrating uniform or singular. Rather, they came from a vast and diverse swath of Europe, from Lithuania and Russia to Romania, Hungary, and even Galicia. Some came fleeing persecution while others sought fortune. Some arrived destitute and desperate, others came comparably wealthy and well educated. They brought such diversity to the already teeming Lower East Side street life, adding new accents, culinary flavors, and religious tradition to an already vibrant tapestry.

Regardless, for later generations of American Jews, the Lower East Side became more than simply a neighborhood where their parents and grandparents once lived among other newly immigrated Jews. As described by Hasia Diner in her 2000 book *Lower East Side Memories: A Jewish Place in America*, these tenement-lined streets became "exemplary of the Jewish experience in America."[47] Even for the not insignificant percentage of Jewish Americans whose ancestors settled not in New York but in Chicago or Los Angeles or elsewhere, the Lower East Side has become a symbolic byword for what it meant to be Jewish and new to America. As lore, "the old country" in Europe was modern-day Egypt and the Lower East Side was the biblical desert into which the Jewish people fled, suffering in the process, but experiencing a purity of faith and community unparalleled in history. To escape the tenements was to emerge from the wandering and re-enter the wider world.

Madison Street from the Manhattan Bridge

Nostalgia notwithstanding, the Lower East Side was, for a brief but pivotal time at the turn of the 20th century, the greatest and densest concentration of Jewish people ever amassed in world history up to that point. An estimated one-third of the entire Jewish population of Eastern Europe moved to the United States in barely more than one generation, swelling New York's Jewish population from 13,000 in 1847 to more than 200,000 in 1890. As they climbed the socio-economic ladder and left for the comforts of uptown and suburbia, the most visible lasting legacy of their presence in lower Manhattan is their many synagogues, some still active but many more long shuttered, which dot virtually every block from Chatham Square to 14th Street east of the Bowery. Easily the most visually arresting of these was built as the Congregation Khal Adath Jeshurun, better known simply as the Eldridge Street Synagogue.

The Eldridge Street Synagogue was constructed by the Herter Brothers, Peter and Frank (not to be confused with the contemporaneous interior decorating firm also called Herter Brothers, Gustave and Christian). It was completed in 1887, spanning three lots at 12–16 Eldridge Street. Its lovely blond-brick facade, elaborated with Moorish arches and terracotta detailing, does little to prepare visitors for what lies within: one of New York's most splendid interior spaces, "a majestic collage of psychedelic polychromy,"[48] with painted ceilings, gilded accents, and a jaw-dropping stained glass rose window, newly created and installed in 2010 as part of the building's decades-long restoration. The Eldridge Street Synagogue represents the imposing wealth that existed on the Lower East Side in the 19th century, bucking its erroneous reputation for entrenched poverty.

During the peak years for Lower East Side Judaism at the turn of the 20th century, the Congregation Khal Adath Jeshurun boasted more than 4,000 members. But Jewish New Yorkers began moving out of the neighborhood in droves in the 1910s and 20s, meaning most local synagogues shuttered by the 1940s. For the Eldridge Street Synagogue, its soaring main worship hall was simply too expensive to maintain and fell into disuse in the 1930s when its remaining congregants began meeting in the basement. It remained closed for decades, falling into disrepair, at the mercy of vandals and the elements. It was rescued in the 1980s and underwent a renovation project which lasted nearly two decades, reopening in 2007 as The Museum at Eldridge Street. From inside or out, it provides an outstanding glimpse of the pinnacle of Jewish life on New York's Lower East Side.

Continue north along **Eldridge Street** and turn right onto **Canal Street**. Follow **Canal** east to the Jarmulowsky building at the corner of **Orchard Street**.

JARMULOWSKY BUILDING

At the corner of Orchard Street and Canal Street is the Jarmulowsky building. This imposing highrise, capped by an ornate cupola that defines the Lower East Side skyline, was built in 1912 to house the banking interests of Alexander "Sender" Jarmulowsky (who was the founding president of the Eldridge Street Synagogue). These were taken over by his sons following his death that June. The bank shuttered in 1917 after a World War I-related run on its holdings and the building deteriorated over the following century.

It was recently restored as luxury hotel, 9 Orchard, with restaurants and event spaces on its ground floor where Jewish immigrants once secured loans and deposited their hard-earned savings.

Continue east for two blocks to where **Canal Street** meets **East Broadway**

Stop 8 → At a plaza called **Straus Square**

THE FORWARD BUILDING

This intersection of Canal, Essex, and East Broadway, is where the story of a Jewish Lower East Side began in the late 19th century. This was where commercial traffic flowing east from Broadway and the Bowery joined the commercial traffic flowing south from Grand Street, mixing with the throngs of residents living on and below East Broadway. It was the center of Yiddish-speaking life in New York for decades, and it pulsed with the sort of sights, smells, and sounds later generations of Jewish Americans would rhapsodize in their novels and essays which attempt to distill just what it meant to live on the Lower East Side during that first wave of migration from the shtetls of Eastern Europe.

Though this area has long since largely emptied of any sizable Jewish population and has been gentrified to within an inch of its life (a certain segment now call the area "Dimes Square" in honor of a local restaurant, but we will not be calling it that), there remain abundant signs of its historic population and identity if one knows where to look. The greatest and most obvious landmark from the neighborhood's Jewish apex is the Forward Building, which looms over East Broadway with the word "*FORWARD*" picked out in orange brick near the top of its dozen stories. This was, for more than 60 years from its construction in 1912, the headquarters of *The Jewish Daily Forward*, a progressive Yiddish- and English-language newspaper first established in 1897.

The Forward, as it is now known, was far and away the most widely read of the many Jewish dailies which sprang up at the turn of the 20th century. At its peak during World War I, it boasted nearly 200,000 subscribers, making it one of the most widely distributed papers in the nation. It was the default resource for the local Jewish population and every other Lower East Side newspaper positioned itself to the left or right of *The Forward*. Its readership declined through the 20th century, and it departed its East Broadway headquarters in 1974. The building has been converted into apartments, part of the neighborhood's larger transformation over the past half-century, but the *FORWARD* remains, at least in brick lettering, as a reminder of what this place used to be.

From **Straus Square**, walk north along **Essex Street** then turn left onto **Hester Street**

THE PIG MARKET

Situated between the wholesale business district of Canal Street and the retail district of Grand Street, Hester Street was the center of the push-cart business world of the 19th- century Lower East Side. Every morning, hundreds of merchants and hawkers would roll up to the curb, forming an unbroken wall of micro-shops selling everything from apples to fabric scraps, their touts melding into a cacophonous din of Yiddish and English. The busiest intersection of this very busy street was that of Hester and Ludlow, called the *Khazzer-Mark* or "pig market," where small-scale garment manufactory contractors would hire day-rate laborers. "This is how the sweating-system worked," explains Ronald Sanders in his 1979 book *The Lower East Side*. "The small contractor, working with a margin of capital thin as a thread, would obtain raw material and an order for finished goods from one of the large merchants. He would then obtain the workers he needed for the assignment, very often in a public shape-up that took place each morning at the intersection of Hester and Ludlow Streets."[49]

Continue west along **Hester Street** before turning right onto **Orchard Street**. Walk north one block to the corner of **Grand Street**, where a stately cast-iron edifice fills the southwestern blockfront

Stop 9 → At the corner of **Grand** and **Orchard Streets**

RIDLEY & SONS DEPARTMENT STORE

While Canal Street was for wholesale business and Hester Street was for pushcarts, Grand Street is reserved for the world of retail and dry-goods stores. True to its name, Grand Street is indeed quite grand, wider than neighboring thoroughfares. Shoppers poured in from all across the city, a flow of humanity greatly aided by the Grand Street Ferry, a pre-Williamsburg Bridge connection to Brooklyn. The greatest of Grand Street's many impressive commercial structures was the department store known as Ridley & Sons. Founded in 1848 by English immigrant Edward Ridley, the store grew to occupy much of the southwest blockfront of Grand and Orchard Streets. Originally a cobbled-together jumble of several older buildings, Ridley & Sons was completely rebuilt in 1886 to roughly its current appearance, with five stories of sturdy cast-iron facade topped by a heavy cornice and arched top-floor windows. Even painted blush pink, as it has been for the past four decades, it holds dignified court over the scruffy streetscape below.

Despite Ridley & Sons' new building, most other department stores were leaving Grand Street by 1890, lured uptown to new shopping districts like Ladies' Mile and Herald Square. Though it was rumored to be planning to follow its competition uptown, Ridley & Sons, with an estimated 2,500 employees, shut down for good in 1901. The Ridleys retained ownership of the building, however, and leased it out as commercial space until at least the 1930s. During that time, Allen Street to the west of the store was widened as part of an overall attempt to open up the Lower East Side and provide increased greenspace in the densely populated district. This gave the old cast-iron Ridley's building a corner location on Allen, with a new deco-inflected brick facade on that street. Its presence is a reminder of the long-ago heyday of Grand Street's mainstream retail supremacy.

From the old **Ridley Building**, walk north along **Orchard Street**

Stop 10 → At the corner of **Delancey** and **Orchard Streets**

THE TENEMENT MUSEUM

Orchard Street is lined with countless shops selling clothes, books, snacks, and all sorts of oddities which serve as a faint echo of the chaotic shopping district the area once was. At Delancey Street, the Tenement Museum has held sway as the *de facto* authority on the Lower East Side immigrant experience since its founding inside a preserved tenement building in 1988.

BANK OF THE UNITED STATES

Next to the Tenement Museum on Delancey Street is the former Bank of the United States which, with its impressive columned edifice and official-sounding name, was one of the more popular banks among the area's immigrant population. It failed in 1931 as a result of the Great Depression and the building was taken over by the Hebrew Publishing Company, one of the foremost publishers of Hebrew- and Yiddish-language books and publications. Notably, its simple brick western facade was exposed by the 1930s widening of Allen Street.

Follow **Allen Street** north from **Delancey Street**, taking note of the rear sides of the buildings along the east side of the street, exposed by its widening in the 1930s.

Turn right onto **Rivington Street** and walk one block east.

ROUMANIAN SYNAGOGUE AND TALMUD TORAH

On Rivington Street, just east of Orchard, sits an empty lot which was once home to the 1860s church-turned-synagogue of the First Roumanian-American Congregation, who acquired the structure in 1902. Though it was demolished in 2006 after its roof partially collapsed, its *Talmud Torah*, or Hebrew school building, still stands next door at No. 95. The carved stone archway above the door attests to this lost bit of history.

Continue along **Rivington** to **Essex Street**, passing the always-worth-a-visit **Economy Candy**. Turn left on **Essex** then right on **Stanton** then turn left on **Norfolk Street**

Stop 11 → On **Norfolk** between **Stanton** and **Houston**

THE CITY'S OLDEST SYNAGOGUE BUILDING AND A LENIN STATUE

At 172–176 Norfolk Street stands the former Synagogue Ansche Chesed. Completed in 1850, it is the oldest surviving structure in New York which was built as a synagogue (any older synagogue buildings have either been demolished or were originally built as something else, such as a church). Following the establishment of New York's first Jewish congregation in 1654 (today's Sephardic Congregation Shearith Israel), the city's Jewish population remained small well into the 19th century. Political upheaval in central Europe, particularly Napoleon's wars and

Economy Candy

Corner of Essex and Rivington

2nd Avenue at 6th Street

German revolutions from the 1810s through the 1840s, sent significant waves of Ashkenazi Jews across the Atlantic for the first time. This ballooned New York's Jewish population from just 400 in 1812 to 10,000 in 1846. Since the majority of these new arrivals were Ashkenazi (Germanic) as opposed to Sephardic (Iberian), they soon splintered from Shearith Israel to found their own congregations.

Ansche Chesed was established in 1828, making it one of the city's first Ashkenazi congregations. As it grew, it moved around various rented or repurposed spaces on the Lower East Side before purchasing three building lots in 1849 on Norfolk Street just below Houston Street on which they set about building a new synagogue. In a bit of a full-circle moment, this land would have originally been part of the country estate of Peter Stuyvesant, whose "less than enthusiastic welcome for the Jews when they first arrived on these shores"[50] in 1654 is a vital part of the story of religious liberty in the United States. The new synagogue building was completed in 1850 in a rich Gothic revival style (compare this to other Gothic revival landmarks from the same era, such as Trinity Church and Grace Church, both completed in 1846) to designs by Alexander Saeltzer. With space for 1,200 worshippers, it was the largest synagogue in New York.

This Norfolk Street synagogue changed hands numerous times over the next century, as various congregations chased their congregants around the rapidly changing city. By 1974, dwindling attendance forced the building's closure and abandonment. It was finally sold in 1986 to Spanish artist Angel Orensanz, who uses the building as an art studio, gallery, and performance space. It also hosts The Shul of New York, a liberal, non-denominational synagogue, restoring some semblance of the building's, and indeed the neighborhood's, Jewish history and heritage.

Next to the Angel Orensanz Foundation, at No. 178 Norfolk Street, stands a rather nondescript tenement building. What makes it unusual is what stands atop its roof: an 18-foot (5.5-meter) statue of Vladimir Lenin, father of the Soviet Union. The statue's journey to the Lower East Side is as strange and apocryphal as one might imagine. It was the work of artist Yuri Gerasimov, and was commissioned by the Soviet government just before its collapse in 1989. That same year, a 130-unit apartment building named "Red Square" was completed at No. 250 Houston Street, visible at the end of the block here. The building's owners reportedly found the statue in the backyard of a dacha outside Moscow and had it shipped to New York, where they installed it on the roof of Red Square in 1994, noting that "Lenin faces Wall Street, capitalism's emblem, and the Lower East Side, the home of the Socialist movement."[51] When Red Square was sold to new owners in 2016, Lenin was removed, popping up the following year just around the corner atop No. 178 Norfolk.

After peering up at Lenin, walk north to **Houston Street** and turn left to go through foodie heaven. Continue west to **Forsyth Street** just past **Yonah Schimmel's**

GASTRONOMIC LANDMARKS

This stretch of Houston is an elite display of long-lasting New York City gastronomic landmarks so make sure you look out for them along the way. In rapid succession, one passes Katz's Delicatessen at No. 205, established in 1888; Russ & Daughters Appetizers at No. 179, established in 1914; and Yonah Shimmel's Knish Bakery at No. 137, established as a pushcart in 1890 and opened at this location in 1910. All three are representative of the area's long Jewish and German history and are worthy of a belly-filling visit.

SARA ROOSEVELT PARK

Just past Yonah Schimmel's is Sara Roosevelt Park. This unusual greenspace is just one narrow block wide but stretches all the way from Houston Street south to Canal Street at the entrance to the Manhattan Bridge. A century ago, this landscape would've looked no different from any other block on the Lower East Side, packed with shops, churches, synagogues, and tenements, but it was emptied and demolished in 1929 in an attempt to bring light and air to the crowded district. The park was dedicated in 1934 and was named in honor of Sara Roosevelt, mother of then newly elected President Franklin Roosevelt (she was alive at the time and vocally protested the honor, proposing it instead be named for former park commissioner Charles Stover, who "was well-known on the East Side"[52]).

Cross **Houston Street** and follow **2nd Avenue** to **2nd Street**. In doing so, you cross from the traditional **Lower East Side** into the **East Village**, though historically, the two were part of one large and contiguous neighborhood. Turn right on **2nd Street**

Stop 12 → In front of the **New York City Marble Cemetery**

MARBLE CEMETERIES

Two unusual and oft-overlooked cemeteries lie hidden on 2nd Street, each occupying the center of its respective block. One, the New York Marble Cemetery, lies on the west side of 2nd Avenue between 2nd and 3rd Streets, while this, the New York *City* Marble Cemetery, lies to the east of 2nd Avenue between 2nd and 3rd Streets. Their neighboring locations and confusingly similar names only add to their mystery. These two burial grounds were established in 1830 and 1831 respectively as the city's first cemeteries unaffiliated with any specific religious organization. These were non-sectarian, for-profit cemeteries, a novel concept at the time.

New York Marble Cemetery (west of 2nd Avenue) is by far the more obscure of the two, being that it is almost completely hidden from view. It is only barely visible through its iron entry gate on 2nd Avenue, and even then there isn't much to see, as it lacks headstones. Far easier to admire is New York City Marble Cemetery (east of 2nd Avenue), which is open to 2nd Street behind a high iron fence. Among its more notable burials was former President James Monroe, who died in New York in 1831. His remains were interred in the New York City Marble Cemetery but were removed to Hollywood Cemetery in Richmond, Virginia, in 1858. Obscure as they are, these twin marble cemeteries straddling 2nd Avenue are a delightfully macabre East Village secret.

After peeking at the marble cemeteries, continue north along **2nd Avenue** before turning left onto **4th Street**

Stop 13 → In front of **No. 74 4th Street** with the three carved heads above its second-floor windows

4TH STREET GERMAN BUILDINGS

In crossing north of Houston Street, visitors not only cross into what is now known as the East Village (so named in the 1950s and 60s to capitalize on the popularity of Greenwich Village and to differentiate it from the less desirable Lower East Side), but they shift from a neighborhood which is largely defined by its Jewish immigrant history to one defined largely by its earlier German immigrant history. These blocks of tenements and townhouses between the Bowery and Tompkins Square Park were first populated by immigrants fleeing the German Revolutions of 1848–49. These were joined by further German immigrants who fled Chancellor Bismarck's 1878 anti-socialist laws. These new arrivals, a mixture of German-speaking Jews and Christians, were solidly middle class if not outright wealthy. They brought with them the linguistic, architectural, and gastronomical traditions of their homeland, and established this neighborhood as *Kleindeutschland*, or Little Germany.

Much of this German culture, particularly the food traditions of *Kleindeutschland*, would be adopted by and folded into the cultures of later waves of Eastern European Jewish immigrants who began settling in the area in the 1870s. *Kleindeutschland* food purveyors "transformed the newcomers into the consumers of delicatessen meats, including corned beef, salami, and tongue."[53] But aside from food culture, evidence of this area's German roots can be found in its architecture. On East 4th Street between 2nd Avenue and the Bowery stand three important German-American landmarks.

No. 74 East 4th was built in 1873 as the *Aschenbroedel Verein*, or "Cinderella Club." Founded in 1860, the Aschenbroedel was one of the foremost social clubs to emerge from *Kleindeutschland*, counting among its members many of the city's leading orchestral musicians during the 19th century, including cellist and conductor Carl Bergmann, conductor and founder of the Chicago Symphony Orchestra Theodore Thomas, and composer Walter Damrosch, who is credited with convincing Andrew Carnegie to fund his eponymous music hall on 57th Street, which opened in 1891. The *Aschenbroedel Verein* moved to Yorkville in 1892, following the uptown flow of New York's German population, and their old East 4th Street building was altered at this time to feature the busts of three great German composers above its second-story windows: from left to right, Mozart, Wagner, and Beethoven. It served for many years as an event hall before being purchased in 1967 by the La Mama Experimental Theater Club, an off-off-Broadway company which remains there today.

Nos. 66–68 East 4th were originally built as two fine townhouses in the 1830s, part of a speculative residential row called Albion Place. These two were altered in 1871 to house the *Turn Verein*, a German fraternal and gymnastics club "with Socialist political leanings."[54] Aside from being a handsome structure, the *Turn Verein* hosted what is thought to be the first Yiddish-language theatrical production in the United States. In staging *Koldunye*, or "The Witch," the *Turn Verein* heralded the beginnings of what would become the so-called Yiddish Rialto of 2nd Avenue. Like the *Aschenbroedel*, the *Turn Verein* also moved to Yorkville, decamping in 1897. Its old headquarters on East 4th Street went through a succession of owners and uses before being acquired by La Mama in 1974.

No. 62 East 4th is perhaps the most architecturally interesting structure on the block. It was completed in 1890 as the Metropolitan Assembly Rooms, a business venture conceived by Victor Eckstein. A restaurant occupied the ground floor, with leasable event spaces on the floors above that. The eight-member Eckstein family lived in an apartment on the uppermost floor, which by law required a fire escape to be added to the building's facade. To avoid marring its architectural dignity, the fire escape was spiraled and creatively enclosed by a metal grille. It remains an ornament, far more beautiful than its utilitarian intentions. Eckstein sold the building in 1903 and thereafter it served a variety of functions, including as an illegal gambling hall. It became a theater in 1956 and, despite changing hands several times, has been lovingly restored and continues to house venues for music, theater, and dance today.

Backtracking to **2nd Avenue**, walk north from **4th Street** to **6th Street**. Turn right onto **6th Street**

Stop 14 → At **No. 325 6th Street** in front of the little red-brick synagogue

GERMAN EVANGELICAL LUTHERAN CHURCH OF ST MARK

A quaint, squat little building, the former church at No. 325 East 6th Street played a pivotal role in "the greatest steamboat disaster ever known in this city"[55] in 1904. Now home to the 6th Street Community Synagogue, it was originally built as St Mark's Evangelical Lutheran Church. This German congregation was established in 1847 to serve the rapidly growing German Lutheran population filling the blocks between the Bowery and Tompkins Square at that time. For half a century, the congregation thrived at the heart of *Kleindeutschland*. By the 1890s, many of the neighborhood's Germans had decamped in search of greener pastures uptown in Yorkville, but little St Mark's on East 6th Street continued to act as a cultural touchstone. One tradition which brought the community together each year was an excursion to picnic on the north shore of Long Island. This was more than simply an opportunity to escape the summer heat; it was a cherished time to commune and reconnect with hundreds of friends, neighbors, and relatives, rekindling some of the *Kleindeutschland* neighborliness their older generations had known downtown.

On June 15, 1904, St Mark's Church chartered the steamboat *General Slocum* to carry 1,358 people, mostly women and children, to a picnic at Locust Grove on Long Island. It was a beautiful sunny day, and after taking on passengers at its 3rd Street pier, the boat disembarked heading northward up the East River. It was just after 9:00 a.m. and the mood was lively. The *General Slocum* was filled to capacity for the three-hour journey, with hundreds of children racing up and down its decks as a band played happy tunes. The ship passed the west side of Blackwell's Island (now Roosevelt), then turned to pass east of Wards Island via a treacherous strait known as Hell Gate. Around 10:00 a.m., as it rounded the bend somewhere near 130th Street in the Bronx, passengers began to smell smoke.

Likely caused by a discarded cigarette, fire quickly raged through the boat's lower deck, fueled by piles of oily rags and straw. It started at the front of the vessel and was carried back through the entire body by the wind. Panicked passengers struggled to get to the upper decks. The boat's life vests were useless, crumbling to bits from a decade of open exposure to the elements. Many who jumped into the river couldn't swim and simply sank, dragged down by their heavy clothing. Within minutes the entire ship was aflame and the desperate shrieks of its passengers could be heard all the way over in Manhattan. The *Slocum* ran aground in a rocky cove of North Brother Island and there burned until its decks collapsed and it partially sank into the river.

In all, more than 1,000 people died, either in the fire or by drowning. There wasn't a German in New York unaffected by the tragedy. Everyone knew someone killed in the disaster; every block from *Kleindeutschland* to Yorkville was plunged into mourning. Bodies washed up on nearby shores for weeks, many unidentified. It was the deadliest incident in New York until September 11, 2001. New York's German community never truly recovered and the *Slocum* disaster is credited with accelerating the breakdown and disappearance of *Kleindeutschland* which had for so long defined this swath of the East Side. The population shift from downtown to Yorkville accelerated after 1904, and by 1940 St Mark's Church shuttered, its building sold to become the Community Synagogue. A monument to the dead stands in Tompkins Square Park. Dedicated in 1906, it features a quote from poet Percy Bysshe Shelley's *Canto VIII*: "They were earth's purest children, young and fair."

From the former **St Mark's Church**, return to **2nd Avenue**. Turn right to head north on the avenue.

MIDDLE COLLEGIATE CHURCH

On 2nd Avenue, you'll pass the former site of Middle Collegiate Church at the southeast corner of East 7th Street. This church, constructed in 1892, traced its lineage back to old Fort Amsterdam and the city's Dutch foundation. Collegiate churches in New York are descendants of the original Dutch Reform congregation which formed within the fort's walls in the 1620s. Middle Collegiate's 2nd Avenue edifice was a major landmark on the low-slung skyline of the East Village until it burned in a six-alarm inferno in December of 2020. The bell which hung in its tower was New York's Liberty Bell, having been rung in celebration of the nation's Declaration of Independence in 1776. It survived the blaze and is now on view at the New-York Historical Society.

Turn left onto **East 7th Street** and walk west toward **3rd Avenue**.

EAST 7TH STREET

Take note of Nos. 33–39 on this block, four surprisingly intact homes from the early 1830s when this area was only just beginning to be developed as a suburban residential district. Next to them, at No. 31, is the Hebrew Actors' Union Building, a relic from the age when 2nd Avenue was the Yiddish Rialto and the heart of the Jewish theatrical universe. The HAU was established in 1888, making it the first theatrical labor union in the nation, which only disbanded in 2002.

At No. 15 East 7th Street, not far from 3rd Avenue, stands what is thought to be the oldest bar in New York: McSorley's Old Ale House. Early records are murky, but it is likely that McSorley's has operated on this lot in some form since 1854, meaning it has served beer to countless customers over the span of 17 decades, through the area's Irish, German, Jewish, Ukrainian, Hippie, and Hipster eras. Through it all, very little has changed at McSorley's, a stalwart outlier in a city famous for its dispassionate commitment to whatever's new and next. To pass through McSorley's time-beaten saloon doors is to step into a time capsule. Sawdust covers the wood-plank floors, wishbones hang from the lanterns over the bar, and beer is served just two ways: light or dark. Cash-only and resistant to change, McSorley's famously did not admit women until forced to do so in a 1970 court case. Today, a new generation of neighbors and tourists have discovered the old ale house's charms, and it seems likely that McSorley's will last another century or more.

Go past **McSorley's**

Stop 15 → On **3rd Avenue** to admire the stately brownstone structure that is the **Cooper Union for the Advancement of Science and Art**

THE COOPER UNION

The Cooper Union, the importance of which is discussed in further detail in Walk No. 6 (page 141), was the pet project of Peter Cooper, perhaps the greatest inventor, thinker, and philanthropist of New York's 19th century. Born poor in 1791, the industrious Cooper amassed his first fortune as a glue manufacturer. In the following decades, he designed the first commercial steam locomotive in the United States, revolutionized iron beam manufacturing, oversaw the laying of the nation's first transatlantic telegraph cable, and in 1845 he patented a condensed edible gelatin which would later become Jell-O. Despite a long life filled with countless triumphs, Peter Cooper considered this school to have been his greatest achievement.

Through The Cooper Union for the Advancement of Science and Art, Peter Cooper sought to provide a world-class education to industrious New Yorkers whose wealth, circumstances, or social position might not otherwise afford them the sort of upward mobility he'd enjoyed in life. By 1854, he'd purchased land near Astor Place and spent an estimated $600,000 building a school which he envisioned as a place not just of technical mastery and entrepreneurial skill, but one of creativity and dedication to social justice. When it opened in 1859, the Cooper Union was free to all, including women, who were admitted as students in co-ed classrooms. The school offered evening classes to allow students to work during the day, and kept its library and reading rooms open to the public until late at night, providing a quiet and enriching hideaway for those aspirant academics not officially enrolled at the Cooper

The Cooper Union

German-American Shooting Society Clubhouse

Deutsches Dispensary

Union. In perhaps its most famous role as part of broader American history, the Cooper Union hosted a rousing speech by Abraham Lincoln in 1860 which is largely credited for securing his eventual nomination as President.

Walk north one block along **3rd Avenue** and turn right onto **St Mark's Place**

Stop 16 → On **St Mark's Place**

ST MARK'S PLACE

If the East Village has a Main Street, it must certainly be St Mark's Place, the three-avenue stretch of East 8th Street between Astor Place and Tompkins Square Park. Laid out in 1826, it was renamed St Mark's Place in the 1830s to make it sound fancy at a time when waves of wealthy New York families were moving uptown to escape the increasing density and commercialization of the old city downtown. Somewhat unexpectedly, St Mark's Place would quickly evolve into something special: one of those rare New York City streets whose very name conjures a whole world history in itself. Wall Street means finance; Broadway means theater; St Mark's Place means myriad things, often unique to whichever generation a person belongs to. It's been called home by everybody from Leon Trotsky to Lenny Bruce and has long symbolized the very essence of intellectual, musical, and counter-cultural movements.

Each successive wave of St Mark's residents believes its time there was the best, the most important, and also the last. In her seminal book *St Mark's is Dead*, local native Ada Calhoun explains: "Disillusioned St Mark's Place bohemians—those who were Beats in the fifties, hippies in the sixties, punks in the seventies, or anarchists in the eighties—often say the street is dead now, with only the time of death a matter of debate."[56] Walking St Mark's, particularly the block between 2nd and 3rd Avenues, is to take the pulse of the East Village. Dead or not, it is the main thoroughfare connecting the neighborhood to the rest of the city. There is no better place to go to people-watch and to sense, even for a moment, the ephemeral optimism of youth that only a place like St Mark's can retain through layered centuries of history.

During the Dutch colonial period, the land where St Mark's Place now runs was part of Peter Stuyvesant's vast farm. The area was first developed as a wealthy suburb in the 1830s, a time of exponential growth in New York following the opening of the Erie Canal in 1825 and the population boom that came with it. Though St Mark's remained relatively affluent well into the mid-19th century, many nearby streets soon became home to waves of first Irish and then German immigrants, imbuing the neighborhood with a sense of eclecticism that remains to this day. Pubs and beer halls dotted the landscape, turning St Mark's into an extension of the entertainment district developing nearby on the Bowery, all in the shadow of the Cooper Union and its culture of democratic inclusion and blurred socio-economic lines.

From farmland to wealthy suburb to a community of immigrants from Ireland, Germany, and Eastern Europe, St Mark's has since evolved into the center of New York's counter-cultural movements. Its architecture reflects its two centuries of change, with buildings from every era standing side by side. Of particular historical note on this block between 2nd and 3rd Avenues are Nos. 4, 12, and 19–23.

No. 4 St Mark's Place is among the most intact of the original speculative homes built on the street in the early 1830s. It is a gracious 26 feet (8 meters) wide with Flemish-bond brick (in which every other brick is turned skinny-side out), high parlor floor windows, and a pitched roof with dormers, every bit an exemplary high-class house for the era. It is the sort of home more commonly found closer to Washington Square or 5th Avenue, and is a delightfully surprising survivor on a block such as this which has seen so much change. Built in 1832 by real estate speculator Thomas Davis, it was purchased in 1833 by Col. Alexander Hamilton, Jr, son of Founding Father Alexander Hamilton, who lived in it along with his mother, Elizabeth Schuyler Hamilton, and his sister, Eliza Hamilton Holly, and her family. They remained at No. 4 St Mark's Place until 1842, and the building is now landmarked as "The Hamilton-Holly House." The only other home from Thomas Davis' 1831 development which has survived similarly intact is the Daniel Leroy House at No. 20 St Mark's Place.

No. 12 St Mark's Place is an architectural standout on St Mark's, with its highly unusual mansard roof and elaborately decorated facade. This building was completed in 1888 as the *Deutsch-Amerikanische Schützengesellschaft*, a name which is emblazoned above its second-story windows in bold terracotta. This translates to "German-American Shooting Society," one of countless such fraternal social clubs in New York's *Kleindeutschland* in the 19th century. Clubs like this provided not just opportunity for German-Americans to meet and socialize, but often provided financial or educational support for newly arrived immigrants. Additionally, No. 12 St Mark's boasts a highly unusual Germanic architectural design, providing a nostalgic visual link to club members' homeland. *Kleindeutschland* reached its zenith in the 1880s when it was home to roughly 250,000 German-Americans, comprising a quarter of the city's entire population. It waned thereafter as later generations moved uptown to Yorkville and to the suburbs, an exodus accelerated by the tragedy of the 1904 *General Slocum* disaster (page 79). The Shooting Society sold the building in 1920, though its splendid Germanic facade remains intact as a reminder of *Kleindeutschland's* heyday.

While the Hamilton-Holly House represents the history of St Mark's in the 1830s and the Shooting Society Building represents the history of St Mark's in the 1880s, Nos. 19–23 St Mark's Place represent all of that and more. They were originally built around 1832 as three rowhouses developed, like the Hamilton-Holly House, by speculator Thomas Davis. In 1870, Nos. 19 and 21 were converted into the Arion Society, a German music club which moved uptown in 1887. The clubhouse was then combined with No. 23 to become Arlington Hall, a ballroom and meeting space which remained there until the 1920s. It was thereafter transformed into a Polish restaurant and event space, reflecting a demographic shift in the neighborhood from Germans to Eastern Europeans. By the 1950s, the Beat movement arrived in what was being rebranded as the East Village, and in 1967, a nightclub called The Electric Circus opened in the buildings. The club featured major acts including the Velvet Underground, the Grateful Dead, and Tina Turner, helping cement the status of St Mark's as the most vital cog in the city's new musical movement. Though the Electric Circus shuttered in 1971, the buildings remain, now nearly 200 years old, bearing witness to the entirety of this neighborhood's many peaks and valleys.

These stories barely scratch the surface of the history of St Mark's Place, and entire books could be (and are) dedicated to that topic.

Moving east, turn left onto **2nd Avenue**

Stop 17 → In front of the spectacularly ornate red-brick and terracotta buildings midway between **St Mark's** and **East 9th Street**

GERMAN CLINIC AND LIBRARY

Perhaps the loveliest pieces of architecture which exemplify this neighborhood's history as New York's *Kleindeutschland* are the neighboring *Freie Bibliothek und Lesehalle* (free library and reading room) and *Deutsches Dispensary* (German clinic and medical dispensary). Both were built in 1884, funded by gifts from the wealthy Ottendorfers, Oswald and Anna, whose philanthropy was widespread during the late 19th century. Anna was born in Bavaria in 1815 and immigrated to the United States in 1837. Her first husband, Jacob Uhl, was a printer who in 1845 purchased the important and influential German-language newspaper, the *New Yorker Staats-Zeitung*. After Uhl died in 1852, Anna oversaw the paper's continued expansion, and in 1859 she married its editor, Oswald Ottendorfer.

In 1883, the Ottendorfers funded the construction of a new library and clinic on 2nd Avenue, in the heart of *Kleindeutschland*. Designed by German-American architect William Schickel, their facades display the sort of busy elaboration common in Germanic buildings throughout the neighborhood (such as the Shooting Society at No. 12 St Mark's Place, the clubhouses and music halls at Nos. 62–74 East 4th Street, and the Scheffel Hall beer garden at No. 190 3rd Avenue). Unfortunately, Anna Ottendorfer died in 1884, shortly before the library and clinic were completed, and their dedication doubled as a memorial service for her.

The library, originally part of the New York Free Circulating Library, became a branch of the New York Public Library system in 1901. It remains open to the public, the oldest library building still in use for its original purpose, and a rare example of a building the interior and exterior of which are both designated city landmarks. The German Dispensary, as an institution, would ultimately evolve into the modern Lenox Hill Hospital, though its Ottendorfer building was sold off in 1906. It changed hands and names numerous times before shuttering as a clinic in 2006. After receiving a thorough restoration in 2009, it is now used as office space.

Passing the **Ottendorfer buildings**, continue north along **2nd Avenue**

YIDDISH RIALTO

While you are on 2nd Avenue, take a note of (and perhaps grab a bite to eat at) Veselka, a mainstay for Ukrainian comfort foods like pierogies and borscht at the southeast corner of East 9th Street. One block north, at East 10th Street, stop to appreciate the Yiddish Theater Walk of Fame. This monument to 2nd Avenue's history as the Lower East Side's answer to mainstream Broadway was begun in 1984 when this corner (now a bank) was home to the 2nd Avenue Deli. It features dozens of starred pavers which celebrate icons of Yiddish theater such as Abraham Goldfaden and Lillian Lux. When the deli moved in 2006, the walk of fame remained. For more Yiddish theater history, walk up to the Village East Cinema at East 12th Street. This elaborately decorated theater was built in 1926 as a Yiddish playhouse and while it has been carved up into a multiplex, much of its beautiful Moorish interior design remains intact.

Before leaving 2nd Avenue altogether, stop in the small triangular plaza at the northwest corner of 10th Street. Abe Lebewohl Park was named in honor of the Polish-born founder of the 2nd Avenue Deli who was murdered in 1996. Facing the plaza is one of the oldest and loveliest landmarks in all of Manhattan: St Mark's Church in-the-Bowery.

ST MARK'S CHURCH IN-THE-BOWERY

The cornerstone for St Mark's Church was laid in 1795, and it opened for services in 1799, making it one of a small handful of 18th-century buildings to survive on Manhattan Island. As old as it is, it replaced an even older chapel which was built on the same site by the Stuyvesant family in 1651, back when New York was still New Amsterdam and Peter Stuyvesant was the colony's director-general. When he died in 1672, he was interred beneath the family vault here, which now lies beneath St Mark's Church. Stuyvesant's great-grandson, Petrus Stuyvesant, sold the old chapel in 1793 to the local Episcopal Church for $1 in exchange for the promise that a new church building would be erected on the site to serve the residents of "Bowery Village," the community which had grown up around the Stuyvesant family's long-held bowery, or farm. Interestingly, the lawyer enlisted to incorporate the new congregation was none other than Alexander Hamilton.

When St Mark's Church was completed in 1799, the city had not yet conceived of its street grid system which would determine the layout of all the lands north of Houston Street. The grid plan, unveiled in 1811, made limited allowances for the preservation of pre-existing streets, most notably those of Greenwich Village. But thanks to the influence of the Stuyvesant family, little Stuyvesant Street, oriented to true east-west rather than to the riverfront like the city's grid plan, was likewise allowed to remain. The odd orientation of Stuyvesant Street helps to explain the unexpected cockeyed angle of St Mark's Church. Its shadowy churchyard and lofty spire have served as charming axes of the East Village for more than two centuries.

As early as the 1870s, much of the wealthy population who had originally surrounded St Mark's Church had moved uptown as the neighborhood transitioned into a home for less affluent immigrant populations. In 1878, in one of the more notorious abuses of the church's sanctity, the body of department store magnate Alexander Turney Stewart was stolen from its vault and held for ransom. This shocking outrage motivated several of the church's wealthier families to remove their loved ones' remains from St Mark's. By the 1960s, the church was suffering witheringly regular burglaries, including one 1968 instance of thieves breaking into coffins to steal jewelry from the dead. "During this macabre incident," reported *The Times*, "a witness saw the thieves tossing the heads of corpses around playfully."[57]

St Mark's Church in-the-Bowery was nearly destroyed by a fire in 1978 but reopened in 1986 after a total restoration funded by millions of dollars in donations. Today, it remains an active parish as well as a center for the arts, acting as a grounding influence in a neighborhood which has seen so much change over so many years.

From the church, walk east along **10th Street** to **Avenue A**

Stop 18 → Tompkins Square Park

TOMPKINS SQUARE

To truly experience the Lower East Side and East Village of the modern era, there are few better places to visit than Tompkins Square Park. This 10½-acre (4.2-hectare) square lies between Avenues A and B, from 7th to 10th Streets, in the eastern segment of the East Village known as Alphabet City due to its lettered avenues. A quirk of the numbered grid system is that some portions of Manhattan extend east of 1st Avenue; these were given letter names which ascend from Avenue A eastward. In uptown neighborhoods, the lettered avenues have been rebranded over the years. Avenue A becomes Sutton Place, York Avenue, and Pleasant Avenue. Avenue B becomes East End Avenue. But here, downtown, the letters remain, giving identity to this dense and historically gritty corner of the island.

The park which would become Tompkins Square was first laid out in 1834, just seven years after Washington Square opened a mile to the west. The new park was handsomely laid out with shade trees and an iron perimeter fence. It was generally expected to attract members of the city's wealthy elite, but ultimately was deemed too far east and too removed from the social and commercial vitality of Broadway. Beginning in the 1840s, the streets surrounding Tompkins Square filled with tenements and houses which "were decidedly not for the upper class which had, 10 years earlier, been expected to live there."[58]

Thanks in part to its location at the heart of a less-wealthy district, Tompkins Square quickly earned a reputation as a site of civil unrest, starting with riots in 1857, 1863, and 1874. That reputation endures today, with Tompkins Square used as a rallying point for anti-war demonstrations in the 1960s and clashes over the removal of unhoused people from the park in the 1980s and 1990s.

Since the riots, gentrification of Manhattan's Lower East Side and East Village has taken off at a fever pitch. Luxury towers pock the skyline and rents have risen to numbers unthinkable on such blocks just a decade ago. Global chain stores and restaurants have elbowed into the neighborhood, pushing out local landmarks like Gem Spa and Mars Bar. It feels as if the counter-culture movement has gone dormant, or at least been pushed to the outer fringes of the city where life remains something close to affordable. What such gentrification means for a neighborhood whose very identity is rooted in being a cradle for immigrants, laborers, artists, musicians, and all the countless others who landed here when there was nowhere else to go, is yet an open question.

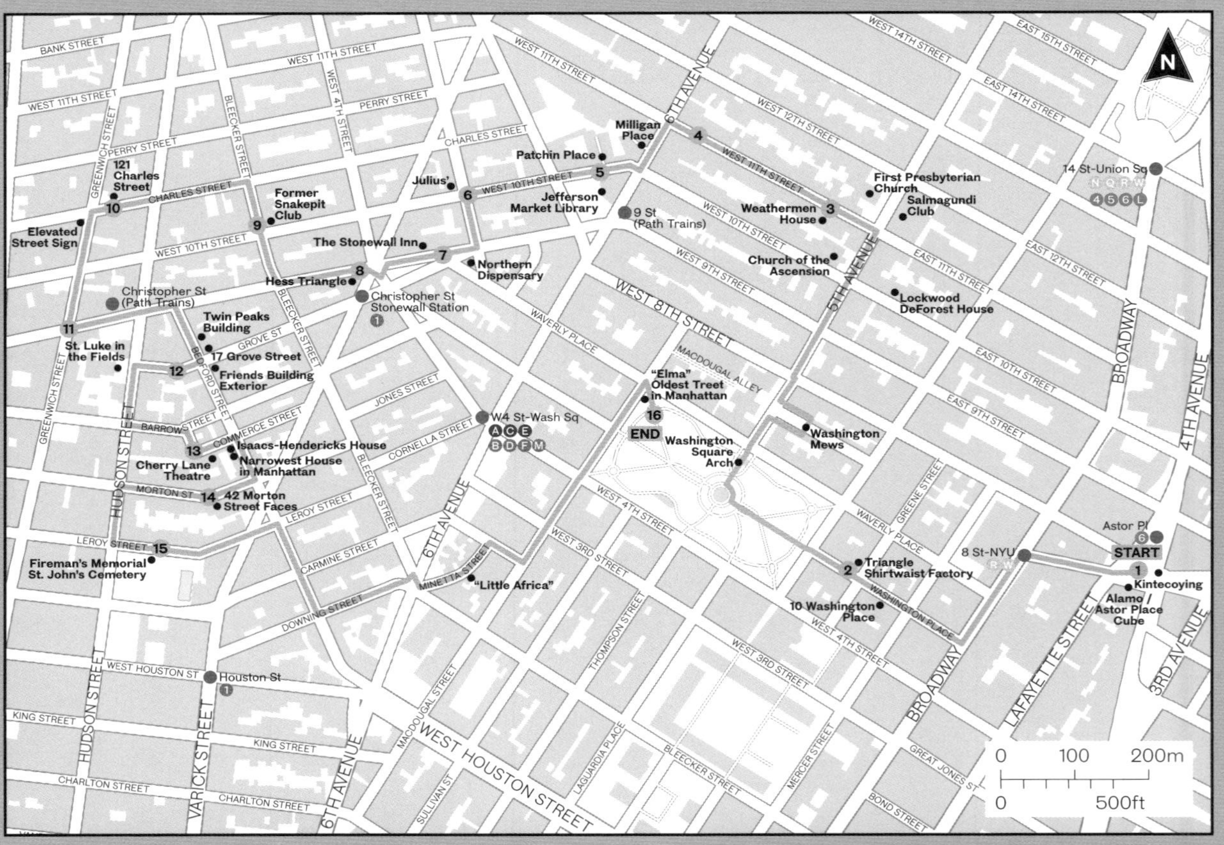
START
1 Kintecoying
Alamo / Astor Place Cube
Astor Pl
8 St-NYU
2 Triangle Shirtwaist Factory
10 Washington Place
Washington Mews
5th Avenue
3 Weathermen House
First Presbyterian Church
Salmagundi Club
Church of the Ascension
Lockwood DeForest House
4
Milligan Place
5 Patchin Place
Jefferson Market Library
9 St (Path Trains)
6 Julius'
7 Northern Dispensary
The Stonewall Inn
8 Hess Triangle
Christopher St Stonewall Station
9 Former Snakepit Club
10 121 Charles Street
Elevated Street Sign
Christopher St (Path Trains)
11 St. Luke in the Fields
Twin Peaks Building
17 Grove Street
Friends Building Exterior
12
13 Isaacs-Hendericks House
Narrowest House in Manhattan
Cherry Lane Theatre
14 42 Morton Street Faces
15 Fireman's Memorial St. John's Cemetery
"Little Africa"
W4 St-Wash Sq
16 END "Elma" Oldest Treet in Manhattan
Washington Square Arch
14 St-Union Sq
Houston St
West 8th Street
West Houston Street
Broadway
6th Avenue
4th Avenue
3rd Avenue
Lafayette Street
Hudson Street
Varick Street
Greenwich Street
Bleecker Street
Charles Street
Perry Street
Bank Street
West 11th Street
West 10th Street
West 4th Street
Waverly Place
Macdougal Alley
Jones Street
Cornella Street
Barrow Street
Commerce Street
Bedford Street
Grove St
Morton St
Leroy Street
Carmine Street
Downing Street
Minetta Street
King Street
Charlton Street
West Houston St
Macdougal Street
Sullivan St
Thompson Street
Laguardia Place
Mercer Street
Greene Street
Washington Place
West 3rd Street
Great Jones St
Bond Street
West 14th Street
West 12th Street
West 9th Street
East 15th Street
East 14th Street
East 12th Street
East 11th Street
East 10th Street
East 9th Street
0 100 200m
0 500ft

GREENWICH VILLAGE

Easily one of the most charming corners of Manhattan, Greenwich Village has always marched to the beat of its own drum. Now known as the West Village (to differentiate it from the East Village), its street grid makes no sense, its bar and restaurant scene is unsurpassed, and its architecture represents a jumbled mixture of eras, the parts of which form a cohesive and pleasing whole. Its story is one of boundless progression in the arts, music, philosophy, fashion, and individual liberty. Today, beneath its gentrified surface, the Village retains much of its inherent vitality: America's Little Bohemia, awaiting its next act.

ROUTE STOPS

1. Astor Place
2. Triangle Shirtwaist Factory
3. No. 18 West 11th Street
4. Second Jewish Cemetery
5. Jefferson Market
6. Julius' Bar
7. The Stonewall Inn
8. The Hess Triangle
9. The Snake Pit
10. No. 121 Charles Street
11. Christopher Street
12. Grove Court
13. Commerce Street
14. Morton Street
15. St Luke's Place
16. "Elma" in Washington Square

DISTANCE
2¾ miles (4.5 km)

TIME ALLOWED
2–3 hours

ROUTE No. **04**

AMERICA'S LITTLE BOHEMIA

In modern parlance, there are three Villages in New York: the East Village and the West Village, with Greenwich Village saddled between them. Together the Villages cover a whole swath of lower Manhattan from river to river between Houston and 14th Streets. Historically speaking, however, there was only one village called Greenwich, encompassing the areas now referred to as the West Village. Over the centuries, the Village became one of the loveliest, most vital neighborhoods in New York, attracting successive waves of artists, musicians, writers, and thinkers to its crooked, tree-shaded warrens, earning it the nickname "America's Little Bohemia."

It wasn't until the 1950s that New Yorkers, seeking to capitalize on the romance and popularity of Greenwich Village, rebranded the northern swath of the Lower East Side as the *East* Village. This reflected that area's emergence as a newly hip neighborhood and also helped lure higher-paying tenants to its warren of aging tenement blocks. By necessity, thereafter, the original Greenwich Village had to be rebranded as the *West* Village in order to differentiate the two. In time, the catch-all area in between, previously broken up into micro-neighborhoods defined by their central landmarks (Washington Square, Astor Place, 5th Avenue) came to be known as Greenwich Village. In the spirit of historical accuracy, this discussion of Greenwich Village will focus on the original village: the one now known as the West Village.

Start 1 → At **Astor Place**

ASTOR PLACE

Greenwich Village started out as *Sapokanikan*, a settlement of Canarsee (a band Munsee-speaking Lenape) people established long before European arrival. The village was centered around a spring-fed stream called the Minetta, which began in modern Chelsea and snaked its way south through what would become Washington Square before curving off to the west to empty into the Hudson. Its fertile banks grew tobacco well, and its original name, *Sapokanikan*, may indeed have meant something to that effect. After Dutch settlement of the island began in 1624, the Minetta lands were taken by the Dutch West India Company and granted to Wouter van Twiller, Director of the colony from 1633–38. In its early Dutch days, the Village was called *Noortwijck*, or the Northern District, as it lay several miles north of the city of New Amsterdam. By the 1670s, however, it was renamed *Greenwijck*, likely after a now-lost estate of the same name on Long Island. This would later be anglicized as *Greenwich*.

For centuries, both before and after European arrival, there was only one real route to take to *Sapokanikan* or Greenwich: the only major road which ran unbroken from the island's southern to northern tips, the *Mohican* or *Wickquasgeck Trail*. The Dutch would rename this undulating highway *The Bowery Road*, which meant *The Farm Road*, since it connected New Amsterdam with farmlands to the north. Following the Bowery Road north from the city, travelers to Greenwich Village would turn west at an intersection called *Kintecoying*, or what is today Astor Place. From there, a winding path which exists today in segments (Stuyvesant Street, Astor Place, Greenwich Avenue, and Gansevoort Street) led out to the Village on the Hudson Riverfront.

By the 18th century, Greenwich was becoming an increasingly popular seasonal settlement, particularly for wealthy city dwellers seeking a respite from the crowded city's malodorous summer months. This seasonality took on an increasingly desperate nature in the years following the American Revolution, when annual waves of infectious disease, such as typhoid or yellow fever, ravaged New York. Those with the means to do so would pick up and relocate to the relative safety of Greenwich, where the promise of clean water and air beckoned miles north of the afflicted city.

Even centuries later—New York City's relentless growth having long since enveloped and obscured the original pastoral nature of the Village—it still gives off an air of peaceful and inviting escape from the stressors of urban life. There are now countless ways to reach the Village, by foot, car, bus, or subway, but by beginning at Astor Place, a visitor can quite literally follow in the same footsteps as the area's first Dutch and English settlers and, before them, its original Native inhabitants making their way out to *Sapokanikan*. Though *Kintecoying* would later be renamed Astor Place in honor of John Jacob Astor, who developed the area into a residential district in the 1830s, it remains a vital crossroads between the Village and everywhere else.

ALAMO

Before leaving, notice the beloved cuboid sculpture in the middle of the plaza. Called *Alamo*, it was designed by artist Tony Rosenthal and installed in 1967. Spinning it has been a delight for generations of New Yorkers and tourists alike. It was not intended to spin, however. Rosenthal thought it would be locked into place, but this unintentional interactivity only added to its popularity. After breaking in 2022, it was repaired and reinstalled with a sturdier base, meant to be spun, in 2023.

From ***Alamo***, follow **Astor Place** west to **Broadway**. Turn left and walk south two blocks to **Washington Place**. Turn right onto **Washington Place** and walk to the corner of **Greene Street**

Stop 2 → At the corner of **Greene Street** and **Washington Place**

NO. 10 WASHINGTON PLACE

Along the way, take note of No. 10 Washington Place, now the site of a lovely late-19th-century factory loft building which is owned by NYU. This address was once the site of the first Manhattan home of Cornelius Vanderbilt, patriarch of the Vanderbilt dynasty, who moved his family here from Staten Island in 1846. He remained on Washington Place until his death in 1877, after which time the neighborhood went into steep decline as a mansion district. One by one, its fine residences were sold off and torn down, replaced by large, mostly speculative industrial buildings which produced garments to be sold in the vast dry-goods emporia lining Broadway.

TRIANGLE SHIRTWAIST FACTORY

Easily the most famous of the many factory buildings crowded onto the blocks east of Washington Square is the 10-story edifice at No. 23 Washington Place. Completed in 1901 for real estate investor Joseph Asch, the building was leased out floor-by-floor to small-scale garment manufacturing businesses. One of its first tenants was the Triangle Waist Company, which produced shirtwaists, "a high-necked blouse usually made of crisp, light, translucent cotton or sheer linen,"[59] which were extremely popular in an era when women were gaining increased autonomy. Shirtwaists, able to be tucked into skirts, were far easier to wear than full dresses, and were able to be swapped out more readily for changing looks, moods, and weather. The Triangle Waist Company leased the eighth floor of the Asch Building, eventually expanding to occupy the ninth and tenth floors as well, employing hundreds of mostly young women and girls from the immigrant districts east of the Bowery.

On March 25, 1911, Rose Rosenfeld was two days shy of her 18th birthday. An Austrian immigrant, Rose was working at the Triangle Waist factory when flames ripped through the factory, which was stuffed with piles of dry fabric. In an era before most workplace safety laws, the factory exits were locked to prevent unapproved breaks (or union organization efforts). The air was soon thick with smoke and screams. As panic spread, Rose stopped to consider what the company executives were doing during the fire. Assuming they would know how to keep themselves safe, she ran to their offices on the tenth floor of the building and found them taking the freight elevator to the roof. From there, firemen pulled them to a neighboring roof as horrors unfolded at the factory: the building's top three floors were fully engulfed.

Tall buildings were still a relative novelty in New York, and the fire department had not kept apace. Their ladders only reached the sixth floor, far below the trapped workers at the Triangle factory. There was a fire escape, but it collapsed under the weight of so many panicked bodies climbing onto it. In desperation, some who were still trapped upstairs jumped down the elevator shaft. Others, many with their hair and clothing aflame, jumped from the windows. "Perhaps these women realized they could not save their lives," supposed *The Times* in a 2001 retrospective. "They knew that those who stayed inside the building would be incinerated beyond recognition. They may have thought that it would be a comfort to their families to have something to identify and then bury."[60] Firemen held nets to try to catch them, but those were not built to withstand the impact of people falling from such great heights, and all died on impact.

"The Row," north side of Washington Square

One hundred and forty six people died in the fire, 62 from jumping, in barely a half-hour. "Of those who stayed behind it is better to say nothing—except what a veteran policeman said as he gazed at a headless and charred trunk on the Greene Street sidewalk hours after the worst cases had been taken out: 'Is it a man or a woman?' asked the reporter. 'It's a human, that's all you can tell,' answered the policeman. It was just a mass of ashes, with blood congealed on what had probably been the neck."[61] The company owners were tried for manslaughter and acquitted. A civil suit brought against them in 1914 by the families of 23 victims forced them to pay restitution of $75 each. If there was any silver lining in the aftermath of the fire, it was the rise of organized labor activism which used the tragedy as an example of corporate indifference to workers' lives. "It should never have happened," insisted Rose Rosenfeld nearly 90 years later. "The executives with a couple of steps could have opened the door. But they thought they were better than the working people. It's not fair because material, money, is more important here than everything."[62]

Rose Rosenfeld, married name Freedman, fought for workers' rights for the rest of her life. She was the last living survivor of the fire, dying in 2001 at age 107. The building at No. 23 Washington Place was repaired and reopened for business within a year. It was taken over as part of NYU's sprawling Washington Square campus in the 1920s. A memorial was finally unveiled on the building's exterior in 2023. Designed by Richard Joon Yoo and Uri Wegman, it features slabs of black stone at waist height, engraved with quotes from survivors and witnesses to the event. Reflected in the stone are the names and ages of the victims, backlit against the sky where so many of them met their tragic end.

Beyond the tragedy of the Triangle fire, the rapidity with which Washington Place transformed from a colony of fine mansions, home to the likes of Cornelius Vanderbilt, to the site of a deadly industrial fire, speaks volumes about the chaos of the city's growth in the 19th century. Neighborhoods like this were built and rebuilt half a dozen times often within one person's lifetime. This sort of redevelopment would by and large bypass historic Greenwich Village to the west, where narrow, crooked streets made it a less-desirable site for industrial and commercial encroachment. Thanks to this, Greenwich Village has remained mostly low-scale and residential in nature throughout its history, adding to its overall charm.

From the **Triangle Shirtwaist** memorial, walk west and pass through **Washington Square** toward the white marble arch on its northern side

From the arch, walk north on **5th Avenue**, stopping along the way to admire the diminutive charm of **Washington Mews** (page 137). Turn left on **11th Street**

Stop 3 → In front of **No. 18 West 11th Street**

WEATHERMEN HOUSE

No. 18 West 11th Street is an oddly modern home in the middle of a row of tidy red-brick townhouses from 1844. On March 6, 1970, all was quiet on West 11th Street, one of the most intact and charming blocks in the neighborhood. Then-married actors Anne Byrne and Dustin Hoffman lived at No. 16. Mel Brooks also lived on the block with his wife Anne Bancroft, who starred opposite Hoffman in the 1967 movie *The Graduate*. At noon on March 6, however, the tranquility of West 11th was shattered by a series of three blasts at No. 18. The first blew apart the facade of the 126-year-old townhouse. The next two explosions brought its four floors crashing down into a flaming pile of brick and rubble. Unbeknownst to neighbors, the house at No. 18 was a bomb-making workshop for the Weather Underground, a militant wing of the Weathermen, themselves a radical outgrowth of the anti-war movement of the late 1960s. Their actions grew increasingly violent until 1970, when they began an arson and bombing campaign against major symbolic targets.

The bombs being assembled on March 6 were destined for the main library at Columbia University. Five members of the group were at home at No. 18 when the dynamite detonated prematurely in the basement, killing three of them: Terry Robbins, Ted Gold, and Diana Oughton. The two survivors, Kathy Boudin and Cathy Wilkerson, were pulled from the wreckage and escaped (they wouldn't be captured until the 1980s). The blast was so powerful that neighbors felt their houses shake more than a block away. Early reports assumed it had been caused by a gas leak, but within days the true story emerged. Crowds gathered at the police barricades, partly to see the chaos and partly for a chance at meeting Dustin Hoffman, who signed autographs when he could. Once the blast site was cleared, in March of 1971, the Landmarks Preservation Commission approved a controversially modern design for the house's replacement which was finally built in 1977. Designed by Hugh Hardy, its facade is turned at a sharp angle to the street, though its cornice and red brick pay homage to the 19th-century townhouse it replaced.

Continue walking west along **11th Street** almost to **6th Avenue**

Stop 4 → On the **south side** of the street at the unexpected sight of a tiny triangular cemetery

THE SECOND CEMETERY OF THE SPANISH AND PORTUGUESE SYNAGOGUE

The little triangular cemetery on West 11th Street is a decidedly inconspicuous landmark. Many lifelong New Yorkers admit to never noticing it despite having walked past it countless times over many years. As far as cemeteries go, it's rather small, measuring only 50 square feet (4.6 square meters) or so, shielded from the sidewalk by a shoulder-high brick wall topped by an iron railing. But for such a small plot of land, it boasts impressive ties to the history of the Village and the wider city.

As the plaque affixed to its exterior wall attests, this is the Second Spanish and Portuguese Cemetery. The First cemetery is down near Chatham Square (page 66); established in 1683 and used until the 1830s, but even as early as 1800 it was beginning to fill up. Representatives of the Jewish congregation sought another piece of property on the new edge of town on which to establish a new burial ground. The parcel they acquired in 1804 sat on the outskirts of the village of Greenwich, at that time still separated from New York City by several miles of open fields and marshland. Situated just east of Greenwich Lane (today's Greenwich Avenue), the land was a sizable rectangular plot, angled to the same cockeyed degree as the streets of neighboring Greenwich Village. It accepted its first burial in 1805.

Just six years later, in 1811, a commission tasked with planning for future development up the length of Manhattan Island unveiled their design: a rectilinear grid plan which would sweep northward from Houston Street to 155th Street. The plan called for numbered streets and avenues across every inch of the island, regardless of property lines or topography, with the notable exception of Greenwich Village, which was largely spared for the time being. But that fortune did not carry over to the Jewish cemetery near Greenwich Lane. In 1829, the city informed the congregation that their burial ground lay in the path of 11th Street. Any bodies in the new road's path were disinterred. Some were moved to a new cemetery uptown in Chelsea (The Third Spanish and Portuguese Synagogue Cemetery, which remains on 21st Street today (page 124)). Others were squeezed into this remaining triangle of land on the south side of the street.

And so, not only is the Second Cemetery of the Spanish and Portuguese Synagogue a vital piece of the history of the oldest continuously active Jewish congregation in the Western Hemisphere, but it is also a tangible bit of physical evidence depicting the clash between old Greenwich Village and the much larger city that gobbled it up two centuries ago. Though the cemetery faces onto 11th Street, its rear walls remain slanted at an angle parallel with the diagonal blocks of the rest of Greenwich Village west of 6th Avenue.

From the **cemetery**, walk west and cross **6th Avenue**, then proceed south down **6th Avenue** and turn right onto **10th Street**

Stop 5 → In front of the gate for **Patchin Place**

MILLIGAN PLACE AND PATCHIN PLACE

When 6th Avenue and 11th Street were laid out here, old property lines at the fringe of Greenwich Village were often left in places. One particular landowner, Samuel Milligan, worked with his son-in-law, Aaron Patchin, to make best use of the oddly shaped parcel they owned here along 10th Street between 6th and Greenwich Avenues. Not only did they build the row of shops here on 6th Avenue between 10th and 11th Streets, but they cut little dead-end streets into the center of their property, lining them with small, simple rowhouses.

These dead-end streets, now gated and private, are among the most unusual and charming houses in the Village. Hidden on 6th Avenue, be sure to peek inside the metal gate labeled "Milligan Place" where four little houses huddle around a courtyard. As you turn onto 10th Street, you'll see the 10 little houses of Patchin Place all in a row, basking in the shadow of the glorious red-brick clock tower of the old Jefferson Markey Courthouse.

JEFFERSON MARKET LIBRARY

As the population of Greenwich Village swelled in the early 19th century, a permanent marketplace was constructed at the western foot of Christopher Street by 1819. Though convenient to river traffic, it was far from the Village's population center and so was replaced by a new market built into the wedge

Astor Place

Washington Square

Triangle Shirtwaist Factory

Washington Mews

18 West 11th Street, Weathermen House

West 11th Street

Jefferson Market Library

of land where Greenwich Lane (now Avenue) intersects 6th Avenue. The new market opened in 1833 and was named in honor of former President Thomas Jefferson who died in 1826. The Jefferson Market complex was more than just an outlet for foodstuffs; it also boasted a police court, assembly halls, a jail, and a watchtower from which firefighters could look for smoke on the horizon.

Though useful, Jefferson Market was a ramshackle collection of wooden buildings and was considered an eyesore by the 1860s. It was demolished and replaced by a spectacular new courthouse building which was designed by Frederick Clarke Withers, a partner of Calvert Vaux, of Central Park fame. The courthouse opened in 1877 and new matching market stalls were completed around it by 1883. Like its predecessor, the new complex also featured a jail as well as a lofty fire watchtower, though this one was integrated into the courthouse itself. With ornate brickwork and a four-faced clock beneath a steeply pitched roof, the Jefferson Market Courthouse instantly became the most visible and beloved landmark of Greenwich Village.

Public markets fell from favor in New York, and by 1927, the Jefferson Market's produce stalls were demolished along with the original jail to make way for an immense new Women's House of Detention. This Art Deco slab of off-white brick loomed over the neighborhood as "an architectural monstrosity and a blight on the area."[63] Though the House of Detention remained in use until 1971, the Jefferson Market Courthouse was shuttered in 1946 as part of an overall effort to centralize the city's court functions. The building, "one of the nation's finest pieces of [Victorian Gothic] architecture,"[64] sat largely unused for the next 20 years.

Threatened with demolition in the 1950s, the old Jefferson Market Courthouse was saved by Greenwich Village residents who rallied to get it landmarked and restored for use as a branch of the New York Public Library. It reopened in November of 1967 after nearly three years of construction and was further beautified following the demolition of the neighboring Women's House of Detention in 1973. The site is now a lovingly tended garden, which is open to the public from April through October. The Jefferson Market Library remains a vital and highly visible piece of the Greenwich Village streetscape.

From the **courthouse**, follow **West 10th Street** west to **Waverly Place**

Stop 6 → At **Julius' Bar, No. 159 West 10th Street**

JULIUS' BAR

A bar of some sort has operated here at the corner of 10th Street and Waverly Place since at least 1900, gaining the name Julius' by 1930. The building housing Julius' is far older, with parts dating back to approximately 1826, which were altered and extended over the next century. Though it wasn't an explicitly gay bar, by the 1940s, Julius' had become a popular watering hole for Greenwich Village's sizable gay population. This was also a time of increasing legal oppression of homosexual and gender-nonconforming people in New York and across the nation. While it wasn't technically illegal to *be* gay, virtually all aspects of gay life were illegal, making homosexuality a *de facto* crime by the 1950s. By the 1960s, more than "100 men were arrested each week in bars or cruising areas following their entrapment for 'homosexual solicitation.'"[65]

Against this backdrop, the Mattachine Society was formed in Los Angeles in 1950 as one of the first gay rights organizations in the nation. A New York branch was established in 1955, and in 1966 executed their most famous protest of anti-gay injustices by staging what came to be known as "the sip-in" at Julius'. At the time, it was illegal in New York State to serve alcohol to "disorderly persons," and gay people were by default considered disorderly. With press reporters in tow, Mattachine Society members Dick Leitsch, Craig Rodwell, and John Timmons went to Julius' and declared that they were gay, that they planned to remain orderly, and that they'd like to be served a drink.

The bartender, fearing legal ramifications, refused them service. Reporters photographed the interaction, and the next morning, Julius' was front-page news in *The Times*, *The Post*, and *The Village Voice*. In response, the State Liquor Authority clarified that the law did not prohibit service to gay patrons, marking one of the first victories of the nascent pro-gay movement and easily the most significant instance of gay rights activism prior to the Stonewall Riots of 1969.

From **Julius'**, follow **Waverly Place** to **Christopher Street** and turn right

Stop 7 → Midway between **Waverly** and **7th Avenue**

THE STONEWALL INN

"The old Stonewall establishment was not a nice place," said city councilman Thomas Duane in 1997. "It was a crummy, mob-run firetrap, basically."[66] The buildings which house the Stonewall Inn were built around 1845 as a pair of horse stables. Located at Nos. 51–53 Christopher Street, the stables were later converted into commercial storefronts, changing hands several times before opening in 1934 as Bonnie's Stonewall Inn, a restaurant owned by Vincent "Bonnie" Bonavia. It remained a popular Village spot for three decades before closing in 1966 after a kitchen fire. The next year, it was acquired by the Genovese crime family who owned and operated several gay bars in the Village at the time. They kept the name and converted the Stonewall into a gay bar which opened in 1967.

This was a common arrangement at a time when homosexual acts and gender nonconformity were illegal: the mob made money while the city's queer community had a place to come together. A place like the Stonewall differed from nearby Julius' in that it was an explicitly gay bar, in direct conflict with a slate of laws against its clientele. Its patrons were often those members of society least welcome in more mainstream bars: sex workers, drag kings and queens, and youths with nowhere else to go. In exchange for turning a blind eye to the bar's illegal operation, the local police regularly raided the Stonewall and other similar establishments around the Village. Such a raid was executed at Stonewall around 3:00 a.m. on June 28, 1969, but instead of fleeing or surrendering, its patrons fought back. The melee evolved into a multi-day riot "with all the fury of a gay atomic bomb."[67]

The crowds of several hundred outside the Stonewall finally dispersed on July 3, but the winds of change could be felt across the nation. A march commemorating the anniversary of the riots was held on June 28, 1970. Several thousand people walked from the former Stonewall Inn up 6th Avenue to Central Park, where a "gay-in" was held in the Sheep Meadow. This was a stunning act of bravery at a time when gay life was still widely criminalized and homosexuality was still considered a mental disorder by the American Psychiatric Association. "We're probably the most harassed, persecuted minority in history," declared Michael Brown, founder of the Gay Liberation Front. "But we'll never have the freedom and civil rights we deserve as human beings unless we stop hiding in closets and in the shelter of anonymity."[68]

The so-called Christopher Street Liberation Day March in 1970 served notice "on every politician in the state and nation that homosexuals are not going to hide any more," said Martin Robinson, founder of the Gay Activists Alliance. "This march is an affirmation and declaration of our new pride."[69] Today, Pride celebrations all around the world are held in June in remembrance of the Stonewall riots which forever changed the cultural narrative. This former horse stable, nearly 200 years old, remains a symbol of the ongoing queer liberation movement and of the people who risked everything for a better future.

"The Stonewall establishment is not what is remembered," concluded councilman Duane in 1997. "It's the actions of gay men, lesbians and drag queens who fought back against the police that we honor with the name Stonewall."[70] Some of those individuals, including Stormé DeLarverie, Sylvia Rivera, and Marsha P Johnson, are memorialized in photos affixed to the perimeter fence of Christopher Park across from the Stonewall Inn. The bar and the park were made National Monuments in 2016.

From the **Stonewall Inn**, walk west and cross **7th Avenue**

Stop 8 → At the **old Village Cigars store** at **No. 110 7th Avenue South**

HESS TRIANGLE

In front of the former Village Cigars shop, you'll see a little mosaic triangle embedded in the sidewalk. As originally conceived in 1811, Manhattan's street grid plan ignored Greenwich Village and its pre-existing jumble of charming, confounding lanes. As the city grew northward and enveloped Greenwich, the rigid straight lines and numbering system simply ended at the Village's borders. This allowed Greenwich Village to remain a proverbial island unto itself. Even as surrounding neighborhoods changed and modernized, evolution largely bypassed the Village, allowing it to remain a charming backwater and a hotbed of counter-culture creativity.

Soon after New York's first subway line opened in 1904, plans were floated to expand it to better connect more of the city. Within a decade, particularly thanks to the opening of Penn Station on the west side, construction was set to begin on a new leg of subway running south from Times Square beneath 7th Avenue. At the time, however, 7th Avenue dead-ended at Greenwich Avenue, the northern boundary of the Village. Simultaneously, automobile use was increasing in Manhattan, and the Village's cockeyed streets blocked the flow of cars between Downtown and Midtown. In short, the stage was set for Greenwich Village to be cracked open and connected to the rest of the city.

The plan was for the new 7th Avenue subway extension to slash directly through the heart of the Village, connecting to Varick Street at Carmine Street. Not only would this project fundamentally upend the area's social and physical makeup, it would require the demolition of more than 200 structures in its path. "Old Greenwich Village will never be the same again," lamented one resident in 1914 while "gazing disconsolately at the wreckage"[71] of his neighborhood. Many owners fought the city, but all lost that fight, and 7th Avenue plowed its way south, opening to traffic by 1918.

Among the hundreds of building owners displaced by the avenue's extension was David Hess, a real estate investor from Philadelphia. He had owned a five-story apartment block called "The Voorhis," which sat on West 4th Street between Christopher and Grove Streets, overlooking Christopher Park. The Voorhis was demolished, but once when the dust settled, and 7th Avenue was complete, Hess made a discovery: by a technicality, the city had forgotten to obtain legal rights to the entirety of his building's plot. A tiny, 500-square-inch (0.3-square-meter) wedge was left over, outside the city's domain, along the sidewalk of the new avenue. The plot's value was assessed at $100. Hess filed notice of retention, and it was granted.

In 1922, the Hess family laid a mosaic on their little plot. A triangle of yellow and black tiles, it read "PROPERTY OF THE HESS ESTATE WHICH HAS NEVER BEEN DEDICATED FOR PUBLIC PURPOSES." This was the Hess family's permanent reminder to the city and to future generations of New Yorkers that people had once been forced out of this space against their will, and that they wouldn't go quietly. They sold it to neighboring Village Cigars in the 1930s for $1,000. The tiny triangle remains embedded in the sidewalk today, visible to all passersby as a quirky and poignant remnant of the destruction wrought on Greenwich Village when 7th Avenue sliced through its heart.

From the **Hess mosaic**, follow **Christopher Street** one block west to **Bleecker**. Turn right onto **Bleecker** and walk one block north to the corner of **West 10th Street**

Stop 9 → At the top of the stairs leading down into the basement of **No. 215 West 10th**

THE SNAKE PIT

Though there was a noticeable uptick in publicity and organization during the months following the Stonewall Riots of 1969, little fundamentally changed for New York's queer community. State laws still criminalized much of their daily existence, they were still maligned by mainstream society, and policestill regularly raided their bars and clubs, subjecting them to humiliation and abuse.

Homophile organizations hoped to stage an anniversary march in honor of the riots in 1970, but enthusiasm flagged in the face of so much of the same oppression.

Julius' Bar

The Hess Triangle

St Luke's Place

Minetta Lane at MacDougal Street

Commerce Street

In the pre-dawn haze of March 8, 1970, an after-hours gay bar called the Snake Pit was subjected to a police raid. The bar, located in the basement of No. 215 West 10th Street, was among a handful of gay-owned gay bars in Greenwich Village, but was accused of operating illegally. The raid was carried out by Deputy Inspector Seymour Pine, the very officer who'd carried out the initial raid at the Stonewall Inn eight months earlier. Eager to avoid a similar calamity, Pine ordered everyone in the bar arrested regardless of whether they were visibly breaking the law or not. 167 patrons were thus hauled to the 6th Police Precinct House a few blocks away at No. 135 Charles Street. There, they were held in a chaotic scene of fear and confusion.

One of those arrested that night was Diego Viñales, a 23-year-old Argentinian whose student visa had expired. Fearful of deportation, Diego fled from the group up a flight of stairs and attempted to jump from the Precinct House to a neighboring building. He missed or slipped and instead fell onto a spiked fence below which impaled his legs and torso. Ultimately, the Fire Department was summoned to cut the fence and bring it, with Diego still attached to it, to St Vincent's Hospital. Diego did survive his ordeal, having endured many hours of surgery, but a rumor got out that he had died of his injuries. As word of the Snake Pit raid spread through the neighborhood, hundreds turned out in anger against the continuation of such cruelty by the authorities.

Several homophile organizations took charge of the ensuing protests, with the Gay Activists Alliance distributing leaflets which read, in part, "Any way you look at it—that boy was PUSHED!! We are ALL being pushed." It encouraged people to rally at Sheridan Square for a march on the 6th Police Precinct House followed by a death watch vigil outside St Vincent's Hospital. "Stop the Raids! Defend Your Rights!"[72] An estimated 500 people turned out for the march, and its success is credited with bolstering enthusiasm for the commemorative march honoring the anniversary of the Stonewall Riots that June. Called the Christopher Street Liberation Day March, it is heralded as the first Gay Pride Parade in the world.

Though today we rightfully celebrate the events which transpired at the Stonewall in 1969, the Snake Pit raid of 1970 has been largely forgotten. While the Stonewall is now a National Monument, the Snake Pit has been reverted into a nondescript basement beneath a clothing store, with nary a plaque to remind passersby of its importance. As for Diego, he was released from the hospital after three months of recuperation and had his criminal charges dropped by the city. However, his immigration status remained in limbo and there is no record of his life after 1971.

From the site of the **Snake Pit**, walk north along **Bleecker Street** and turn left onto **Charles Street** and continue for two blocks

Stop 10 → At **No. 121 Charles Street** at the corner of **Greenwich Street**, site of the strangest house in **Greenwich Village**.

GOODNIGHT MOON HOUSE

To be called the strangest house in Greenwich Village is an honor not lightly bestowed in such a quirky neighborhood. But No. 121 Charles Street, nestled behind a vine-draped fence at the corner of Greenwich Street, is a worthy contender for the title. In a city of cold glass, stone, and skyscrapers, this lopsided little house is a joy to behold. Every wall and surface seems to slant at odds with how a house should be pieced together. It's become a local landmark and is part of the Greenwich Village Historic District, which was designated in 1969. But it wasn't always located in the Village. In fact, it only arrived in the neighborhood in 1967, two years before the historic district was established. So how did this little interloper find its way onto this leafy Village block? Its story is fittingly unusual.

The original portion of No. 121 Charles Street is the boxy three-window-wide section with the brick chimney sticking out of it. No one knows precisely how old it is. When it was built, why, and by whom remains a mystery. Various news articles claim it was built any time from the 1760s to the 1810s, but it doesn't appear on any maps until the 1890s. For most of its history, it lay hidden behind another two-story brick house at No. 1335 York Avenue in Yorkville, on Manhattan's Upper East Side. It was separated from the front house by a stone walkway, earning it the nickname Cobble Court. It may have been built as a farmhouse or as an outbuilding or, more likely, it may have been built as a rear house to earn rental income for the front house's owners.

Regardless of its age or provenance, it achieved some fame in the 1940s when children's author Margaret Wise Brown rented it for use as her studio. She worked out of it from 1942 until 1952, and in that decade, she published 100 books, including the iconic *Good Night Moon*. Tragically, Brown died at age 42 following surgery for a ruptured appendix while in France. Following her death, the little rear house on York Avenue fell into disrepair. It was rented in 1960 to Swedish-born Sven Bernhard who, along with his wife Ingrid, spent countless hours and thousands of dollars rehabilitating it. In 1965, however, the whole block was sold to the Catholic Archdiocese who wished to build a retirement home on the site.

Sven and Ingrid went to court, insisting they'd put enough time, energy, and money into Cobble Court to claim it as their own. They were granted ownership of the house but not of the land beneath it, forcing them to seek a new home for their home. With the help of architect William Shopsin, the Bernhards acquired a large triangular plot at the corner of Charles and Greenwich Streets, and then turned their attention to the far more complicated matter of moving a six-room, 12-ton house more than 5 miles (8 km) across the city.

With help from Mayor John Lindsay, Cobble Court was hoisted onto a flatbed truck on the cold, blustery morning of March 5, 1967. It was hauled south along York Avenue to 57th Street, where it headed west to 2nd Avenue. There, it turned south and continued all the way to 14th Street. Turning west again, it crossed the width of Manhattan to Washington Street, before zigzagging its way through the neighborhood to Charles Street, where it was carefully lowered into place. They even brought with them the cobbled courtyard from Yorkville, which now forms the house's driveway. The Bernhards moved into newly designated No. 121 Charles Street in 1968 and remained in the little house until 1985. Later owners added extra rooms to the house, but thankfully built them just as lopsided and charming as Cobble Court was meant to be.

THE 9TH AVENUE ELEVATED TRAIN

Just across the intersection from the Good Night Moon House, the five-story apartment building at No. 128 Charles Street bears evidence of a long-lost piece of New York City transit infrastructure. Greenwich Street, which stretched south from here all the way to the World Trade Center, was laid out in the first half of the 18th century to provide a more direct path from New York to Greenwich. Before this, the usual route was to take the Bowery Road, a long and circuitous journey. Greenwich Street was built right along the riverfront, offering the most direct route between the city and the village.

In 1873, the 9th Avenue IRT Elevated Train opened along this stretch of Greenwich Street, with stations nearby at Christopher and Bethune Streets. Ultimately, it would run from South Ferry all the way up to the Bronx, serving as the first rapid-transit connection between the city's whole west side. Though it was demolished in the 1940s, having been replaced by the subway, evidence of the old 9th Avenue El survives today at the corner of Greenwich and Charles Streets. Look up to the space between the third and fourth floors of No. 128 Charles Street there. Perplexingly, there is a large sandstone block embedded into the building's corner, carved with the names of the streets. This wayfinding sign is too high to be useful for pedestrians; it was meant for the passengers of the elevated trains who would've been at eye-level with it as they rattled their way uptown or downtown.

Walk south along **Greenwich Street**

Stop 11 → At **Christopher Street**

CHRISTOPHER STREET

Note that Christopher Street is almost double its normal width from Greenwich Street to the Hudson River. This is a surviving incongruity from the brief period when the south side of Christopher down to the water was home to the 1819 Greenwich Village Market, which would move to 6th Avenue in 1833 as the Jefferson Market (page 96). The choke of wagon traffic and produce stalls along these blocks of Christopher Street necessitated its widening here, a quirk of the Village grid which endures to this day, almost two centuries later.

Christopher Street serves as the spine of Greenwich Village, marking the boundary between the straight-line grid north of it and the bent streets to its south. This is because Christopher Street was originally the southern border of the country estate of Sir Peter Warren, an Irish-born British naval officer who married into the prominent De Lancey family of New York in 1731. Lauded as a hero, he was granted a vast tract of land at Greenwich to use as his country seat. Following his death in 1751, the estate was carved up into development plots with streets named after various Warren family members: Abingdon Square was named for Sir Peter Warren's son-in-law, Willoughby Bertie, 4th Earl of Abingdon; Charles, Christopher, and Amos (later renamed 10th) Streets were named for Charles Christopher Amos, one of Warren's heirs.

In contrast to the relatively well-organized street grid of the Warren estate north of Christopher Street, the streets south of it are a crooked jumble. Grove, Morton, Leroy,

Clarkson, and Downing Streets are all bent in the middle, reflecting the collision of historic land tracts. The area west of the bend was owned by Trinity Church while the land east of it passed through various hands over the centuries. Understanding that the intersection of Christopher and Bedford Streets marks the meeting point of these three historic properties, each with their own grid system, goes a long way toward helping Greenwich Village's confounding streets make sense.

Walk east along **Christopher Street** to **Bedford** and turn right

Notice how much narrower the sidewalks are here when compared to the blocks north of Christopher. At Bedford and Grove Streets, navigate through the tourist crowds taking photos of the tenement building at No. 20 Grove Street (its exterior was used in the establishing shots of the TV show *Friends*) and instead notice the odd gray building at No. 102 Bedford Street which is colloquially known as "Twin Peaks." Built as a regular dormered house in the 1830s, it was radically altered in 1925 by the artist Clifford Reed Daily who used funds from his wealthy patron, Otto Kahn, to transform it into an "inspiring home for creative workers."[73]

Next to Twin Peaks, sits No. 17 Grove Street, is one of a mere handful of wooden buildings left standing in Manhattan, where such construction was banned in 1866 to mitigate against fires. The little shop behind it was built in 1833 and has served variously as a workshop, apartment, and cafe over the years. The house also holds a tantalizing secret in its basement: a tunnel of uncertain age and provenance that is thought to have at one time connected to Chumley's, a legendary former speakeasy down the block at No. 86 Bedford Street.

From **Bedford Street**, turn right onto **Grove**

Stop 12 → At the bend in the block, in front of the little brick-and-iron gate labeled **Grove Court**

GROVE COURT

Grove Court is one of the more charming pockets of Greenwich Village, with six diminutive townhouses hidden in a gore lot filling the crack between Nos. 10 and 12 Grove Street. The houses were constructed in 1854, wedged into an otherwise hard-to-utilize piece of land in a manner similar to Milligan Place and Patchin Place (page 96). Like those quaint alleys near Jefferson Market, these Grove Street houses were meant for a less-affluent populace than otherwise dominated Greenwich Village in the 19th century. What is now romantically labeled Grove Court was long known as "Pig Alley" or "Mixed-Ale Alley," reflecting its lowly reputation as a home for laborers and poor immigrants, inhabited "largely by Irish families headed by women."[74]

Grove Court was gated in the 1920s as part of a wave of such projects at the height of the Village's first Bohemian age. Artists, writers, and other creative types coveted the charms of such secluded enclaves. A century later, as gentrification reached its zenith in the neighborhood, the house at No. 5 Grove Court sold for a reported $3,400,000, a sum likely unimaginable for the residents of old Mixed-Ale Alley.

From **Grove Court**, walk west to **Hudson Street**

A PEACEFUL SPOT AT ST LUKE'S

Admire the little brick Church of St Luke in the Fields, so named because when it was built in 1822, it stood in the middle of open fields. It is an Episcopal congregation, built on land which was originally part of the farm given to Trinity Church by Queen Anne in 1705. Take advantage of the respite offered by St Luke's walled garden, accessible by a small gateway on Hudson Street near Barrow. It is one of the quietest escapes from daily life to be found in the city.

Turn left (east) onto **Barrow Street** and continue onto **Commerce Street**

Stop 13 → At **No. 38 Commerce Street**

CHERRY LANE THEATRE

The Cherry Lane Theatre has operated at No. 38 Commerce Street since 1923, making it the oldest Off-Broadway theater in New York. It was established by a group of theatrical artists, such as Eugene O'Neill and Edna St Vincent Millay, who had grown disillusioned by the increasing commercialism of Broadway and other mainstream theaters at the time. To combat that slide, they converted this former brewery and box factory, constructed in 1836, into an intimate playhouse called the Cherry Lane, the original name for Commerce Street. In its century of existence, the Cherry Lane has fostered some of the most innovative, envelope-pushing theater in the nation.

Passing the **Cherry Lane**, turn right onto **Bedford Street**

No. 77 Bedford, is the oldest known house in Greenwich Village, dating back to 1799. It is officially known as the Isaacs-Hendricks House and, while it has been greatly altered over the years, retains much of its original charm, including an unusually generous entry portal. Note the exposed brick openings in the house's Commerce Street facade: these are its fireplaces, left exposed to vent heat and prevent accidental ignition of the clapboard siding.

Next to the Isaacs-Hendricks House stands No. 75½ Bedford Street. It was constructed in 1873 to fill in a disused alley which formerly ran between the houses on either side. At just 9 feet 6 inches (2.9 meters) wide, it is the narrowest house in New York.

Passing the **skinny house**, continue along **Bedford Street** to **Morton Street**, then turn right

Stop 14 → In front of the elaborately carved tenement building at **No. 42 Morton Street**

MORTON STREET FACES

No. 42 Morton Street is not inherently unique. It is one of countless similar tenement buildings which proliferated across New York's cityscape in the latter half of the 19th century as a steady flow of immigrants put incredible pressure on the city's housing stock. By the 1880s, Greenwich Village had begun to transform from an enclave of wealthy homeowners into a far more socio-economically stratified district of artists, musicians, and immigrants. In response, some property owners demolished older single-family homes like the one next door at No. 44 Morton, replacing them with far larger tenements which not only stood five or six stories, but held as many as four apartments per floor. This allowed for the squeezing of 20 or more rent-paying tenants onto a plot intended for one.

When building such tenements, owners often gave the architects and artisans assigned to the site a surprisingly free hand in their design choices. Beyond basic requirements for the building's dimensions, sculptors and masons could let their imaginations run wild in the details. With thousands of immigrant laborers working on such projects, many hailing from nations with long traditions of masonry like Italy and Germany, some of the results are extraordinary. No. 42 Morton is a sublime example of such work, which is far more beautiful than might otherwise be expected for a project as prosaic and utilitarian as a tenement block. Its entryway is particularly gorgeous, with birds, floral festoons, and delicately carved faces coaxed out of the soft, time-worn blocks of brownstone. (This building is also an excellent example of real brownstone, heavily damaged by the years, as yet unrepaired.)

Interestingly, though, one side of the building appears to have been executed with a defter hand than the other. It is possible that a more experienced mason carved one side while an apprentice carved the other. Or one mason did it all and simply achieved finer results on one side than the other. Regardless, it is a fascinating peek inside a brief historical moment, only a handful of years before more streamlined architectural fashions would all but eliminate such stonework from New York's streetscape.

Follow **Barrow Street** west to **Hudson** and turn left. At **St Luke's Place** (part of Leroy Street), turn left

Stop 15 → along the imposing stone and iron fence of **James J Walker Park**, across from **No. 5 St Luke's**

ST JOHN'S CEMETERY

Most people who pass by James J Walker Park in the West Village would never guess that thousands of people lie buried beneath its playgrounds and ballfields. But as early as the 1790s, this patch of ground was set aside as St John's Cemetery, a rural graveyard for the area's Episcopal congregations. A succession of epidemics in the first half of the 19th century filled the graveyard with thousands of bodies, mostly those of the city's less-affluent dead who couldn't afford to be buried in more exclusive cemeteries downtown. By 1860, St John's stopped accepting burials, and within decades, the city had grown up around it.

In 1887, New York City authorized the seizure of small parcels of land in crowded districts to create public parks, and city leaders soon earmarked old St John's Cemetery for such a conversion. By then, the century-old burial ground had grown decrepit: "The monuments have toppled over," reported one funerary journal in 1894, "and of the tombstones have fallen. In Summer it has been filled with a growth of rank grass, noxious weeds, and shrubbery run riot."[75] It was surrounded by a high wooden fence which was missing several planks, allowing neighborhood children to sneak through and play among the graves. A row of tenements was constructed on the east side, and the residents took to tossing their household trash out their rear windows.

City residents were given notice in 1894 that they must relocate any bodies of loved ones from the graveyard, lest they be covered by a new park. A few wealthier families did so, but the vast majority were the so-called "friendless dead," and were left in place. Their headstones were laid face-down and covered with dirt. The cemetery reopened in 1899 as Hudson Park, a bucolic jewel box designed by Carrère and Hastings. Though many New Yorkers objected to such disregard for the sanctity of a burial ground, the new park was lauded for its beauty, featuring fountains, playgrounds, sculpted stone ramparts, and a stretch of green lawn.

Much of the park's original Carrère and Hastings design was destroyed during a 1939 renovation which added more active-play space, including the present ballfield which faces Hudson Street. During construction, workers uncovered an impressive cast-iron casket with a glass window in its lid which revealed the body of six-year-old Mary Elizabeth Tisdall, a girl who'd died in 1850. Her burial dress was reportedly still freshly white and her hair was visibly blond after nearly a century underground. Mary is one of an estimated 10,000 New Yorkers still hidden beneath James J Walker Park.

Today, the only visible remnant of the former cemetery on St Luke's Place is an oversized marble monument dedicated to two firemen killed in the line of duty in 1834. As one of the only grave markers too large to bury during the cemetery's conversion to a park in 1898, it now serves as the lone memorial to the many New Yorkers resting quietly six feet below.

From **James J Walker Park**, walk east and across **Varick Street**. Turn right onto **Bedford** then left onto **Downing Street**. Follow **Downing** to **6th Avenue** and cross over to the east side and up **Minetta Street**

Downing and Minetta Streets trace the original path of Minetta Brook, a river which once marked the eastern and southern boundary of Greenwich Village.

This crooked, closely shaded little street is one of the only vestiges of a once-vibrant community called "Little Africa," home to generations of Black New Yorkers since the Dutch era of the 17th century. The neighborhood slowly depopulated, in part due to the rising importance of first 53rd Street and then Harlem as Black districts. It was all but eliminated by the cutting through of a new stretch of 6th Avenue and the subway lines which run beneath it in the 1930s. But for centuries, and not all that long ago, this was one of the most vital nodes of Black life in the city.

Follow **Minetta Street** north, following the curving path of the old brook which still flows underground, to **Minetta Lane**. Turn right and follow it to **MacDougal Street**. Turn left on **MacDougal** and walk north all the way to **Washington Square**

ELMA

Just inside the northwest entrance of Washington Square, look for a truly immense tree, towering more than a dozen stories above the ground, it is thought to be the oldest in Manhattan. It is so mighty that you'd be forgiven for missing it as you walk by; its first branches don't start until at least 30 feet (9 meters) overhead. The last time it was measured, it stood more than 130 feet (40 meters) tall, and best guesses put it at a minimum of 300 years old, though it is likely decades older. It may have been a sapling when the British took New Amsterdam from the Dutch. It would have been a century old when George Washington was inaugurated as the nation's first President on Wall Street. It turned 200 just after the Civil War, and 300 some time in ours or our parents' lifetimes. It is undoubtedly one of the oldest trees in the city, as most of its contemporaries fell long ago (the great Tulip Tree in Inwood and the Stuyvesant Pear Tree on 3rd Avenue to name a few more prominent documented losses).

"Elma", the oldest tree in Manhattan

This tree, a non-native English Elm, was planted during the city's colonial period on a stretch of open farmland north of the city. It stood on the western bank of Minetta Brook, a well-stocked waterway which originated as a cluster of springs beneath modern Chelsea. In 1825, the tree was taken, along with the neighboring potter's field across the brook, and landscaped as part of a newly designated public common now known as Washington Square. Somewhere along the way, the old tree gained the macabre nickname the Hangman's Elm, and unfounded rumors abound that it was used for executions. But no evidence supports this legend, not to mention the fact that the elm stood across the Minetta Brook from the graves, and the few executions which did occur in the area utilized a gallows, so the tree is likely innocent and undeserving of this dark moniker. Knowing neighbors instead call the tree Elma.

Regardless of its name, the tree is a living link to the Village's whole history: one of a dwindling number of great trees who've known New York since before it truly existed. It has lasted through every stage of Greenwich Village's origins and evolution, a living witness all it ever was and hopefully will be.

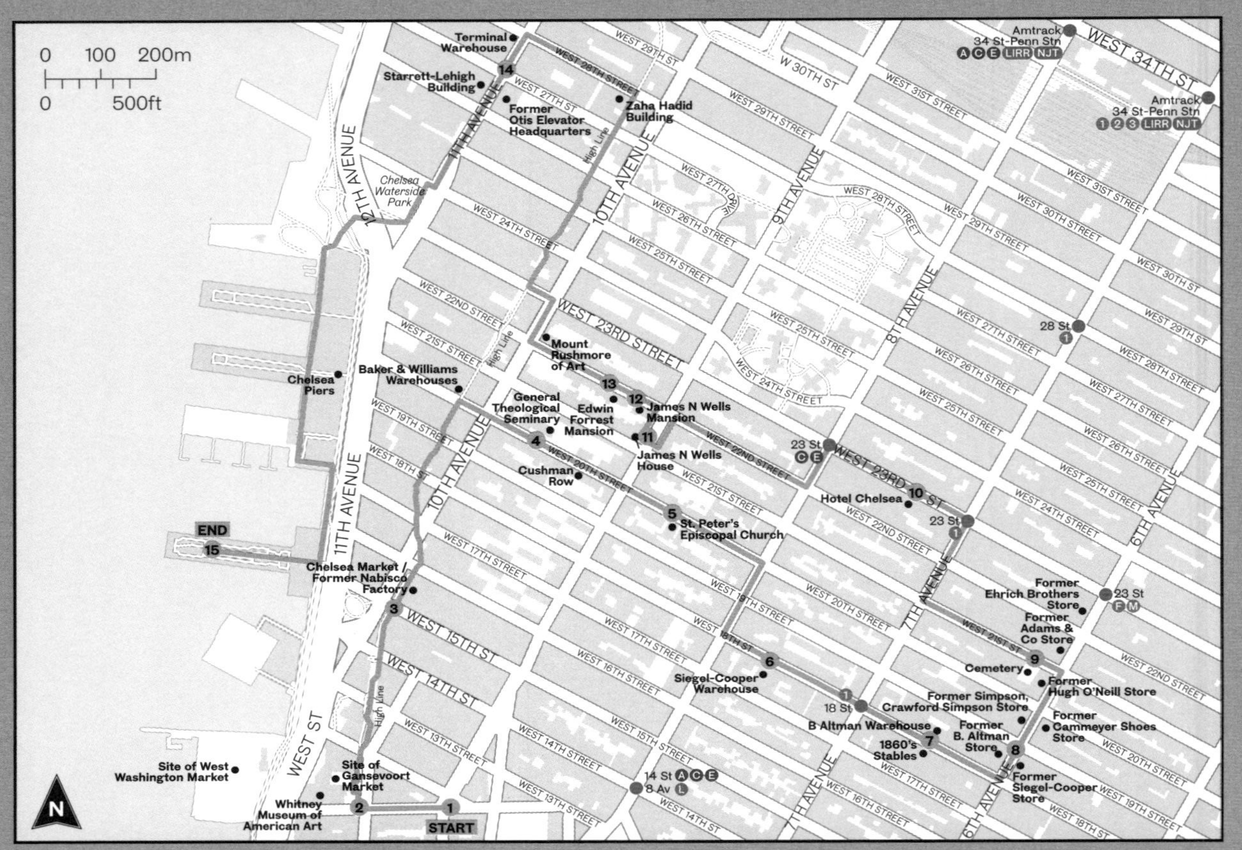
0 100 200m
0 500ft
N
START
1
2
3
4
5
6
7
8
9
10
11
12
13
14
15
END
Site of Gansevoort Market
Whitney Museum of American Art
Site of West Washington Market
Chelsea Market / Former Nabisco Factory
Chelsea Piers
Baker & Williams Warehouses
General Theological Seminary
Cushman Row
St. Peter's Episcopal Church
Siegel-Cooper Warehouse
B Altman Warehouse
1860's Stables
Former B. Altman Store
Former Siegel-Cooper Store
Former Cammeyer Shoes Store
Former Simpson, Crawford Simpson Store
Former Hugh O'Neill Store
Cemetery
Former Adams & Co Store
Former Ehrich Brothers Store
Hotel Chelsea
James N Wells House
James N Wells Mansion
Edwin Forrest Mansion
Mount Rushmore of Art
Zaha Hadid Building
Former Otis Elevator Headquarters
Starrett-Lehigh Building
Terminal Warehouse
Chelsea Waterside Park
High Line
WEST ST
11TH AVENUE
12TH AVENUE
10TH AVENUE
9TH AVENUE
8TH AVENUE
7TH AVENUE
6TH AVENUE
WEST 14TH ST
WEST 15TH ST
WEST 23RD STREET
WEST 23RD ST
WEST 34TH ST
W 30TH ST
WEST 27TH DRIVE
14 St
8 Av
18 St
23 St
28 St
34 St-Penn Stn
Amtrack
LIRR
NJT

CHELSEA AND LADIES' MILE

Chelsea is in many ways a world unto itself. Filling a wide swath of Manhattan's west side between the Village and Penn Station, its long, verdant blocks contain some of the loveliest rows of 19th-century townhouses to be found anywhere in New York. On its eastern edge lies the so-called Ladies' Mile, once the city's grandest shopping district, where the hulking remains of long-shuttered department stores recall the early days of conspicuous consumption. To the west, the High Line bisects Chelsea's industrial waterfront, now filled with galleries and food halls. Taken together, Chelsea is a city within the city.

ROUTE STOPS

1. Gansevoort Plaza
2. High Line
3. Nabisco Sky Bridge
4. General Theological Seminary
5. St Peter's Church
6. Siegel-Cooper Warehouse
7. B Altman Warehouse
8. Ladies' Mile
9. 2nd Jewish Cemetery
10. Hotel Chelsea
11. James N Wells House
12. James N Wells Mansion
13. Edwin Forrest Mansion
14. Industrial West Chelsea

DISTANCE
3¾ miles (6 km)

TIME ALLOWED
2–3 hours

ROUTE No. 05

BEAUTY BEYOND THE HIGH LINE

To understand Chelsea, one must understand the context in which it exists today. Historically, Chelsea was meant to be a wealthy, somewhat cloistered community of fine mansions and lofty church spires. Its development began in the 1830s with great optimism. It was expected to pull the social center of gravity to the west, offering a quieter alternative for the city's elite families who wished to live away from the bustle of Broadway and 5th Avenue. Instead, as urbanity swelled around Chelsea's leafy blocks, the neighborhood became an island unto itself, surrounded on all sides by commerce, industry, and the unrarefied realities of living in a modern metropolis.

Chelsea, as an historic entity, is centered around the General Theological Seminary, which occupies the block east of 10th Avenue between 20th and 21st Streets. To the west lies the industrial waterfront of Chelsea Piers and the High Line; to the north, Penn Station and the skyscraping lofts of the Garment District. To the east is the historic Ladies' Mile, once New York's greatest shopping district, with the crowds and transit infrastructure to match. And to the south lies the Meatpacking District, once the larder for millions. It is there that this walk begins.

Start 1 → At **Gansevoort Plaza**

THE MEATPACKING DISTRICT

Gansevoort Plaza sits on the border between Greenwich Village and Chelsea, where charming rows of brick and brownstone townhouses give way to the faded industrial grit of the Meatpacking District. The small brick buildings across the street at Nos. 3–7 9th Avenue are among the oldest in the neighborhood, having been built in the early 1840s as single-family homes. Soon after their construction, however, this area began to be consumed by commercial development, with many farm stalls relocating here from the older Washington Market downtown (where the World Trade Center now stands). Gansevoort Street acted as the conduit funneling goods from the Hudson River waterfront to the rapidly growing population centers of Greenwich Village, Chelsea, and Union Square.

This area's commercialization was accelerated by the 1884 opening of the Gansevoort Market (for farmed foodstuffs) and the 1887 opening of the West Washington Market (for meat and dairy products). By the 1950s, the sale and packing of meat products had become the area's chief economic driver. The commercial vitality of the neighborhood continued well into the 1970s but entered a rapid decline with the advent of modernized shipping and refrigeration techniques which allowed for the centralization of meatpacking plants elsewhere. Abandoned commercial buildings became home to nightclubs and restaurants and, in a trend not unlike what happened in SoHo and Tribeca a generation earlier, artists transformed the Meatpacking District into a vibrant cultural enclave.

Gentrification and tourism have transformed the Meatpacking District in recent years as the last of the actual meatpackers have departed one by one. Less than a dozen remain today, all under one roof beneath the High Line, adjacent to the Whitney Museum of American Art. When their lease expires in 2032, it is quite likely that the Meatpacking District will cease to live up to its name.

Walk west along **Gansevoort Street** to **Washington Street** and the southern end of the High Line, which can be accessed via stairs or elevator

Stop 2 → On the **High Line**

HIGH LINE

Emerging atop the High Line is always a treat. This linear park extends from Gansevoort Street all the way uptown to 34th Street near the Jacob Javits Convention Center. It opened to the public in phases between 2009 and 2014, with later additions like the Spur at 30th Street and a bridge connecting the High Line to Moynihan Train Hall opening as recently as 2023. Walking the High Line offers a unique perspective of the city, bringing visitors eye-level with buildings boasting two centuries of architectural evolution. There is also no better way for pedestrians to traverse such a long stretch of Manhattan without ever having to interact with cars, bicycles, or other street traffic.

But the High Line wasn't always such a bucolic spot, nor was it built to be a park. The High Line began life as an elevated freight line, carrying its first trains in 1933. Its purpose was to replace the much older street-level freight lines which had long carried trains down the middle of 11th Avenue on their way to and from the freight terminal at St John's Square (page 44). Not only did these trains snarl traffic along the west side, but they routinely maimed or killed people unlucky enough to be in their path as they rumbled through the area's densely built neighborhoods. Such was their reputation that, as early as 1907, *The New York Times* referred to 11th as "Death Avenue."[76] Removal of the tracks was debated for decades, with ever more people dying in the meantime.

Finally, in 1929, plans were approved for the "West Side Improvement," a colossal redevelopment scheme which would not only replace Death Avenue with an elevated freight line but would also bury the tracks of the New York Central Railroad's freight lines north of 72nd Street, allowing for the expansion of Riverside Park on the Upper West Side. The transformation of such a vast swath of the cityscape was hailed as "the greatest single public improvement ever undertaken on Manhattan Island, with the single exception of the subways."[76]

Despite being an unquestionable success in making the streets safer for west-side residents, the elevated freight line was rather late to the party. After World War II, trucking rapidly outpaced rail as the nation's preferred mode of commercial transportation, and train traffic dwindled. The last trains passed along the West Side Improvement in 1978, and by 1984 it was abandoned. A segment of the elevated line was demolished in the early 1990s, from Gansevoort Street south to the old St John's Freight Terminal at Clarkson Street, and it seemed likely that the whole structure might, and perhaps ought to, likewise be dismantled.

Happily, nature was working a bit of unanticipated magic on the remaining segments of the elevated tracks. Borne by the wind, wild plant life began to sprout in the trackbeds, forming a sort of ad hoc savannah of native grasses, flowers, trees, and shrubs. Urban explorers who scaled the structure were so taken with its rustic beauty that they formed the non-profit conservancy, Friends of the High Line, in 1999 in order to advocate for its preservation and, ultimately, adaptive reuse as a permanent public space. Inspired by the *Promenade Plantée* in Paris, the group proposed transforming the west side viaduct into a linear park. Above the protest of neighboring homeowner groups, which had long fought for the High Line's removal, the park plan went ahead, and the High Line began opening to the public in 2009. It is now one of the city's must-see attractions and a joy to explore in all seasons.

Follow the **High Line** north to **15th Street**

Stop 3 → On the **High Line**, looking east along **15th Street**

CHELSEA MARKET

Stand where you can see a graceful pedestrian sky bridge off to the right and admire the sprawling complex of stout red-brick buildings all around. Now home to Chelsea Market and a cluster of high-end restaurants, gyms, and offices, this former industrial compound was once home to the National Biscuit Company, a conglomeration of bakeries better known today as Nabisco. The company was formed in 1898 and remained active at its Chelsea campus, filling the air "with the fresh-baked aromas of vanilla wafers and Marshmallow Fancies, animal crackers and Fig Newtons"[78] until it decamped to New Jersey in 1958. It was here, in 1912, that Nabisco first produced the Oreo cookie.

Continue north along the **High Line** to **20th Street**

RADIOACTIVE STORAGE

Before descending, look left at the three unassuming brown-brick warehouses on the north side of the street adjacent to the High Line. These buildings, at Nos. 513 through 535 West 20th Street, were built at the turn of the 20th century as the Baker & Williams Warehouses but were used during World War II by the United States Army Corps of Engineers as short-term storage for uranium concentrates and other materials later used in the development of the atomic bomb. More than 200,000 pounds (90,000 kg) of radioactive materials were held in these buildings, which returned to civilian use after the war. Amazingly, the radioactivity wasn't measured or remediated until the 1990s.

Take the stairs down to street level, cross to the east side of **10th Avenue** and walk partway down the block

Stop 4 → In front of the rectangular, light-gray stone building at **No. 445 West 20th Street**

GENERAL THEOLOGICAL SEMINARY

The gray-stone building at roughly 445 West 20th Street, with its high stoop, cream-colored doors, and pointed Gothic window frames, is the oldest surviving part of the General Theological Seminary and the geographic center of historic Chelsea.

The General Theological Seminary is a fanciful surprise when first glimpsed from the High Line. Much of its campus is made of rich red brick with a brownstone base, an English collegiate fantasy with spires, dormers, and bay windows to delight the eye wherever they land. The seminary was established in 1817 as a training school for the Episcopal Church, which itself had only been established in 1785 in a break from the Church of England following the American Revolution. The new seminary was meant to operate independent of any particular Episcopal congregation or governing body, hence the General in its name. It would be a seminary for all.

In 1818, the seminary was given a full city block bound by 20th and 21st Streets between 10th and 9th Avenues. This block forms the heart of Chelsea, the former estate of Major Thomas Clarke, a British officer who stayed in New York after serving in the French and Indian War (the American theater of the Seven Years' War). The estate, named in honor of the Royal Chelsea Hospital in London, encompassed everything between 19th and 24th Streets from 8th Avenue to the river. It eventually passed to Clarke's grandson, the writer Clement Clarke Moore, whose greatest claim to fame is his purported authoring of *A Visit from Saint Nicholas*, though there is some debate as to whether he actually wrote it.

Moore gave this parcel of land, once the family's apple orchard, to the seminary with an eye toward Chelsea's future: he intended the seminary's campus to act as a sort of town square for the wealthy residential enclave he hoped would grow around it. To that end, the first seminary building opened on 20th Street in 1826 with a twin constructed next to it five years later. The first structure was later demolished, but the twin remains, its light-gray rough-stone walls a reminder of the area's more bucolic origins. Most of the rest of the campus dates to the 1880s and 1890s, designed in the fashionable Collegiate Gothic style.

In the interceding century, financial pressure has seen the seminary sell off or redevelop several buildings. In 2024, it was announced that the Seminary had inked a 99-year lease with Vanderbilt University which will turn this historic Chelsea campus into a satellite for the Nashville institution while allowing the Seminary to continue to operate alongside them. Otherwise, changes to the General Theological Seminary have been happily subtle, providing Chelsea with a unique architectural focal point, anchoring the historic landscape which radiates outward from it.

Clement Clarke Moore, in addition to providing land for the construction of the

General Theological Seminary, also oversaw the development of the surrounding blocks of fine houses which would give Chelsea its particular residential flavor. The houses which face the seminary on 20th and 21st Streets reflect Moore's guiding hand. Built mostly between 1830 and 1855, these brick and brownstone houses are all set luxuriously far back from the sidewalk, a requirement imposed by Moore to ensure that Chelsea's streets would forever retain the sort of verdant charm which first lured his family to the area in the 18th century.

One of the loveliest house rows in the neighborhood can be admired at Nos. 406–418 West 20th Street. These handsome Greek-revival homes were constructed in 1840 for developer Don Alonzo Cushman, whose descendants later founded the extant real estate firm of Cushman & Wakefield. Cushman was one of the leading developers of Chelsea, working alongside Moore and James N Wells to create a district lovely enough to lure New York's wealthy elites to the far-west side of the island. Though Cushman died in 1875, his daughter Angelica Faber constructed the unusual apartment building at No. 402 West 20th Street in 1897. Above the entryway is the word *DONAC*, short for Don Alonzo Cushman.

Walk east along **20th Street** and cross **9th Avenue**

Stop 5 → On **20th Street** in front of **St Peter's Episcopal Church**

ST PETER'S EPISCOPAL CHURCH

In addition to providing land for the General Theological Seminary, Clement Clarke Moore also donated a smaller parcel on 20th Street just east of 9th Avenue for the construction of an Episcopal chapel to serve the lay population of Chelsea. St Peter's was established in 1831, and Moore submitted initial architectural plans for the church's layout. His vision was for a compound of tetrastyle Greek-revival temples, with a central church flanked by a rectory and parish house. Moore's Greek vision for St Peter's is visible in the rectory, a low red-brick structure consecrated in 1832 immediately west of the main church building. This is among the oldest buildings in Chelsea and one of the first examples of Greek-revival architecture in New York.

In the years between the rectory's completion in 1832 and the church's completion in 1838, architectural tastes had changed. Instead of Moore's proposed Greek style, St Peter's Chapel was instead built in a quasi-Gothic style then fashionable in England. This makes it one of the first such buildings in the nation and would serve as inspiration for later Gothic-revival churches in the city, such as Richard Upjohn's Trinity Church (page 22), and James Renwick Jr's Grace Church (page 142). Instead of a columned Greek portico, St Peter's Chapel was given a lofty tower, complete with a clock and belfry, long making it one of the tallest structures in Chelsea.

Interestingly, though its outward appearance is that of an English country chapel, St Peter's lacks the traditional cruciform shape of a Gothic church. Instead, its main body

The High Line, Standard Hotel

Chelsea Market, former Nabisco factory

Baker and Williams Warehouses, the High Line

General Theological Seminary

20th Street

St Peter's Episcopal Church

retains the rectangular form of its original Greek-revival plan. The clocktower seems to have been tacked onto the facade almost as an afterthought, with the whole project sheathed in fieldstone to distract from the fact that its style had changed so drastically midway through construction. It is an outstanding and unique structure in the pantheon of American architecture, bridging two distinct eras.

The oldest element of the St Peter's Chapel complex is perhaps the easiest to overlook: the wrought-iron fence in front of it, which was originally installed in 1790 downtown at Trinity Church during its reconstruction following the American Revolution. That version of Trinity was demolished in the 1830s, just as St Peter's was being completed, and the disused fence was repurposed here.

Walk east along **20th Street** to **8th Avenue**, the eastern boundary of Clement Clarke Moore's estate. Turn right on **8th Avenue** and walk south. Turn left down **18th Street**

Stop 6 → In front of **No. 236 West 18th Street**

SIEGEL-COOPER WAREHOUSE

Walking east and leaving historic Chelsea behind, its tidy rows of red-brick homes give way to a messier, grittier district of commerce and industry. These are the neighborhood's transitional blocks, situated between Moore's planned community to the west and the density of Midtown and the shopping district of Ladies' Mile to the east. Each block boasts an eclectic mix of building heights, volumes, and uses, with tenements sandwiched between low-slung stables, which are sidled up against loft buildings rising a dozen or more stories. There is a grit to these blocks between 6th and 8th Avenues, enduring even in this age of hypergentrification, thanks in part to the streetscape's pre-zoning-law density which casts the streets in shadow for much of the day.

Lovely enough to rise above the architectural din, 236 West 18th Street runs through the block, becoming 249 West 17th Street on its south side, and both facades are heavily embellished with elaborate brick detailing and terracotta ornamentation. Above the arched entryway, the keystone features interlocking "SC Co.," the monogram of Siegel-Cooper Company, formerly one of the city's great department stores which rivaled Macy's and Saks in its brief heyday. While Siegel-Cooper opened on 6th Avenue in 1896 (and closed barely 20 years later), this building was constructed on 18th Street in 1902 to serve as its warehouse and stables. From here, purchases could be ferried to customers' homes all around the city, a luxury afforded by many of the city's great dry-goods emporia, including B Altman, whose warehouse stands one block to the east.

From the **Siegel-Cooper warehouse**, walk east across **7th Avenue**

Stop 7 → In front of the ruddy-colored B Altman warehouse at **No. 135 West 18th Street**

B ALTMAN STABLES

When Benjamin Altman died in 1913, his memorial service at Temple Emanu-El (page 211) was attended by an all-star list of the nation's retail titans: Isidor Saks and Emanuel Bloomingdale alongside Louis Stern, Isaac and Jacob Gimbel, and Jesse Straus, who'd only just taken over operations of Macy's department store following the death of his father Isidor in the sinking of the *Titanic*. Respect for Altman ran deep across the broad spectrum of New York society. He embodied the classic tale of a man who'd risen to great wealth and success through hard work and integrity. Born to Bavarian Jewish immigrants in 1840, Altman established his retail company at age 25 and amassed an estimated fortune of $50 million by the time of his death at age 73.

B Altman first opened in 1865 at No. 39 3rd Avenue on Manhattan's Lower East Side (sited between 9th and 10th Streets, this would be considered the East Village today). In 1876, it moved uptown to a larger, more modern building at No. 627 6th Avenue at the corner of 19th Street. It would remain on that site for three decades, expanding along with its revenue and the overall success of what came to be known as Ladies' Mile, the city's premier shopping district. The former B Altman building still stands on 6th Avenue, spanning the entire block front between 18th and 19th Streets with a beautifully decorated cast-iron facade featuring unusual Eastlake-inspired embellishment.

In 1896, as part of the store's expansion and modernization, B Altman constructed this imposing sandstone stable and powerhouse on 18th Street, immediately behind the main store. This allowed for easy movement of products to and from the selling floor as well as quick home delivery for customers. Across from the massive Altman stable stands a row of nine smaller individual stables, built in the 1860s when this area was just beginning to develop. Their rounded triple-arch windows echo similar design elements found on contemporary landmarks such as the Astor Library (page 142) and the Cooper Union (pages 81 and 141). Between the Altman stable and the many smaller neighboring stables, it is easy to imagine the bustle, sounds, and smells of this shopping district more than a century ago.

Continue walking east along **18th Street** to **6th Avenue** and the heart of Ladies' Mile

Stop 8 → In front of the former B Altman store at **Nos. 615–629 6th Avenue**

LADIES' MILE

Ladies' Mile earned its name in the 1850s, when New York's high-end shops began to cluster along Broadway between Astor Place and Madison Square. This concentration of respectable retail spaces lured the city's wealthy ladies who could shop for anything imaginable all within one compact district. Ladies' Mile expanded rapidly following the end of the American Civil War as dozens of retail outfits shouldered onto the blocks of 5th and 6th Avenues, creating a shoppers' paradise made all the more accessible by the 1878 opening of the 6th Avenue elevated train line.

By the end of the 19th century, shoppers walking north along 6th Avenue could visit Macy's at 14th Street; B Altman or Siegel-Cooper at 18th; Simpson, Crawford & Simpson or Cammeyer Shoes at 19th; Hugh O'Neill at 20th; Adams & Co. at 21st; and Ehrich Brothers at 22nd. In just a half-mile, New Yorkers could buy anything

Siegel-Cooper store

and everything, from furs to laces and silks to furniture and hats to gowns imported from Paris. "Shopping on Sixth Avenue," read *The Times* in 1899, "is as cosmopolitan a scene as can be found in New York. Every variety of human being can be seen during a few moments' pause to watch the hurrying shoppers."[79]

The largest of all these was of course Siegel-Cooper, the Chicago-based department store which tried to muscle its way into the New York retail scene in 1896 by building the largest store the city had ever seen. The Siegel-Cooper building occupies the east side of 6th Avenue between 18th and 19th Streets and stretches back roughly 500 feet (152 meters), halfway to 5th Avenue. An estimated 35,000 shoppers passed through the still-unfinished Siegel-Cooper building's monumental triple-arched entrance during a "dress rehearsal"[80] on September 12, 1896.

Inside, New Yorkers found an endless array of wonders and conveniences across nearly 800,000 square feet (74,300 square meters) of selling space. In addition to the expected array of high-end clothing and furniture, Siegel-Cooper also included a soda counter and cafe, a meat counter with the city's largest refrigerator, a seafood counter with live fish, a post office, a dentist, a nursery, and both telegraph and telephone services. The focal point of the store's interior was a central fountain with a 13-foot (4-meter) reproduction of Daniel Chester French's *The Republic* at its center. Siegel-Cooper promoted "Meet me at the fountain" as one of the great store's popular slogans.

Despite Siegel-Cooper's initial success, Ladies' Mile went into rapid decline in the beginning of the 20th century as stores continued to chase their customer base ever farther uptown. One of the first companies to abandon this stretch of 6th Avenue was RH Macy & Co., which moved to Herald Square in 1902, followed by B Altman, which relocated to a palatial new building on 5th Avenue at 34th Street in 1906. Siegel-Cooper acquired the old Altman building on 6th Avenue, briefly making it the world's largest store, but the whole operation shuttered in 1917.

By the mid-20th century, much of the former Ladies' Mile was either abandoned or being used as warehouse space. It experienced a resurgence in the 1980s when, in an echo of what had been done previously in SoHo and Tribeca, New Yorkers began to convert the expansive floor plates of the former stores into residential lofts. The area became a designated historic district in 1989 and today enjoys renewed success as a shopping district, with sometimes half a dozen stores occupying the ground floors of these former palaces of retail trade.

Keen-eyed explorers will easily spy remnants of the area's faded glory: the iconic red star logo of Macy's is still visible on the facade of 55 West 13th Street; thistles picked out in tile mosaic celebrate the Scottish heritage of the founders of Simpson, Crawford & Simpson at No. 641 6th Avenue; and the interlocking "SC Co." of Siegel-Cooper can be seen on the facade of Nos. 616–632 6th Avenue, echoing the similar logo found on their former warehouse at No. 135 West 18th Street.

From the former Siegel-Cooper building, walk north along **6th Avenue**

Admire the beauty of the streetscape. Note how most of the former department stores on the avenue boast double-height show windows. Those on the ground floor were for pedestrians and passersby while those on the second floor were for passengers of the former 6th Avenue elevated trains. At 20th Street, take a moment to gaze at the little brownstone chapel complex, originally built in 1852 as the Episcopal Church of the Holy Communion. It is perhaps the only vestige of this area's more rural appearance from an age when Clement Clarke Moore's Chelsea estate was still developing on the west side. It would become far more famous in 1983 when it reopened as the nightclub, Limelight.

At **21st Street**, turn left

Stop 9 → On **West 21st Street** in front of the small gated **cemetery**

THIRD CEMETERY OF THE SPANISH AND PORTUGUESE SYNAGOGUE

Tucked away on 21st Street, just west of 6th Avenue, behind a high iron fence, is the third of three historic Jewish cemeteries on Manhattan Island. The oldest is located on St James Place just south of Chatham Square (page 66). It was used from 1682 until 1833 when it was deemed too full. The second cemetery is located on West 11th Street near 6th Avenue (page 95). It was established in 1805 to replace the Chatham Square location but was shuttered in 1830 when 11th Street was cut through the middle of it, leaving only a small triangular patch of its original grounds. The third cemetery, here in Chelsea, was opened in 1829 to receive many of the bodies displaced from the 11th Street location. It remained in use until 1851 when New York passed a law forbidding burials south of 86th Street.

All three are relics of bygone eras and survive as testaments to the long and complex history of religious liberty in this city and nation. The synagogue associated with these graveyards, Shearith Israel, traces its origins to the arrival in New Amsterdam of 23 Sephardic Jews in 1654. Shearith Israel exists today on Central Park West, making it the oldest active Jewish congregation in the Western Hemisphere.

Today, the cemetery lies almost hidden behind the 1887 Hugh O'Neill store, a cast-iron marvel with twin gilded domes which were actually removed a century ago and were only recreated during the building's 2004 conversion for residential use.

Continue walking west along **21st Street** to **7th Avenue**. Turn right and walk north to **23rd Street**, then turn left on **23rd Street**

Stop 10 → In front of the elaborate facade of the **Hotel Chelsea**

HOTEL CHELSEA

The Hotel Chelsea opened in 1884 amidst a wave of luxury apartment construction in New York. The 1882 Knickerbocker (now demolished) on 5th Avenue at 28th Street, the 1884 Dakota on Central Park West, and the 1885 Osborne on 57th Street at 7th Avenue together marked the beginning of a gradual shift among wealthy New Yorkers away from the expense and obligation of mansion living and toward the thrifty convenience of apartments. But this shift

Hotel Chelsea

would take time and many of the city's early apartment buildings struggled to fill themselves with the sort of well-heeled clientele they initially sought. Such was the case for the Chelsea, which sat just a bit too far west to be considered acceptable to the *bon ton*.

In place of socialites and millionaires, the hotel attracted tradesmen and artists, establishing an early reputation as a sort of luxurious melting pot. In its first decades, it was home to writers such as Thomas Wolfe, O Henry, Dylan Thomas, and Arthur Miller. When Chelsea began entering a sort of creative renaissance in the 1950s, the Hotel Chelsea benefitted likewise, attracting residents such as Bob Dylan, Patti Smith, and Robert Mapplethorpe. In many ways, it reflects the neighborhood's continuing proclivity for refusing to live up to its founders' high-minded plans. Just as Chelsea never attracted the sort of elite, highly pedigreed residents envisioned by Clement Clarke Moore for his rows of fine townhouses in the 1840s, the Hotel Chelsea has never quite evolved into the sort of genteel fortress typified by its uptown contemporary, the Dakota. It is more independent, more egalitarian, and more interesting than it was ever meant to be.

Continue walking west past the **Hotel Chelsea**. At **8th Avenue**, turn left and then right again onto **22nd Street**

Here, we re-enter Clement Clarke Moore's Chelsea estate and notice an accompanying shift in architectural scale and pedigree. Much of this block dates to the 1830s and 1840s, part of Chelsea's earliest development.

Follow **22nd Street** west to **9th Avenue** and turn left

Stop 11 → At the little dormered brick house at **No. 183 9th Avenue**, the northwest corner of **21st Street**

JAMES N WELLS

Clement Clarke Moore first moved full-time to his family's country estate at Chelsea in the 1820s, and soon thereafter began plotting how best to transform this bucolic farmland into a modern and desirable neighborhood. To that end, he enlisted the architect James N Wells to act as his planner and developer. At that time, Wells was best known for building the Church of St Luke in the Fields (page 108) on Hudson Street down in Greenwich Village. By 1833, he and his family had moved uptown to Chelsea, settling in this little red-brick two-and-a-half-story house at the northwest corner of 9th Avenue and 21st Street.

It was from this house that Wells oversaw the initial plans for Chelsea and likely concocted many of the rules which would dictate the neighborhood's development: required building materials, forbidden land uses, and mandatory setbacks and gardens, among other things. Much of the loveliness baked into historic Chelsea is a direct result of Wells' ideas, and much of those ideas were first conceived and implemented while he lived at No. 183 9th Avenue. By 1835, however, Wells and his construction company were flush from working on dozens of houses all across the district. Reflecting his success, Wells relocated his family to a newly completed mansion just around the corner.

Walk north from the little Wells house on **9th Avenue** to **22nd Street** and turn left

Stop 12 → In front of the surprisingly palatial **Wells mansion**, at Nos. 414-416 West 22nd Street

WELLS MANSION

The Wells mansion is one of the grandest townhouses in all of Manhattan, more than 40 feet (12 meters) wide and boasting five generously proportioned bays, which allow for an unusual central stoop and doorway, something all but impossible in a typical townhouse of half the width. It was originally designed in the Greek revival style but was redone in the fashionable Italianate in the 1860s. James N Wells died in 1860 and the mansion was sold by 1870 to become the Samaritan Home for the Aged, which remained here until 1929. Next, the house became a women's shelter until 1952 when it was reverted to mainstream residential use. This spacious home which once housed "the man who planned Chelsea,"[81] is now chopped up into unremarkable apartments.

Walk west from the **Wells mansion** along **22nd Street**

Stop 13 → At **No. 436 22nd Street**

FORREST MANSION

Like the Wells mansion, this once-grand home was also built in 1835. Unassuming today, one of its original residents played an outsize role in New York's theatrical history. In 1839, it was purchased by the wealthy actor Edwin Forrest, allegedly to escape his unhappy marriage and overbearing in-laws. Edwin and his wife, the English actress Catherine Norton Sinclair, would endure years of scandal culminating in a messy and highly public divorce in 1852.

But Edwin's great claim to notoriety remains his role in the deadly 1849 Astor Place Riot (page 140), in which he riled antipathy for the English actor William Macready who'd been hired to play Macbeth at the opera house there. Thousands turned out to protest, and in the ensuing melee, at least 30 people were killed and more than a hundred more injured. Forrest sold his 22nd Street house in 1856 and its once-stunning interiors were shamefully gutted in the 1940s while being converted into apartments. Outside, mismatched bricks tell the tale of a missing stoop and original entryway. Despite this abuse, the Forrest home remains a vital piece of Chelsea history nearly two centuries on.

Continue walking west along **22nd Street**, passing leafy **Clement Clarke Moore Park** before turning right onto **10th Avenue**. Turn left onto **23rd Street** and ascend the **High Line** once more

SECOND PHASE OF THE HIGH LINE

This portion of the High Line was the second completed phase, opening from 20th to 30th Street in 2011. Unlike the original segment which begins at Gansevoort Street, this segment runs entirely midblock, sandwiched between buildings, some of which are close enough to touch. It is an intimate and unusual way to see the city and occasionally catch voyeuristic glimpses of people at home or in their offices.

James Wells House, 9th Avenue at 21st Street

The High Line near 24th St

Empire Diner and *Mount Rushmore of Art*

The High Line near 27th Street with the Zaha Hadid building (left) and Hudson Yards (middle)

As you exit the High Line at 28th Street, admire the black sinuous lines of No. 528 West 28th Street, the only building in New York designed by Zaha Hadid. The High Line has acted as a magnet for high-profile architects, and the Hadid building sits within shouting distance of projects by everyone from Norman Foster and Jean Nouvel to Bjarke Ingels and Renzo Piano.

Exit the High Line at **28th Street**. Descending from the High Line, walk west along **28th Street** to **11th Avenue**, then turn left

Stop 14 → At the corner of **27th Street**

TERMINAL WAREHOUSE

Chelsea can generally be divided into three distinct sub-districts. The original Chelsea, as developed in the 1830s by Clement Clarke Moore and James N Wells, sits neatly between 8th and 10th Avenues, defined by rows of tidy brick and brownstone homes with high stoops and front gardens. To the east of that, between 6th and 8th Avenues, is the more commercial Ladies' Mile, defined by immense department stores alongside their supporting stables and warehouses. Lastly, to the west of 10th Avenue, lies the neighborhood's industrial waterfront, defined by colossal warehouses and industrial lofts which once served the countless west side docks and freight rail lines. Residential, commercial, and industrial: Chelsea has it all.

The industrial waterfront of Chelsea is a far cry from the lovely streetscapes which define the rest of the neighborhood to the east. Here, landfill pushed Manhattan's riverfront far out into the Hudson River during the late 19th century, allowing for highly lucrative development which took full advantage of the area's position at the juncture of road, rail, and waterborne traffic. Many of the city's more historic industrial buildings can be found in far west Chelsea, clustered between the High Line and the West Side Highway. In fact, the intersection of 11th Avenue and 27th Street sits directly at the center of the West Chelsea Historic District, officially designated in 2008 to protect the area's unique architectural character.

One of the oldest buildings in the West Chelsea Historic District stands at the northwest corner of 11th Avenue and 27th Street. The Terminal Warehouse, its name emblazoned on its 11th-Avenue facade, is technically a complex of 25 warehouses and cold-storage facilities built to look like one unified structure. The block it occupies had only just been reclaimed from the Hudson River a few years prior to its completion in 1891. At that time, freight trains of the New York Central Railroad ran directly down the middle of the avenue here, and the Terminal Warehouse was built with a double-track spur, allowing train cars to pull directly inside through the building's enormous arched entryway.

Though the freight trains which once ran down the middle of 11th Avenue were diverted to the elevated tracks now known as the High Line in 1933, the Terminal Warehouse remained in use for another half-century. By the 1980s, however, industry had largely vacated west Chelsea, and the old Terminal Warehouse building was transformed into an 80,000-square-foot (7,500-square-meter) nightclub known as The Tunnel, which operated until 2001. Today, the Terminal

Warehouse has been reimagined again, this time as a complex of art galleries, restaurants, and office space.

OTIS ELEVATOR COMPANY

Diagonally across from the Terminal Warehouse, at the southeast corner of 11th Avenue and 27th Street, stands a beautifully elaborated seven-story brick tower with a heavy copper cornice which stands out among the otherwise quite utilitarian neighborhood. Constructed in 1911, this was for more than six decades the headquarters for the Otis Elevator Company, which was established in 1852 by Elisha Otis. In 1853, Otis demonstrated his new safety elevator at the World's Fair in what is now Bryant Park, a technological advancement which heralded the impending skyscraper age. During its time in Chelsea, Otis was responsible for crafting and installing elevators and escalators for some of the world's tallest and most notable structures, including the Woolworth Building, the Empire State Building, and the original World Trade Center. They abandoned their 11th-Avenue building in 1974, but the elevators crafted here can still be found and ridden all around the globe.

STARRETT-LEHIGH BUILDING

Directly across the avenue from the former Otis building is the monumental Starrett-Lehigh Building. Completed in 1931, this 19-story edifice contains more square footage than the Empire State Building, which was completed the same year and boasts more than 100 stories. Like its neighbor to the north, the Terminal Warehouse, the Starrett-Lehigh Building was designed to maximize its industrial utility. But in the four decades since the Terminal building was completed in 1891, architecture and engineering had advanced at a rapid clip, and the Starrett-Lehigh Building was hailed as a paragon of modernism and a symbol of the future metropolis. Its most striking features are its windows, forming unbroken ribbons of glass across its brick facade. It offered tenants direct access to rail piers on the Hudson River waterfront and elevators capable of carrying trucks to each floor for easy loading and unloading.

The Starrett-Lehigh Building takes its name from the Starrett Corporation, formed in 1922 as a real estate development firm, and the Lehigh Valley Railroad which partnered with them to build a new freight terminal on Manhattan's west side. The building was originally supposed to be symmetrical, with fifteen stories across a full city block. But when construction began, it was discovered that, because its plot sat mostly on landfill, bedrock lay 45 feet (14 meters) down on its east side but 145 feet (44 meters) on its west. Rather than fight such uneven topography, the building's center of gravity was shifted eastward, explaining why its 11th-Avenue wing is fully twice as tall as its Hudson River wing.

As industry declined in western Chelsea in the 1980s, the Starrett-Lehigh Building began to fill with new types of tenants such as art galleries, photographers, and fashion companies drawn to the building's ample floor space and sweeping river and city views. It was extensively renovated in the 2020s, adding convention and exhibit space along with restaurants and retail spaces on the ground floor. As the Starrett-Lehigh Building approaches its 100th birthday, it appears to have a new lease on life, not unlike the nearby High Line and much of formerly industrial west Chelsea.

From **27th Street**, walk south along **11th Avenue** to **23rd Street**

Notice the massive stone bull heads on display inside the playground at Chelsea Waterside Park. These are relics from a long-lost New York Butchers' Dressed Meat Company Building, constructed in 1919 on 11th Avenue at 39th Street. When the building was demolished in 1991 for an expansion of the Javits Center, the bulls and rams which adorned its facade were salvaged and reinstalled here at this playground in 2018.

Walk through the park at **23rd Street** and cross **12th Avenue** to enter the park along the **Hudson River waterfront**

CHELSEA PIERS

Walking south through the waterfront park, at 22nd Street you may enter Chelsea Piers, the 1990s entertainment complex cobbled from the remnants of what was once the city's greatest passenger ship terminal. These west side piers, constructed by the city in 1910, welcomed such liners as the *Lusitania* and the *Olympic*, sister to the *Titanic*, during the golden age of ocean travel. But by the 1960s, with larger modern ships unable to fit at Chelsea's antiquated piers, a new terminal was built uptown near 42nd Street and these piers entered a slow decline. They were saved in 1994, when work began on converting them into a complex of gyms, event spaces, and restaurants.

Emerging from **Chelsea Piers** at **17th Street**, follow the waterfront just a bit farther south to **Pier 57**

PIER 57

Built in 1954, this pier was recently renovated as a cavernous food hall with offices above and a beautifully well-hidden rooftop park. Ride the public elevators up to the roof and take in the sweeping views and cool river breezes. From this vantage point, it is easy to see why Chelsea has for so long seemed to sit at the center of New York's urban and industrial development: it is indeed a city within a city.

View of Chelsea from Pier 57

0
200
400m
0
1000ft
START
Washington Square
1
2
3
4
5
6
7
8
END
34 St-Herald Sq
Empire State Building
B Altman Store
Marble Collegiate Church
Little Church Around the Corner
Evelyn Nesbit Mural
Site of Madison Square Garden
Madison Square Park
Flatiron Building
Metropolitan Life Tower
Calvary Episcopal Church
Mayor's Lamps
Gramercy Park
National Arts Club/ Tilden Mansion
The Players/ Booth Mansion
Fish Mansion
Union Square
14 St-Union Sq
Grace Church
8 St-NYU
Astor Place Opera House Location
Astor Pl
The Cooper Union
LeGrange Terrace
Former Astor Library
W4 St Wash Sq
5TH AVENUE
6TH AVENUE
7TH AVENUE
8TH AVENUE
BROADWAY
4TH AVENUE
3RD AVENUE
2ND AVENUE
1ST AVE
PARK AVE
PARK AVE STH
MADISON AVENUE
LAFAYETTE ST
IRVING PLACE
WEST 23RD STREET
EAST 23RD STREET
EAST 14TH ST
WEST 8TH STREET
WAVERLY PLACE
WASHINGTON PLACE
N

The Gilded Age in New York played out during the half-century between the American Civil War and World War I. It was a time of boundless economic growth and an opportunity for the city's wealthiest families to flaunt their status as never before. Though the heyday of the Gilded Age took place uptown in what is now considered Murray Hill, Midtown, and the Upper East Side, its origins lie downtown. This walk explores the neighborhoods which birthed some of the era's most notable dynasties, including the Astors and the Vanderbilts, whose ostentation would redefine what it meant to be wealthy in the United States.

ROUTE STOPS

1. Washington Square
2. Washington Mews
3. Astor Place
4. Grace Church
5. Union Square
6. Gramercy Park
7. Madison Square
8. Murray Hill

THE GILDED AGE: ITS ORIGINS AND EARLY YEARS

DISTANCE
2¼ miles (3.6 km)

TIME ALLOWED
2–3 hours

ROUTE No. 06

FROM WASHINGTON SQUARE TO MURRAY HILL

Historians generally agree that New York's Gilded Age took place from the 1860s to the 1910s, during the 50-year period between the end of the American Civil War and the start of World War I. In that brief half-century, a level of wealth, opulence, and ostentation emerged which was unlike anything Americans had ever seen before. This glittering age of excess would fundamentally change New York City, from the filthy colonial port town it had so recently been into a world-class urban agglomeration more akin to the New York we know it to be today. How did this happen? It shouldn't be taken for granted that New York's rise was inevitable. Far from it. At the turn of the 19th century, New York was locked in economic competition with a dozen or more rival port towns up and down the eastern seaboard of the newly formed United States: Boston, Newport, Philadelphia, Baltimore, Charleston, Savannah, New Orleans. Each stood poised and eager to become the axis around which the nation's economy spun. But thanks to a series of massive infrastructure projects undertaken by New York's city and state leadership, this chaotic and strangely Dutch city would emerge as the unquestioned economic capital of the country and, in time, the world.

Chief among the infrastructure projects which positioned New York for success was the Erie Canal. Completed in 1825, it physically connected the Great Lakes and the heart of the North American continent to the Atlantic Ocean for the first time. Stretching nearly 400 miles (650 km) from Buffalo on the shores of Lake Erie to the Hudson River near Albany, the canal allowed for the cheap and easy transport of goods and travelers to and from newly acquired lands west of the Appalachian Mountains. Almost overnight upon its completion, roughly half of the nation's GDP was funneled through the canal, down the Hudson River, and into New York Harbor. With this flow of commerce came an economic and population explosion for New York City. That, combined with the genius of the city's 1811 street grid plan and its 1842 Croton Aqueduct, which supplied Manhattan with a seemingly limitless supply of clean drinking water, meant that New York barreled through the first half of the century at a breathtaking clip of growth and prosperity.

All that growth meant that by the time the nation plunged into its devastating Civil War in 1861, New York was far and away its largest and most important city. A hub for both sea and rail, it industrialized rapidly during the war, giving rise to an entirely new generation of wealthy families, most of whom had not been steeped in the conservative traditions of New York's social inner circles. They were rich and they wanted everyone to know it. Led by the Vanderbilts, these new-money New Yorkers built colossal mansions up and down 5th Avenue, forever changing the city's relationship with wealth, status, and hubris.

But this rising tide did not lift all ships, and for most New Yorkers, the decades following the Civil War were anything but golden. Hence the reason we call this era the "Gilded Age" and not the "Golden Age." Gilding is a thin layer of gold applied to something less valuable. This was precisely the situation in New York in the late 19th century: a few dozen ultra-wealthy families enjoyed their economic fruits while the vast majority of New Yorkers continued to live in the city's often-squalid boarding houses and tenements. The silken finery, endless cotillions, and palatial summer cottages of the elite may as well have been a fairy tale to the less-fortunate masses for whom life was inescapably difficult and often too short. This is a vital point to keep in mind when discussing New York's Gilded Age. Its stories often revolve around those few dazzling families with the means to enjoy the era's prosperity. But in many ways, these stories are the ones we associate with the era because, as a rule, history is written by the victors. We remember their names and preserve their mansions (some of them, anyway) because they are well documented and because they could often afford to affect history by their deeds and monuments.

And so, while we explore the Gilded Age history of New York, always bear in mind that behind the finery and excess are a million unremembered stories of a different, less rarefied world, existing contemporaneously and often within a few short blocks of the families whose lives were truly gilded.

Start 1 → At Washington Square

WASHINGTON SQUARE

In that spirit, we begin our journey at Washington Square, a 9¾-acre (4-hectare) rectangle of greenery which functions as the buzzing heart of modern Greenwich Village. This is not a spot most people would immediately associate with the Gilded Age, but it serves as an outstanding jumping-off point for understanding how it came to be. Here were sown the seeds of what would eventually grow into the Gilded Age, because this was essentially Manhattan's first suburb. After the opening of the Erie Canal in 1825, rich New Yorkers fled northward in search of quiet, fresh air, and clean water. Down at the southerly tip of the island, any vestige of the quaint Dutch town New York had once been was wiped from the slate in the name of exponential economic expansion. The old Knickerbocker families whose mansions had long defined the harborfront now fled uptown, whether to escape the noise and bustle, or to reap immense profits from selling their newly valuable landholdings.

The area now known as Washington Square was, until that time, so far away and isolated from the population center that it was taken in 1797 to serve as the city's public burial ground, or potter's field. Most of those buried here were victims of successive waves of infectious disease, primarily yellow fever, and it was thought to be a good idea to keep those bodies as far from the city as possible. But with the opening of the Erie Canal in 1825 and the anticipated population growth that came with it, city leaders shut the land to burials and began converting it into a public park, which opened in 1827. They declined to move the bodies buried here, however, and today there are still something like 25,000 New Yorkers buried beneath Washington Square.

With the potter's field shuttered and the city's wealthy population looking for new places to live away from the chaotic waterfront, the land around this new park became exponentially more valuable and attractive as a development site. Block by block, the swath of land around Washington Square was filled with row upon row of high-end speculative houses, built to be sold off to wealthy families eager to move uptown. By the 1840s, the park and surrounding thoroughfares – like 5th Avenue, University Place, Lafayette Place, and, of course, Broadway – were among the choicest, loveliest neighborhoods the city had yet seen.

The problem which became readily apparent for these new uptown residents, and which would become the theme of New York's urban development for the next century, was that anywhere rich folks went, businesses naturally followed in search of their customer base's money. Wherever businesses went, so went factories which produced the myriad products being sold in those stores. And wherever factories went, so went an impoverished, often immigrant population in search of jobs. And so, within as little as sometimes 15–20 years, wealthy families found themselves surrounded by the very urbanity from which they'd attempted to flee. If they could afford it, they'd pick up stakes and move another few blocks or so up the island to start the whole process again.

It was by this pattern that the island of Manhattan essentially filled up between the middle of the 19th and beginning of the 20th centuries. Wealthy, mansion-dwelling families played hopscotch, moving from the old town at the tip of the island to new neighborhoods like St John's Square and Lispenard Meadows, then on to Greenwich Village and Washington Square. From there, they moved to Astor Place, Union Square, Chelsea, Gramercy Park, Madison Square, Murray Hill, Vanderbilt Row, the Upper East Side, and so on until there was no more room to move uptown. And in that messy cycle of endless movement and rebuilding, the story of the Gilded Age nests as part of the overall story of Manhattan.

The white marble arch which defines Washington Square's landscape was constructed in 1892 to designs by the architectural firm of McKim, Mead & White. It was built to replace an older arch which formerly stood astride 5th Avenue just north of the park. Built of wood and plaster, that arch was meant to be temporary when it was constructed in 1889 as part of the city-wide celebration of the 100th anniversary of George Washington's inauguration (he was inaugurated on Wall Street in 1789 during New York's brief stint as the national capital). Citizens raised money to build a permanent version of that original plaster arch inside the park, and thus we have the starting point for this walk and story.

From the **Washington Square Arch**, walk east along **Waverly Place** (also called Washington Square North here) to **University Place**

THE ROW

Along Waverly Place, admire the stately red-brick and marble townhouses on your left, built in 1831 as a row of speculative mansions which attracted some of those first wealthy suburbanites discussed earlier. These impressive Greek-revival houses, often simply referred to as "The Row," are among the most built as a direct result of the city's growth after the opening of the Erie Canal. The one obvious outlier within the row is No. 3, which was altered to be a multi-unit apartment building later in the 19th century. Notably, this is where the artist Edward Hopper lived and worked from 1913 until his death in 1967.

This whole row was originally constructed by the Sailors' Snug Harbor, a charitable home for retired seamen. When the wealthy sea captain Robert Richard Randall died in 1801, his will decreed that the land he owned – encompassing roughly the area bound by today's 5th Avenue, University Place, Waverly Place, and 8th Street – would become a sailors' retirement home, or a "snug harbor" for them. (Interestingly, the lawyer who aided Captain Randall in this endeavor was none other than Alexander Hamilton.)

A legal battle broke out, however, when two nephews of the childless Captain Randall challenged his will in court. In the end, a compromise was reached whereby the nephews could develop the land, but profits from the project must fund a Snug Harbor elsewhere in the city. Thus, the charitable old captain's land on Washington Square was filled with rows of fine and lucrative townhouses and stables, and Sailors' Snug Harbor was built instead on the north shore of Staten Island. Its sprawling neo-classical campus remains there today, now used as a cultural center.

At **University Place**, turn left. Midblock on the left, turn through a brick-arch gateway and step into a charming stone alley

Stop 2 → Inside **Washington Mews**

WASHINGTON MEWS

Washington Mews is that most unexpected of Manhattan anomalies: a true alleyway in the middle of the city. A mews is, by definition, a group of stables clustered around an alley, often with lodging rooms above them for staff. This particular mews began attracting artists in the 1910s when this area, along with all of Greenwich Village, was in the midst of its first wave of Bohemianization. In the late 19th century, wealthy residents began abandoning the area in favor of newer neighborhoods uptown, and in their wake Greenwich Village became a haven for artists, musicians, immigrants, and a whole tapestry of interesting and exciting counter-cultural communities. In 1915, the whole north side of the mews was stylishly renovated. "Out with the horses, in with the artists!" heralded the *Times* in 1915, in announcing the transformation of this "unsightly row of stables into a square of artists' studios, the double of which can be found only in one of the 'rues' of the Latin Quarter of Paris."[82]

As originally built, Washington Mews was nothing more or less than a private carriageway tucked behind the row of townhouses which face the northeastern edge of Washington Square. The north side of the mews are the oldest of the block, built in the early 1830s as, one for each of the residences. Today, their oversized entryways, big enough for a horse to walk through, hint at their original utility.

The south side of the block has a slightly more eclectic history. The six buildings on the east end, closest to University Place, were built individually between the 1850s and 1880s, mostly as supplemental carriage houses sited squarely in the rear gardens of the Washington Square houses. This accounts for their varying heights and styles. The newest and tallest of these, the five-story No. 14A, was built as "bachelor studio apartments" in 1884 in conjunction with the similarly renovated building behind it on Washington Square (the aforementioned Edward Hopper residence).

The 10 remaining buildings on the south side of Washington Mews, closer to 5th Avenue, were built far later, in 1939, specifically to serve as residences. Despite being a century younger than their neighbors across the alley, this stucco-faced row retains the scale and much of the aesthetic spirit of Washington Mews.

NEW YORK UNIVERSITY

Today, after nearly two centuries of evolution and alterations, Washington Mews remains one of the more eye-catching and unusual streets in Manhattan. Most of its buildings, as is the case with much of the area around Washington Square, are now owned by New York University (NYU) which has had a presence on the Square since 1833 when the cornerstone was laid for its first permanent building on the east side of the park. Near the end of the century, NYU sought roomier and more bucolic surroundings when it purchased a vast tract of land in the southwest Bronx. There, on a bluff high above the Harlem River, a new campus was built to designs by Stanford White, with a grassy quadrangle centered on a beautiful copper-domed library building. NYU moved most of its undergraduate students, faculty, and staff to its University Heights campus, which opened in 1894. The school remained in the Bronx until the early 1970s, when NYU sold the campus due to rising debts, falling enrollment, and increasing citywide crime. It was then that NYU began aggressively snapping up real estate around Washington Square, retrenching itself in the neighborhood it had long called home. Understanding this late-20th-century return from the Bronx helps to explain NYU's outsize presence in the neighborhood, including its many idiosyncratically modern buildings. The old NYU campus in the Bronx was purchased by the City University of New York (CUNY) which operates it today as Bronx Community College.

With **Washington Mews** in mind, follow **University Place** north to **8th Street** and turn right. Follow this all the way east, across **Greene Street**, **Mercer Street**, and **Broadway** until you come to a wide-open plaza

Stop 3 → At **Astor Place**

LAFAYETTE STREET

Lafayette Street lies just east of Broadway, stretching south from Astor Place to Worth Street. Originally, it dead-ended at Great Jones Street, but was elongated in the 1900s thanks to the construction of the city's first subway line which runs beneath Lafayette today as the 4/5/6 Trains. While the areas west of Broadway were developed mostly piecemeal by individual landowners, the development of Astor Place and Lafayette

Street was largely the work of one man: a German immigrant named John Jacob Astor.

John Jacob Astor was born in 1763 in the small town of Walldorf (in the southwest of modern Germany). The son of a butcher, young Astor moved to London in 1779 before sailing to the newly independent United States in 1783. He arrived in 1784 nearly penniless and barely literate. He settled in New York, then a city of just 30,000 which had been half-destroyed during the Revolution. Astor quickly insinuated himself into the fur trade, buying pelts from indigenous people, cleaning and tanning them, and selling them to Europe at great profit. By 1800, he was worth an estimated $250,000.

In 1808, he established the American Fur Company and the next year, he sent the first of a series of ships to the Columbia River where he established a trading post (today's Astoria, Oregon). From there, he sold furs to China in exchange for "teas, china, silk, silk thread, vermillion, handkerchiefs, crapes, &c."[83] He ultimately created a global trade empire, making himself one of the world's richest men. War with Britain in 1812 upended his plans out west, and Astor thereafter turned his focus back to New York, where he'd spent years buying up cheap real estate, guarding it with patient tenacity, correctly trusting that it would eventually pay dividends to him or his heirs as the city grew up and around it.

In the 1830s, he developed one such tract of land (then at the very northern edge of the city) into a fine residential enclave. Already hemmed in by Broadway to the west and the Bowery Road to the east, Astor cut a new street through the middle which he called Lafayette Place. He then carved it all into building lots which attracted prominent Knickerbocker families to its tree-lined streets.

So-called Knickerbockers were those families of Dutch origin whose lineage stretched back to the colonial era. The name was coined in 1809 by the author Washington Irving, who created the character Diedrich Knickerbocker as a personification of old New York. His high breeches and tri-corner hat soon became "the pictorial embodiment of the city that was once Dutch New Amsterdam and is now metropolitan and cosmopolitan New York."[84] The moniker was readily adopted by the members of this old guard, much to Irving's delight, and offered a shorthand differentiation between those New Yorkers whose ancestors had laid the foundation for the great metropolis enjoyed by later parvenus.

This is important: until this point, the Astors were not viewed with great esteem by the city's dynastic elite. For John Jacob Astor, wealth did not translate into likability. Though his bootstraps rags-to-riches life story would become the stuff of American legend, he was by most accounts crude, mean, and "absent of charitable benevolence." His reputation threatened to bar the entire Astor lineage from social acceptance. But Lafayette Place attracted the sort of genteel residents who would otherwise shun the Astors. This allowed Astor's grandsons to grow up alongside, and eventually marry into, many of the city's best families, cementing the Astor name atop the social heap.

Today, Lafayette Street bears little resemblance to the fine mansion district it was nearly two centuries ago. What happened? Even as the neighborhood was being developed in the 1830s and 40s, residents looked downtown in horror as the formerly exclusive residential district known as Lispenard Meadows (today's Tribeca and SoHo) was slowly upturned in favor of commerce and industry. One by one, its sturdy old brick houses were sold off and demolished to make way for factories and dry-goods emporiums. The cast-iron loft buildings that define SoHo's ultra-pricey real estate market today are, in fact, remnants of this era of upheaval.

ASTOR PLACE OPERA HOUSE

Up on Lafayette, wealthy residents oversaw the construction of a major cultural institution which would, they hoped, prevent a similar incursion of industry into their neighborhood. Thus the Astor Place Opera House opened in late 1847 as the pride of New York's so-called "uppertens" who chafed at the city's unrefined reputation. By then home to nearly half a million people, New York was ascendant, its population swollen by immigrants, many of them Irish fleeing the great famine there. The divide between rich and poor had never been greater, as a small but powerful clutch of wealthy families lorded over the impoverished masses of the city's overcrowded tenement districts. Exacerbating this was a bitter rivalry between two great actors: the Englishman William Macready and the American Edwin Forrest. Both specialized in Shakespeare plays, but in vastly different styles. While Macready was classically trained, imbuing his roles with nuance and tenderness, Forrest was butch and bombastic, the new American ideal.

In New York, the wealthy favored Macready and his tasteful English pedigree. The city's underclasses favored Forrest from a mix of American pride and an aversion to anything English. Trouble erupted on May 7, 1849, when Macready attempted to play Macbeth at the Astor Place Opera House. Dozens of protestors in the balcony assailed Macready the moment he took the stage, pelting him with rotten food and debris, shouting so he couldn't be heard. He fled the theater and planned to leave New York entirely but was convinced to try again.

On May 10, he retook the stage, but by now emotions citywide were at a fever pitch. Egged on by Forrest and local nativist groups, tens of thousands turned out in Astor Place to protest. Things quickly turned violent as the police began arresting people and the crowd assailed them with paving stones. The national guard was called up but they too were met with a volley of stones, quickly losing control of the situation as their horses spooked. In desperation, the soldiers opened fire on the crowd, killing at least 24 people and wounding dozens more. "Many a wife sat watching at home, in terror and alarm for her absent husband. It was an evening of dread—and it became a night of horror, which on the morrow, when the awful tragedy became more widely known, settled down upon the city like a funeral pall."[85]

The long-term impact of these Astor Place Riots was that the neighborhood began to steadily decline. Residents moved uptown, seeking newer, quieter districts untarnished by Shakespearean violence. One by one, mansions and townhouses were sold, demolished, and replaced by large-scale factories, warehouses, and department stores: exactly the fate their original tenants had sought to avoid. The Opera House, so briefly the pride of New York, shuttered in 1852. The building was repurposed as the home of the city's Mercantile Library. It was finally demolished in 1891 when the current structure was built on the site (Nos. 13-25 Astor Place, it housed a Starbucks in its base from 1994-2024). In 1854, a new opera house and event space called The Academy of Music opened its doors on 14th Street just east of Union Square at the corner of Irving Place. The Academy would remain the cultural heart of Gilded Age New York until it was usurped by the Metropolitan Opera House, which opened on Broadway at 39th Street in 1883.

COOPER UNION

Even as the Astor Place Riots were unfolding in 1849, several other notable landmarks were in the planning or early construction stages in the immediate vicinity. Among these was the Cooper Union for the Advancement of Science and Art (page 81), which rises like the prow of a great brownstone ship from the east side of Astor Place. The Cooper Union was established by lifelong inventor and philanthropist Peter Cooper who wished for New York to have a creative and scientific academy akin to Paris's *École Polytechnique*. Today, it remains "dedicated to Peter Cooper's radical commitment to diversity and his founding vision that fair access to an inspiring free education and forums for courageous public discourse foster a just and thriving world."[86] In that spirit, the school made a tradition out of inviting speakers of all stripes and beliefs to address the public from its Great Hall. Famously, in February of 1860, it hosted a lesser-known Illinois politician named Abraham Lincoln, who gave a rousing speech about the importance of preserving the Union.

For most in attendance that evening, it was their first time seeing or hearing this peculiar man, and newspapers attempted to describe his appearance, which is now so well known as to be a caricature. Calling him "another Republican on the stump," the *New York Herald* printed the following on February 28, 1860: "Mr. Lincoln is a tall, thin man, dark complexioned, and apparently quick in his perceptions. He is rather unsteady in his gait, and there is an involuntary comical awkwardness which marks his movements while speaking. His voice, though sharp and powerful at times, has a frequent tendency to dwindle into a shrill and unpleasant sound. His enunciation is slow and emphatic, and a peculiar characteristic of his delivery was a remarkable mobility of his features, the frequent contortions of which excited the merriment which his words alone could not well have produced."[87]

Life was never the same for Abraham Lincoln. Thanks in part to the notoriety brought by his Cooper Union Speech, he secured his party's nomination and was elected to the presidency that November. The Civil War began shortly thereafter. Following his assassination in 1865, Lincoln's funeral procession crisscrossed the nation, and when it came through New York, his body was carried up Broadway from City Hall to Union Square, passing just steps away from Astor Place and the Cooper Union where it all began five years before.

From **Astor Place**, walk south along **Lafayette Street** to the building now housing the **Public Theater**.

ASTOR LIBRARY

Around the corner from the Cooper Union, on Lafayette Street, stands another 1850s landmark: the former Astor Library. When John Jacob Astor died in 1848, his last will and testament was printed in newspapers across the nation, "a spectacular invasion of the private affairs of an ordinary citizen."[88] The document, begun in 1836 and amended with codicils numerous times over the last years of his life, divided his cash, stock, and extensive real estate holdings among his children, grandchildren, and various charitable organizations. One such codicil, signed December 22, 1839, left explicit instructions for one piece of his legacy: "Desiring to render a public benefit to the City of New York and to contribute to the advancement of useful knowledge and the general good of society I do by this Codicil appropriate four hundred thousand dollars out of my residuary estate to the establishment of a Public Library in the City of New York."[89]

Astor's Library was incorporated by the New York State Legislature in January of 1849, at a time when libraries were not generally open and accessible to the city's masses. After spending several years in temporary space at 32 Bond Street, the Astor Library opened in 1854 on the east side of Lafayette, just south of Astor Place. "A better location could hardly have been selected," gushed *The Tribune*, "for though it is between Broadway and the Bowery, it seems to be almost entirely exempt from the clamor of the city."[90] The Astor Library was expanded twice, with north wings added in 1859 and 1881 (a slight difference in the color of the building's bricks serves as evidence of these expansions even today).

By the 1880s, the library was wanting for funds, and citizens were beginning to clamor for a truly public lending-library system. The trustees of the Astor Library and the similarly privately funded Lenox Library agreed to merge. (The Lenox was formerly located on 5th Avenue at 70th Street. It was later demolished and replaced by the Frick Collection (page 217) in 1912.) Bolstered by a substantial bequest from Samuel J Tilden, the wealthy and book-loving former governor of New York who died in 1886, the New York Public Library (page 173) was officially created in 1895. When the new main branch of the NYPL opened in Bryant Park in 1911, the old Astor Library closed. After serving as home to a Jewish charity for half a century, the building reopened as The Public Theater in 1967.

From **Astor Place**, follow the **Bowery** (here called 4th Avenue) north to **10th Street**. Turn left and follow **10th Street** to **Broadway**, then turn right

Stop 4 → On **Broadway** in front of **Grace Church**

GRACE CHURCH

When it opened in 1846, Grace Church was one of the tallest structures in New York. At 230 feet (70 meters), its soaring spire (originally wood, rebuilt with marble in 1883) would have been visible from miles away, including from the congregation's original location down on lower Broadway at Rector Street. This was an important nostalgic touch for Grace Church, and this particular location was carefully selected due to the bend here in Broadway, which otherwise runs in a straight line up from the Battery. Standing on the front steps of Grace Church even now, with the city's densely built skyline all around, one can see the sun shining on the harbor more than two miles south.

The story of what makes this vista possible is a partially apocryphal tale of land ownership and city planning, difficult to prove but easy to believe. It is a fact that the land now occupied by Grace Church was once the property of the Brevoort family. Their 86-acre (35-hectare) estate stretched diagonally from the Bowery westward to the now-buried Minetta Brook (roughly today's 5th Avenue between 9th and 10th Streets).

In 1815, in anticipation of the city's northward growth, it was announced that Broadway would be cut through as far as 23rd Street. (The notion that Broadway was an ancient Native American highway is only partly true: though the portions south of City Hall Park and north of 169th Street follow the original Lenape route, the rest of Broadway is a series of other roads cut through and cobbled together during the 18th and 19th centuries.)

If Broadway continued its northward path in a straight line to 23rd Street, it would cut through the Brevoort family farm to intersect with the pre-existing Bowery around 12th Street. It is believed that city leaders altered its course out of respect for Henry Brevoort, Sr, who then still lived in the family homestead on the Bowery Road, directly in Broadway's proposed path. And so Broadway was bent at 10th Street, finally intersecting the Bowery several blocks north in a tangle of major roads known as Union Place. This would be organized and formalized as Union Square in the 1820s.

As for this land, the family held onto it until Mr Brevoort's death in 1841, after which when it was finally sold to Grace Church for $40,000. The new building was designed by James Renwick, Jr, a member of the Brevoort family through his mother Margaret. Trained as an engineer, Renwick had up to that point designed little more significant than a fountain and a portion of the old Croton Distributing Reservoir. But the young man (not yet 25 when he received the Grace Church commission) had an eye for beauty and an appreciation for architectural history. The completion of this new church in 1846 not only helped launch the Gothic Revival movement in the United States, but it launched Renwick's remarkable career in architecture. Less than a decade later, he won the design competition for St Patrick's Cathedral on 5th Avenue (page 180).

In addition to getting Broadway to bend at 10th Street, the Brevoort family also successfully fought against the city's attempts to cut 11th Street through their property between Broadway and the Bowery. The opening of this single block had been delayed "out of respect to Mr Brevoort who then resided in the old Homestead that stood directly in the street"[91] and was never laid out. To this day, 11th Street is split in half to the east and west of Grace Church, allowing room for a gracious Gothic Revival rectory and ample gardens where there would otherwise be traffic and asphalt.

Walk north from **Grace Church** and cross 14th Street to enter **Union Square**

Stop 5 → At **Union Square**

UNION SQUARE

Union Square did not get its name from its long history as the preferred site for labor union rallies, marches, and organization. Nor did it get its name from the Union Army of the American Civil War, despite being the site of one of the nation's first memorial statues of Abraham Lincoln. No, Union Square's name is far simpler and more prosaic: it describes the fact that this has been, for at least three centuries, where all of the island's most important north–south thoroughfares came together. It is a literal union of traffic flow, a glorified intersection.

The oldest road running through Union Square is the Bowery, though here it's been rebranded as 4th Avenue. The Bowery was originally the Wickquasgeck Trail, the oldest and most important of the highways laid out by Manhattan's Native residents long before European contact, following high ground from the southern tip of the island up to Spuyten Duyvil, the marshy inlet which separates Manhattan from the mainland. Most of that ancient route was later erased in favor of the 1811 grid plan, but from Madison Square down to Battery Park, it still follows roughly the same path.

In 1707, the Bowery Road was joined by the Bloomingdale Road, which forked off to the west near where the Flatiron Building stands today on 23rd Street. It got its name not from the famous department store, but rather from the collection of villages dotting the hills and valleys along the west side of Manhattan. Originally called *Bloemendahl* by the Dutch, which means "flowering valley," its name was anglicized as Bloomingdale around the same time *Nieuw Amsterdam* became New York. The Bloomingdale Road served to connect what is now the Upper West Side to the city and harbor miles to the south. It would later be straightened, widened, and renamed Broadway by the end of the 19th century.

Splitting off from the Bowery and Bloomingdale Roads were a number of other old roads and paths, many of which have been forgotten to time, but suffice it to say that the area between modern-day 10th and 26th Streets has been a teeming web of traffic and commerce for centuries. By the time the city's population began to grow up and around Union Square, those New Yorkers who could afford to do so were increasingly choosing to live in neighborhoods close enough to major thoroughfares that they could still easily venture there to shop and socialize, but far enough away that they didn't have to endure the associated noise and smells and kicked-up dust. Hence the rise of districts like Washington Square and Lafayette Place: both sit comfortably close-but-not-too-close to Broadway.

This sort of neighborhood development reached its apogee at Union Square thanks in large part to a wealthy lawyer and landowner named Samuel Ruggles, who'd also been one of the masterminds behind the transformation of Union Place into Union Square.

From **Union Square**, follow **4th Avenue** (the east side of Union Square) north to **17th Street** and turn right. Pause near **Irving Place.** Turn left and head north along **Irving Place**, named for the writer Washington Irving

Stop 6 → At **20th Street** next to the high iron fence of **Gramercy Park**

GRAMERCY PARK

As you arrive on Irving Place, marvel at how quiet it becomes. Just one block from Union Square, it's an entirely different world. This is no mistake; it is evidence of Ruggles' success some 200 years ago. Just east and north of Union Square, Ruggles created an entirely new neighborhood known as Gramercy Park, modeled in part on older garden districts downtown and in London, which survives today as one of the most fascinating and intact pieces of 19th-century urban planning ingenuity in the nation.

Samuel Ruggles was born in Connecticut in 1800 but moved to New York in 1822 determined to make his way in the world's most exciting and rapidly changing urban center. He watched as the city's population grew and pushed inexorably northward, filling Manhattan block after block with densely built rows of houses, stables, shops, hotels, and whatever else could turn a quick profit. In 1831, Ruggles purchased the swampy 22-acre (9-hectare) tract of land known as Gramercy from the Duane family and set out to transform it into something truly great.

To appreciate Gramercy as a piece of Manhattan's rich tapestry, it is important to understand just what Gramercy is. The name comes from the Dutch *Krom Moerasje*, which itself is thought to be a crude interpretation of a far older Lenape name for the swampy stream that ran through the area. As purchased by Ruggles in 1831, it was a broad swath of land, curving out to the east from the main road (modern Broadway) to a point near where 21st Street meets 2nd Avenue today.

On this land, Ruggles hoped to create a neighborhood which would be more than just another short-lived mansion district, the likes of which had multiplied across the city in recent years. Lovely and ephemeral, they were inevitably crushed beneath the wheels of progress as soon as denser commercial or industrial development became more lucrative for its residents. Ruggles envisioned Gramercy as enduring beyond the short term, achieving through careful planning and prescience an unprecedented sort of staying power. His success in this remains unmatched in all of Manhattan's history.

To transform Gramercy, Ruggles oversaw the draining and flattening of the land, welcomed the grading of new streets through it, and began carving it up into valuable building lots. Most importantly, he plotted out a 2-acre (0.8-hectare) park at the heart of Gramercy, a verdant respite from city life which would anchor and enrich the neighborhood. In many ways, Gramercy echoed the charming aesthetics of Chelsea, which was being developed by Clement Clarke Moore on his family's west side estate around the same time (page 117).

There were, in fact, numerous well-to-do neighborhoods scattered all around Manhattan at the time of Gramercy's inception, often of similar scope and aesthetic to what Ruggles hoped to achieve. Chelsea, Washington Square, Stuyvesant Square, Tompkins Square, St John's Square, Greenwich Village: each was lovely, expensive, exclusive, but, as Ruggles saw it, also inherently flawed. These other neighborhoods lacked a sense of centralized cohesion and control, dooming them to eventual failure.

Houses surrounding Gramercy Park

For example, Washington Square is a city-owned public space, and the homeowners living around it have never been bound by any sense of neighborly responsibility for the fate of the district writ large. Looking at it, Ruggles recognized that its makeup meant fragility should the winds of socio-economic change ever blow through the area. (Ruggles was proven to be prescient in this, as Washington Square did indeed devolve into a hodgepodge collection of boarding houses, apartment buildings, and factories by the end of the 19th century.)

Similarly, the now-lost neighborhood of St John's Square (page 44) was a fine and attractive place to live in the 1830s when Ruggles was designing Gramercy. Situated near the Hudson River waterfront south of Canal Street, on the western edge of modern TriBeCa, St John's Square was laid out by Trinity Church on land they had been granted by Queen Anne as part of the "Church Farm" more than a century prior. The neighborhood was laid out and developed by the church as an investment property; Trinity retained ownership of the land beneath its houses as well as the lovely fenced-in park which anchored it. Ruggles recognized that, because of this, the church could quite literally pull the rug out from beneath the area's homeowners at any moment. (Again, he was proven to be prescient, as in the 1860s, the park itself was sold to Cornelius Vanderbilt, who ripped it out and built a freight train terminal on the site, effectively killing St John's Square as a desirable neighborhood. Today, the square of land which was once such a lovely park is the exit roundabout for the Holland Tunnel.)

With this impressive foresight, Samuel Ruggles laid out his new neighborhood. It would be anchored by a park, yes, but rather than have it be publicly owned like Washington Square or institutionally owned like St John's Square, Gramercy would instead function as a sort of neighborhood collective. Each of the 60 lots overlooking Gramercy Park would include a share of ownership in the park itself. Owners would therefore be financially responsible for the upkeep of the park but would also therefore be the only people to have access to the park.

This sort of neighborly cohesion would ultimately foster an incomparable sense of desirability and exclusivity in Gramercy which has allowed it to remain a high-end mansion district for nearly two centuries. Today, Gramercy remains a private park, the only such greenspace in all of Manhattan. Residents who live within those original 60 lots around the park receive (or at least have access to) keys which open the heavy iron gates on its four sides. Other New Yorkers may walk by and peer through the fence but cannot enter. To find a way into Gramercy Park is a bucket-list item for many New Yorkers, a badge akin to eating at Rao's or visiting the City Hall Subway Station.

Thanks to the early planning of Samuel Ruggles, Gramercy is one of the most special and unusual places in New York. And thanks to his designs for the neighborhood, by the time New York's Gilded Age was in full swing in the 1880s and 90s, Gramercy was still one of the choicest residential districts in the city despite being so far downtown and despite being relatively old by the city's late-19th-century standards. Gramercy welcomed its first residents in the early 1840s, but within a decade, wealthy families had begun pushing northward into Murray Hill as far as 40th Street, fully a mile north of Gramercy. And in the 1880s, spurred on by the newly ascendant Vanderbilt family, the city's *nouveaux riches* were living as far north as Central Park at 59th Street. By all metrics, Gramercy should have been too old, too old-fashioned, and definitely too far downtown to still be fashionable during the Gilded Age. But thanks to Ruggles and his co-operatively owned park, this proved not to be the case.

MRS FISH

Proof of Gramercy's staying power is the impressive roster of luminaries and socialites who called the neighborhood home during the Gilded Age's peak years. A prime example of this is Marion Graves Anthon Fish, an undisputed leader of New York Society, who lived at the southeast corner of Irving Place and Gramercy Park South from 1887–1900. Mrs Fish was a force to be reckoned with in Gilded Age New York. She was second to none as leader of Society, Mrs Astor included, for Mrs Fish had "more ancient claims to distinction"[92] than even she. Despite her noble pedigree, Mrs Fish was most notorious for her fearsome personality and extravagant entertainments. Unlike Mrs Astor, who shied from the press her whole life, Mrs Fish relished the quotes and tales attributed to her in the nation's newspapers.

Mrs Fish was 23 years Mrs Astor's junior and saw fit to lead the younger generation of society's *bons vivants*. Born Marion Graves Anthon on Staten Island in 1853, she married Stuyvesant Fish, descendant of Peter Stuyvesant and president of the Illinois Central Railroad, in 1876. She strove to outshine her peers, quite literally, by wearing a diamond tiara to public events, reminding them all of her unimpeachable lineage. She and her sidekick, "America's court jester"[93] Harry Lehr, threw entertainments the likes of which Society had never seen. "She is the genius of society whose special fate and forte is to drive away its blues,"[94] declared *The St Louis Republic* in 1902. The Fish family only left Gramercy Park in 1900 to take up residency in a new Standford White-designed mansion on East 78th Street (page 226).

THE PLAYERS

Just a few doors west of the Fish house stands a massive and beautiful brownstone mansion which is now the private clubhouse of The Players, a theatrical social club formed by the renowned tragedian Edwin Booth in 1888. Booth's name likely sounds familiar to modern ears due to the fact that it was his younger brother, John Wilkes Booth, who assassinated President Abraham Lincoln in 1865. However much Edwin loved his brother, he was a staunch supporter of Lincoln and the Northern cause. He had nothing to do with the assassination and in fact went on to have a lucrative and much-celebrated career for many years thereafter.

Despite his success, Booth's life was defined by tragedy. He spent much of his youth looking after his father, the acclaimed Shakespearean actor Junius Brutus Booth, who was reckless with alcoholism. Edwin himself would later struggle with the same affliction. Junius Booth died in 1852 while on a voyage without Edwin, leaving the then-teenaged boy crushed with by notion that he might have been able to save his father had he been with him.

In adulthood, Edwin Booth was married twice, but both wives died. He was first married to the actress Mary Devlin Booth in 1860, and the happy young couple had a child named Edwina in 1861. But in 1863, while Edwin was away in New York for an acting run, Mary fell severely ill at their home in Dorchester, Massachusetts. Despite being summoned multiple times, Edwin was in a drunken stupor and missed the last train to Boston. By the time he got to his wife's side, she was dead. She was just 22 years old.

Grief-stricken, Booth continued acting, though he lamented that Mary's death had stripped it of all meaning. "Her applause was all I valued – gaining it I felt there was something noble in my calling; her criticism was the most severe and just – feeling this I felt also there was something higher to be attained; but now I can only regard my profession as the means of providing for the poor little babe she has left with me – the beauty of my art is gone – it is hateful to me – it has become a trade."[95]

In March of 1865, Edwin Booth rescued a young man who'd fallen on the train tracks at Jersey City, New Jersey. In a somewhat macabre coincidence, this turned out to be Robert Todd Lincoln, eldest son of President Abraham Lincoln. Neither man could have known that on April 15, less than a month after Booth saved young Lincoln, the President would be killed by Booth's own brother. The American Civil War officially ended on May 26, kicking off an era of excess and inequality that would come to be known as the Gilded Age.

With the war ended, Booth's life appeared to get back on track to some semblance of happiness. In February of 1869, he opened the lavish Booth's Theatre, on 23rd Street at the southeast corner of 6th Avenue, with a performance of Romeo and Juliet starring himself opposite the actress Mary McVicker. Off-stage, the pair were married that June. But following the death of their infant son the following year, Mary's mental health declined rapidly. "The mental disturbance, which became sadly obvious in her last days, early made itself manifest to her husband, who watched and tended her with patient devotion throughout the vicissitudes of painful sorrow and decay."[96] During her years of illness, Booth was forced into bankruptcy in 1874, losing the theater which bore his name. As for Mary, she died in 1881, aged 33. The 1885 marriage of his only daughter, Edwina, meant that Edwin found himself unhappily alone.

Late in life, in the gloomy aftermath of so much loss and trial, Booth founded a social club called The Players, the purpose of which was to help elevate the social and educational status of those working in the theatrical arts and industries ("players"). Up to that time, actors were generally looked down upon as lowly, crass, and uneducated. Booth hoped "to establish an institution in which influences of learning and taste should be brought to bear upon the members of the stage – a place where they might find books and pictures, precious relics of the great players of the past, intellectual communion with minds of their own order, and with men of education in other walks of life, refinement of thought and of manners, innocent pleasure, and sweet, gracious, ennobling associations."[97]

The club was incorporated on January 7, 1888, by Booth and other interested members including Samuel Clemens (Mark Twain). That December, The Players officially opened at No. 16 Gramercy Park in the gracious brownstone-front mansion which remains the club's home to this day. The mansion, originally built in 1847 as part of Gramercy Park's initial wave of development, was extensively renovated by the architect Stanford White, who also happened to live in a rented home (since demolished) just across the park on 21st Street at the corner of Lexington Avenue.

When Edwin Booth died in 1893, he left the mansion to the club he'd founded. His bedroom on the third floor is preserved exactly as he left it, complete with his slippers on the floor next to his bed. A painting of his likeness, executed by John Singer Sargent in 1890, hangs in the parlor (it is now a reproduction, as the original was sold to the Amon Carter Museum of Fort Worth, Texas, in 2013), and there is a statue depicting Booth as Hamlet standing in the center of Gramercy Park. That statue, the work of fellow Players member Edmond T Quinn, was unveiled in 1918. More than a century later, Booth's legacy lingers over Gramercy and indeed over the whole of the theatrical world.

THE NATIONAL ARTS CLUB

Just next door to The Players stands easily one of the most impressive mansions in all of Manhattan. Home to The National Arts Club since 1906, it was originally built in the 1840s as two side-by-side townhouses, Nos. 14 and 15 Gramercy Park. In 1863, the eastern home (No. 15) was purchased by the wealthy politician Samuel J Tilden. Tilden was elected Governor of New York State in 1874, and that same year he purchased the neighboring house at No. 14 Gramercy Park, intending to combine the two into one massive house for himself. For though he was a lifelong bachelor, Tilden was a prolific entertainer and collector of books who felt that his home was increasingly too small for his needs.

Before Tilden could combine his two houses, however, he was chosen as the Democratic nominee for the presidency in 1876. It was a raucous, violent, and corrupt election year in a nation still licking its wounds from the devastating Civil War. Ulysses S Grant shocked the nation by announcing he would not seek a third term as President, and both major political parties sought to bend the nation's fate to their will.

It is important to note that the political alignment of the United States in the mid-19th century was roughly flipped from what it is today. The Democratic party was largely the party of agrarianism and individual liberty and was therefore more closely aligned with the American South and the former Confederacy. The Republican party, the party of abolition and of Abraham Lincoln, was more closely aligned with the far more industrialized American North. Despite this, New York City remained an outlier. So much of the city's economy relied on its ability to trade freely with the South that it tended to vote far more for the Democratic party than the rest of the North. Understanding this alignment helps to explain the selection in 1876 of Samuel J Tilden, the Democratic governor of New York, to run against Rutherford B Hayes, the Republican Governor of Ohio.

Election day in 1876 was rife with violence and corruption. There were widespread accusations of voter intimidation and fraud hurled from both sides of the political aisle. In the end, Tilden won the popular vote (4,286,808 to Hayes's 4,034,142) but Electoral College

The Row, Washington Square

Public Theater, former Astor Library

Grace Church

Union Square

Washington Mews

Gramercy Park

votes for four states, South Carolina, Florida, Louisiana, and Oregon, could not be decided. For those unfamiliar with the Electoral College: in the US Presidential Election, the popular vote is tallied individually in each of the 50 states and various territories. Each possesses a number of electoral votes relative to its population. These votes are awarded to the candidate who wins each state's popular vote, most in a winner-take-all fashion. It is these Electoral Votes which actually decide the winner of the Presidency, a quirk of the nation's 18th-century formation.

Corruption of the 1876 election left 20 Electoral Votes unallocated (seven from South Carolina, four from Florida, eight from Louisiana, and one from Oregon), meaning neither Tilden nor Hayes could legally claim the presidency.

Ultimately, the matter was settled by the so-called "Compromise of 1877" which historians continue to debate. The Compromise allegedly awarded the presidency to Hayes in exchange for Republicans' removal of Federal troops from formerly Confederate states in the South. This ended the period known as Reconstruction, allowing the South to regain legalistic sovereignty, and ushering in a century of increasingly segregationist legal structures which are collectively known to history as the "Jim Crow" era. (Jim Crow was a minstrel character introduced to American audiences in 1832 by blackface comedian Thomas Dartmouth Rice. The name became shorthand for Black Americans and, in time, for the laws which defined their subjugation.)

Defeated, and his reputation in tatters over his machinations to take the presidency, Tilden returned to his home at No. 15 Gramercy Park. In 1878, he turned his attention back to domesticity, hiring the architect Calvert Vaux to finally combine his two houses into one. Vaux is far and away best known for his role in designing the architectural elements of Central Park in partnership with landscape architect Frederick Law Olmsted. But his deft hand worked wonders on Tilden's new double-mansion, executed in what an 1884 edition of *Artistic Houses* described as "a free adaptation of the Gothic style of architecture."[98] Bands of dark granite and marble columns break up the monotony of its brownstone facade, with florid punctuations of naturalistic plant motifs.

The most joyful of the Tilden mansion's many eccentricities are the six busts which adorn its parlor-level facade. Carved from Belleville (New Jersey) brownstone, five found between the house's bay windows depict great writers from history: William Shakespeare, John Milton, Benjamin Franklin, Johann Wolfgang von Goethe, and Dante Alighieri. Lest any passersby doubt Tilden's appreciation of arts and letters, a sixth bust, generously bearded, hangs over the house's western entrance: Michelangelo.

When Samuel J Tilden died in 1886, he left much of his estate (an estimated $2,400,000) to the creation of the Tilden Trust, the purpose of which was to establish and maintain "a free library and reading room in the City of New York."[99] His gift would eventually be combined with the collections of the Astor and Lenox Libraries to create the New York Public Library in 1895. A panel above the entrance to the main Library building on 5th Avenue at 42nd Street reads: "The Tilden Trust Founded By Samuel Jones Tilden to Serve the Interests of Science and Popular Education."

As for Tilden's home on Gramercy Park, it was rented out as a boarding house for nearly two decades before it was purchased by the National Arts Club for use as their new clubhouse. They've remained there ever since, preserving for posterity a splendid mansion as well as its many fascinating ties to local and national history.

Mamie Fish, Edwin Booth, and Samuel Tilden were three tremendous social, cultural, and political leaders of New York with three wildly different stories but one unifying trait: each was prominent enough, wealthy enough, and well-connected enough to live quite literally anywhere they chose. And all three chose to live on Gramercy Park at the apex of the city's Gilded Age when most wealthy New Yorkers lived more than a mile away uptown on Murray Hill or Vanderbilt Row. And this in an era when Gramercy's housing stock was already several decades older than most of the city's mansion districts. Gramercy's ascendance and endurance as a wealthy enclave is testament to the success of Samuel Ruggles' plans for the neighborhood two centuries ago.

BROWNSTONE

On the west side of Gramercy Park stands one of the most intact rows of 1840s townhouses in the whole neighborhood. These five homes are rather typical for their era: nondescript brick facades, raised stoops, and bracketed pressed-metal cornices. Their most unique feature is the elaborate cast-iron balconies stretched across the parlor levels of three of them. But perhaps even more incredible is the fact that these homes boast a brown, sandy material on their stoops, basements, and windows. These are among the very first New York City houses to feature brownstone. Brownstone: the darling of NYC real estate. Its chocolatey hue defines vast swaths of the city from Harlem to Brooklyn and beyond. But what is it exactly? Scientifically speaking, brownstone "is a conglomerate of particles of sand cemented together by a ferruginous (rust-colored) and argillaceous (clay-filled) cement." So it is a sandstone, "exceedingly porous,"[100] which was used extensively in construction all across the city during the latter half of the 19th century. Nearly all of New York's brownstone originated in quarries near Middletown CT, where an immense outcropping of the stuff was first noted by English settlers in 1665. It was used extensively in the region for more than a century before its popularity spread to New York.

The first use of brownstone on a NYC house occurred in 1840, when Connecticut native Newton Perkins had it added to his new double-wide mansion at 11 West 9th Street, which still stands today. "The house when it was built was so far uptown as to be on a country road,"[101] explained Perkins' daughter Elizabeth in 1926. But the Perkins house wasn't alone for long. As Gramercy Park began developing half a mile uptown from the Perkins home, brownstone quickly became a favorite design element in virtually all its houses, schools, clubs, and churches.

By the 1860s, as the city continued to grow and sprawl, brownstone became ubiquitous. Homeowners employed it as an economical alternative to harder, pricier marble, granite, or limestone. Speculative developers slathered it onto the facades of thousands of townhouses, making them look far more expensive than they would with a simple brick facade. But by the 1880s, the stone's reputation was faltering. Called "too dark and gloomy,"[102] it was also found to weather badly, cracking and flaking after just a few years. Porous as it was, it absorbed water which froze and expanded in winter, splitting the stone to pieces.

New York's "brownstone age" was said to be "coming to a close"[103] in 1926, as hundreds of the aging houses were cleared away to build apartment towers and newer homes in brick or limestone. Countless others had their brownstone fronts shorn off, the homes modernized beyond recognition. But a funny thing happened in the years after World War II: New Yorkers rediscovered the charms of brownstone homes. Particularly in Brooklyn, their architectural details, convenient locations, and affordable prices made them attractive starter homes for young families who rejected the lure of suburbia. Thousands were renovated or restored, often at great expense, by shaving off their broken facades and replacing them with a brown concrete mixture which mimics brownstone without the risk of breaking apart. Today, these fake-brownstone beauties fetch millions.

THE MAYOR'S LAMPS

Before leaving Gramercy, take note of the lamps in front of the house at No. 4 here on the park's west side. The tradition of Mayor's Lamps is thought to have begun in the earliest days of New Amsterdam when the *Burgomaster*, or Dutch Mayor, would be escorted home by the light of two lanterns. Upon reaching his home, the lanterns would be hung outside to alert the townsfolk within. Well into the 20th century, every Mayor of New York was granted the privilege of having two lamps erected outside his home. The only two noted exceptions were Robert Van Wyck (Mayor 1898–1901), who refused the offer, and John Purroy Mitchel (Mayor 1914–17), who lived in an apartment during his time in office.

The last Mayor to receive the lamps, so far as research can tell, was Jimmy Walker (Mayor 1926–32), who lived on St Luke's Place in Greenwich Village. His successor, John O'Brien (Mayor 1933), did not receive them, nor did Fiorello LaGuardia (Mayor 1934–46). Thereafter, Mayors lived at Gracie Mansion on the Upper East Side, which does not have the traditional lamps. Most former Mayors' homes have long since been demolished; many of those that remain had their lamps removed. Only two are known to still exist: the aforementioned West Village townhouse of Jimmy Walker, and this splendid townhouse at No. 4 Gramercy Park, home to James Harper (Mayor 1844–45) after his time in office. He apparently took his lamps with him when he moved from No. 50 Rose Street to this new home in 1847. This quirky tradition, a legacy of the city's Dutch origins, has been all but forgotten, lost to history like so much else.

CALVARY EPISCOPAL CHURCH

Around the corner from Gramercy Park, on Park Avenue at 21st Street, stands Calvary Episcopal Church. Designed by James Renwick, Jr, and completed in 1848, the church's exterior is composed of solid brownstone blocks which remain largely unrestored. Here, passersby have the opportunity to see and (gently) touch

LaGrange Terrace

Madison Square

Flatiron Building

Appellate Division Courthouse of New York State

Empire State Building

actual Connecticut brownstone. Cracked and flaking, it is a rare surviving example of the ephemerality of this material which has for so long been so closely associated with the New York City streetscape.

From **Calvary Church**, walk north along **Park Avenue** for one block. Turn left onto **22nd Street** and continue on to **Broadway**, where you will encounter the Flatiron Building. Turn right, cross **23rd Street**, and

Stop 7 → Inside **Madison Square**

MADISON SQUARE

Madison Square is a 6¼-acre (2.5-hectare) park situated between 23rd and 26th Streets where 5th Avenue meets Broadway. It first opened as a public park in 1847, when it and the adjoining Madison Avenue were both named in honor of President James Madison (1751–1836). Similar to Union Square, Madison Square sits at the junction of numerous heavily trafficked thoroughfares, making it from its inception a busy, bustling nexus of urban life. As the city continued to grow, grand buildings rose all around its perimeter, transforming Madison Square into the next, greatest wealthy residential enclave at the edge of town.

But as New Yorkers moved north of 23rd Street in the 1850s and 1860s, they found themselves unexpectedly hemmed in on both sides by unappealing urban developments. On the west side, Broadway had been given over almost entirely to the city's entertainment industries. Hotels, restaurants, dry-goods emporia, and theaters brought raucous crowds both day and night. Beyond that lay a thriving red-light district, its workers attracted by the many high-end hotels and the deep-pocketed guests they guaranteed. In time, much of the west side of Manhattan devolved into one of the world's most notorious vice districts, nicknamed the Tenderloin in the 1870s, as police officers stationed there learned how wealthy they could become from the many kickbacks and bribes they received (tenderloin being among the choicest cuts of beef).

The situation was similarly dour on the east side, where the city's first steam-powered train line ran directly down the center of 4th Avenue. Belching soot and smoke, the New York and Harlem Railroad began operating in the 1830s, connecting Manhattan to the mainland for the first time, but also making 4th Avenue a decidedly unpleasant place to live. Like the Tenderloin to the west, everything east of the train tracks devolved over time, becoming a dense and expansive district of tenements, factories, and hospitals all the way to the East River.

In short, by the start of the Gilded Age, everything from Broadway to the Hudson and from 4th Avenue to the East River was a no-go zone for the city's elite residents. In effect, this funneled New York's mansion districts into one narrow strip of land between Madison and 5th Avenue as they pushed ever farther uptown into first Murray Hill, then north of 42nd Street, and ultimately onto the Upper East Side.

Back down on Madison Square, growth was fueled in large part by the New York & Harlem Railroad, which had its main depot spread across a full city block at the northeast corner of 26th Street and Madison

Avenue. This depot opened in 1845 and made Madison Square the primary point of disembarkation for countless travelers from all points north. Though the city passed a law in 1858 forbidding smoke-producing trains from passing south of 42nd Street, it wasn't until 1871 that Madison Square's depot became obsolete, superseded by Cornelius Vanderbilt's new uptown Grand Central Depot.

Removed from rail service, Madison Square Depot was repurposed as an entertainment venue. In 1873, it was leased to PT Barnum, who transformed the space into a facsimile of the Roman Hippodrome. It was there that he hosted what is thought to be the world's first three-ring circus. In 1879, the venue was renamed Madison Square Garden, hosting all manner of entertainments both high-brow and low. But by the mid-1880s, the Garden's profitability was faltering. It was demolished in 1885 and its land was sold off by the Vanderbilt family to a syndicate which sought to reimagine it as something far grander.

The new Madison Square Garden was designed by the architect Stanford White and opened to the public with a performance of Edward Strauss's orchestra on June 16, 1890. "A new and uncommon place of amusement," reported *The New York Times*, Madison Square Garden boasted restaurants, theaters, concert halls, and an enormous elliptical arena for horse races and circuses. It was "a wildly eclectic pleasure palace at an unprecedented scale"[104], all executed in a soaring Moorish revival style by White, who capped his design with a tower more than 300 feet (90 meters) tall modeled on La Giralda, an ancient minaret-turned-bell-tower in Seville, Spain. Atop the tower, the highest point for miles in any direction, stood a gilded statue of the goddess Diana as sculpted by Augustus Saint-Gaudens. Her lithe, nude figure was floodlit at night, adding an element of golden titillation to the entire city.

The greatest drama to play out on Madison Square occurred in 1906 when Stanford White, architect of Madison Square Garden, was gunned down at its rooftop theater by Harry Kendall Thaw, wealthy husband to one of White's many former teenaged paramours, the model and actress Evelyn Nesbit. Born on Christmas Day in 1884, Evelyn made her Broadway debut in 1901 as a "Florodora Girl" at the Casino Theater. There, she met 47-year-old architect Stanford White, a notorious womanizer who used his wealth and status to woo young Evelyn with lavish gifts. The pair made frequent visits to his apartment on West 24th Street, which was festooned with velvet and had mirrored walls and ceilings.

Evelyn was the focus of White's affections for about two years, when in 1903 she caught the eye of Harry Kendall Thaw, heir to a Pittsburgh coal and railroad fortune. Thaw saw Evelyn perform in the Broadway show *The Wild Rose* 40 times, obsessing over her. Stanford White warned Evelyn against him (he was prone to violence and emotional volatility, and it is thought that the term "playboy" was coined to describe Thaw). Despite this, Evelyn saw Harry as perhaps her last, best chance at an advantageous union. They were married on April 4, 1905. Evelyn wore black.

Thaw obsessed over Stanford White. Beyond his abuses of Evelyn, Thaw blamed White for his inability to enter New York's inner social circles. Things came to a head on the evening of June 25, 1906, when the Thaws attended a show at Madison Square Garden. At 10:55 p.m., White arrived and took his seat near the stage. Thaw marched over to confront him, firing three shots into White's head. His body tumbled to the floor as pandemonium broke out and Thaw was arrested. The ensuing trial was dubbed the Trial of the Century and helped usher in a new era of tabloid journalism. Thaw was found not guilty by reason of insanity and spent much of the next four decades moving in and out of maximum-security facilities in New York and Pennsylvania.

As for Evelyn, she divorced Thaw in 1915 and moved to California. There, she struggled with addictions, supporting herself as a dancer when she could. In 1955, she sold the rights to her life story, which was turned into a film called *The Girl in the Red Velvet Swing* starring Joan Collins. Evelyn died in a nursing home in California in 1967 at age 82. Her whole life had been defined by the dramas of her youth. Her obituary, she was quoted as lamenting: "Stanny White was killed, but my fate was worse. I lived."[105]

The murder of Stanford White and the ensuing trial did much to erode the decorum which had hitherto defined much of Gilded Age life. Increasingly, wealthy families shied from the spotlight, preferring the privacy of rural estates or highrise apartments over the grand city mansions of previous generations. With the outbreak of World War I, the imposition of new taxes, and the stock market crash of 1929, New York's Gilded Age was at an end barely half a century after it began.

Exit **Madison Square's northwest corner** onto **5th Avenue,** taking note of the large mural of Evelyn Nesbit by artist Tristan Eaton which bedecks the facade of **No. 236 5th Avenue.** Follow **5th Avenue** north to **34th Street**

Stop 8 → On **5th Avenue** between **33rd and 34th Streets**, directly across from the Empire State Building

MURRAY HILL

Little remains of the gracious mansion district Murray Hill once was. On 29th Street, you may visit the Marble Collegiate Church or Church of the Transfiguration (known as the Little Church Around the Corner) to gain some perspective on the now-lost neighborhood's scale and style. Look down side streets for surviving brownstone townhouses, scattered here and there in various states of degradation. This is all that survives of Murray Hill's Gilded Age glory days.

34th Street and 5th Avenue is the heart of historic Murray Hill. In the 1850s, decades before Stanford White's murder, a generation of young heirs and heiresses chose to bypass the crowds of Madison Square on their march uptown, favoring Murray Hill to its north as the site for their newest residential enclave. This stretch of undulating fields and pastures was originally called Inclenberg, the storied estate of the Murray family whose farmhouse once stood on a hill near the modern-day intersection of 37th Street and Park Avenue. The farm was leveled, gridded, and opened for development almost in tandem with Madison Square.

Among the first residents of Murray Hill were two grandsons of John Jacob Astor: John Jacob III and William Backhouse, Jr. Both brothers had grown up wealthy, well-educated, and exposed to all the pedigreed finery of the city's Knickerbocker aristocracy. When it came time to wed, each made advantageous matches, marrying well above their social station and helping to elevate the Astor name to the very pinnacles of New York Society. John married Charlotte Augusta Gibbes in 1846 and William married Caroline Webster Schermerhorn in 1853.

At this time in American Society, the titles of Mr or Mrs had become essentially an honorific bestowed upon the leaders of the nation's great families. By this logic, all other couples were distinguished by the husband's given name. John Jacob was the original Mr Astor; his wife Sarah was the original Mrs Astor. When they died in the 1840s, their titles passed to their son William and his wife Margaret. When they died in the 1870s, their titles passed to their eldest son John Jacob III and his wife Charlotte. This was a thorn in the side of their sister-in-law and neighbor, Caroline Webster Schermerhorn, who coveted the title of "Mrs Astor."

Descended from many of the city's oldest Knickerbocker families, Caroline (or Lina) was a powerful force in New York Society, serving as an arbiter of good taste and comportment. Despite her power and pedigree, though, she had married William, the younger Astor brother, and was therefore relegated to the decidedly less prestigious title of "Mrs William Astor" for much of her adult life, to her chagrin.

The waters muddied when Charlotte died in 1887, followed by her husband in 1890. Caroline, now the eldest Astor woman, seized her opportunity and ordered new calling cards, styling herself "Mrs Astor of New York." This likely wouldn't have caused an issue, as Caroline was already viewed as the most socially prominent woman in the Astor family (and arguably the entire city). But the late John and Charlotte had a son, William Waldorf Astor, who believed the titles, such as they were, should have passed patrilineally down to him and his wife, Mary Dahlgren Paul Astor.

Mary jockeyed for position against Caroline by ordering cards which read "Mrs Astor of Newport," but in the end, she could not overcome Caroline's influence. In protest, she and William moved their family to England. They then ordered the family house on 5th Avenue demolished, replacing it with the 13-story Hotel Waldorf, which opened in 1893 directly next to Caroline's brownstone mansion. The crowds and chaos it brought to the block were too much for Caroline Astor. Within a year, she ordered a new home built uptown at 65th Street. Back on Murray Hill, she had her 34th Street mansion torn down and replaced by the Hotel Astoria, even larger than the neighboring Waldorf. (The two were combined as the Waldorf-Astoria in 1897.)

This marked a major inflection point for Murray Hill, seat of the city's Old-Money smart set for more than a generation. With Mrs Astor gone, few of her neighbors were willing to hold the old neighborhood together. One by one, their mansions and brownstones were sold off and demolished, replaced by ever-larger shops and factory lofts. Within a decade, Murray Hill was transformed into the city's densest commercial district, ending one of the final chapters of the Gilded Age's rise and fall. Murray Hill's decline, commercialization continued its stronghold inexorable uptown.With Murray Hill's decline, commercialization continued its exorable uptown push, bringing businesses within striking distance of the new-money stronghold north of 42nd Street.

0
200
400m
0
1000ft
START
END
Site of 1853 World's Fair
New York Public Library
Site of Latting Observatory
Site of Wendel Mansion
Arnold Constable Store
Lord & Taylor Building
Bonwit Teller Store
Former Tiffany Store
DeLamar Mansion
Gorham Silver Store
Robb Mansion
Lanier Mansion
Hotel Vanderbilt
Murray Hill Tunnel
One Vanderbilt
MetLife Tower
Helmsley Building/ New York Central
Grand Central-42 St
Chrysler Building
LIRR
METRO-NORTH
New JP Morgan Tower
St Bartholomew's Church
Waldorf-Astoria Hotel
Villard Mansions
Saks Fifth Avenue
St Patrick's Cathedral
Rockefeller Center
Site of Vanderbilt Triple Palace
Plant Mansion
Site of Vanderbilt Petit Chateau
Site of Twombly-Webb Mansions
St Thomas Church
University Club
Gotham (Peninsula) Hotel
St Regis Hotel
Fifth Avenue Presbyterian Church
5 Av/53 St
57 St
7 Av
50 St
49 St
47-50 St's Rockefeller Ctr
Times Sq-42 St
42 St Bryant Pk
5 Av
33 St
Lexington Av/53 St
51 St
WEST 57TH STREET
EAST 60TH STREET
EAST 59TH STREET
WEST 54TH STREET
WEST 53RD ST
WEST 49TH STREET
WEST 50TH STREET
WEST 46TH STREET
WEST 45TH STREET
WEST 42ND STREET
WEST 37TH STREET
WEST 36TH STREET
EAST 34TH ST
EAST 36TH STREET
EAST 37TH ST
EAST 45TH ST
EAST 46TH ST
EAST 49TH STREET
EAST 50TH STREET
EAST 53RD STREET
EAST 54TH STREET
EAST 46TH STREET
EAST 45TH STREET
6TH AVENUE
5TH AVENUE
7TH AVENUE
BROADWAY
PARK AVENUE
MADISON AVENUE
LEXINGTON AVENUE
3RD AVENUE
2ND AVENUE
VANDERBILT AVE
N

THE GILDED AGE: OLD MONEY / NEW MONEY

What did it mean to be part of the "old" or "new" social set during New York's Gilded Age? For generations, access to the city's innermost circles depended more on one's lineage than one's bank account. The American Civil War and the industrial wealth it created in New York gave rise to a whole new generation of millionaires whose unbridled willingness to flaunt their earnings sent shockwaves through high society. Through their comportment, patronage, fashion, and architecture, these parvenu families would forever alter the city and the nation. This walk explores the gulf which existed between the old and new families across the very neighborhoods and spaces in which they once glittered.

DISTANCE
2¼ miles (3.6 km)

TIME ALLOWED
2–3 hours

ROUTE No. **07**

ROUTE STOPS

1. The Morgan Library
2. 34th Street and Park Avenue
3. The Robb & Lanier Mansions
4. The De Lamar Mansion
5. The Weird Wendels
6. The New York Public Library
7. Grand Central Terminal Exterior
8. Grand Central Terminal Interior
9. St Patrick's Cathedral
10. The Plant Mansion & Vanderbilt Row
11. Grand Army Plaza

FROM MURRAY HILL TO CENTRAL PARK

The great divide between "Old Money" and "new money" in Gilded Age New York was a phenomenon which is too often distilled into a somewhat petty dichotomy pitting Mrs Astor's old guard against the likes of Mrs Vanderbilt. The truth of the matter is both simpler and more consequential. Prior to the American Civil War, the prerequisites for joining Society's inner circle were incredibly strict. A person's lineage mattered far more than their bank accounts. Respectability was earned over generations and could not be purchased.

It is important, too, to take into account the timeline of New York's growth and wartime history: neighborhoods like Washington Square, Astor Place, and even Gramercy Park were developed in the 1830s and 1840s, mere decades after the American Revolution. New Yorkers of not terribly advanced age during this period would have grown up during the war and almost certainly would have seen relatives fight or die in the name of American independence. Since most Loyalist families fled New York during the Revolution, those that remained had often risked quite literally everything in support of the patriotic cause. They are likely to have attended George Washington's 1789 inauguration on Wall Street or known Alexander Hamilton and Aaron Burr before their fateful 1804 duel. In short, America's founding and inherent fragility was not lost on New York's leading families in the first half of the 19th century.

With this in mind, it begins to make sense that New York's old guard – the Old-Money folks of the impending Gilded Age – lived lives still informed by the stoicism of the nation's Puritan and stolid Dutch founders. There was an understanding that wealth and social prominence came with certain responsibilities: that the egalitarianism envisioned for this new nation must be upheld through example. At a time when the United States was still largely looking inward to determine its future, New Yorkers erred on the side of conservatism of dress, carriage, and comportment. This played out in virtually every aspect of early 19th-century life, but most notably in architecture, which remained uniformly mundane. "Gotham was, architecturally speaking, a monotonous grid of virtually identical brownstone row houses,"[106] with divergence frowned upon if not outright forbidden.

Everything changed during the American Civil War, which raged from 1861–65. Northern urban centers like New York rapidly industrialized to feed the national war machine, giving rise to an entirely new generation of wealthy families whose fortunes came from manufacturing, banking, and railroads. These *nouveaux riches* lacked the sense of conservative responsibility so long fostered by the old guard and were instead eager to flaunt their riches with as much glitz as possible. Thus began the usurpation of New York's former leading class, with its dowdy restraint, sterling pedigrees, and quiet adherence to tradition. These new-money folks, led by the likes of Vanderbilt, Carnegie, Rockefeller, and Huntington, spent lavishly on the fastest horses, the finest French fashions, and the largest, gaudiest mansions that money could buy.

In diamonds, mahogany, and limestone, these new-money titans redefined what it meant to be rich in America and in so doing, they helped usher in New York's Gilded Age. But their ostentation not only flew in the face of social tradition; it raised the question of what sort of nation the United States ought to become. Would it still attempt to uphold some notion of egalitarianism or would the nation's grand experiment devolve into a sort of capitalistic monarchy, one in which its people pay homage to millionaires and industrial masters in place of the sort of hereditary monarchy it had so recently fought to cast off? This is the essence of the conflict between Old Money and new money: a divide which would come to define the era forever.

Start 1 → At the **Morgan Library,** on **Madison Avenue** at **East 36th Street**

MORGAN LIBRARY

One of the greatest surviving instances of new money blending with Old Money is the Morgan Library & Museum on Madison Avenue between 36th and 37th Streets. J Pierpont Morgan, the man behind the library's establishment, was a titan of Wall Street and founder of United States Steel, the nation's first billion-dollar corporation. Unlike other parvenus of his generation, Morgan chose to resist the allure of building for himself a big, gaudy, new, uptown mansion. Instead, in 1881, he purchased and renovated the 1853 brownstone mansion of John Jay Phelps at the northeast corner of 36th Street and Madison Avenue.

This was perhaps Morgan's way of showing his Knickerbocker neighbors (page 139) that he had enough good taste to live the way they lived. After all, Mrs Astor lived just around the corner at 34th Street and 5th Avenue until her departure from Murray Hill in 1895. Morgan stayed put, even as the neighborhood around him began to devolve into a crowded commercial district, and by 1904, he'd created family.

What had initially been a cluster of four large houses built in the 1850s for the intermarried Phelps, Dodge, and Stokes families, was acquired by Morgan house by house as their original owners moved on. Ultimately, Morgan retained No. 219 Madison Avenue as his own. He demolished No. 225 to build a garden, and he gifted No. 229 to his son Jack. He likewise purchased No. 31 East 36th Street, just behind his home, which is where his splendid library building now stands.

Like many wealthy men of his day, Morgan was an avid collector of rare and expensive items. He accumulated paintings and tapestries, but his keenest interest was reserved for books and manuscripts. He scoured the globe, enlisting a team of field agents to help him find new and interesting artifacts. By 1902, it was clear

Morgan Library

that his brownstone mansion could no longer contain his holdings and he set out to build a proper library and office for himself. For this project, he enlisted the renowned architect Charles F McKim of McKim, Mead & White.

When the elder Morgan received the keys to his library in late 1905, the interiors were nearing completion. Three levels of colorfully bound books, many priceless and irreplaceable, were to be displayed behind glass within sumptuous cases made of walnut and bronze, all beneath a richly painted ceiling by artist Harry Siddons Mowbray depicting various artforms and the 12 signs of the Zodiac. Two spiral staircases were hidden within the walls so as to not disrupt the room's purity of design. For Morgan, perfecting this library meant having a fitting showcase for his cherished collections.

For McKim, the project meant perhaps much more. It would ultimately be one of his last works before his untimely death in 1909, its clean lines a glorious testament to his masterful restraint. A McKim biography written in 1913 by Alfred Hoyt Granger marvels at the library's aesthetic success: "Here was an opportunity for every form of lavish expenditure, for this was the private toy of a multi-millionaire who never discussed the price when gratifying his desires. In this building restraint and discrimination are carried to the nth power. These are the two characteristics which American architecture most sadly lacks, and in a careful and exhaustive study of the Morgan library as a whole and in detail, one strengthens the belief that no great architecture can exist without them."[107]

The library's exterior is made of Tennessee pink marble, constructed employing interlocking techniques such that virtually no mortar was used. Set back from the street behind an imposing gate, the entrance is flanked by stone lions sculpted by Edward Clark Potter, who would later produce *Patience* and *Fortitude*, the lions outside the New York Public Library's main branch on 5th Avenue. Construction on the Morgan Library was completed in 1906 after four years of intense secrecy and widespread curiosity. No members of the press or public were allowed inside, and speculation swirled as to what treasures hid within the building's 4-foot (1.2-metre) thick walls. "Mr J Pierpont Morgan is probably the greatest collector of things splendid and beautiful and rare who has ever lived," gushed the first reporter to visit the new library. "There is no one with whom we can compare him except, perhaps, Lorenzo de Medici, and he surpasses even that Prince in the catholicity of his taste."[108]

Integral to the expansion of Morgan's collection was his longtime librarian, Belle da Costa Greene. She was introduced to Morgan in 1905 while working at the Princeton Library by his nephew Junius who was a student there. Belle's story is singularly fascinating. Born Belle Marion Greener, she was the daughter of Richard Howard Greener, who was the first African-American person to graduate from Harvard. When he moved to Siberia, leaving his family behind in America, they changed their names and began to pass as white in society. Belle adopted the middle name "da Costa" to suggest Portuguese heritage and explain her complexion.

Greene became Morgan's right hand in the library, co-ordinating purchases for him from around the globe, particularly in illuminated medieval manuscripts. One of the most extraordinary acquisitions made during

Morgan's lifetime came in 1910, when a bundle of 9th-century Coptic scripts was found in a desert well, untouched by hands or sunlight for a thousand years. Ultimately, Greene stayed on at the Morgan Library for nearly four decades, assembling one of the greatest collections of literary treasures ever amassed.

Morgan was in Egypt in 1913, sailing up the Nile to Khartoum, when he fell ill and was rushed to Rome for treatment. He died there, 75 years old and one of the richest men in history. His will was vague about the fate of his library and its holdings: he left his collections largely to his son, saying only that "it has been my desire and intention to make some suitable disposition [...] which would render them permanently available for the instruction and pleasure of the American people."[109] Thankfully for future generations of scholars, Jack Morgan fulfilled his father's wish. Following his mother's death in 1924, he demolished their brownstone mansion and built an annex in its place, doubling the size of the library with gallery and exhibition space. The new, expanded Morgan Library opened to the public on October 1, 1928.

Jack Morgan died in 1943 and Belle Greene died in 1950. Over the decades, the Morgan Library has continued in its mission to make its collections available to the public through decades of cultural upheaval, expansion, and war. Its collections were scattered to the countryside for safekeeping during World War II, part of a mammoth wartime effort by New York's cultural institutions, now largely forgotten. By the 1980s, the institution had outgrown its original buildings and purchased the neighboring brownstone mansion, formerly home to Jack Morgan, in 1988. It currently houses the Library's gift shop, offices, and conservation areas.

In 2002, the Morgan enlisted architect Renzo Piano to sketch out plans that would maximize its available space while preserving its landmarked original structures. Piano designed an airy glass polygon which fit into the courtyard between the McKim building, the 1928 annex, and the Jack Morgan brownstone, pushing the Morgan to the edge of its footprint. They also drilled 80 feet (24 meters) down into the lot's bedrock, installing waterproof vaults for the collection's most fragile and valuable pieces. Today, the Morgan Library & Museum continues to make its incredible collection of books, documents, and artwork available to the public more than a century after Morgan's death.

From an architectural standpoint, the Morgan is one of the greatest juxtapositions of Gilded Age styles to be found in the city: the old-money brownstone grandeur of Jack Morgan's mansion connected via a 21st-century atrium to Charles McKim's new-money masterpiece of a library. Looking at the Morgan complex is an excellent way to begin understanding the complexities of the city's social and stylistic evolution at the end of the 19th and beginning of the 20th centuries.

From the **Morgan Library**, walk east along **36th Street** to **Park Avenue**. Turn right and walk south to **34th Street**

Stop 2 → At **34th Street** and **Park Avenue**

MURRAY HILL

Calling any part of Midtown Manhattan a hill feels like a misnomer. Manhattan is famously flat, at least below the rocky heights on the island's northern leg. But it wasn't always such an even plane. Manhattan's landscape was originally made up of countless hills, ridges, marshes, creeks, and ponds. Most aberrations were erased in the 19th century to allow for easier development and street grading. Ponds and marshes were drained, creeks were buried as sewers, and hills were shaved down to manageable proportions. Understanding this history helps make sense of the name Murray Hill. There once was a hill here, and it was at one time owned by the Murray family.

Generally, Murray Hill is flat land today, but in certain places it remains physically true to its name. Specifically, standing at the corner of 34th Street and Park Avenue, looking downtown, astute explorers will notice how precipitously the avenue drops away on its journey toward Union Square one mile south. This incline is a remnant of Murray Hill's true form. Incredibly, despite centuries of terraforming, it really is still a bit of a hill.

In the 1830s, Murray Hill was still largely open fields and farmland, miles north of the city. This began to change when New York's first railroad company, the New York & Harlem, was incorporated in 1831. Within a year, tracks were being laid down the middle of Park Avenue (then called 4th Avenue) en route to connecting New York at the south end of the island to Harlem and its river at the north end. Murray Hill, too steep for early rail technology to surmount, stood in the way of the new route. It, along with Mount Prospect (now called Carnegie Hill) near 92nd Street, would need to be tunneled if the New York & Harlem Railroad were ever to live up to its name.

THE RAILROAD LINKS

Finally, in 1836, a tunnel was completed through Mount Prospect from 92nd to 94th Streets, and a wooden viaduct was built across the marshy lowlands of East Harlem from 103rd to 106th Streets. The following year, in 1837, a cut was completed through Murray Hill, from 32nd to 42nd Streets, allowing for uninterrupted rail service from Madison Square all the way to the Harlem River. The Murray Hill cut was covered in 1850, turning it into a true tunnel, carrying countless New Yorkers and visitors in and out of the city for a generation. In short order, rail would do more to revolutionize New York's developing cityscape than any single other technological advance.

In 1858, New York City passed a law forbidding steam-powered trains below 42nd Street. Shortly thereafter, the New York & Harlem was purchased by Cornelius Vanderbilt as part of his late-in-life pivot from ferries to rail. Vanderbilt consolidated numerous rail lines throughout the region, including the Harlem, New Haven, and Hudson lines in Manhattan, and united them under one roof at his new Grand Central Depot up on 42nd Street. With that now-demolished Grand Central opened in 1871, the old tracks south of the station were taken out of regular rail use and returned to horse-drawn streetcar service.

Though the tunnel's tracks were electrified in 1898, it remained a streetcar line until 1935, when it was given over to a newer piece of technology which would, in many ways, signal the beginning of the end of the rail age altogether: the automobile. Standing at 34th Street and Park Avenue, the old tunnel is still visible as it vanishes beneath the rise of Murray Hill. It is an unassuming piece of early transit development hiding in plain sight. And, importantly, it is also a visual reminder that Murray Hill's name is still apt even after so many years and so much change.

From **34th Street**, walk north along the east side of **Park Avenue**

Stop 3 → At **35th Street**

ROBB MANSION

Even after the burial and eventual removal of steam-powered trains along 4th Avenue (which was renamed Park Avenue in an attempt to attract higher-end investment) in the late 19th century, Murray Hill's wealthy residents remained largely concentrated on 5th and Madison Avenues, while 4th Avenue was long seen as the dividing line between millionaires in their mansions to the west and less affluent rows of middle-class brownstones to the east. Things began to change at the end of the 19th century thanks in part to the 1895 departure of Caroline Astor from the area. With her gone, ever more Old-Money families fled Murray Hill in favor of greener pastures uptown on the Upper East Side.

As the old guard departed, their mansions were sold off and demolished. One saving grace for Murray Hill was the stubbornness of some of its residents, including J Pierpont Morgan, who refused to leave. Their presence empowered a respectable number of other wealthy families to stay. However, as 5th Avenue north of Madison Square began to transition increasingly to commercial development, Murray Hill residents began to shift eastward, building new mansions on and east of Park Avenue, crossing the traditional boundary of the neighborhood's rarefied heart.

The Gilded Age divide between rich and not-so-rich is rarely so blatantly visible in the modern streetscape as it is at the northeast corner of 35th Street and Park Avenue. In dramatic fashion, construction of the Robb house here broke with architectural convention for the area. Importantly, it was a stylistic leap forward thanks to its architect, Stanford White, who designed it as a sort of American take on a Roman renaissance-revival palazzo. This was particularly notable in the 1890s, when the residential style of choice was far more French-inflected chateauesque or beaux arts. As noted in the house's 1998 landmark designation report, its design was celebrated as "the most dignified structure" in all of Murray Hill, "not a palace, but a fit dwelling house for a first-rate citizen."[110]

James Hampden Robb was a wealthy Philadelphia-born banker, politician, and club man. When completed in 1892, the home White designed for him and his wife, Cornelia, was (and remains) dramatically out of scale with its older brownstone neighbors along 35th Street. Those houses, most of them just two bays wide, are relics from the 1850s, when the blocks east of the New York & Harlem Railroad tracks were significantly less affluent than those to the west. The Robb house quite literally looms over them, occupying the same footprint as perhaps half a dozen of the smaller brownstones. The house was built at the height of Stanford White's fame and popularity; work concluded on his new and glorious Madison Square Garden on 26th Street in 1890, while the Robb house was nearing completion.

Jack Morgan House

Murray Hill from the Empire State Building

Lanier Mansion

36th Street

De Lamar Mansion

The Robbs remained at No. 23 Park Avenue until their deaths, hers in 1903 and his in 1911, after which point it passed to their grandson, who leased it out as a boarding house. In 1923, the home was sold to the Advertising Club of New York, which remained there until 1977, through a devastating fire in 1946 which destroyed some of the original interiors. After the club moved out, the house was converted for residential use once more, sliced into a dozen luxury apartments which fetch millions today.

LANIER MANSION

Just east of the Robb house, midblock on the north side of 35th Street, stands another splendid example of the area's Gilded apogee: the James FD Lanier home at No. 123. Completed in 1902, a decade after the Robb house, the Lanier mansion features a beaux-arts facade, more typical of the late Gilded Age, executed with obvious skill by the architectural firm of Hoppin & Koen (Francis Hoppin and Terence Koen met while working as young draftsmen for McKim, Mead & White). With its rusticated ground floor, red-brick body set off by iron balustrades and light stone pilasters, and copper-clad mansard roof, the home is "elegant and dignified, one that could be at home in Paris as well as in New York." [111]

Situated as it is between much older and smaller brownstone houses, the Lanier home is an outstanding example of the stylistic and socio-economic changes wrending Murray Hill's easterly blocks at the turn of the 20th century. Though families like the Robbs and the Laniers took a bet on Murray Hill's staying power, it is obvious from the surrounding streetscape that they were ultimately among the minority in Gilded Age Society, which otherwise abandoned the area in favor of newer, more fashionable districts uptown. Astoundingly, despite its proximity to Midtown and its commercial chaos, the Lanier home has never been significantly altered or converted for multi-family use. Both its interior and exterior remain intact, hinting at a type of residential dignity largely lost across the rest of the city during the interceding century.

On **35th Street**, walk east to **Lexington Avenue** and turn left. Following **Lexington** for one block, then turn left onto **36th Street** and walk back to **Park Avenue**, admiring the largely homogenous rows of brownstone townhouses along the block. At **Park Avenue**, turn right and then left again onto **37th Street**

Stop 4 → Near the corner of **Madison Avenue**, between the **Morgan Library** and the **De Lamar Mansion**, which is now home to the Polish Consulate

DE LAMAR MANSION

Standing at the northeast corner of Madison Avenue and 37th Street is a most unusual mansion. It's one of the last true Gilded Age palaces in Murray Hill, an area which lost its social primacy a century ago. The mansion was completed in 1905, long after most wealthy families had decamped for greener pastures uptown. A pile of heavy gray-stone beaux-arts excess, its facade is perhaps too heavy, its dimensions stretched, its mansard roof too steep. It's an interpretation of a French chateau verging on caricature. Its builder was

Joseph Raphael De Lamar, born in Holland in 1843. He left home as a sailor at a young age, traveling the globe before settling on Martha's Vineyard, by 1870. There, he made a living raising shipwrecks, but in 1878, De Lamar headed west, lured by the metals boom then occurring in Colorado.

He was "of small stature," described *The Sun* in 1894, "with shrewd, twinkling eyes, large features, and an energetic, pushing manner."[112] He bought and sold several mines, reaping vast profits before moving to Washington DC in 1891, "seeking a wife."[113] There, he spent lavishly on parties for the town's elite, but quickly learned that money does not necessarily guarantee social acceptance, and he failed to find a bride. Instead he moved to New York in 1893 and ultimately was wed to a young beauty of no particular social standing named Nellie Sands. She was 17, he was 49. The couple had a daughter, Alice, in 1895, and lived in a fine house at No. 109 Madison Avenue.

Joseph believed that Nellie's youth and beauty, tied to his wealth, would make them a more socially acceptable couple. But both in New York and at Newport, the De Lamars continued to be iced out, and instead spent increasing time in Paris where one's pedigree mattered less than one's wealth and affability. In 1897, however, Joseph discovered that Nellie had been carrying on a long-distance love affair with another man. He divorced her and took Alice back to New York. In 1902, determined that young Alice would enjoy a better social life than he or Nellie ever had, Joseph hired architect CPH Gilbert to build for him a grand new mansion on Murray Hill. Father and daughter moved into this "monument to extravagance"[114] in 1905 along with nine servants.

Though Joseph was never really embraced by Gilded Age Society, Alice was, by all accounts, a lovely, well-educated, and well-liked girl. Her debut ball in 1915 was a resounding success, with more than 400 well-heeled attendees. Afterward, she was widely expected to become one of the city's most eligible bachelorettes, particularly following her father's death in 1918. As his sole heir, Alice inherited an estate worth an estimated $30 million. Instead of taking her rightful place atop the social heap, however, Alice largely retreated from the spotlight altogether, serving in the Women's Motor Service Corps and later the Red Cross in support of the American war effort in World War I.

She sold her father's Murray Hill house in 1923 to the New York Democratic Club and spent the next six decades enmeshed in the world of wealthy east coast Bohemians. She mainly split her time between Palm Beach, Florida, and her primary residence in Weston, Connecticut. At her Connecticut compound, Alice bought up dozens of surrounding properties and rented them at low rates to friends and creatives, attracting an impressive list of notable neighbors. Never married, Alice maintained a number of long-term relationships (romantic or not), including with actors Eva Le Gallienne and Mercedes De Acosta. When she died in 1983, Alice left $1 million to Eva. The rest went to charity.

As for the De Lamar home on Murray Hill, it was sold in 1973 by the Democratic Club to the Government of Poland, which has used it as their New York City consulate building to this day. Architecturally, it is a visually arresting reminder of the neighborhood's twilight years as a bastion of Gilded Age excess, standing in stark contrast to the stolid brownstone cube that is the old Morgan house across the street. There is perhaps no greater visual representation for the gulf that existed between old and new money during the 19th century than this. Additionally, the stories behind the De Lamar mansion, of Joseph's humble origins and Alice's emergence as a truly modern heiress, mark one of the final instances of Manhattan's many Gilded Age dramas.

From the **De Lamar Mansion**, walk west to **5th Avenue**. Turn right onto **5th Avenue** and walk north to **39th Street**

Stop 5 → At the northwest corner of **39th Street**

WENDEL MANSION

At the northwest corner of 5th Avenue and 39th Street, where a modern skyscraper now stands, there once stood one of the last of the neighborhood's pre-Gilded Age mansions, that of the so-called "Weird Wendels."

The tale of New York's Wendel family is too often overlooked. For three generations, the Wendels built one of the nation's greatest fortunes in real estate and fur trading, only to hide for decades in paranoid isolation. Johann Gottlieb Wendel, the family patriarch, was born in 1767 in Schleswig-Holstein (near modern-day Hamburg, Germany). His wife, born Elizabeth Astor, was a sister of John Jacob Astor, who learned the fur trade working in Wendel's shop on Pearl Street in lower Manhattan. Johann and Elizabeth had one son, John David Wendel, born in 1800. He took over his father's fur business and multiplied the family's wealth by investing heavily in New York real estate. John and his wife Mary had one son: John Gottlieb, Jr, and seven daughters: Mary Eliza, Henrietta, Rebecca, Augusta, Josephine, Georgiana, and Ella.

In 1856, the family moved into a large brick-and-brownstone mansion here on 5th Avenue at the northwest corner of 39th Street. John David Wendel died in 1876, followed by his wife Mary in 1894, leaving nearly the entire $10 million Wendel estate to their son. Whereas his parents had been frugal, John G was tyrannical in his protection of the family fortune. He forbade his sisters from marrying, insisting that no property leave the Wendel name. (A sign hung on his office door saying "We do not sell property."). He resisted new technology, freezing their home in time with no electricity or modern conveniences. The siblings sewed their own clothes for decades, all black, in the style of the 1890s. They closed their shutters against the world outside, and soon became known as "the house of mystery."[115]

One sister, Georgiana, attempted to leave the family home at age 50 in 1900, checking herself into the Park Avenue Hotel. For that, her brother declared her insane and had her institutionalized at Bellevue Hospital until she relented and agreed to return home. The only sister to succeed in breaking away was Rebecca; at age 60, over her brother's "violent opposition," she married teacher Luther Swope and lived many years thereafter at 249 Central Park West.

John Gottlieb Wendel, the "recluse of 5th Avenue,"[116] died in 1914, leaving behind four surviving sisters, three of whom remained in the family home on 5th Avenue. It became almost comically anachronistic as the area rapidly transformed into a commercial center; the massive department store Lord & Taylor opened next door in 1914. One by one the remaining Wendel sisters passed away: Mary in 1922, Georgiana in 1929, and Rebecca in 1930. That left the youngest Wendel, Ella, alone in the house, living much as she had since the 1850s even as the Empire State Building neared completion four blocks away.

The last Wendel stayed on in the house, alone but for her dog Tobey, until Ella died in 1931. Her funeral, "a ritual as simple, frugal and quiet as her long life had been,"[117] was attended by only a handful of surviving family friends. With no heirs to inherit it, the Wendel fortune was ultimately broken up and given to various charities, including the Drew Theological Seminary in New Jersey. The Wendel Mansion was torn down in 1935, ending nearly a century of residential tradition on a storied stretch of a storied avenue. In its place rose a Kress discount store which has since been replaced by a glass tower which bears a plaque marking the site of the strange old home. The Wendels, so protective of their fortune and legacy, have become a quirky footnote to history.

From the **Wendel plaque**, walk north along **5th Avenue**, across **40th Street**

Stop 6 → In front of the **New York Public Library's** monumental main building

NEW YORK PUBLIC LIBRARY

Prior to 1895, New York City did not have an official public library system. There were, of course, academic and religious libraries throughout the city, but these were not open to the general public. There were also subscription libraries, which charged a fee for access, as well as privately run libraries, which set their own rules for who could or couldn't rifle through their stacks. Two of these last sorts were the Astor Library on Lafayette Place (page 142) and the Lenox Library on upper 5th Avenue between 70th and 71st Streets (page 217).

Neither the Astor nor the Lenox Library was a truly public institution. The Astor was criticized for its strict rules which limited access to its collections and prevented public circulation of books. The Lenox was likewise strict and charged a fee for access. Most New Yorkers remained largely cut off from any meaningful literary access until the death, in 1886, of prominent lawyer, politician, and book-lover Samuel J Tilden (page 150). His will left the bulk of his estate, more than $2,000,000, plus his personal collection of some 20,000 books to the creation of a truly public, city-wide library system. After years of delay and debate, it was decided to combine Tilden's gifts with the collections of the Astor and the Lenox Libraries, creating the New York Public Library in 1895.

Until this time, the west side of 5th Avenue between 40th and 42nd Streets was dominated by the enormous, rough-stone walls of the Croton Distributing Reservoir, which was built as part of the city's first water supply system in 1842. It was one of the architectural and engineering wonders of the city when it

New York Public Library

was new, and to walk along its walls was a popular pastime for generations. Behind the reservoir, fronting 6th Avenue, was a public park originally called Reservoir Square, which was renamed Bryant Park in 1884.

In 1853, the park hosted the Exhibition of the Industry of All Nations, the first World's Fair to be held in the Western Hemisphere. The Fair served as solid proof of the emerging industrial greatness of the United States, featuring an impressive Crystal Palace in echo of the one built at London's much-lauded Great Exposition two years earlier. New York's Fair also featured the Latting Observatory, a 315-foot (96-meter) tower made of wood and iron which offered sweeping views of the city from its lookout platform. It made a particular impact on one park attendee, a young French engineer named Gustave Eiffel, who later used the Latting Observatory as his inspiration for building his eponymous tower for Paris's 1889 World's Fair.

The Exhibition ended in 1854, the Latting Observatory burned down in 1856, and the Crystal Palace likewise burned down in 1858. Nothing but the park and the reservoir remained on the site by the 1860s, by which time Murray Hill had become a thickly settled district of mansions. As the Gilded Age got underway after the Civil War, newly flush families like the Vanderbilts began to move north of 42nd Street, building a colony of immense chateaux and palazzi where once there had been nothing but shacks, stables, and dirt pits. The old Croton Distributing Reservoir acted as a physical and psychological barrier between the old guard on Murray Hill and the new-money families north of it. Considered a colossal eyesore in one of the choicest locations in the city, the reservoir was demolished beginning in 1897. In its place rose a spectacular new monument to the city's democratic greatness: the New York Public Library.

The New York Public Library's main branch was designed by the architectural firm of Carrère and Hastings, who envisioned it as "very monumental in character, with classical proportions, and very big and impressive in scale."[118] It was one of a grand new generation of public buildings to rise across the city at the turn of the 20th century, part of the City Beautiful movement inspired by Chicago's 1893 World's Columbian Exposition. Buildings such as the library, the new US Custom House on Bowling Green (page 10), and the new Police Headquarters on Centre Street, were meant to imbue the city with grandeur and instill in its citizenry a sense of civic responsibility and pride.

Construction began on the library building in 1900; its cornerstone was laid in 1902 and its exterior was largely complete by the end of 1907. Its facade is made almost entirely out of white marble quarried at Dorset, Vermont. Nearly two-thirds of all the marble brought to the library site was rejected for lack of quality or impurity of color. Some of the rejected marble was used to build the present campus of Harvard Medical School in Massachusetts.

The New York Public Library was completed in 1911, opening to the public on May 23 following the several months' work required to move more than one million books from the Astor and Lenox Libraries into the new building. Once emptied, the old library buildings were sold off. The Lenox, designed by Richard Morris Hunt, was purchased by Henry Clay Frick who demolished it and replaced it with his own new home and art gallery, now known as The Frick Collection.

The Astor was used for half a century by the Hebrew Immigrant Aid Society, meeting the needs of the increasingly Jewish immigrant population of the surrounding neighborhood. After their departure in 1965, the building was saved from demolition and repurposed as The Public Theater under the direction of Joseph Papp.

Standing in the plaza in front of the New York Public Library on 5th Avenue, be sure to look up above the three entry arches. There, on prominent and permanent display, are memorial plaques to the three founding bodies of this great institution: the Astor Library, the Lenox Library, and the Tilden Trust. The library is open to the public and its interior is well worth a visit.

Before moving on take a moment to appreciate the two enormous stone lions which flank the library's front steps. These are the work of artist Daniel Clark Potter and were sculpted by the Bronx-based Piccirilli Brothers. They have become the mascots of the city's library system, beloved symbols of the universality of reading and knowledge. Their original nicknames, *Leo Lenox* and *Leo Astor*, were replaced in the 1930s by Mayor Fiorello LaGuardia, who renamed them *Patience* and *Fortitude* in honor of those attributes shown by New Yorkers during the Great Depression. To remember which lion is which, remember that *Patience* is near 40th Street, while *Fortitude* is near Forty-Two Street.

From the **NYPL**, walk up to **42nd Street**, turn right, and continue east to the plaza at **Pershing Square**

Stop 7 → Directly across the street from Grand Central Terminal

GRAND CENTRAL TERMINAL

Grand Central Terminal as it looks and functions today was completed in 1913. But it is not the first Grand Central building to occupy the site. The first was Grand Central Depot, which opened in 1871, shortly after Cornelius Vanderbilt took over operations of the New York & Harlem Railroad, the city's oldest train line which had previously terminated at Madison Square (page 156). Vanderbilt likewise controlled the New York & Hudson River Railroad, as well as the New York & New Haven, and consolidated passenger movement for all three lines at this new depot on 42nd Street. He called his new company the New York Central Railroad and therefore named its new station Grand Central Depot.

When it opened in 1871, Grand Central Depot was heralded as a massive improvement over the city's previous rail infrastructure, though there were complaints about its far-flung location, "practically as far as Harlem from the City Hall."[119] Thankfully, the city quickly grew up around it and by 1890, Grand Central could at last honestly be called *central*, with some of the world's largest and finest hotels, office towers, clubhouses, cathedrals, and mansions all within a short walk's distance. By 1897, the depot was at capacity and so underwent an extensive modernization which saw much of its headhouse rebuilt, its waiting rooms combined, and its railyards reconfigured. Work was completed in 1900, with the building rechristened Grand Central Station.

Importantly, for decades, the New York Central was the only rail company with stations located on Manhattan Island. All of its competitors terminated on opposite sides of the East and Hudson Rivers, forcing their passengers to disembark and board ferries for the final leg of their journey, an indignity made infinitely worse in bad weather. In 1900, however, the Central's chief rival, the Pennsylvania Railroad Company, purchased the Long Island Railroad and began buying up property on Manhattan's west side. Their goal was to build a series of tunnels beneath the rivers, connecting them at an enormous new station in the heart of New York which would strike a direct blow at the Vanderbilts and their railroad's long-held monopoly of traffic in and out of the city.

Because the Pennsylvania trains would need to run underground, their engines, tunnels, and stations in New York would all be electrified to reduce the need for ventilation. The Central had long resisted the expense of electrifying its system, meaning its trains were still the sorts of steam-powered, smoke-and-soot-spewing behemoths used a generation before. This fact became a focal point of press coverage in the aftermath of a deadly train crash on January 8, 1902, in which a train from Danbury, Connecticut, was rear-ended by one from White Plains, New York, in the approach tunnel to Grand Central. Fifteen people died at the scene, and another seven died of their injuries in the days after.

Later investigations into the crash revealed that the White Plains conductor had effectively been blinded by the darkness of the tunnel which was filled with the smoke and soot of the hundreds of coal-fired trains which passed through it every day. Unable to see the lights or the Danbury train ahead of him, the conductor rammed into it full speed near 56th Street, telescoping his engine into its rear two cars. Following the crash, New York State ordered the electrification of all rail lines within city limits, forcing the New York Central to completely reimagine its whole system. The Central was electrified, allowing its tracks and yards to be buried, and the first electrified train departed from Grand Central on March 14, 1910.

As part of the overhaul of the system, and to better compete with the new Penn Station across town, the company made plans to demolish Grand Central Station barely two years after its completion. In its place, the architectural firm of Warren & Wetmore designed a radically modern new structure called Grand Central Terminal, which was completed in 1913 to great fanfare. With its trains electrified, the building did not have to account for smoke ventilation, allowing them to essentially float the new terminal atop its cavernous warren of platforms. Aside from being beautiful, Grand Central Terminal was innovative in its design, providing grade-separated streets for local and through traffic as well as a system of ramps which allowed passengers to get to and from their trains without ever having to navigate up or down stairs.

Before entering Grand Central, be sure to look closely at its 42nd Street facade. Warren & Wetmore displayed a deft hand in the building's scale, which appears far smaller from the outside than it actually is. It is in fact the same height as a 15-story building, with its main interior hall soaring 125 feet (38 meters) from floor to ceiling. From outside, this scale can best be appreciated by looking up at the colossal-scale statue grouping on the roofline. Called *A Tribute to Commerce*,[120] it was executed by French sculptor Jules Alexis Coutan and features Mercury, god of commerce and travel, flanked by Vulcan, god of fire and technology, and Minerva, goddess of wisdom and the arts.

The whole grouping stands 48 feet (15 meters) tall, 66 feet (20 meters) wide, and weighs an estimated 1,500 tons. Adding to the list of superlatives, the stained glass clock embedded below Mercury measures an astounding 14 feet (4 meters) wide. The clock is often attributed to Tiffany Studios, though it is unsigned and there is no record of it being the work of Tiffany.

Walk across **42nd Street** and enter **Grand Central** beneath the **Pershing Square viaduct**. Pass through the grandeur of **Vanderbilt Hall**, the terminal's former waiting room, and enter the main hall just beyond it

Bask in the scale of things. Listen to the hum of voices, the blare of track announcements, and the clatter of luggage and footfall as crowds swirling to and fro, some running to catch a train, but so many more simply staring upward in slack-jawed wonder. 125 feet (38 meters) overhead, a mural of the night sky designed by French artist Paul César Helleu depicts the January to June zodiac: Aquarius (water-bearer), Pisces (fish), Aries (ram), Taurus (bull), Gemini (twins), and Cancer (crab). It also includes Pegasus (winged horse), Orion (hunter), Triangulum (triangles), and Musca (fly).

For reasons not entirely clear, with the exception of Orion, the entire mural is reversed from reality. It is likely that this was merely a mistake of the artists in their attempt to translate sketches onto the vast ceiling, but some sources posit that the sky depicts the stars as viewed from Heaven, as was common in the Middle Ages. Regardless, it is an amusing quirk.

After peaking during World War II, train ridership in the United States plummeted in the face of increased competition from air travel and private automobiles. In 1968, facing bankruptcy, the New York Central merged with its longtime rival, the Pennsylvania Railroad, creating the short-lived Penn Central Transportation Company. Demolition had only just wrapped up at Penn Station when, that same year, Penn Central proposed building a 55-story office tower atop Grand Central. The tower, designed by Marcel Breuer, would spare the grand celestial concourse inside, but would otherwise "scoop out" much of the terminal's interior, "using the old facades as a kind of classical window dressing."[121]

Thankfully, these plans did not come to fruition, thanks in no small part to support from former First Lady Jacqueline Kennedy Onassis, who defended the doomed building, saying "if we don't care about our past, we cannot hope for our future."[122] The fight to save Grand Central dragged on until 1978, when the United States Supreme Court ruled against Penn Central's attempts to demolish the landmark building. Despite this, the near-bankrupt rail company retained ownership of Grand Central and allowed it to decline for the next decade.

It wasn't until 1996 that work got underway to restore Grand Central to something like its original appearance. The two-year project cost nearly $200 million but marked a turning point for Midtown, the city, and the relationship between its people and its transit hubs. Eight decades of grime and tobacco stains were cleaned from the terminal's walls and ceilings, revealing the beauty most New

New York Public Library

Grand Central Terminal and Chrysler Building

Cartier, former Plant Mansion

St Patrick's Cathedral spires from Olympic Tower

Yorkers had forgotten existed at Grand Central. Today, it serves upward of a million passengers each day, with countless more tourists visiting simply to gawk.

One remnant of Grand Central's pre-restoration appearance survives, however. High on the ceiling near the crab symbol of Cancer, look for a little dark rectangle. This patch of filth was left in place to remind future generations of preservationists what was done during the restoration project in the 1990s as well as to give visitors a small taste of just how far gone this beloved building once was. Imagine that dark patch expanded across the entire ceiling. It seems unfathomable today but it was reality not all that long ago.

To leave **Grand Central**, take the escalators behind the information booth up and into the **MetLife Tower**, a much-maligned brutalist pile built on the site of Grand Central's former baggage building in 1962. Pass through the public base of the tower and emerge on **East 45th Street**. Cross the street and walk through the pedestrian tunnel marked **Park Avenue West**. Exiting the tower on **46th Street**, look north along **Park Avenue**

Standing on 46th Street, the splendid Helmsley Building looms behind. With its ornate decoration and elaborate spherical clock overlooking Park Avenue, it was originally built as the headquarters for the New York Central Railroad in 1929. Looking north, everything in view as far as the Waldorf-Astoria Hotel at 49th Street is built atop Grand Central's still-active railyards underground. In fact, standing atop many of the sidewalk grates in the area affords a peek down to Metro-North Trains sitting at their platforms below.

Walk west along **48th Street** and turn right onto **Vanderbilt Avenue**

Towering overhead is the newly constructed No. 270 Park Avenue, world headquarters for JP Morgan Chase. At 1,388 feet (423 meters) tall, it is one of the city's tallest buildings and is rather astoundingly balanced atop some of the busiest active train tracks in the nation. It is also worth noting that the company building it (Morgan) and the street at its base (Vanderbilt) retain names of some of the city's most powerful new-money Gilded Age families.

Walk west along **47th Street** before turning right on **5th Avenue**. Continue walking north through what was once the seat of new-money power and prestige a century and a half ago

Stop 8 → On **5th Avenue** on the front steps of **St Patrick's Cathedral**

ST PATRICK'S CATHEDRAL

St Patrick's Cathedral feels as if it has always existed on 5th Avenue, so familiar is its silhouette against the surrounding skyscrapers. But its cornerstone was laid only in 1858, making it a veritable baby compared to the many ancient cathedrals of Europe. It was dedicated in 1879, largely complete but for its twin pointed spires, which were topped out at 330 feet (100 meters) tall in 1888.

The impetus for building such a splendid cathedral in New York was sparked by an enormous influx of Catholic immigrants during the 19th century. Previously relegated to minority status, Catholics were long outnumbered by the city's Protestants who, particularly within the Episcopal, Presbyterian, and Dutch Reformed congregations, counted most of the city's oldest and most well-heeled families among their ranks. Irish-born Archbishop John Hughes believed that Catholics would one day lead the city, and so set about planning for the construction of a great cathedral which would symbolize their rise.

St Patrick's Cathedral was designed by the architect James Renwick, Jr, whose career was launched by his splendid work on Grace Church (page 142), one of the city's leading Episcopal congregations, which was completed in 1846 near Union Square. For this cathedral, Renwick produced a work of art and architecture which was instantly hailed as one of the great ornaments of the city. It proved that American artisans and architects were capable of greatness comparable to that achieved in Europe. It also proved to the city's Protestant elites that New York's Catholics were driven by the same spiritual and civic animation which they held. In short, St Patrick's helped pave the way for the acceptance of a Catholic majority in this city.

By the time the spires of St Patrick's were completed in 1888, the land around it, which had so recently been mostly empty fields and dirt pits, had been filled by some of the city's most outlandishly ostentatious homes. The new-money families of the Gilded Age, with the Vanderbilts setting the example, strove to outshine one another in fashion, carriage, and architectural excellence. Diminishingly few of these mansions would survive more than a generation as the demands of commerce washed over what is now Midtown. But a walk up 5th Avenue today offers an opportunity to hunt for remnants and survivors from that age of glamor.

Walk one block north of **St Patrick's Cathedral** on **5th Avenue**

Stop 9 → At the Cartier store at the southeast corner of **52nd Street**

PLANT MANSION

The Cartier store at No. 653 5th Avenue is a rare Gilded Age survivor. It is the last of what was once an unbroken chain of mansions stretching from Murray Hill to Central Park. Home to Cartier since 1917, it was built in 1905 for Morton F Plant, heir to a railroad and steamship empire. Plant's home stood directly across from several members of the Vanderbilt family, who were, by the time Plant moved in, desperately trying to fend off the encroach of commerce by buying up neighboring properties. "It is an expensive luxury to live in 5th Avenue and keep business encroachments at a distance," explained *The New York Times* in 1904. "To protect that part of 5th Avenue in the immediate vicinity of their residences from undesirable forms of structures has already cost the Vanderbilt family nearly $4,000,000."[123]

Morton Plant bought one of the Vanderbilt plots, promising to keep it residential for 25 years. He moved in with his wife Nellie and son Henry in 1905. Nellie died of typhoid fever in 1913, and Morton was soon remarried to recent divorcee Maisie Manwaring. He was 62, she was 33. By then, the Vanderbilts were already losing their battle against commercialism on the avenue. The Plants decided to follow Society uptown, building a large new home at on 5th Avenue at 86th Street. This is where the story of the old Plant Mansion gets hazy, morphing into legend. The tale is that Cartier had a double strand of perfect natural pearls in its shop window at No. 712 5th Avenue. Maisie Plant, a friend and regular customer of Pierre Cartier, coveted the pearls, which were worth an estimated $1,000,000. Seated next to him at a dinner party, Maisie proposed a trade: Cartier would pay the Plants $100 plus the pearl necklaces in exchange for the Plants' old 5th Avenue home, which would become Cartier's new shop.

It's an attractive and romantic tale, oft repeated despite Cartier's reluctance to confirm or deny its veracity. Whatever the details of the exchange, Cartier moved into the Plant mansion in 1917 and has remained there ever since, making only cosmetic changes to the building's exterior. It offers a rare glimpse of Midtown 5th Avenue's more rarefied residential past. Morton Plant died in 1918, but Maisie lived until 1956. Her "dust-filled house of romantic memories"[124] at 86th Street was demolished, its contents auctioned off the next year. Among the items sold: a pair of remarkable pearl necklaces by Cartier with diamond and platinum clasps. They brought $165,000 and have not been seen since.

From the former **Plant Mansion**, now the Cartier store, walk north along **5th Avenue** toward **Central Park**

VANDERBILT ROW

Walking north along 5th Avenue from the Cartier Store, ghosts of the Gilded Age swirl all around. From the 1880s through the 1920s, this strip of pavement was the most expensive, exclusive residential enclave the city had ever seen. It is fittingly known to posterity as Vanderbilt Row, since that family built no fewer than seven enormous mansions for themselves on the west side of the avenue between 51st and 58th Streets. Not a single one of them has survived to the present day.

The Vanderbilt family sailed to New Netherland colony in the 1640s, settling in what would later become Brooklyn and, later, across the narrows on Staten Island. There, in 1794, a boy named Cornelius was born to a family of poor but respectable farmers. Cornelius's father, also named Cornelius, farmed first at Port Richmond then Stapleton and used a crude sailboat to transport his produce to Manhattan for sale. The younger Cornelius felt drawn to the water and quickly proved adept at driving the boat himself. This would be the beginning of his extraordinary career.

In 1810, Cornelius turned 16 and borrowed $100 from his mother to buy a small boat of his own which he ran across the bay almost constantly. By day, he transported goods from market to market, and by night he hired himself out for pleasure cruises from the Battery. He repaid his mother within a year. Cornelius became known for his reliability and fair prices. He won lucrative contracts and watched his fortune grow. By 1817, age 23, he commanded half a dozen ships, earning the teasing nickname "Commodore," and boasted a bank account worth $9,000. Unafraid of innovation, Cornelius sold his fleet that year in favor of steamboats. He grew to dominate the American steam trade, even running ships to California via Nicaragua during the 1840s gold rush.

In 1846, Cornelius moved his family to Manhattan, occupying a splendid mansion near Washington Square (page 91). In his 60s, when most men of his stature might consider retirement, Cornelius instead began dabbling in railroads. At a time when many fledgling rail lines were teetering on the brink of insolvency, he sold off his shipping empire and used that liquidity to buy up the New York & Harlem, New York & Hudson River, and a slew of other train companies. In 1869, to convey the grandeur of his newly consolidated rail empire, he ordered a vast new Grand Central Depot to be built on 42nd Street, the predecessor to today's Grand Central Terminal (page 176). It opened in 1871.

By the time Cornelius died in 1877, he was worth an estimated $100 million and his rail network stretched as far as Chicago. Most of this was passed on to his son William who, along with his eight children, would come to define the opulence of the Gilded Age.

William Henry Vanderbilt was never supposed to inherit his father's empire. The eldest son of the Commodore, William was often disregarded as feckless and incapable, unworthy of being the great patriarch's heir. At 17, William began clerking on Wall Street, working ceaselessly to prove himself and earn the respect of his employers. In 1841, he married Maria Louisa Kissam, daughter of a Brooklyn preacher, and the couple formed a happy home on East Broadway, free from Cornelius's condescension.

But when William's health began to fail in 1849, he was sent to recover on a Staten Island farm. William ran the farm so well that he not only turned a profit but greatly expanded his landholdings. He was likewise successful in heading the Staten Island Railroad, greatly impressing Cornelius. When his younger brother George (long his father's favorite) died unexpectedly in 1863, William was thrust into the role of heir apparent. He, Maria, and their eight children moved back to Manhattan, into a gracious brownstone mansion on 5th Avenue at 40th Street. By the time Cornelius died in 1877, this formerly scorned son's redemption arc was complete.

Of the Commodore's $100 million estate, more than $90 million went directly to William. Unfortunately, this effectively cut out his dozen siblings, several of whom sued William for a larger piece of the fortune. The ensuing court battle was bitter and humiliating for the family, with their personal grievances aired in newspapers across the nation. His relationship with his siblings never fully healed, and largely because of this, he decided to split the family fortune more evenly among his children. This allowed them all to live lavishly during the Gilded Age, but also began the gradual breakup of the Vanderbilt empire which would diminish precipitously through the ensuing generations.

Building their way to social primacy, William and his children built a row of colossal new mansions between Bryant and Central Parks, outstripping in opulence anything the city had yet seen. The largest of these was William's so-called "Triple Palace" which occupied the entire western blockfront of 5th Avenue between 51st and 52nd Streets. Completed in 1882, it was a sprawling brownstone interpretation of a Venetian palazzo designed by John B Snook and Charles B Atwood. William, Maria, and their youngest son, George, occupied the southern half, while his two eldest daughters,

Margaret Shepard and Emily Sloane, and their families, split the northern half.

Across 52nd Street from the Triple Palace, William's second son, William Kissam Vanderbilt, and his wife, Alabama-born Alva Erskine Smith, hired Richard Morris Hunt to design for them a splendid "Petit Chateau" made of nearly white Indiana limestone. This house marked a major aesthetic leap forward for the city, shifting popular taste decidedly away from the darker hues of traditional brick and brownstone blocks. It was in this home, in March of 1883, that Alva threw perhaps the most famous costume ball of the Gilded Age, one which helped launch the Vanderbilts to the forefront of high society.

One block north of William K and Alva's Petit Chateau, next to St Thomas Episcopal Church, stood two more Vanderbilt mansions, these belonging to William Henry's younger two daughters, Florence Twombly and Eliza Webb, and their families. These attractive, many-turreted townhouses are less well remembered than other Vanderbilt houses but did much to extend the family's presence along 5th Avenue.

Lastly, on 5th Avenue at the northwest corner of 57th Street, stood the red-brick chateau of the family's eldest son, Cornelius II, his wife Alice, and their children. As originally constructed in 1883, Cornelius's house was large but not otherwise overly remarkable. This would change following the premature death of patriarch William Henry in 1885.

In the eight years between the Commodore's death in 1877 and William's death in 1885, the latter's dedication and hard work as head of the family doubled his inheritance to more than $200 million. Possibly due to the stress of such responsibility, he died at age 64, passing the mantle of leadership to Cornelius II. In order that his home might better reflect his new, more public and highly scrutinized role as head of the Vanderbilt family, Cornelius purchased the rest of the blockfront between 57th and 58th Streets, cleared the land, and expanded his chateau at No. 1 West 57th Street into the largest single-family home ever constructed in the city's history.

Like his father, Cornelius II didn't get to enjoy his place at the top of the family for long. He died in 1899 following a series of strokes, aged just 55. His widow, Alice, remained in the home with their younger children who one by one married and moved away. By the 1920s, owning and operating such massive houses as the Vanderbilts' was becoming increasingly unappealing. Not only had World War I heralded the imposition of a slate of new taxes which broke apart such familial empires, but commercialism had begun to push into the area, making 5th Avenue an increasingly unpleasant place for a home. Additionally, increased automobile use in the city necessitated the widening of the avenue in 1911, which stripped the area's mansions of their stoops, gardens, and other decorative projections. Not only was this costly and inconvenient, but it eliminated any protective barrier between home and sidewalk, allowing tourists and passersby to peer directly into families' windows.

All this is to say that, by the 1920s, the Vanderbilts and their Gilded Age neighbors on 5th Avenue began to one by one sell off their homes in favor of the peace, privacy, and economy of country estates and high-rise apartments. Never again would such architectural opulence be concentrated in one place like this. By the time the Great

Depression began in 1929, all but one of the Vanderbilt mansions which had made up "Vanderbilt Row" had been demolished, each replaced by the sort of larger, more lucrative commercial towers which now define the avenue.

The last to go was William Henry and Maria's half of the Triple Palace at the corner of 51st Street. It hung on until 1947, before it, too, met the wrecking ball, signaling the end of the Gilded Age in Midtown. "The sound of sledge-hammers and creaking timbers marked the passing of the costly landmark that for nearly 70 years had stood as a symbol of residential luxury in the old New York style."[125]

Walk to the fountain in front of the Plaza Hotel at **58th Street** and **5th Avenue**

54th Street from MoMA

PULITZER FOUNTAIN

This walk ends at the Pulitzer Fountain outside the Plaza Hotel. Though the Vanderbilt mansions are gone from New York today, the Plaza was built in 1907 and retains much of the sort of glamor which Gilded Age families would have expected in their daily lives. The Bergdorf Goodman department store, which sits on the block formerly occupied by the palatial chateau of Cornelius Vanderbilt II, caters to the deep-pocketed shoppers of this century's new Gilded Age.

Plaza Hotel

0
400
800m
0
2000ft
N
START
END
The Blockhouse
Great Hill
North Woods
The Pool
Loch & Ravine
Conservatory Garden
North Meadow
97TH STREET TRANSVERSE
Jacqueline Kennedy Onassis Reservoir
86TH STREET TRANSVERSE
The Great Lawn
American Museum of Natural History
81 St - Museum of Natural History
Swedish Cottage Marionette Theatre
Delacorte Theatre
Cleaopatra's Needle
Metropolitan Museum of Art
John Lennon Memorial
Bow Bridge
The Boathouse
Tavern on the Green
Former Bandstand Site
Naumburg Bandshell
Site of Former "Casino"
Sheep Meadow
THE MALL
65TH STREET TRANSVERSE
The Dairy
Central Park Zoo
Delacorte Clock
Wollman Rink
Sherman Statue
5 Av/59 St
Lexington Av/63 St
68 St Hunter College
72 St
77 St
86 St
96 St
103 St
79 St
CENTRAL PARK WEST
COLUMBUS AVENUE
AMSTERDAM AVENUE
BROADWAY
RIVERSIDE DRIVE
WEST DRIVE
EAST DRIVE
CENTER DRIVE
5TH AVENUE
MADISON AVENUE
PARK AVENUE
LEXINGTON AVE
3RD AVENUE
2ND AVENUE
1ST AVENUE
YORK AVENUE
FDR DRIVE
CENTRAL PARK STH
WEST 57TH ST
WEST 72ND ST
WEST 79TH ST
WEST 86TH STREET
EAST 72ND STREET
EAST 79TH ST
EAST 86TH ST

Central Park is perhaps the greatest work of art ever created in the United States. From Bethesda Terrace to Harlem Meer, every inch of its landscape was specifically designed to surprise, delight, and cradle untold generations of New Yorkers in the leafy bosom of nature. Masterminded by landscape architect Frederick Law Olmsted and his partners, Calvert Vaux and Jacob Wrey Mould, Central Park is a masterpiece unlike anything previously conceived. It would redefine the very meaning of parkland and landscape manipulation. This walk, stretching nearly the full length of the park, attempts to illuminate the genius behind the greensward.

CENTRAL PARK

ROUTE STOPS

1. 59th Street and 5th Avenue
2. The Arsenal on 5th Avenue
3. Goat Wall
4. Balto Statue and Willowdell Arch
5. The Mall
6. Bethesda Terrace
7. Bow Bridge and the Ramble
8. Belvedere Castle
9. Shakespeare Garden and Swedish Cottage Marionette Theater
10. Seneca Village
11. Jacqueline Kennedy Onassis Reservoir
12. The Ravine and Loch
13. The Pool

DISTANCE

more than 3+ miles (more than 5+ km)

TIME ALLOWED

2–4 hours depending on pace and preference

ROUTE No.

A PARK FOR THE PEOPLE

The germ of an idea to build Central Park began in the 1840s, at a time when New York City's population was growing exponentially thanks to the completion of the Erie Canal and the Croton Aqueduct system. Manhattan's population had more than tripled to 312,710 residents between 1820 and 1840. It would surpass one million by the early 1870s. Prior to the 1840s, however, the need for parkland in the city was not seen as a pressing matter. Much of Manhattan Island remained open fields and bucolic pastureland. In a city so driven by monetary gain, to carve out space specifically for recreation seemed wasteful if not ridiculous.

But by the 1840s, whole swaths of Manhattan were being consumed by expanding development, and city leaders at last began to recognize how imminently life on the island might be choked out by brick and asphalt if action wasn't taken soon. The pocket parks found downtown, like the Battery, City Hall Park, Washington Square, and Madison Square, were insufficient to the needs of the sort of metropolis New Yorkers now anticipated their city would become. The first proposal for a permanent uptown park was for the city to acquire a beloved parcel known as Jones Wood. But at 150 acres (60 hectares), it was decried as too small. Further, it was located on the East River between 66th and 75th Streets, considered too far from the majority of the island to be convenient or useful.

Instead, in 1853, New York's Common Council approved the acquisition of a vast rectangular tract of land at the island's center, encompassing everything between 5th and 8th Avenues from 59th Street to 106th Street (later extended to 110th). Much of the property taken for the park was part of the "common lands" already owned by the city, but roughly 1,800 people were evicted from privately owned parcels, including the residents of Seneca Village on the west side near 86th Street and those of the Academy of Mount St Vincent on the east side near 105th.

"The process to create Central Park was an almost endless battle," wrote Sara Cedar Miller, park historian emerita for the Central Park Conservancy. "Properties had to be evaluated, landowners' petitions had to be heard, the Supreme Court had to approve the commissioners' reports, and the City of New York had to take the land through eminent domain."[126] It took four years to acquire and clear the land. Finally, in 1856, exponentially over budget, the daunting tasks of surveying the terrain and planning the park landscape could begin.

It is a mistake to believe that Central Park is in any serious way a reflection of Manhattan's primeval appearance. The land that would become Central Park was among the swampiest, rockiest, and least attractive on the whole island, and it would need to be molded and landscaped to within an inch of its life to become the verdant playground it is now. A design competition was held in 1858 to which 33 proposals were submitted. The last of these, handed in on April 1, the last possible day, was the Greensward Plan, devised by the Connecticut-born landscape designer Frederick Law Olmsted and his partner, the English-born artist and architect Calvert Vaux.

Vaux and Olmsted's vision for Central Park was unique in that it sought to achieve naturalistic perfection through careful curation and terraforming of the existing terrain. Every hill, path, and rivulet would be arranged to provide the greatest sense of romantic disorientation for the visitor, allowing them to momentarily forget city life and lose themselves in nature. This meant that virtually no square inch of the park was left untouched. Hills were leveled or added; rocky outcroppings were blasted away or crowned by rustic gazebos; marshes and creeks were dredged out to become lakes or ponds; trees, flowers, and landmarks were arrayed in such a way that visitors to the park were forever drawn further into the landscape, searching for the next delight or surprise.

Start 1 → At **59th Street** and **5th Avenue**

THE SHERMAN STATUE

There are dozens of ways to enter Central Park, but none more formal than the twin plazas at 59th Street and 5th Avenue, the park's southeast corner. Here, the gilded equestrian statue of General William Tecumseh Sherman faces off against Pomona, the Roman goddess of abundance, who surmounts the Pulitzer Fountain. The fountain, which sits directly in front of Bergdorf-Goodman and the Plaza Hotel, was designed by the architect Thomas Hastings with the statue sculpted by Karl Bitter. It was installed in 1916 as a memorial to Joseph Pulitzer (page 222), longtime publisher of *The New York World*.

The Sherman statue, meanwhile, was the last major work by the great artist Augustus Saint-Gaudens. He worked on the piece for a decade before displaying its plaster cast at the 1900 *Exposition Universelle* in Paris. It was afterward cast in bronze and installed atop a stone base designed by the architect Charles Follen McKim in 1903. The statue depicts General Sherman, the great General of the Union Army during the American Civil War, who lived the final quarter-century of his life in New York City. He is depicted on horseback, led by winged Victory. Clutched in Victory's hand is a palm frond, usually a symbol of peace, which here represents Sherman's scorched-earth march through Georgia in 1864. Additionally, there are Georgia pine branches trampled beneath the horse's hooves. Symbolically, this statue represents the brutality of that war, with Sherman a reluctant but steadfast servant to its cause.

When installed in 1903, the Sherman monument would have gazed southward toward a virtually unbroken row of grand mansions, homes for the Vanderbilts, Huntingtons, and Rockefellers, which stretched halfway down the island at the height of the Gilded Age (page 182). Today, those mansions have been replaced by great skyscrapers, hotels, and department stores, but the feeling remains similar: that of a grand and imperial crossroads between the city and its park.

From the **Sherman statue**, enter the park across **60th Street**. Walk north into the Central Park Zoo and look for the tall red-brick fortress of a building on the right. This is the *Arsenal*. Walk around to its eastern side, facing **5th Avenue**

Stop 2 → In front of the *Arsenal*

THE ARSENAL

The Arsenal was completed in 1851, more than a decade before Central Park began opening to the public, making it the second-oldest structure in the park. Only the 1814 Blockhouse in the North Woods is older. When constructed, the Arsenal sat far north of the city, appropriate for its intended purpose as a repository for explosives and munitions used by New York's numerous military regiments. But in 1853, just two years after its completion, the Arsenal was included as part of the land to be taken by the city to build a new central park which was meant to provide permanent recreational greenspace for future generations of New Yorkers.

Amid all the tumult of the park's design and construction, the Arsenal remained. Repurposed as the headquarters for the park's commissioners, it has been left essentially unchanged from its original appearance as constructed in 1851. Most charmingly, many of its architectural flourishes still reflect its original intended purpose: the entry stair rails are made up of cannons and rifles; the lights on either side of the doors are snare drums; the doorway itself is festooned with pikes, sabers, and cannonballs all surmounted by a spread-winged eagle.

Most interesting about the Arsenal, however, is the fact that, since it predates the park, it also predates the grading of neighboring 5th Avenue. While the Avenue was leveled to flatten the adjacent building lots across from the park, the Arsenal was built on the natural elevation of the island as it existed before the city caught up to it. Because the Arsenal sits so far below 5th Avenue, it is one of the only places in the park where visitors must descend a flight of stairs to reach it.

From the **Arsenal**, walk north beneath the **Delacorte Clock** (which chimes and animates every half-hour) to the goat and bunny pens of the **Children's Zoo**

Stop 3 → Near the **northern Zoo entrance**

GOAT WALL

There was a time, not so long ago really, when Manhattan was an island of goats. "Four-footed philistines"[127] they were called as they ran roughshod and unfettered across the island's rural stretches north of Union Square. Harlem, especially, was noted for its large and untenable goat population for much of the 19th century. When Central Park was being laid out in the 1850s, the goats had to factor into its design.

Fully encircling the park is a chest-high wall made of schist and bluestone with tapered

Sherman Statue

The Arsenal

66th Street Transverse Arch

Central Park Zoo

Balto Statue and Willowdell Arch

capstones. Not part of the park's original design, the wall had to be added in the 1860s to prevent goats and other wayward farm animals from wandering in to devour the new park's tender plantings. But building the park took time, and for a good many years goats easily found their way inside. Guards known as "sparrow cops"[128] were positioned at park entrances to fend them off but the goats were known to get a running start and jump over the half-finished walls.

So perhaps it was a fitting adaptation (or comeuppance) when goats were turned into a novel attraction for the new park: a herd of them, kept in the sheep paddock (now Tavern on the Green), were kept happily fed, groomed, and festooned with ribbons and painted horns and hoofs. By day, beginning in 1869, these dandy goats were harnessed into miniature carriages and driven to the park's great mall. There they carried children, who paid a nickel to ride, back and forth between the rows of benches and elm trees. The goat carriages were one of the chief delights of the park, often attracting great crowds on sunny days. The goat carriages remained a fixture of Central Park for at least 40 years, vanishing some time before 1920. By then, most of the feral goats which once roamed the island had been banished.

Today, the only goats remaining in Central Park are those kept at the Zoo. Few New Yorkers could imagine their urban jungle as a goat-infested wilderness; the lower stone wall encircling the park remains a testament to their free-roaming forebears, the four-footed philistines of a bygone era.

Continue past the **Children's Zoo**, beneath the **65th and 66th Street** transverse roads, following the leftward curve of the path past the **Native Meadow** toward the **Balto Statue**

Stop 4 → At the **Balto Statue** and the **Willowdell Arch**

BALTO STATUE AND ARCHES

Balto is among the most beloved statues in Central Park since its installation in 1925. Its flanks and face are rubbed to a brilliant sheen from countless children climbing him and countless hands patting him. The real Balto was a sled dog who made history as part of a legendary mid-winter relay which brought medicine from Anchorage to Nome, Alaska, which was experiencing a deadly diphtheria outbreak. Teams of dogs made the 674-mile (1,000-km) run in just 127½ hours in January 1925, with Balto hailed as the leader of the team which at last entered Nome without a single vial broken.

There was some controversy following the race, questioning whether Balto had actually been the lead dog which entered Nome, as well as the fact that another dog, Togo, had actually run a far longer and more difficult stretch of the route. Regardless, Balto was hailed as a national hero and his statue was sculpted by the artist Frederick Roth to be installed here in Central Park by the end of that very year. Balto was in attendance at its unveiling and actually went on to live until 1933. Today, his statue remains as a monument to all the dogs and people involved in the serum run while his body was stuffed and put on display at the Cleveland Museum of Natural History in Ohio.

Just beyond Balto is the lovely brick-and-stone Willowdell Arch. It is one of 42 arches and bridges in Central Park, each one unique in design. They generally reflect the landscape in which they are placed, with iron bridges crossing the park's bridle paths, rough-stone arches ornamenting the park's more rustic landscapes, and architecturally refined brick or cut-stone arches, like Willowdell, built into the more formal areas of the park.

Walk through the **Willowdell Arch**. On the far side, curve to the left and follow the path around and

Stop 5 → at the southern end of **the Mall**, Central Park's most formal promenade

THE MALL

The Mall is the only straight promenade in Central Park and is by far its most formal element. Throughout the rest of the park, Olmsted generally avoided straight lines altogether, preferring to disorient visitors with curves and undulation. But even he knew that 1860s New Yorkers would demand a more formal promenade for their park, a place to see and be seen. In all, the Mall is 1,212 feet (370 meters) long and 35 feet (10 meters) wide with benches all along its length for resting and people-watching. It is planted on both sides with rows of mighty, curving American elm trees.

If the park needed to have a formal promenade, Olmsted would take steps to make sure that, despite its formality, it would still provide a unique and surprising exposure to nature. To that end, he envisioned the Mall as a sort of woodland cathedral. He lined it on both sides with double rows of American elm specifically for the unique beauty of their form and canopy. When mature, their branches arch sinuously, touching from either side of the pathway high above amblers' heads like Gothic church vaulting. Dappled light streams through their leaves like stained glass. It is hard to deny that walking up the Mall in fair weather is an almost religious experience.

It is important to note that the elm trees lining the Mall are corralled by permanent metal fencing the likes of which is not found anywhere else in the park. This is to protect the trees from premature sickness and death by a vexing fungal blight known as Dutch Elm Disease, which can unwittingly be transmitted by people walking through the grass here. The American elm was once the most ubiquitous urban tree in the United States, but more than 75% of them have been killed by the blight since its initial detection here in 1928. Protected by metal fencing and vigilantly monitored by the Parks Department, Central Park's trees are the largest surviving stand of American elms on earth.

NAUMBURG BANDSHELL

In keeping with Olmsted's ecclesiastical theme, a sense of momentousness builds while processing north along the Mall. (Imagine Wagner's "Elsa's Procession to the Cathedral" playing along the way.) If the elm-shaded walkway is the church's nave, then the Naumburg Bandshell is part of the crossing and transept. The Bandshell was completed in 1923 to replace an older, Jacob Wrey Mould-designed music pavilion which used to stand where there is now a statue of Beethoven on the Mall's west side.

Though lovely in its own right, the Bandshell unfortunately blocks much of the original wisteria arbor and promenade built into the ridge behind it. Behind the arbor, where the Rumsey Playfield and Summer Stage are now, originally stood what was called the park's Casino, a Victorian-era comfort station and rest area. Built in 1864, it was demolished in 1936. Even with the Bandshell blocking the view, standing beneath the wisteria arbor affords a stirring view over the Mall. From there, it is easy to imagine what it might have been like to promenade through the park a century and more ago. Amid the hum of convivial chatter and the lilting strains of classical music, life itself passes by.

From the **Naumburg Bandshell**, walk the short distance to the top of the stairs leading down, then

Stop 6 → At **Bethesda Terrace**

BETHESDA TERRACE

Bethesda Terrace is the heart of Central Park, "the most innovative and elaborate work of civic architecture in America."[129] The culmination of Olmsted's naturalistic church metaphor, the terrace is the choir or high chapel: the most formal, most impactful, and most rewarding space in the park from which all else radiates. Ever since their initial Greensward Plan in 1858, Vaux and Olmsted envisioned a grand terrace carrying walkers down from the end of the Mall to the Lake below. But it was English-born architect and designer Jacob Wrey Mould who elaborated on their idea, transforming the terrace into something truly magnificent.

Though Mould is less well remembered than either Vaux or Olmsted, it is truly his vision on display at Bethesda Terrace. Born in 1825, he studied under noted architect Owen Jones in the 1840s, accompanying him on an extended trip to the Alhambra in southern Spain, where Mould's affinity for sumptuous Moorish polychromy was first developed. Back in England, he did some design work for London's 1851 World's Fair and soon after moved to New York to work on the World's Fair it hosted at what is now Bryant Park in 1853. Over the next three decades, he either designed or contributed to work on Central Park's Dairy, Casino, Music Pavilion, and fountains, as well as the original buildings of the Metropolitan Museum of Art and the American Museum of Natural History.

At Bethesda Terrace, Mould achieved something truly sublime. Taken as a whole, the terrace is a barrage of pleasing sensorial experiences. It is imperative that visitors take time to admire Mould's work here. The patient observer is rewarded with a never-ending feast of details. Virtually every surface is carved and virtually no two carvings are alike. Many of the sculptures are thematic, starting with the columns flanking the top of the stairs connecting the Mall to the tiled arcade below. These represent Day and Night, with Day fittingly represented on the east side of the stairs. The column's eastern face, which first catches the sun's rays each morning, depicts a deeply carved sunrise behind a cluster of sunflowers. The western face depicts a farmhouse surrounded by stacked hay and various farming implements, all representing an industrious start to the day. The southern side of the column, facing the Mall, features the most explicit symbol of morning: a crowing rooster.

The Mall

The Mall

Bethesda Terrace

Springtime, Bethesda Terrace

The Ramble and Bow Bridge

The column to the west of the stairs, representing night, depicts on its eastern face an open Bible and oil lamp. In answer to the Day column's rooster, its Mall-facing side depicts an owl and a bat, heralds of darkness. And lastly, the Night column's western face depicts a witch on a broom flying above a Jack-o-lantern and a small house with a weeping willow (a symbol of death) outside.

Descending from the Mall into the shade of the arcade below 72nd Street, the temperature drops amid echoed voices. Eyes adjusting to the dim light, they are treated to the sight of more than 15,000 elaborately colored encaustic tiles overhead, designed by Mould and executed by Minton & Co. of England (thought to be the only instance in the world in which Minton tiles are hung from a ceiling). Looking ahead, framed by the rounded arches at the far end of the arcade, the angel of the Bethesda fountain beckons visitors onward.

From the fountain plaza, the two external staircases which flank the arcade are on full and glorious display. Look closely and it becomes apparent that each of their four balustrades are themed around the seasons. Viewed from the fountain, from left to right, they depict Spring, Summer, Fall, and Winter in literal but easy-to-overlook ways. The Spring balustrade features flower buds and hatching birds' eggs, all promising warmth and new life. In the Summer balustrade, the flower buds have opened, and the foliage is lush with fruits and roses. The Fall balustrade depicts the end of the fertile season, with birds foraging in preparation for Winter, which is depicted on the westernmost balustrade with pine cones, berries, and holly leaves. The most charming element of the Winter balustrade is the inclusion of a pair of ice skates inset on the lower staircase. Ice skating was a relative novelty to most New Yorkers in the 1860s when the park opened and was one of its chief initial draws.

Aside from the terrace structure itself, the main focal point of Bethesda Terrace is the fountain. Officially titled *Angel of the Waters*, the sculptural body of the fountain was commissioned in 1863 and completed by American-born Emma Stebbins. Born in New York in 1815, Emma moved to Rome in 1856 and joined a community of artist expatriates there which included the actress Charlotte Cushman, her life partner of nearly 20 years. The terrace fountain is by far Stebbins's most famous commission and was the city's first public art commission awarded to a woman. Once the clay models for the fountain were sculpted in 1867, they were sent to Munich to be cast in bronze. Once cast, the fountain was shipped to New York in pieces, arriving in 1871.

In short, Stebbins' angel was inspired by the Biblical tale of a pool in Jerusalem which was "beneficially troubled by an angel, and bathed in by the blind, the halt and the withered."[130] New York in the 1860s was just finishing work on a major expansion of its Croton Aqueduct system which had provided clean drinking water to the city since its construction in 1842. The angel on the fountain is depicted with wings spread and hand outstretched, blessing and purifying the water below. In her left hand she holds a bunch of lilies, symbols of purity, and below her stand four cherubic figures meant to represent temperance, purity, health, and peace (the latter most fitting since work on the sculpture began during the depths of the American Civil War).

When the new fountain was finally unveiled on May 31, 1873, initial reaction was decidedly negative. A harsh account written in *The New York Times* accused the angel of resembling "a servant girl executing a polka [...] in the privacy of the back kitchen."[131] They also lambasted the angel's physical appearance including its wings, which "do not seem to have any anatomical connection with the body, but rather to have been affixed artificially, as in ballets and melodramas." Some of the negativity may have been due to the accusations of nepotism playing a role in Stebbins winning the lucrative commission: her brother, Henry G Stebbins, was chairman of the park's Committee on Statuary, Fountains and Architectural Structure and apparently saw to it that his sister be given the job.

Initial criticisms aside, the angel has silently presided over the life and bustle of the surrounding terrace for a century and a half. She has featured in countless films and television shows. New Yorkers and visitors alike have gained a warm familiarity with the angel which has become "all but synonymous with New York."[132]

Today, one of the most important design elements of Bethesda Terrace has been lost: as originally conceived, Olmsted aligned the Mall and terrace with Belvedere Castle, which should be visible beyond the treetops of the Ramble across the Lake. This was in keeping with Olmsted's picturesque vision for the park.

Having processed through the formal grandeur of the Mall and experienced the unfolding architectural and sculptural drama of the Terrace, visitors should have been enticed to push further into the landscape by the promise of the castle's romantic spires. To this end, the Ramble was carefully planted in such a way that lower-growing trees would create a sort of saddle in the canopy, revealing Belvedere on the distant horizon. Later generations of parks employees, likely unfamiliar with Olmsted's careful design, replanted much of the Ramble with whatever trees were at hand at the moment, ultimately blocking the intended vista. The Central Park Conservancy's long-range goal is to restore the Ramble, and the view from the terrace, to Olmsted's picturesque intention.

From the **Bethesda fountain**, walk northwest around the edge of the Lake toward the **Bow Bridge**. Crossing the bridge,

Stop 7 → As you enter the confounding woodland known as **the Ramble**

BOW BRIDGE AND THE RAMBLE

Part of Olmsted's genius in designing the layout of Central Park was his ability to lure sojourners ever deeper into the landscape. In order to walk from Bethesda Terrace to Belvedere Castle, one must enter the Ramble, so named because it is designed specifically to disorient. Anyone who enters the Ramble must indeed ramble about until they find their way to the other side. It is a delightful and rare sensation to be lost in the middle of a city built on a numbered grid. For a moment, it is almost possible to forget the city exists just steps away. "Here a man may sit for hours and hear no sound but the chirp and twitter of birds, the rustle of the light breeze overhead, or the far-off murmur of the town,"[133] wrote

The Ramble

19th-century author Clarence C Cook on his visit to the Ramble in 1869.

The Ramble encompasses all of the thickly wooded area between the East and West Drives north of the Lake up to the 79th Street Transverse. In truth, it is not a large geographical area, but the tangled web of forked and switched paths makes a walk through it an adventure. Particularly in summertime, when trees are at their leafy fullest, even the hum of automobiles and the surrounding city skyline – urban advances Olmsted could never have anticipated – are masked enough to allow for the sensation of being in a real wilderness. This is, as has been mentioned numerous times regarding the Park's conception, entirely part of Olmsted's plan. "The design in planting the Ramble," wrote Cook, "has been to give, if possible, the delicate flavor of wildness, so hard to seize and imprison when civilization has once put it to flight."[134] Every inch of the Ramble has been landscaped to feel like a hyper-concentrated version of actual nature. In a city and a nation barreling headlong into the industrial age, this was the closest that many New Yorkers could get to it.

Emerging from **the Ramble**,

Stop 8 → at **Belvedere Castle** and its splendid terrace overlooking the Turtle Pond and the Great Lawn

BELVEDERE

Belvedere is easily one of the most charming ornaments of Central Park. It has enchanted generations of New Yorkers and visitors alike, bringing a dash of medieval magic and romance to the middle of this great modern metropolis. That is, in essence, its original reason for being. Built from 1869–72, it is a folly, a structure built for the express purpose of pleasing the eye and decorating the landscape. Calvert Vaux, partnering with Jacob Wrey Mould, conceived of the Belvedere as the greatest of Central Park's follies.

Visible from great distances, including from Bethesda Terrace, one of Belvedere's most important functions was to help draw visitors ever deeper into the park. Perhaps more importantly, it was also conceived as a disguise for the immense, now-demolished Croton Reservoir which once occupied the area now home to the Great Lawn. Though it was a vital cog in the city's early drinking water system, the reservoir was a harsh and ugly rough-stone rectangle, a major impediment to Olmsted's naturalistic vision for the Park. Belvedere, which sits atop an imposing rocky outcropping which once formed the southwest corner of the reservoir, was meant not just to serve as a viewpoint for visitors, but also to help disguise and distract from the reservoir's unforgiving lines.

Construction began on Belvedere, a name which means beautiful view, in 1869. Despite budgetary cutbacks which scaled back its size, it opened to the public by 1872. The reservoir below was drained in the 1920s and demolished in the 1930s (famously, in the years between its draining and removal, a small community of Depression-era New Yorkers lived in a so-called "Hooverville" within the empty pit). It is rather fortunate that the reservoir's removal occurred during the Great Depression, as it meant a lack of funding for any of the more outlandish proposals bandied about regarding what to do with such a large parcel of newly available land. Proposals for the space included "airplane landing ports, radio towers, sports arenas, an opera house, underground parking garages, and even a mausoleum for the storage of motion pictures."[135] Instead, the old Reservoir was replaced by the Great Lawn, 55 acres (22 hectares) of much-used public greenspace.

By the 1970s, both the Great Lawn and Belvedere Castle were in sorry shape. Decades of neglect and overuse had left the lawn a patchy dust bowl. Belvedere was a graffiti-tagged mess, its wooden pavilions long gone, its windows smashed, and whole sections of its stonework toppled to the ground. Vandals repeatedly broke in and destroyed the weather-monitoring equipment inside. Thankfully, a concerted effort to restore the park began in the early 1980s, and Belvedere was pulled back from the brink. It reopened to the public in 1982, looking better than it had since 1872. As ever more funds poured in to support the park's resuscitation, the Great Lawn was likewise refurbished: its hard-pack sod, a legacy of the millions of gallons of reservoir water which once sat atop it, was dredged out and replaced by healthier topsoil. Today, Belvedere and its sweeping views of the lush, verdant lawn below is among Central Park's most beloved landmarks.

From **Belvedere**, descend the terrace's western stairs and follow the path to the Charles B Stover bench

Stop 9 → At the sunken stone area overlooking the **Shakespeare Garden**

SHAKESPEARE GARDEN

Hidden just off the main path below Belvedere Castle is the Charles B Stover memorial bench. Stover was an early-20th-century social activist and parks commissioner who "worked ceaselessly for the development of children's playgrounds,"[136] including Seward Park on the Lower East Side, which opened in 1903 and is considered to be the first municipally operated playground in the United States. Stover died in 1929 and a stone bench proclaiming him *Founder of Outdoor Playgrounds* was installed in Central Park in 1936.

Not only is the Stover bench a welcome spot for shady respite, but it offers a splendid view down and over the Shakespeare Garden which covers the steep hillside below. This garden was begun in 1912 by park entomologist Dr Edmond Bronk Southwick, who planted what he called "The Garden of the Heart" as a teaching tool for local school children. Planted with a wide array of flowers and herbs, it provided "a depot for nature study material, as well as a demonstration garden, as a necessary adjunct to the study of natural history."[137]

While the garden always included a section dedicated to plants mentioned in the works of Shakespeare (Professor Southwick was a fan), it was officially converted into a "Shakespeare Garden" in 1916, the 300th anniversary of the Bard's death. As such, it was sown with as many of the 180 plants mentioned in Shakespeare's works as could be procured. Though many of these died rather quickly (lemon and orange trees struggled to thrive in Manhattan's wintry climate), the garden remained a lovely and popular spot in the park for decades. It began to decline, however, following Dr Southwick's death in 1938. Not only did many of its original plantings wither, but they were too often replaced by plants Shakespeare never could have known such as "Nancy Perkins roses and fancy chrysanthemums."[138]

By the 1970s, the Shakespeare Garden was, like much of Central Park, "a vandalized ruin."[139] A complete redesign was executed in the 1980s, overseen by Bruce Kelly, a landscape architect, friend to the Central Park Conservancy, and fierce advocate for the preservation of the park's Olmstedian principles. The renewed Shakespeare Garden was unveiled in 1989, with bronze plaques scattered throughout which display Shakespearean quotes next to their corresponding plants.

SWEDISH COTTAGE

At the bottom of the Shakespeare Garden is a lovely little log cabin known as the Swedish Cottage Marionette Theater. This unusual little building actually dates to 1876, when it was constructed by the government of Sweden as their pavilion for the Centennial Exposition in Philadelphia. It was designed by prominent Swedish architect Magnus Iseus as a typical one-room schoolhouse with living space for the schoolmaster. After the Exposition, it was purchased by the New York Department of Parks for $1,500 and rebuilt at its current location to serve as an aesthetically pleasing utility shed. It was converted into a puppetry theater in 1947.

DELACORTE THEATER

Occupying the pondside hollow north of the Swedish Cottage and the Shakespeare Garden is the 1,800-seat Delacorte Theater, which opened on June 18, 1962, with a performance of *The Merchant of Venice*. The amphitheater's opening was the culmination of years of advocacy by Joseph Papp, founder of the New York Shakespeare Festival, who believed in theater "as a social force, not just entertainment."[140] As such, the Delacorte (named in honor of publisher George T Delacorte, whose $150,000 gift allowed the theater's completion) has staged hundreds of theatrical performances for millions of New Yorkers over six decades, with the night sky and the towers of Belvedere as a backdrop.

Passing the **Delacorte**, continue northward along the west side of the **Great Lawn**. Look for interpretive signs highlighting long-vanished **Seneca Village**

Stop 10 → Seneca Village

SENECA VILLAGE

The land taken to create Central Park was not an empty wasteland. Indeed, more than 1,000 people are thought to have called the area home prior to the start of construction in 1858. There were farms and gardens, a convent and schools, and a succession of taverns. But by far the most famous settlement in what is now Central Park was the small cluster of homes, schools, and churches on the west side, centered just east of 8th Avenue between 83rd and 87th Streets.

This village, occupying a high, flat ridge, was unusual for its time in that the overwhelming majority of its residents were Black. Though it existed for a mere quarter-century, it has taken on almost mythical importance in the overarching history of both Central Park and Black New York.

The town is known as Seneca Village, and interpretive plaques dot the landscape of its former location in Central Park today, helping visitors to understand and envision what the place might have been like, who its residents were, and why it appeared and disappeared with such rapidity. We don't know what became of most of its residents once their land was purchased for construction of the park. In fact, we don't even know where the name Seneca Village comes from. It is almost certain that residents of the community didn't call it that; not a single document has been found from the time of its existence which refers to it as Seneca Village. Census records and legal documents more often lumped it in with the larger surrounding Bloomingdale area, or referred to landholdings there by their street locations. It is thought that the name Seneca may have actually been chosen as part of an early design for Central Park which envisioned the landscape as a microcosm of New York State, with different sections and roads named for various counties (of which Seneca is one). But as yet, scholarship has not found a conclusive answer.

Regardless of its name's origins, Seneca Village played an outsize role in the post-emancipation rise of New York's upwardly mobile Black community. Manumission began in New York in 1799, when the state legislature ordered all children born to enslaved persons after July 4th of that year to be free. All enslaved adults were to be freed by July 4, 1827. Even as slavery ended in New York, the state's Black population faced enduring hurdles to wealth-building and suffrage. Specifically, in 1821, a law was passed requiring that a person must own at least $250 worth of real estate in order to vote. This by default excluded virtually all Black New Yorkers from the political process.

In 1825, the Erie Canal opened upstate and set New York on a course to explosive growth. That same year, west side landowners John and Elizabeth Whitehead subdivided their vast holdings into some 200 lots which they began selling off, a common scheme at the time as land speculation ballooned property values exponentially year over year. What is interesting about the Whiteheads is that they appear to have sold these lots exclusively to Black New Yorkers, helping dozens of buyers to enter the speculative real estate game, but more importantly, to obtain enough property to be able to vote. These purchases also formed the basis for what would become Seneca Village.

At its peak, Seneca Village was home to 264 people, of whom an estimated three-quarters were Black, a majority not seen in any other Black communities in New York at the time. This would have made Seneca a vital center for Black culture, education, and spiritual enrichment. Prior to its removal, the village boasted a school, three churches, and dozens of houses, some of which included multiple stories and stone-lined cellars. It was not the sort of "filthy, squalid and disgusting"[141] shantytown portrayed by the Central Park Commissioners during their survey for the park's construction in 1856. This denigration was in all likelihood a tool used to push residents out at lower purchase prices.

Jacqueline Kennedy Onassis Reservoir

Glen Span Arch

Conservatory Garden

Aside from its Black majority, Seneca Village was also home to a sizable population of Irish and German residents, many of them employees of the Croton Reservoir, which existed where the Great Lawn is now. While some families lived and farmed on the land they owned, many more Seneca Village residents were renters, making details about their lives difficult to pin down. We know that the community began to disperse by 1855, with many residents likely leaving in anticipation of inevitable eviction for the park's creation. Seneca Village was effectively erased from the map by the time construction began on Central Park in 1858.

The existence of Seneca Village faded from collective memory over the next century and was only revived in the 1980s and 1990s as city historians began to actively research it. An archeological excavation of the village's former location was executed in 2011, unearthing the stone foundations of several buildings alongside nails, iron shingles, a teapot, and even a child's shoe. Though no signs of Seneca Village's brief existence remain visible in Central Park today, these artifacts, along with continued research, shed ever more light on a place of such vital historical importance.

Walk north from the site of **Seneca Village**, crossing the **86th Street** Transverse to meet the southwestern edge of the park's great reservoir. The shortest path to the north end of the park is via the gravel bridle path which runs along the reservoir's western edge. A longer, but perhaps more picturesque route, is to join the jogging path atop the reservoir's edge and to follow it counter-clockwise around its southern and eastern edges. Regardless of the chosen path, the goal is to cross the **96th Street Transverse** via the East Drive near the North Meadow. But first:

Stop 11 → Overlooking the north side of the **Reservoir**

JACQUELINE KENNEDY ONASSIS RESERVOIR

Between the 86th and 96th Street transverse roads, Central Park is almost entirely given over to the Jacqueline Kennedy Onassis Reservoir. This enormous body of water occupies 106 of the park's 843 acres (43 of 341 hectares) and was completed in 1862 as part of an expansion of the city's drinking water system. Its curving, naturalistic shape was a welcome departure from the older rectangular reservoir which once stood atop the current Great Lawn, meant to blend more seamlessly into the park landscape. It was first drawn up in its current form in 1856, part of an early park layout proposal by engineer Egbert Viele. Though the park would ultimately be designed (over Viele's protestations) by Frederick Law Olmsted, the reservoir's shape was retained, providing the only lasting evidence of Viele's original vision.

The reservoir remained in use until 1993, when a greatly modernized water system rendered it obsolete. The next year, it was renamed in honor of former First Lady Jacqueline Kennedy Onassis, who lived at No. 1040 5th Avenue from 1964 until her death in 1994. She was known to regularly walk or jog "half hidden behind dark glasses"[142] along the 1½-mile (2.5-km) track which encircles the reservoir. In honor of her many civic contributions, including her valiant crusade to save Grand Central Terminal from demolition, this reservoir now bears her name.

At the very northern tip of the reservoir, cross the **96th Street Transverse** and follow the path which cuts directly through the middle of the **North Meadow**

Here, the tourist crowds thin to a trickle. The people walking their dogs, reading a book under the trees, playing tennis or baseball on the courts and fields, are invariably locals. There is a sense of calm familiarity in these northernmost reaches of Central Park which can be difficult to find in the more social-media-friendly landscapes below the reservoir.

Reaching the north end of the **North Meadow**, continue heading straight downstairs and through the partly hidden **Springbanks Arch**. Emerging from its shadowy tunnel,

Stop 12 → To absorb the verdant solitude of **The Ravine**, possibly the park's most stunningly beautiful and least-known landscape

THE LOCH AND POOL

The Loch, like the Pond and the Lake at the southern end of the park, was created by dredging out a naturally occurring waterway here, transforming what was originally a marshy valley into a long, narrow, slow-moving loch (hence its name). The trees here are taller and straighter than in the similarly rustic Ramble, with less brambly undergrowth to block any view of the all-encompassing woodland. Keep left as the path meets the waterway, following it to and through the imposing rough-stone Glen Span Arch. Through the arch, ascend the hill past the waterfall to the more manicured landscape of the Pool, an oval-shaped body of water ringed with paths, willows, and reeds.

From the Pool, exploring the park's northern reaches is a bit of a choose-your-own-adventure. Much of the area north of 103rd Street is consumed by the rustic landscapes of the Loch, the Great Hill, and the North Woods. In the latter, it is possible to find the Blockhouse, built in 1814 as a defensive battery in case of a British land invasion during the war of 1812. This is the oldest manmade structure in the park (excepting, of course, the 3,000-year-old obelisk behind the Metropolitan Museum of Art, gifted to the city by Ottoman Egypt and installed in the park in 1881).

It is also a supremely satisfying end to a long walk to meander downhill to the Conservatory Garden, which sits along 5th Avenue between 103rd and 106th Streets. Actually composed of three distinct gardens, one English, one Italian, and one French, this formal, fenced landscape was designed in 1937.

Wherever one's Central Park adventure ends, re-entering the city's busy streets can be jarring. There is nothing quite like the hustle and bustle of Manhattan's ceaseless urbanity to help one appreciate the beauty, ingenuity, and foresight inherent in Central Park's design. The fact that it exists at all, enriching the lives of generations of New Yorkers and visitors alike, is a minor miracle, and one which must not be taken for granted.

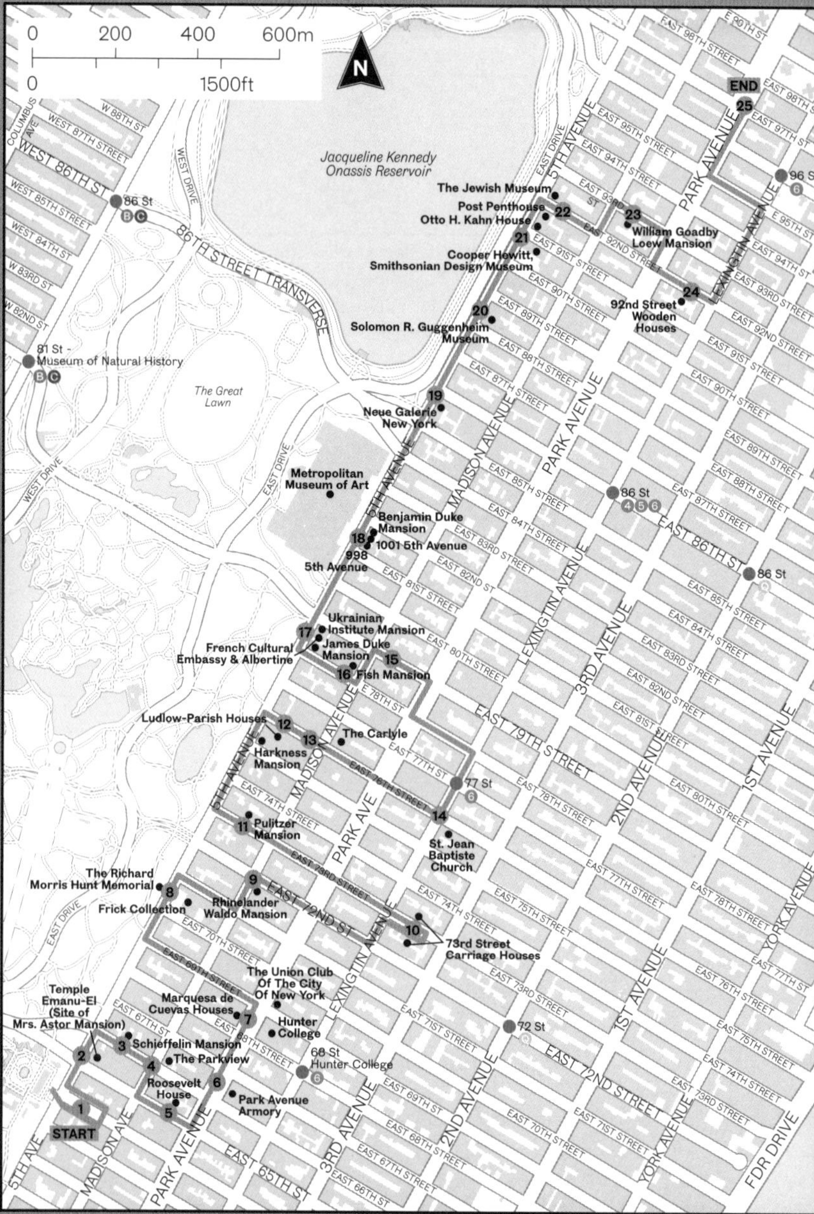

0
200
400
600m
0
1500ft
N
Jacqueline Kennedy Onassis Reservoir
The Great Lawn
START
1
2
Temple Emanu-El (Site of Mrs. Astor Mansion)
3
Schieffelin Mansion
4
The Parkview
Roosevelt House
5
6
Park Avenue Armory
7
Marquesa de Cuevas Houses
The Union Club Of The City Of New York
Hunter College
68 St Hunter College
8
The Richard Morris Hunt Memorial
Frick Collection
9
Rhinelander Waldo Mansion
10
73rd Street Carriage Houses
11
Pulitzer Mansion
12
Ludlow-Parish Houses
13
Harkness Mansion
The Carlyle
14
St. Jean Baptiste Church
77 St
15
16
Fish Mansion
17
Ukrainian Institute Mansion
French Cultural Embassy & Albertine
James Duke Mansion
18
Benjamin Duke Mansion
1001 5th Avenue
998 5th Avenue
Metropolitan Museum of Art
19
Neue Galerie New York
20
Solomon R. Guggenheim Museum
21
Cooper Hewitt, Smithsonian Design Museum
Otto H. Kahn House
22
Post Penthouse
The Jewish Museum
23
William Goadby Loew Mansion
24
92nd Street Wooden Houses
25
END
86 St
81 St - Museum of Natural History
96 St
72 St
86TH STREET TRANSVERSE
WEST DRIVE
EAST DRIVE
5TH AVENUE
MADISON AVENUE
PARK AVENUE
LEXINGTIN AVENUE
3RD AVENUE
2ND AVENUE
1ST AVENUE
YORK AVENUE
FDR DRIVE
COLUMBUS AVE
WEST 86TH ST
EAST 86TH ST
EAST 79TH STREET
EAST 72ND ST
EAST 72ND STREET
EAST 65TH ST

The Upper East Side is a neighborhood of great beauty and great contrast. It is one of the wealthiest enclaves in the nation, boasting endless stands of luxury apartment towers along its storied avenues. Tucked away on its side streets are some of the most gloriously intact rows of Gilded Age townhouses remaining in New York. East of Park Avenue, a less rarified history is on display, with wooden, brick, and brownstone houses dating back to the Civil War era. In all, the Upper East Side is a surprisingly fascinating and diverse cross-section of the city's architectural, cultural, and social history.

THE UPPER EAST SIDE

ROUTE STOPS

1. No. 3 East 64th Street
2. No. 840 5th Avenue
3. No. 5 East 66th Street
4. No. 45 East 66th Street
5. Nos. 47–49 East 65th Street
6. Park Avenue Armory
7. Hunter College
8. The Frick Collection
9. No. 867 Madison Avenue
10. 73rd Street Carriage Houses
11. No. 11 East 73rd Street
12. Nos. 6–8 East 76th Street
13. The Carlyle
14. St Jean Baptiste Church
15. The New York Society Library
16. No. 25 East 78th Street
17. 5th Avenue at East 78th Street
18. 81st and 82nd Streeta
19. Neue Galerie
20. Solomon R Guggenheim Museum
21. Cooper-Hewitt Museum
22. No. 1107 5th Avenue
23. No. 56 East 93rd Street
24. Nos. 120 and 122 East 92nd Street
25. Park Avenue at East 97th Street

DISTANCE
4 miles (6.4 km)

TIME ALLOWED
2–3 hours

ROUTE No. **09**

A CODA FOR THE GILDED AGE

When construction began on Central Park in 1858, its footprint lay more than a mile north of the city's built-up area. Development had only just begun to push north of Madison Square into Murray Hill.

It wasn't until the end of the 19th century that meaningful residential development arrived on this stretch of 5th Avenue. Even as some forward-thinking speculators threw up rows of tidy brownstones on the cheaper side streets, 5th Avenue north of 59th Street remained largely undeveloped even into the early years of the 20th century.

Though the Upper East Side is rightfully celebrated for its many grand mansions, it would be overly generous to say that the Gilded Age played out on these streets. No, the Gilded Age's headiest years took place south of the park, in older neighborhoods which have largely been swept aside by commercial redevelopment. Astor Place, Union Square, Madison Square, Murray Hill, Vanderbilt Row: these are the neighborhoods where the Astors and the Vanderbilts peacocked, where the battle between the Academy of Music and the Metropolitan Opera played out, and where great glittering parties such as Alva Vanderbilt's legendary 1883 costume ball took place.

The vast majority of this area's most notable homes were built and demolished within a generation, falling to make way for modern, more lucrative highrise apartment towers. Nevertheless, some late-stage Gilded Age mansions survive on the Upper East Side, many of them tucked away on the side streets just off of 5th Avenue, offering a glimpse of what life was like in those final glorious years of unmitigated excess before two World Wars and a Great Depression brought this gilded house of cards tumbling down.

Start at **5th Avenue** at **64th Street**, Central Park's Arsenal Entrance. Cross **5th Avenue**

Stop 1 → In front of **No. 3 East 64th Street**, now home to the Consulate General of India

CARRIE ASTOR WILSON HOUSE

These blocks, lovely as they are, are where the Gilded Age came to an end. The grand homes which comprise its historic districts today were mostly built between 1895 and 1930, as the glamor faded and fortunes dwindled. Many of the best houses on the Upper East

Side were built by or for younger generations of the city's great families, given as wedding gifts or investments. Here, the free-wheeling spirit of the Gilded Age faded into something more modern and pragmatic: still lovely but never again quite so ostentatious.

One of the best mansions to survive on the Upper East Side is the palatial townhouse at No. 3 East 64th Street. Completed in 1903, it was designed by the architectural firm of Warren & Wetmore, the same men who would be immortalized a decade later by designing the masterpiece that is Grand Central Terminal (page 176). The home was built for Marshall Orme Wilson, scion of a wealthy southern cotton-merchant family known pejoratively in social circles as "The Marrying Wilsons" for their uncommonly advantageous marital matches.

For newly wealthy families in 19th-century New York, to be labeled a social climber was among the most unforgivable sins. To aspire above one's station was antithetical to the very notion of pedigree and good breeding. One either belonged to the so-called Knickerbocracy (page 139) or one did not. Few families succeeded at breaking through: the Vanderbilts are the greatest example, having risen from unremarkable Staten Island farmers to Gilded Age supremacy. But theirs was an unusual case, and one which developed over the course of three generations.

The Wilsons rose through the ranks far more quickly, a remarkable feat by family patriarch Richard Thornton Wilson. Born a poor Georgia farm-boy, Richard succeeded as a cotton merchant during the Civil War. He and his wife, the Tennessee-born Melissa Clementine Johnston, rode a wave of postbellum wealth north to New York City, where Richard established a lucrative banking outfit. The Wilsons lived with their five children in brownstone refinement at No. 511 5th Avenue, just north of Bryant Park.

By all accounts, the family was well liked despite Society's distaste for Richard's self-made status. His children ultimately married into many of the era's most respectable pedigrees. The eldest, Mary Rita Wilson, was wed in 1878 to Ogden Goelet, heir to a storied New York City real estate empire. In 1888, middle sibling Leila "Belle" Wilson married Sir Michael Henry Herbert, later British Ambassador to the US. The youngest sibling, Grace Graham Wilson, was wed in 1896 to Cornelius Vanderbilt III, a union considered "most unsuitable"[143] due to the bride's lack of pedigree. In 1902, Richard Thornton Wilson, Jr, married Boston socialite Marion Steedman Mason.

But it was eldest son Marshall Orme Wilson's 1884 marriage to Society belle Carrie Astor, daughter of *The* Mrs Astor (page 210), that really cemented the family's status atop the New York social heap. Their marriage, called "the principal social event of the season," took place at the storied home of Carrie's parents at No. 350 5th Avenue (a site now occupied by the Empire State Building), which was bedecked with "an extraordinary display of floral decorations."[144] In addition to gifts of jewelry, fine china, and silver service, the young couple was given a home at No. 414 5th Avenue on Murray Hill, just steps from Carrie's sisters and parents.

But Murray Hill's pre-eminent position as the city's choicest neighborhood began to decline in the 1890s as commerce muscled its way in. In 1895, Carrie's mother, the formidable Caroline Webster Schermerhorn

Astor, decamped for a new mansion more than a mile north at No. 840 5th Avenue, at the corner of 65th Street. Carrie and Marshall Wilson followed suit shortly thereafter, hiring Warren & Wetmore in 1900 to build for them a new Upper East Side mansion befitting their wealth and status.

The result, as can be plainly seen today, is marvelous. Five bays wide with a massive central entryway, the house boasts three full floors clad in limestone surmounted by two additional floors tucked within a grand double-mansard roof. It is among the more imposing homes to survive from this era. Additionally, it is one of the best examples of the standard of living enjoyed by the likes of Marshall and Carrie Astor Wilson. They were among the younger generation of Gilded Age notables whose fame and wealth were gleaned more from their parents than from their own doings. This is not a slight against them; merely, it illustrates a generational difference between those wealthy elites who ruled society during the Gilded Age and those who later built their mansions on the Upper East Side. Beautiful as it is, the Astor-Wilson home at No. 3 East 64th Street represents the ending of an era.

BROWNSTONE SURVIVORS

Across from the Astor-Wilson mansion, take note of the varying styles of the townhouses present here on the south side of this block of 64th Street. Columns and mansards and bow-fronted parlors all jockey for attention, with hints of neoclassical, beaux-arts, and even Egyptian-revival architectural elements to be found among them. Most of these, with their marble or limestone facades, were initially built as speculative brownstones in the 1870s and 1880s, part of a wave of development on these side streets following the arrival of elevated train lines on nearby 2nd and 3rd Avenues.

But as ever more young heirs and heiresses followed the example of the Astor-Wilsons in the early 20th century, ever more of these old brownstones were stripped down and modernized to within an inch of their lives, producing the eclectic assemblage as it exists today. Hidden among the more modern limestone houses are a handful of brownstone survivors, including the twins at Nos. 12 and 14 East 64th Street as well as another with a gorgeous triple-height bay window down the block at No. 17. Though all three have lost their stoops, they hint at what this neighborhood would have looked like in the 1870s, decades before the young and fashionable set barged in.

Return to **5th Avenue** and walk one block north

Stop 2 → At **65th Street**

TEMPLE EMANU-EL / SITE OF CAROLINE ASTOR'S MANSION

Here at the northeast corner of 65th Street and 5th Avenue, from 1896 until its demolition in 1926, stood the home of Mrs Caroline Webster Schermerhorn Astor, better known to history as *The* Mrs Astor. The family feud which erupted over her claiming this honorific is the stuff of Gilded Age legend: her nephew, William Waldorf Astor, was so incensed that she'd taken a title which he felt by all rights belonged to his wife, Mary, that he transplanted his family to London. Back in

New York, to make Caroline's life miserable, he built the 13-story Hotel Waldorf directly next to her Murray Hill home. In response, she abandoned Murray Hill altogether, replacing her mansion there with the even larger Hotel Astoria, creating what would soon after be consolidated as The Waldorf-Astoria.

Mrs Astor's departure from Murray Hill in many ways signaled the beginning of the end for the Gilded Age. No longer would Society revolve around her stodgy brownstone palace at 34th Street. Instead, she hired the architect Richard Morris Hunt to design for her a new home, resplendent in French chateauesque detail, so fashionable at the time thanks to the influence of the new-money Vanderbilts and their many similar palaces. Her new home at No. 840 5th Avenue, completed in 1896, was in fact two residences in one: Caroline, by now a widow, occupied the southern half while her son, John Jacob Astor IV, occupied the northern half with his first wife, the former Ava Lowle Willing, and their son, Vincent.

This mansion, regrettably torn down a century ago, signaled to the rest of society, particularly those Old-Money families who'd long stayed on Murray Hill to be in close proximity to the Astors, that the Upper East Side was now ascendant. One by one, wealthy New Yorkers of good old Knickerbocker stock abandoned Murray Hill and its seemingly endless rows of brownstone for the thrill of ostentatious modernity east of the park.

Caroline Astor, *The* Mrs Astor of the Gilded Age, held court from her new home for less than a decade before declining health forced her to retreat from the limelight by 1905. She died in 1908, marking for many the end of an age. By then, Society had simply become too big and "divided into too many independent cliques"[145] to be effectively ruled by one person. Her double-mansion here at 65th Street passed to her son, John Jacob IV, better known as Jack. He took swift advantage of his staunchly anti-divorce mother's absence to end his long-unhappy marriage in 1910. The very next year, he married Madeleine Talmage Force, a beautiful socialite nearly 30 years his junior.

To escape the negative press surrounding his divorce and remarriage, and to allow time for his newly inherited mansion to be modernized for his use, Jack and Madeleine fled to Egypt and then France, where they discovered Madeleine had become pregnant. Desiring a return to the comforts of home, the Astors booked passage back to New York aboard the RMS *Titanic*. Though Madeleine survived the ship's sinking, Jack did not, making him the wealthiest man to die in the tragedy. He was buried in Harlem's Trinity Cemetery with his parents. As for his house on 5th Avenue, it passed to his son, Vincent, who sold it in 1926 to the Temple Emanu-El, which had just consolidated with Beth-El to form one of the city's most prominent Jewish congregations. The mansion, once home to New York's most prominent social leader, was "borne away in commonplace trucks," remarked *The Times*, "about each block of debris clustering recollections of an earlier day."[146] In its place rose the present edifice of Temple Emanu-El, completed in 1930 and now itself a designated landmark as part of the Upper East Side Historic District.

Walk north to **66th Street** and turn right

Stop 3 → In front of the Lotos Club at **No. 5 East 66th Street,** the William and Maria Schieffelin Residence

SCHIEFFELIN RESIDENCE

Among the very finest beaux-arts homes ever built in New York, No. 5 East 66th Street was designed by prolific Gilded Age architect Richard Howland Hunt. Completed in 1900, it was commissioned by Margaret Vanderbilt Shepard for her eldest daughter, Maria Louise, and her husband, William Jay Schieffelin, who was partner and later chairman of his family's lucrative pharmaceutical firm. He was among the fifth generation of his family to run the business and was also a direct descendant of American Founding Father John Jay. Maria Louise was a great-granddaughter of Cornelius Vanderbilt and heiress to his railroad fortune. (Her sister Edith, known to Society as Mrs Ernesto Fabbri, lived in a similarly luxe mansion at No. 11 East 62nd Street, likewise a gift from her mother in 1899. It is worth a short detour to visit this house just a few blocks away.)

The Schieffelins were among the wave of wealthy heirs and heiresses relocating to the Upper East Side as the formerly exclusive residential blocks south of Central Park were infiltrated by ever denser commercial development. Since their marriage in 1891, the couple had lived in a more traditional brownstone home on 57th Street. The 1900 census[147] found them already settled into their new double-wide mansion at No. 5 East 66th Street, which they shared with their four young children and a retinue of 10 servants. Next door at No. 3, though sadly demolished in 1933, once stood the brownstone home where former President Ulysses S Grant spent much of the final decade of his life alongside his wife Julia. With the old Grant home next door and the Astors around the corner, this would have been one of the most illustrious blocks of early 20th century New York.

It wasn't until 1946 that the Schieffelin family at last sold their mansion, one of the last great Gilded Age homes still in private hands following the tumult of World War I, the Great Depression, and World War II. It was purchased by the Lotos Club, a private social club focused on literature and the arts, which was founded in 1870. The club reopened in the Schieffelin residence the following year, maintaining it ever since with only the most minimal alterations made over the decades.

Of note, the home next to the Lotos Club at No. 9 East 66th was constructed in 1909 for publishing scion Charles Scribner. It was designed by noted architect Ernest Flagg, who also happened to be Scribner's brother-in-law.

Walk east to **Madison Avenue**

Stop 4 → To admire the handsome and heavily embellished apartment building at the northeast corner of the intersection, **No. 45 East 66th Street**

THE PARKVIEW

When completed in 1908, the Parkview would have sent shockwaves through the neighborhood. Apartment buildings were still eyed suspiciously by many of the city's wealthiest families who viewed single-family mansion living as the only acceptable lifestyle for those in good social standing.

Apartment buildings had found more fertile territory on Manhattan's west side, with luxury landmarks such as the Dakota

(1884; page 247), the Ansonia (1903; page 244), and the Dorilton (1902; page 243) introducing what were then referred to as "French Flats" to thrifty millionaires. But the Upper West Side in general attracted a more eclectic demographic, one which was less beholden to tradition and social expectations. The Upper East Side was still very much a world apart, its streetscape dominated by splendid mansions belonging to families bearing household names. And so it came as something of a shock when the 10-story Parkview began rising above the uniform skyline of Madison Avenue.

The Parkview was designed by the architectural firm of Harde & Short, who were also responsible for the spectacular Alwyn Court at No. 180 West 58th Street, completed in 1909. Like that terracotta masterpiece, the Parkview takes full advantage of its corner plot, with a rounded facade which makes it appear as a ship's prow breaking through a wave. Its facade boasts intricate Gothic terracotta tracery set off against a rich red-brick background. Inside, the building held just two apartments per floor, each containing a dozen or more rooms.

Over time, tastes changed and the Parkview has been all but engulfed by less-flamboyant apartment buildings which have risen all around. Most of its original apartments were long ago carved up into more manageable spaces, and even its original corner entrance was shifted around to a more conservative side-street location. But following an extensive restoration in the 1980s and another in the 2010s, it looks much the same from the outside as it did more than a century ago.

Turn right on **Madison Avenue** and then left to walk east along **65th Street**

Stop 5 → In front of the tidy brick-and-limestone townhouse at **Nos. 47–49 East 65th Street**

ROOSEVELT HOUSES

The extra-wide townhouse standing here was actually built as two houses cloaked by one unified facade. They were completed in 1908, with wealthy heiress Sara Delano Roosevelt living in No. 47 and her son, Franklin, living in No. 49 with his new bride, Eleanor. The young couple had only just been wed in 1905, at which time Franklin was attending Columbia Law School. He passed the New York State Bar in 1907 and began practicing in 1908, the same year he, Eleanor, and Sara moved into their new 65th Street home.

Following Franklin's polio diagnosis in 1921, 65th Street would take on increased importance for the Roosevelts. After being discharged from the hospital, the future President insisted on convalescing at the townhouse, rather than the privacy of the family's country retreat at Hyde Park in the Hudson Valley. The home's 4th floor became "the scene of the most critical struggle" in his life: "his determined recovery from the illness and his gradual resumption of an active life."[148]

As his health improved, Franklin Roosevelt re-entered public and political life, spending ever less time at his Manhattan townhouse. In 1928, he was elected Governor of New York State and never returned to 65th Street for any significant stretch of time thereafter. His mother, however, stayed on in the house until her death in 1941. The following year, it was purchased by a group of concerned citizens who gifted it to nearby Hunter College for use as classroom and event space. This reportedly delighted Franklin, who believed such usage would have pleased his mother. In that spirit, he "furnished the library at No. 47 and donated a large number of books for it."[149] The Roosevelt House, now known officially as The Public Policy Institute at Hunter College, remains a well-used and lovingly maintained piece of the school's campus.

Walk east to **Park Avenue** and turn left

Stop 6 → Between **66th** and **67th Streets**

PARK AVENUE ARMORY

The imposing crenelated red-brick edifice known as the Park Avenue Armory was completed in 1881 to house the 7th Regiment, one of the most storied state militias in American history. Armories such as this proliferated in cities across the nation in the mid- and late-19th century, built to not only house the militia itself but to provide "space for drills, stables, storage, and administrative and social functions."[150] Other armories were built prior to this one, but none did more to establish an elevated standard for their design and beauty. Designed by Charles W Clinton, the Park Avenue Armory fills the block between 66th and 67th Streets all the way back to Lexington Avenue. Inside, its offices, library, and boardrooms boast sumptuous decoration by Louis Comfort Tiffany, Stanford White, and Herter Brothers.

The 7th New York Militia Regiment first formed in 1806 and was widely known as the Silk Stocking Regiment for its well-heeled members and benefactors. The wealth behind the regiment is reflected in the beauty of its design and furnishings. "Taking the building all in all," reported *The Times* in 1880, "it is probably the most complete of its kind in the world, while the interior fittings, the finish of all the rooms, halls, corridors, &c., is so rich and elaborate that the place rather deserves the name of a military palace than a regimental armory."[151]

Architecturally, the armory remains little changed from its initial construction. The most obvious alteration was made in 1909 when a high belfry, which once crowned its central tower on Park Avenue, was removed. Otherwise, it remains an imposing presence in the neighborhood. The building remained in active military use through World War II, after which time the specter of demolition hung over it rather constantly. Happily, it was landmarked instead and now serves primarily as an arts and event space, hosting concerts, fairs, exhibitions, and theatrical productions. The Park Avenue Armory, "a very palace in point of elegance and comfort,"[152] remains a vital piece of the Upper East Side's social and cultural landscape today.

Walk north along **Park Avenue**

Stop 7 → At **68th Street**, where the main building of Hunter College presides over the east side of the street

HUNTER COLLEGE

Hunter College was established in 1870 as "The Female Normal and High School," soon thereafter renamed "The Normal College of the City of New York." Its purpose was to provide a free, high-quality education to women and girls who were at that time unable to study at the boys-only College of the City of New York. Initially housed at No. 694 Broadway, the school was granted this parcel of land on Park Avenue (then known as 4th Avenue) in 1870 and construction soon commenced on a grand new academic edifice. The new building opened in 1873 as a soaring Collegiate-Gothic affair with a high central tower and pointed-arch windows. In the rear, on Lexington Avenue, were the elementary and high schools. That structure stood, more or less intact, until it was devastated by fire in 1936.

The Normal College was renamed in 1914 to honor Thomas Hunter, the man who had served as the school's first president from 1870 until his retirement in 1906. Hunter College remained a women-only school well into the 20th century, gaining a reputation as one of the nation's pre-eminent public institutes of higher learning. When its main building on Park Avenue burned down in 1936, Hunter had already built for itself an annex campus in the northwest of the Bronx. While there was some push to relocate the school entirely to the new campus after the fire, administrators chose instead to rebuild on its ancestral site.

The new building was completed in 1940, designed in a stark International Style by the architectural firm of Shreve, Lamb & Harmon, who had only a decade before designed the Empire State Building. The 16-story tower included every modern amenity found lacking in the original building and provided space for a new library, theater, gallery space, and classrooms for 10,000 students per day across its daytime and evening courses. Mayor Fiorello LaGuardia, speaking at the dedication ceremony, called the new building "New York City's gift to girlhood,"[153] heralding it as the latest word in educational design.

Hunter College became part of the sprawling City University system which was established in 1961. In 1964, the school began admitting men as part of the overall opening up of the system's enrollment, and in 1967, its Bronx campus was spun off as Lehman College. Hunter's original Park Avenue campus remains a bustling hive of academia, with more than 20,000 students enrolled at its compact skyscraper campus.

UNION CLUB

Just north of Hunter College, at the northeast corner of 69th Street, stands an imposing limestone building, its oversized mansard roof giving it the appearance of "a Fifth Avenue mansion gone wild."[154] Since its completion in 1933, this structure has been home to the Union Club, one of the most exclusive of New York's many historic social clubs. The Union was formed in 1836 as a place where members of the city's oldest and most pedigreed families could gather to socialize, drink, dine, play cards, and smoke cigars. It also functions as a hotel, providing comfortable lodging to visiting members and guests from reciprocal clubs. It is "generally considered the cynosure of men's organizations in New York."[155]

The club moved several times in its first few years, slowly making its way uptown from Nos. 343 to 376 Broadway in 1842, then to No. 691 Broadway in 1851. It finally commissioned a custom clubhouse for itself in 1855, occupying the northwest corner of 5th Avenue and 21st Street. They remained there until 1903 when the club moved uptown again, this time to a gracious limestone edifice at the northeast corner of 5th Avenue and 51st Street, directly north of St Patrick's Cathedral and across the avenue from the Vanderbilt clan. They remained there for more than a quarter-century, finally announcing their evacuation before the encroachment of commerce in 1927.

New York's zoning laws, imposed in 1916, forbade the sort of aggressive redevelopment which had pushed the city's wealthy residents and organizations ever farther uptown. That law would "assure the club against commercial invasion."[156] And so, when the Union Club announced it would relocate to the corner of Park Avenue and 69th Street, the new location was described as "one of the largest and finest private home centres on Manhattan Island."[157] The new clubhouse was designed by the firm of Delano & Aldrich, who had already built new spaces on the Upper East Side for the Colony (No. 564 Park Avenue) and Knickerbocker (No. 807 5th Avenue) Clubs.

MARQUESA DE CUEVAS MANSIONS

The 1960s were a difficult time for New York preservationists. All across the city, beautiful and beloved architectural monuments were falling before the wrecking ball of so-called progress and modernity. Demolition began on Penn Station in 1963, on the Brokaw Mansions in 1964, and on the Singer Building in 1967. Other landmarks, including the old Astor Library (page 142) and the Jefferson Market Courthouse (page 96) came perilously close to vanishing as well. Among the more unusual bright spots during this time of architectural loss was the rescue, at the last possible moment in 1965, of a cluster of splendid Park Avenue mansions on the Upper East Side.

Filling the blockfront opposite Hunter College, on the west side of Park Avenue between 68th and 69th Streets, are four homes which were all built between 1911 and 1926. Made of red brick and marble, they form one of the most picturesque and cohesive streetscapes in the city. The houses were built by highly prominent architectural firms: McKim, Mead & White designed Nos. 680 and 684; Delano & Aldrich designed No. 686; Walker & Gillette designed No. 690. After World War II, the northern two houses were sold to the Italian government which transformed them into a consulate and cultural institute. As for the southern two houses, however, wreckers arrived in 1964 with orders to demolish them to make way for a luxury apartment tower.

As workers erected scaffolds and began wrenching out elaborate parquet floors, paneling, and mantles, it seemed New York was set to lose yet another piece of its more glamorous past. But in January of 1965, it was announced that "an unidentified New Yorker, described only as 'a person of immense good will,'"[158] had paid $2 million to acquire the houses. Demolition was immediately halted and the blockfront was saved. Dubbed the "Miracle on 68th Street,"[159] the generous act proved that it was possible and, indeed, imperative for New York's leadership to pass the landmarks bill then being debated by the City Council. It was signed into law that very April, creating the Landmarks Preservation Commission which today oversees the designation and protection of thousands of buildings of "historical or architectural merit."[160]

Those wondering who the mysterious savior of the Park Avenue houses might be needn't have looked far: days after the sale was announced, the purchaser was revealed to be the Marquesa de Cuevas, nee Margaret Rockefeller, who just so happened to live across from the houses at Nos. 52–54 East 68th Street. The Marquesa's story is one of countless tales of glittering eccentricity which define so much of the history of the Upper East Side. As a granddaughter of John D Rockefeller, she inherited a reported $25 million on his death in 1937. Her husband was Chilean ballet impresario George de Cuevas whose claim to the title Marques is up for debate. Regardless, the couple spent Margaret's inheritance traveling and funding ballet companies around the world until George's death in 1961.

As a widow, the Marquesa de Cuevas won widespread praise for saving the Park Avenue mansions in 1965. She oversaw their restoration before giving No. 680 to the Center for Inter-American Relations and No. 684 to the Spanish Institute. She remarried in 1977 and soon thereafter moved to Madrid, where she died in 1985. Back at Park Avenue, her largesse continues to pay dividends to countless modern passersby who are able to enjoy the beauty of this block which she rescued from the rubble heap.

Walk north on **Park Avenue**, turn left onto **69th Street**, and walk all the way to **5th Avenue**. Turn right and walk one block north

Stop 8 → At the Frick Collection at **70th Street**

FRICK COLLECTION

Henry Clay Frick moved to New York from his native Pittsburgh in 1905. He brought along a fortune worth tens of millions of dollars and a vast art collection which he had amassed over many years of scrupulous collecting. In New York, he rented the immense brownstone mansion at No. 640 5th Avenue which had once belonged to William Henry Vanderbilt. There, he began experimenting with how to best display his artwork for public enjoyment as he searched the city for a place to build himself a home and gallery befitting his collections.

He found such a site in 1911, when the beloved Lenox Library on 5th Avenue between 70th and 71st Streets shut down to be consolidated as part of the newly formed New York Public Library system. Frick acquired the old library, which had been built in 1877 to designs by Richard Morris Hunt and was widely considered a local landmark. Such was its importance in the pantheon of Hunt's career that a memorial to him was erected directly across 5th Avenue from it.

Dedicated in 1898, the memorial was completed in 1901 with the addition of the two bronze figures, designed by Daniel Chester French, which flank its benches. The left figure represents *Painting and Sculpture* and "holds in her hand the 'Theseus' from the pediment of the Parthenon." The right figure represents *Architecture* and holds a model of the Administration Building of the 1893 World's Columbian Exposition in Chicago, which was considered "one of Mr Hunt's masterpieces."[161] As an interesting aside, the statues were actually stolen in 1962 and sold as scrap to "the factory of a beltbuckle manufacturer."[162] Happily, they were rescued before being melted down and were reinstalled where they remain today.

But the placement of Hunt's memorial at this location here, across from the grand library he'd designed, would only remain apt for a few years. The Lenox Library, along with the Astor Library on Lafayette Street, was subsumed into the new Public Library system and was soon sold to Henry Clay Frick. In the summer of 1912, wreckers began "to tear down the heavy, dignified building," which was called "one of the most solidly built structures in the city."[163] In its place, Frick hired Carrère and Hastings, the very architectural firm who had only just finished work on the new main library building in Bryant Park, to design for him a palatial new home and art gallery.

Construction wrapped up on the new Frick home in 1914 as the press breathlessly reported his rapidly growing art collection. "Lorenzo the Magnificent of the modern world," the *Washington Herald* called him, "who now stands as the most magnificent patron of the arts in the world."[164] Frick snapped up works by Rembrandt, Vermeer, Hals, Goya, Renoir, Turner, and a set of Fragonard panels for which he had his drawing room especially remodeled. Following his death in 1919, Frick's wife, Adelaide, and their daughter, Helen, remained in the home. After Adelaide died in 1931, the Frick home was renovated to be reopened as a public art museum, which it did in 1936.

Go past the Frick Collection, turn right onto **71st Street**, left on **Madison Avenue**

Stop 9 → At the corner of **72nd Street**

RHINELANDER MANSION

On a Saturday morning in late May of 1914, a funeral was held at Manhattan's Hotel Netherland. Lying in repose there was Gertrude Rhinelander Waldo, a singularly unusual figure in New York society. Once heir to a vast fortune from one of the city's oldest dynasties, she died alone, mired in debt. Her brother Charles, "90 years old, deaf, lame and suffering from many of the infirmities of old age,"[165] was one of the few to attend her funeral, despite not having spoken to her in decades. "She is dead," he declared. "I feel no bitterness toward her memory."[166]

Gertrude's life had been dominated by her eccentric personality, her general misanthropy, and in the end, her woeful fiscal mismanagement. "Mrs Waldo was a woman of forceful manner and some unusual views," the *New York Sun* proclaimed after her death in 1914. "She had no hesitation in declaring her opinions on women's dress, art, music, and society."[167]

Her most lasting legacy today is the mansion she commissioned in 1895 for herself at the southeast corner of Madison Avenue at 72nd Street. Five stories tall and more than 100 feet (30 meters) long on the avenue, it is a mini chateau, reportedly inspired by one she'd seen on a trip to France. Inside, the home boasted enormous halls, galleries, banquet rooms, and a full-floor ballroom, as well as a bowling alley and swimming pool. She filled its sumptuous interiors with crates of furniture, art, and antiques, but never actually moved in. The mansion instead sat empty and fell into rapid decline. The stone exterior became streaked with filth, its windows broken, its immense glass rooftop dome collapsed by heavy snowfall.

The Frick Collection

Over the years, Mrs Waldo would occasionally entertain the possibility of selling her neglected Madison Avenue property, only to call off the deal at the last moment. It rotted away, becoming a derelict symbol of the passing age of New York's gilded palaces. Her death in 1914 exposed her to be deeply in debt; her home and possessions were sold off to settle her accounts.

The Rhinelander mansion gained its first residents in the 1920s when it was carved into palatial apartments. When it was landmarked in 1976, the preservation commission called it "an exceptionally large and imposing structure, its opulence a reminder of the lavish scale on which many rich and fashionable New Yorkers lived in the late 19th century."[168]

Gertrude's much-abused home was given another new lease on life when it opened in 1986, following an extensive renovation, as the new flagship store of Ralph Lauren, the New York-based fashion company. It stands today as a testament to a lost age of wealthy eccentricity in New York, when fortunes were made, inherited, and lost over generations of diamond-encrusted heirs and heiresses. For every mansion like Gertrude's which has survived today, a dozen more like it were lost to the wrecking ball of progress, and with them went a version of New York that will never return.

The Ralph Lauren store is open to shoppers, providing an excellent opportunity to go inside a real Gilded Age mansion. Perhaps more impressive is the Ralph Lauren women's store across the street at No. 888 Madison Avenue. While it appears, inside and out, to be another grand palace of a century ago, it was actually built in 2010 by the fashion company, employing time-honored craftsmanship to create a store which seems to transcend time. The coffee shop inside No. 888 is worth a visit, if only to ogle the beautiful interiors.

Walk east along 72nd Street to **Lexington Avenue**. Turn left onto the avenue, then right onto **73rd Street**

Stop 10 → Mid-block, east of **Lexington**

73RD STREET CARRIAGE HOUSES

Here on 73rd Street, between Lexington and 3rd Avenues, stands an exceedingly rare surviving cluster of carriage houses, relics from the late Gilded Age. These would have once housed the horses and conveyances of some of the city's wealthiest families who could be shuttled to their front door, dropped off safely and soundly, before their horse, carriage, and staff vanished into such stables at a respectable distance, out of sight, out of smell, and out of mind.

One perennial criticism of Manhattan's grid system is that it lacks alleyways where the many unsightly necessities of urban life might be tucked neatly out of view. In truth, Manhattan does have alleyways. Or, rather, it has streets which function as alleyways without bearing the official title. Certain streets, like this block of 73rd Street, were long ago earmarked as service corridors, given over to those uses which might offend the residents and gentility of the main residential or commercial streets nearby. Most of the carriage houses on this block of 73rd Street were erected in the 1890s to serve the many grand mansions then proliferating along 5th and Madison Avenues to the immediate west, near Central Park.

Decades prior to the arrival of mansions so far uptown, this area was largely undeveloped, with farmhouses and wooden shacks defining its landscape. The largest concentration of buildings belonged to the community known as Yorkville, centered around 3rd Avenue in the East 80s, which sprang up in the mid-19th century following the 1834 arrival of the New York & Harlem Railroad in the area. Streetcars arrived in the 1850s, supplemented by elevated train lines along 2nd and 3rd Avenues in the 1870s. Yorkville was accessible but affordable, attracting waves of less-affluent residents to its rows of humble but comfortable newly constructed homes.

"Nearly 2,000 houses were built between 1859 and 1864,"[169] including two which now stand on this block of 73rd Street, huddled between the carriage houses which later replaced their original neighbors. Nos. 171 and 175 East 73rd Street provide an exemplary idea of what this area on the south end of old Yorkville would have looked like in its earliest, more bucolic days. With their high stoops, decorative railings, and bracketed cornices, they were originally part of a matching row of "modest rowhouses" built on speculation to attract the sort of "lower-middle-class and working-class families"[170] moving to the area in the 1860s.

By the 1890s, New York's Gilded Age elite had pushed into the park-facing blocks to the west, a continuation of their perpetual uptown migration as they tried to keep ahead of the commercial redevelopment which followed them. In short order, mock chateaux and manor houses filled 5th and Madison Avenues all the way up to 96th Street, transforming the area into New York's newest social center. This brought immense change to blocks like this one on 73rd Street, which were conveniently near to the new mansions but just far enough away to allow for rarefied usage. One by one, humble brick and wooden houses east of the 4th Avenue railroad tracks were torn down and replaced by carriage houses for the elite.

On this block, all but two of the original working-class houses were demolished by 1900. Some of the carriage houses built in their place are quite opulent, like the neo-Flemish Renaissance one at No. 168 East 73rd Street, built for the Baylis family in 1899. Its unusual stepped-gable roofline is a romantic nod to New York's Dutch heritage, a style which enjoyed notable popularity in the 1890s. With the decline of the horse-drawn era, many of these carriage houses were adapted for automobile use. But by the 1920s, in the shadow of World War I's aftermath and the Great Depression, such private garages had become an unnecessary extravagance. Most were sold and converted into charming homes which today sell for many millions.

In all, 13 carriage houses occupy the north and south sides of this short block of 73rd Street, giving it an unusually low-scale profile. But it's the two surviving brick houses hidden in their midst which tell the richer story of this neighborhood's early development. From such humble beginnings, the Upper East Side and Yorkville have become some of the world's wealthiest enclaves. No. 171 East 73rd Street, built for working-class families, is currently listed for more than $13 million.

Walk west along **73rd Street**, crossing **Lexington**, **Park**, and **Madison Avenues**

Stop 11 → At the immense **Venetian palazzo** at **No. 11 East 73rd Street**

PULITZER MANSION

The transition of the Upper East Side from a far-flung working-class neighborhood into an elite enclave of the city's wealthiest and most influential titans is exemplified by this enormous mansion on the north side of 73rd Street. Completed in 1903, it replaced five normal-sized townhouses which had been built here in the 1870s, barely three decades prior. The new home was designed by Stanford White, who modeled it on numerous 17th-century Venetian palazzi in a style which is also evident in the cast-iron facades of SoHo, including most notably the EV Haughwout Building at Broadway and Broome Street (page 46). Here, instead of iron, White employed more luxurious limestone, creating a beautifully light and balanced mansion whose symmetrical facade is centered on a gracious triple-wide entryway.

The man for whom Stanford White built this palazzo was Joseph Pulitzer, the Hungarian-born newspaper baron whose *St Louis Post-Dispatch* and *New York World* ushered in an era of journalistic sensationalism better known as *yellow* or *tabloid* journalism. Pulitzer commissioned this new structure in 1901 after his previous home at No. 10 East 55th Street burned down. Pulitzer had a longstanding fixation on and devotion to the number 10, and his new home would not deviate from that. It would replace Nos. 7, 9, 11, 13, and 15 East 73rd Street. By Pulitzer's eccentric calculations, "Seven plus nine, plus eleven, plus thirteen, plus fifteen, equals fifty-five; and five plus five equals ten."[171] Even 73rd Street was hand-selected, as 7 plus 3 equals 10. It was, to Pulitzer's mind, a highly auspicious location.

Pulitzer retained the home as his primary residence until his death in 1911. In his will, he endowed journalism programs at the University of Missouri and Columbia University, both of which are among the oldest and most prestigious such programs in the world. Additionally, he set aside funds for the creation of the Pulitzer Prize for Journalism (now also awarded for various achievements in arts and letters) which were first distributed in 1917.

As for his home on 73rd Street, it was retained for use by his widow, Kate, and their son, Ralph, who lived next door at No. 17. After Kate's death in 1927, the home's furnishing and art collection were sold off and in 1934, it was announced that the mansion in which Stanford White had taken "personal pride" in designing would soon "go the way of many other dwelling landmarks in the Fifth Avenue area"[172] and be demolished to make way for a modern highrise. Instead, the home was carved up into palatial apartments which largely preserved its splendid interiors intact.

Walk west to **5th Avenue** and turn right. Walk north, with **Central Park** on the left.

As you go, take note of Nos. 925 and 926 5th Avenue, two delicate yellow-brick townhouses designed by renowned architect CPH Gilbert and completed in 1899.

At the corner of 75th Street, take note of the Edward S Harkness mansion, built in 1907 of brilliant white Tennessee marble. Harkness was the primary beneficiary of his father's early

Temple Emanu-El

Pulitzer Mansion

East 76th Street

Fish Mansion

Ukrainian Institute

investments in Standard Oil, making him one of the wealthiest men in the nation. Today, the home is occupied by the Commonwealth Fund, a charitable organization founded in 1918 by Harkness' mother, Anna.

Turn right onto **76th Street**

Stop 12 → In front of the light-brick twins at **Nos. 6–8 East 76th Street**

LUDLOW-PARISH HOUSES

Of the many spectacular mansions and rowhouses which populate the side streets of the Upper East Side, these two at Nos. 6–8 East 76th Street do not immediately stand out. Built of gray brick and limestone, their style is more muted than was typical for the city's moneyed elite when they were completed in 1896. The two homes were designed by the firm of Parish & Schroeder for Edward Ludlow and his wife, Margaret, both of whom came from old and illustrious New York families. The Ludlows lived in No. 6 and gave No. 8 to their daughter, Susan, and her husband, wealthy banker Henry Parish, Jr.

In addition to claiming blood ties to the Livingston family, one of the oldest and wealthiest dynasties in the Hudson Valley, the Ludlows and Parishes were also related to the Roosevelts through Margaret's brother, Valentine Hall, whose daughter, Anna, married Elliott Roosevelt. Anna and Elliott both died tragically young less than two years apart, she in 1892 at age 29 and he in 1894 at age 34. Their children, Eleanor and Gracie, were thereafter taken in by the Ludlows and Parishes of 76th Street.

A decade later, Eleanor Roosevelt was introduced to her distant cousin, Franklin Delano Roosevelt, and the pair were engaged in 1903. Their marriage took place here at the Parish-Ludlow mansions on March 17, 1905. Without a father to walk her down the aisle, Eleanor was given away by her uncle, President Theodore Roosevelt. In 1908, the young couple moved into a new double-mansion on 65th Street which they shared with Franklin's mother, Sara (page 213). Franklin would, of course, also go on to become President of the United States, with Eleanor as his First Lady, serving from 1933 until his death in 1945. Together, they ran the nation for more than a decade, longer than any other pair in American history. Their union began right here on 76th Street.

Walk east along **76th Street**

Stop 13 → At **76th** and **Madison**

THE CARLYLE

At Madison Avenue, look up at the Carlyle Hotel, one of the tallest structures on the Upper East Side. Built in 1929, "its towering form and crisp art deco detailing command attention and admiration."[173] Over nearly a century, the Carlyle has hosted an exhaustive list of the world's richest, most famous, and most powerful figures. Everyone from John F Kennedy and Marilyn Monroe to Michael Jackson and Princess Diana have walked its corridors. Its Bemelmans Bar was a favorite of Anthony Bourdain; Broadway legend Elaine Stritch lived at the hotel for nearly a decade prior to her death in 2014. Her farewell cabaret performance at the Café Carlyle was attended by Tom Hanks, Tony

Bennett, Liza Minnelli, and a host of other luminaries. The Carlyle remains a beacon of glitzy excitement in the middle of an otherwise buttoned-up neighborhood.

Walk east along **76th Street**, across **Park Avenue** to **Lexington Avenue**

Stop 14 → At **76th** and **Lexington**

CHURCH OF ST JEAN-BAPTISTE

The southeast corner of Lexington Avenue and 76th Street is dominated by the "ordered but vital monumentality"[174] of the Catholic Church of St Jean-Baptiste. Its dome rises 180 feet (55 meters) above the sidewalk behind twin bell towers and a flank of granite columns topped by finely carved Corinthian capitals. The church was completed in 1913 for a congregation which had been established in 1882 to serve the sizable Francophone population of Yorkville. Funding for its construction was provided by wealthy financier Thomas Fortune Ryan who, along with his wife Ida, gave prodigiously to build religious, medical, and academic buildings across the nation. The aim was to produce a church building which might rival the grandeur of St Patrick's on 5th Avenue and, in its way, St Jean-Baptiste succeeds. Its interior, recently restored, is among the most splendid spaces in New York.

Walk north along **Lexington Avenue** to **78th Street**. Turn left onto **78th Street** and walk to **Park Avenue**. Turn right onto **Park Avenue** and walk to **79th Street**, then turn left again

Stop 15 → In front of **No. 53 East 79th Street**, the New York Society Library

SOCIETY LIBRARY

The New York Society Library is far older and more historic than any building it occupies. This is not a claim made lightly, especially considering that the library is currently housed within a dignified limestone mansion "of exceptional character and distinction,"[175] built in 1917 to designs by the renowned architectural firm of Trowbridge & Livingston. The library, by comparison, was established in 1754 as one of the first such institutions in New York. It began as a subscription library housed within Colonial Hall down on Wall Street (page 21) and received an official charter from King George III in 1772.

During New York's brief stint as the national capital in 1785–90, the newly formed House and Senate first assembled within Colonial Hall, renamed Federal Hall. Thanks to its proximity, the Society Library became the first *de facto* Library of Congress. In 1789, George Washington was inaugurated as the nation's first President on the building's upper balcony, and on October 5 of that year, he checked out Emer de Vattel's *The Law of Nations* from the library. He never returned it. It wasn't until 2010, 221 years later, that representatives from Washington's home, Mount Vernon in Virginia, presented the Society Library with a replacement copy of the volume. The library does not plan to collect any late fees, which by some estimates would have amounted to more than $300,000 accounting for inflation.

The Society Library thrived and its collection grew exponentially. After relocating several times, it moved in 1856 into a large, modern new building at No. 109 University Place. It remained there until 1937, when it moved into its current quarters. For now, the Society Library seems content here and has recently begun a renovation project which will greatly expand the storage capacity of its already ample stacks. As it approaches its 300th year, New York's oldest library remains committed to making knowledge and literature publicly accessible. While it is a membership-based institution, anyone is welcome to enter the building and make use of its reading room, which provides free internet, periodicals, and access to the library's extensive catalog of books, any of which a librarian will bring out for perusal.

Walk west to **Madison Avenue** and turn left

Stop 16 → At **No. 25 East 78th Street**

FISH MANSION

Take a brief stop at this light, restrained home which was built in 1898 to designs by Stanford White for that indomitable Gilded Age figure, "the holy terror of New York Society,"[176] Mamie Fish. Mrs Fish and her husband Stuyvesant moved here after more than a decade spent living on Gramercy Park (page 148) as part of the overall uptown shift of the city's wealthy elite. Compared to many contemporary mansions, the new Fish home was rather small, being only two bays wide on the avenue. But Mamie ordered the home designed first and foremost to impress visitors, with its imposing entrance set within the building's broad street facade. Inside, White created for the Fish some of the city's most extravagant rooms, with a marble-covered entry hall and one of the largest private ballrooms ever seen.

Mamie Fish entertained lavishly and regularly within this house until her death in 1915. Her chief desire for her home and fetes, as she was wont to announce often and with relish, was for them to be "an uncomfortable place for anyone without breeding."[177] Since 2006, the Fish home has been occupied by Bloomberg Philanthropies, the charitable organization of former Mayor Michael Bloomberg.

Walk west along **78th Street**

Stop 17 → At the corner of **5th Avenue**

78TH–79TH STREET MANSIONS

The blocks of 5th Avenue which line the east side of Central Park have historically been some of the most valuable real estate in the nation. They were first developed in the 1890s with the extravagant mansions of New York's Gilded Age titans, but by the 1920s, tastes had changed. The costs associated with building and maintaining a private home seemed less and less sustainable, and an ever-higher percentage of the population began to prefer living in modern apartment towers. Developers took quick advantage of this shift, buying up white-elephant mansions for pennies on the dollar, demolishing them, and replacing them with dozens of units which yielded exponentially higher profits for them.

With this in mind, it is truly extraordinary that the block of 5th Avenue between 78th and 79th Street remains intact, with four grand Gilded Age mansions still standing together, just as they have for more than a century. The oldest of the group, at No. 2 East 79th Street, is the Isaac Fletcher House, completed in 1899 to designs by CPH Gilbert. Today, it houses the Ukrainian Institute. Next to it, at No. 973 5th Avenue, is the 1905 Louis Stern Residence, designed by McKim, Mead & White. It remains a private home, recently listed for $58 million.

Next to the Stern Residence, at No. 972 5th Avenue, is the 1906 Payne Whitney House, also designed by McKim, Mead & White. Its original occupants were William Payne Whitney and his wife, Helen, whose sister-in-law was Gertrude Vanderbilt Whitney, founder of the Whitney Museum of American Art. Helen remained in the home until her death in 1944 and, in 1952, it was sold to the Republic of France, which uses it as the Cultural Services branch of its US Embassy.

The last of this mansion grouping to be complete is also its largest, located at No. 1 East 78th Street, which replaced an older mansion which had stood on the site since the 1880s. This new mansion was completed in 1912 as the home of tobacco heir James Buchanan Duke and his second wife, Nanaline. Designed by architect Horace Trumbauer, it is based closely on Château Labottière in Bordeaux. Its limestone facade is "of an unusually fine quality, suggesting marble."[178]

From humble beginnings, the Duke family built a vast tobacco empire in North Carolina after the American Civil War. Their rags-to-riches story saw James lauded as "one of the last of the log-cabin successes of American life."[179] Today, the Dukes are perhaps best known as the namesakes of Duke University. Around the time construction began on his 5th Avenue home, James controlled roughly 90% of the American cigarette market. James made this his primary residence until his death here in 1925, after which it was retained by his widow, Nanaline, and their daughter, the legendary socialite Doris Duke. In 1958, Doris and Nanaline gifted the home to NYU, which now uses it as their Institute of Fine Arts.

Cross to the western side of **5th Avenue** and walk north to **81st Street**

Stop 18 → Between **81st and 82nd Streets**, in front of the Metropolitan Museum of Art

BENJAMIN DUKE MANSION

Compared to the block between 78th and 79th Streets, with its cohesive row of mansions, the block between 81st and 82nd Streets is a jumble of heights, styles, and materials. Here, the impact that highrise construction has had on 5th Avenue is on full display, with just one single-family home remaining from the neighborhood's Gilded Age heyday. That home, at No. 1009 5th Avenue, was once part of a row of four similarly ornate mansions built on speculation in 1901. Its first resident was tobacco magnate Benjamin Newton Duke, who moved to an even newer mansion at 89th Street in 1909. Following his departure, the home was occupied by Benjamin's brother, James, who remained here until his own mansion was completed a few blocks away (page 227). After passing through multiple generations of Duke family ownership, the home was sold in 2006 and has traded hands several times since. Most recently, it was purchased in 2010 by the billionaire telecommunications magnate Carlos Slim.

NO. 1001 5TH AVENUE

Though now protected by landmark status, No. 1009 5th Avenue came perilously close to demolition in the 1970s, when developer Peter Kalikow tore down its three neighbors over the years-long objection of city preservationists. In their place rose the aggressively modern apartment tower at No. 1001, which was designed by Philip Johnson and John Burgee. In 1979, as the building neared completion, it was skewered by legendary *Times* architectural critic Ada Louise Huxtable, who categorized it as "Architectural Pathetic Fallacy." In attempting to blend such an "out-of-context, out-of-scale, discordant structure" with its more historic neighbors, its designers attempt to recall certain surrounding details. "In actual practice, this is almost always hogwash, with results ranging from well-intentioned bungling to pious hypocrisy."[180]

NO. 998 5TH AVENUE

Compare No. 1001 to the 12-story masterpiece next door at No. 998. Completed in 1912 to designs by McKim, Mead & White, it is considered the first modern apartment building to be constructed on this stretch of 5th Avenue. It helped usher in an era of great upheaval, with ever more millionaires eschewing mansion life in favor of such modern, well-appointed towers as this. The apartments here were palatial, with just 15 units in the whole building, some of them encompassing 9,000 square feet (835 square meters) of living space. This "exceptionally handsome" building attracted members of "families who had previously resided in private town houses" but who "decided that for convenience, and often for economic reasons, that it would be more advantageous to live in an apartment house."[181] Within a generation, buildings like No. 998 would dominate the 5th Avenue skyline.

Turn around to face the grand entry stairs of the Metropolitan Museum of Art

METROPOLITAN MUSEUM OF ART

The middle decades of the 19th century saw the flower of New York's Gilded Age begin to bloom. Fantastically wealthy families sought to flex their economic muscle in ways which would simultaneously establish their own positions within Society and cement this city's reputation, then just beginning to emerge, as a cosmopolitan metropolis on par with London, Paris, and Rome. To that end, grand civic buildings and institutions sprang up all across Manhattan. Among the most promising was the so-called Metropolitan Museum of Art, which was incorporated in 1870, opened to the public in 1872, and moved to its current location within Central Park in 1879.

As it currently stands, the Met is a sprawling jumble of galleries and wings designed and built over the course of more than a century. The building is "a microcosm of 150 years of American architectural history," explained museum curator and historian Morrison Heckscher in 2020. "Its classical Fifth Avenue facade masks a Victorian Gothic core and modernist 20th-century extremities, the residue of five master plans and the ministrations of more than a dozen architects."[182] The original structure was a brooding red-brick affair designed by Calvert Vaux and Jacob Wrey Mould, fittingly also the designers of Central Park's architectural elements. But its style had fallen from favor even before it opened, and the building received scathing reviews.

Later expansions of the museum were overseen by Richard Morris Hunt, whose design for a grand new 5th Avenue entrance is the one still in use today. Following Hunt's death in 1895, McKim, Mead & White did some work on the museum, but the outbreak of World War I stymied their vision after just five wings were built. In 1942, the Whitney Museum planned to move into its own wing at the Met but pulled out of the deal in 1948. Much of the following two decades were focused on renovations rather than expansions. Finally, in 1970, Connecticut-based architectural firm Roche-Dinkeloo (successor firm to Eero Saarinen) unveiled a decidedly modern master plan, which included massive glass-clad new wings for the museum's Egyptian, American, African, and Modern art collections. These expansions, completed between 1975 and 1990, gave the museum some of its most iconic gallery spaces.

Incredibly, though, the Met remains unfinished, a fact on quite public display if one knows where to look. On the building's 5th Avenue facade, directly above the pairs of enormous Corinthian columns which flank its main entrance, sit four uncarved piles of stone blocks. These piles, installed as part of Richard Morris Hunt's design scheme, were intended to be carved into sculptural groupings representing Egyptian, Greek, Roman, and Modern eras of art. Budgetary concerns, as well as disagreement over just how "Modern" art should be represented, meant the groupings were never sculpted. The limestone piles remain in place, unfinished, and with no plans to ever carve them.

Today, the museum's greatness is easy to quantify with its many superlatives: more than 1.5 million objects and artworks occupy its 2 million square feet (186,000 square meters) of space, with more than five million guests visiting each year. True to its original aims, the Metropolitan Museum of Art ranks among the greatest museums on earth, helping to cement New York's status as a global cultural capital. Its founders would certainly be proud.

The Met marks the start of a long stretch of 5th Avenue known colloquially as Museum Mile. The moniker was conceived in the 1970s as a way to draw attention to the avenue's embarrassment of cultural riches and invite visitors to patronize other, smaller institutions in the neighborhood.

From the **Met**, walk north

Stop 19 → At **No. 1048 5th Avenue**, at the southeast corner of **86th Street**

NEUE GALERIE

The most recent addition to Museum Mile is the small-but-mighty Neue Galerie, which opened in 2001, mere weeks after the terrorist

The Metropolitan Museum of Art

Neue Galerie

Post Penthouse Driveway

The Solomon R Guggenheim Museum

attacks of September 11. On its opening, the museum was hailed as "little short of superb,"[183] with just over 4,300 square feet (400 square meters) of gallery space dedicated entirely to modernist works from Austria and Germany. Its creation was the long-held dream of founder Ronald S Lauder, son of cosmetics mogul Estée Lauder, and of prominent art collector Serge Sabarsky, and it has become one of the brightest jewels in New York's cultural crown.

Perhaps its most famous work is Gustav Klimt's *Portrait of Adele Bloch-Bauer I,* which was stolen by the Nazis in 1941 and ended up at Vienna's Galerie Belvedere. In 2006, after years of legal battle, the portrait was handed over to Maria Altmann, one of the last of the surviving Bloch-Bauers, who then sold it to Lauder and the Neue Galerie, where it hangs in pride of place to this day. Ms Altmann's saga was the subject of the 2015 film *Woman in Gold.*

The Neue Galerie occupies a stately brick-and-limestone mansion which was built in 1914 and was among the last single-family homes to go up on the avenue. It was designed by the firm of Carrère & Hastings for wealthy capitalist William Starr Miller II and his wife Edith. Following her death in 1944, the house was sold to Grace Wilson Vanderbilt, who is considered one of the last great social hostesses of New York's Gilded Age. Finally, in 1994, the home was purchased by Lauder and Sabarsky, laying the groundwork for its second act as a world-class museum.

Walk north along **5th Avenue**

Stop 20 → At **88th Street**

THE SOLOMON R GUGGENHEIM MUSEUM

This iconic, otherwordly white spiral fills the block up to 89th Street. Solomon Robert Guggenheim was born in Philadelphia in 1861, the son of Swiss-born Meyer Guggenheim, who made his fortune in the mining bonanza of mid-19th century Colorado. Solomon began collecting art in the 1890s and by the 1920s, he had become enamored with the new modern art styles emerging in Europe. His collection growing, in 1937 he created the Solomon R Guggenheim Foundation to manage and display it. Two years later, under the direction of artist Hilla von Rebay, he opened the Museum of Non-Objective Painting at No. 24 East 54th Street.

As the foundation and its collection continued to grow, Guggenheim commissioned architect Frank Lloyd Wright to design a permanent home for it on 5th Avenue. In 1945, Wright unveiled his plans for the building, which would mark a shocking departure from the neighborhood's traditional aesthetic: a huge, conical spiral, widening as it ascends, allowing visitors to view the entire collection from top to bottom in one uninterrupted stride. One goal for Wright was to make the new museum an alternative to the MoMA, which he and Rebay viewed as overly corporate. The building itself was meant to be an artistic experience.

Solomon Guggenheim never lived to see his new museum completed. He died in 1949, and in 1952, the Museum for Non-Objective Art was renamed in his honor. Meanwhile, Wright's outlandish building plan languished in the planning stages for more than a decade. The Solomon R Guggenheim Museum finally opened to the public in 1959. From day one, the Guggenheim was highly divisive, with *Times* architecture critic Ada Louise Huxtable asking "is it a museum, or a monument to Mr Wright?"[184] Wright had long held New York's architectural landscape in contempt, and it is possible that in this building he found a way to thumb his nose at the city forever.

Walk north along **5th Avenue** to the corner of **91st Street**

COOPER-HEWITT MUSEUM

The Cooper-Hewitt is a museum dedicated to design, operating under the umbrella of the Smithsonian Institution. It was conceived in 1897 by sisters Amelia, Sarah, and Eleanor Hewitt, granddaughters of the wealthy inventor and philanthropist Peter Cooper. After years of industrious planning behind the scenes, the Hewitt sisters borrowed part of the 4th floor at the Cooper Union (pages 81 and 141) and there established the Museum for the Arts of Decoration. The new museum was intended to mimic Paris's Musée des Arts Décoratifs, providing New York's artisans with "free and convenient access to the best models of decoration of all kinds,"[185] including textiles, furniture, and works of paper, wood, and metal.

Around the same time the Hewitt sisters were inaugurating their new museum downtown, the Scottish-born steel tycoon Andrew Carnegie was making plans to move uptown. After marrying quite late in life (he was 51; his wife, Louise, was 30 at the time of their wedding in 1887), it was another decade before the Carnegies welcomed their first and only child, a daughter named Margaret, who was born in 1897. Now 61 and a new father, Carnegie wished to make family his top priority, and so quietly purchased land along upper 5th Avenue. Here, he would build a compound befitting his wealth and status which would afford him the space and privacy to enjoy his golden years in domestic bliss.

Carnegie's new home was designed by the firm of Babb, Cook & Willard and was completed in 1902. It occupies the entire block front between 90th and 91st Streets. Taken along with its spacious private gardens, the house fills 20 city lots, making it one of the roomiest residential properties ever built in New York. In addition to his own parcel, Carnegie purchased the 5th Avenue blocks to the north and south of his new home so that he might control who his neighbors would be. This was rather prescient, as it also protected the Carnegie home and yard from the impending arrival of highrise apartment towers which might have otherwise crowded it out or cast it into shadow.

When the Carnegie family arrived at their new home in 1902, having come directly from the ship which had carried them across the Atlantic from Skibo Castle, their Scottish home, these blocks were considered at least a mile north of the established social boundary. The location was "remote, rural, and distinctly unglamorous," sitting surrounded by "a lemonade stand and a series of shanty-like houses"[186] close to the drop-off point where the uplands of Yorkville give way to the tidal flats of East Harlem. Its uptown location jolted Gilded Age New York and helped to pull the center of gravity northward through the blocks of the 70s and 80s.

Andrew Carnegie was lucky enough to enjoy his new home and family for nearly two decades before his death in 1919. His widow, Louise, remained in the house until her death in 1946, and thereafter it was sold by their daughter, Margaret, to become the Columbia University School of Social Work. The school remained at the Carnegie mansion until 1969, allowing it to survive the decades when so many of its neighbors met the wrecking ball. In 1972, the home was given to the Smithsonian Institution, which had recently acquired the Hewitt Sisters' Cooper Union Museum as its first location outside of Washington DC. The museum was at the time being evicted from its longtime quarters on Astor Place and the vacant Carnegie mansion seemed a fortuitous match for its new home. The renamed Cooper-Hewitt museum opened here in 1976, providing public access to one of the greatest private homes ever built in New York.

Additionally, thanks to Carnegie's purchase of the blocks on either side of his new home, this pocket of the Upper East Side is one of the most intact Gilded Age mansion districts in the city. Among the more notable homes is that of wealthy merchant Otto Kahn, which sits at No. 1 East 91st Street, directly across from the Cooper-Hewitt. The house, built in 1914, has been home to the Convent of the Sacred Heart, a private girls' school, since 1934.

From the **Cooper-Hewitt**, walk one block north

Stop 21 → At the corner of **5th Avenue** and **92nd Street**

POST PENTHOUSE

Next to the Otto Kahn mansion used to stand another mansion, long ago demolished, which was built for Isaiah Townsend Burden, heir to a vast ironworks empire. Following Burden's death in 1913, the house was sold in 1916 to cereal heiress Marjorie Merriweather Post. Just 29 years old at the time, Ms Post used the home as her New York pied-à-terre, with the empty lot next door on 5th Avenue turned into her private tennis court. In 1924, after years of negotiations, the house was sold to the developer George A Fuller, who had made a fortune building luxury apartment towers throughout the city. Post, then married to financier Edward Hutton, threw a lavish farewell ball at the home prior to its disposal, with the press speculating that they intended to split their time between a modern apartment somewhere in the city and their new estate in Palm Beach, Florida, known as Mar-A-Lago.

The Post-Huttons did indeed move into an apartment. In fact, their new home would occupy the top three floors of the new tower built in place of their old mansion by George Fuller. Spread out over 54 rooms, it remains the largest such residence ever built in New York. In addition to an endless array of luxurious appointments, including a wine room and a closet just for ball gowns, the apartment could be reached via its own private elevator, which rose from a private lobby on 92nd Street. More than perhaps any other single apartment, Marjorie's home in the sky helped to shift Society's opinion of penthouse living. Upper floors were traditionally the domain of servants and thus, even long after the adoption of elevators and skyscrapers, still largely shunned by the city's moneyed elite. This 54-room palace changed that forever.

When her lease expired in 1941, Marjorie left the penthouse, which ultimately languished on the market for a decade before being carved up into half a dozen smaller, more practical units. Today, little of Marjorie's penthouse remains intact with the notable exception of her private *porte-cochère*, the small, covered driveway built into the 92nd Street facade of No. 1107 5th Avenue. It remains a relic of the extraordinary life of a cereal heiress who lived here a century ago.

JEWISH MUSEUM

Across from Ms Post's driveway, at No. 1109 5th Avenue, stands the former home of the wealthy German-born banker Felix Warburg. Built in 1909 to designs by CPH Gilbert, it has housed the Jewish Museum since 1947. The museum expanded the house in 1994, building a new wing onto its northern side. Incredibly, it hired artisans who recreated, almost perfectly, the châteauesque exterior of the original Warburg mansion. The only giveaway, visible to knowing eyes, is a slight difference in the color of the facade stone. It stands as proof that such architecture can be achieved by modern hands and techniques.

Walk east and turn left on **Madison Avenue**. Turn right on **93rd Street**

Stop 22 → In front of the Spence School at **No. 56 East 93rd Street**

LOEW MANSION

This striking home was completed in 1932 as one of the last truly great single-family homes built in New York at the extreme tail-end of the Gilded Age. "Few town houses in the City have ever had more thoughtful care bestowed upon their design," crowed the Landmarks Preservation Commission in its 1972 designation report, "and few have ever achieved the striking elegance we find here."[187] Its stoic limestone facade and iron grillwork honor its more traditional neighbors while its concave entrance, almost Art Deco in its cleanliness, hints at the sleek modernity which had emerged in New York in the aftermath of World War I.

The house was designed for socialite stockbroker William Goadby Loew and his wife, Florence, by the architect Alexander Stewart Walker of Walker & Gillette. Walker's wife, Sybil, designed and furnished the home's interiors. The Loew family retained the home until 1956, when it was opened for public auction and sold to theatrical producer Billy Rose, who lived here until his death a decade later. Today, it houses the private, all-girls Spence School, which purchased and restored the home in 1999. Built during the depths of the Great Depression, the Loew mansion acts as a bookend to the era of the Upper East Side's Gilded Age, which arguably began with Mrs Astor's arrival in the neighborhood in 1895 (page 210).

Take note of the imposing mansion at No. 60, directly next to the Spence School. This home was built in 1931 for Virginia Graham Fair, one-time daughter-in-law of William Kissam Vanderbilt and his Gilded Age titan of a wife, Alva Erskine Smith. After decades of use as

The Cooper-Hewitt, Smithsonian Design Museum; former Andrew Carnegie Museum

Otto Kahn Mansion

92nd Street Wooden Houses

East 95th Street

a consulate, school, and art gallery, the home was sold in 2022 to a buyer seeking to restore it as a single-family home.

Walk east along **93rd Street** to **Park Avenue**. Turn right then left again onto **92nd Street**

Stop 23 → In front of **Nos. 120 and 122**

92ND STREET WOODEN HOUSES

The contrast between the Gilded Age mansions of 5th Avenue and the simple elegance of these two unlikely survivors could hardly be more extreme. Nos. 120 and 122 East 92nd Street are among a small handful of wooden houses left standing on Manhattan Island, predating the city's 1866 law which forbade wooden construction for fear of fires. The houses were likely built around 1860, when this block sat on the outskirts of rural Yorkville, and similar such houses would have dotted the dusty, goat-strewn landscape.

Separated from the wealthy mansion district which rose along 5th and Madison Avenues a generation later, they represent the height of middle-class comfort available to those New Yorkers willing to move so far uptown long before it was convenient or fashionable. Similar wooden houses may be found at Nos. 412 East 85th, 160 East 92nd, and 128 East 93rd.

Walk east to **Lexington Avenue**, turn left, and walk north to **95th Street**. Turn left and walk west to **Park Avenue**

This block features one of the most intact collections of late-19th-century townhouses this far uptown, located just below the traditional boundary with East Harlem. Of particular note on the block is No. 122, the long-time home of legendary cartoonist Al Hirschfeld, who painted its facade blush pink and filled its interiors with his iconic drawings of actors, musicians, and celebrities.

Walk west to **Park Avenue**, turn right, and walk north to **97th Street**

Stop 24 → Where the tracks of the *Metro-North Railroad* emerge from the earth

METRO-NORTH TRAIN VIADUCT

Though real estate brokers have in recent years tried to push its boundary northward, the Upper East Side ends at 96th Street. Here, the high, hilly terrain which defines most of Manhattan's east side drops away in favor of the lowlands of East Harlem. The drop-off is so dramatic that the tracks of the Metro-North Railroad, originally built as the New York & Harlem Railroad (page 176), are forced to emerge from their tunnel to run along a mighty stone-and-iron viaduct down the middle of Park Avenue from here to the Harlem River.

Here, in the 19th century, the northward growth of New York City collided with the southward growth of Harlem, marking the end of the uptown migration which had defined the city's development for a century. The affluence of the Upper East Side shoulders up against the tenements, hospital

Train Viaduct

buildings, and public housing towers of East Harlem, creating one of the starkest economic divides in the city. Permeating the border, however, are the trains which continue to rumble down the viaduct, in and out of the tunnel, uniting both neighborhoods along Manhattan's spine just as they have done for nearly two centuries.

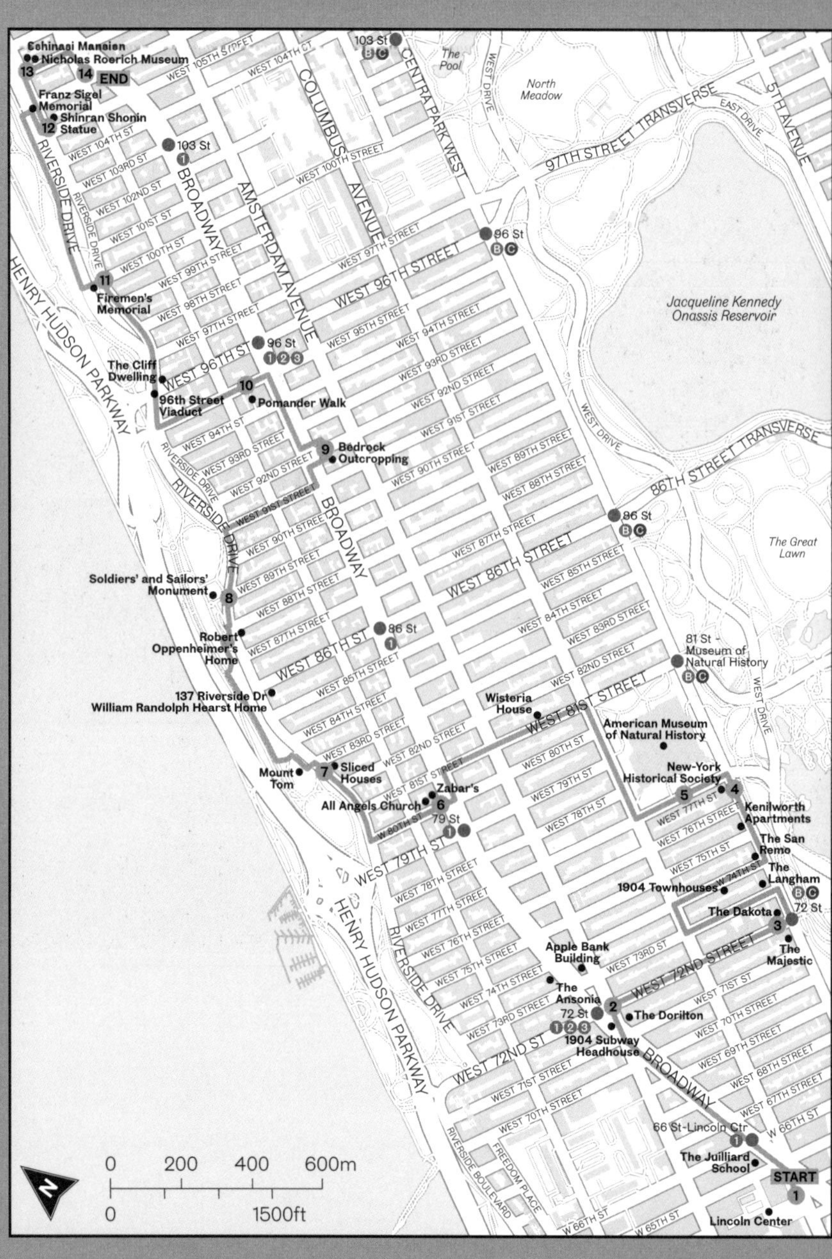

Schinasi Mansion
Nicholas Roerich Museum
13
14
END
Franz Sigel Memorial
Shinran Shonin Statue
12
103 St
1
11
Firemen's Memorial
The Cliff Dwelling
96th Street Viaduct
10
Pomander Walk
96 St
1 2 3
9
Bedrock Outcropping
Soldiers' and Sailors' Monument
8
Robert Oppenheimer's Home
86 St
1
137 Riverside Dr William Randolph Hearst Home
Mount Tom
7
Sliced Houses
Zabar's
All Angels Church
6
79 St
1
Wisteria House
American Museum of Natural History
New-York Historical Society
5
4
Kenilworth Apartments
The San Remo
The Langham
1904 Townhouses
The Dakota
3
72 St
B C
The Majestic
Apple Bank Building
The Ansonia
72 St
1 2 3
2
The Dorilton
1904 Subway Headhouse
66 St-Lincoln Ctr
1
The Juilliard School
START
1
Lincoln Center
103 St
B C
96 St
B C
86 St
B C
81 St - Museum of Natural History
B C
The Pool
North Meadow
Jacqueline Kennedy Onassis Reservoir
The Great Lawn
97TH STREET TRANSVERSE
86TH STREET TRANSVERSE
EAST DRIVE
WEST DRIVE
5TH AVENUE
CENTRAL PARK WEST
COLUMBUS AVENUE
AMSTERDAM AVENUE
BROADWAY
RIVERSIDE DRIVE
HENRY HUDSON PARKWAY
RIVERSIDE BOULEVARD
FREEDOM PLACE
WEST 105TH STREET
WEST 104TH ST
WEST 103RD ST
WEST 102ND ST
WEST 101ST ST
WEST 100TH STREET
WEST 99TH STREET
WEST 98TH STREET
WEST 97TH STREET
WEST 96TH STREET
WEST 95TH STREET
WEST 94TH STREET
WEST 93RD STREET
WEST 92ND STREET
WEST 91ST STREET
WEST 90TH STREET
WEST 89TH STREET
WEST 88TH STREET
WEST 87TH STREET
WEST 86TH STREET
WEST 85TH STREET
WEST 84TH STREET
WEST 83RD STREET
WEST 82ND STREET
WEST 81ST STREET
WEST 80TH ST
WEST 79TH ST
WEST 78TH STREET
WEST 77TH STREET
WEST 76TH STREET
WEST 75TH STREET
WEST 74TH STREET
WEST 73RD STREET
WEST 72ND STREET
WEST 71ST STREET
WEST 70TH STREET
WEST 69TH STREET
WEST 68TH STREET
WEST 67TH STREET
W 66TH ST
W 65TH ST
0 200 400 600m
0 1500ft
N

THE UPPER WEST SIDE

The Upper West Side is a neighborhood defined by its proximity to parkland. To the west lies Riverside Park, the narrow, undulating greenspace which cascades downhill to the banks of the Hudson River. To the east lies Central Park, that masterpiece of 19th-century landscape design and the leafy lungs of Manhattan. Between them, the Upper West Side is one of the most vibrant communities in the city, with generations of New Yorkers living out the theater of city life behind its ornate brownstone facades. From Lincoln Center and the American Museum of Natural History to the Dakota and the Ansonia, this neighborhood is one of real beauty and delight.

ROUTE STOPS

1. Lincoln Center
2. Verdi Square
3. The Dakota
4. The New-York Historical Society
5. American Museum of Natural History
6. Zabar's
7. Riverside Drive & 83rd Street
8. Soldiers' and Sailors' Monument
9. 92nd Street Bedrock Outcropping
10. Pomander Walk
11. Firemen's Memorial
12. Shinran Shonin Statue
13. Schinasi Mansion
14. Straus Park

DISTANCE
4½ miles (7 km)

TIME ALLOWED
2–3 hours

ROUTE No. **10**

HOME BETWEEN TWO PARKS

The Upper West Side encompasses a long, hilly strip of land sandwiched between Central Park to the east and Riverside Park to the west. With Broadway as its spine, the neighborhood is home to roughly 200,000 New Yorkers, representing a heady cross-section of the city's demographic diversity. Long preserved as an under-developed landscape of rural estate houses, ramshackle farms, and country churches, this area was originally called *Bloemendahl* by the Dutch. This nickname, anglicized as Bloomingdale, remains in use at least for a portion of the neighborhood to the present day.

But the modern Upper West Side is defined by its locational relationship to Central Park and the Upper East Side, its fraternal twin across the way. Bloomingdale began to develop in earnest only in the 1880s following the arrival of the 9th Avenue elevated train and, two decades later, the city's first subway line beneath Broadway. Its cross streets are filled with some of the loveliest and most eclectic townhouses ever assembled in this city. In contrast, its avenues are lined with grand century-old apartment buildings, many boasting the sorts of spires, domes, and mansards people imagine when they think of New York.

Home to *Seinfeld*, *Will & Grace*, *30 Rock*, and *Sesame Street*, the Upper West Side is a location scout's dream. For visitors, it is the version of Manhattan they picture from television and the movies. For locals, it is simply a wonderful place to live. Its diners, cafes, specialty grocers, easy transit access, and close proximity to some of the city's choicest greenspace makes the Upper West Side the sort of place where notoriously nomadic New Yorkers happily put down roots. From Columbus Circle to Morningside, it represents a microcosm of the best the city has to offer.

Start 1 → at the fountain plaza in **Lincoln Center**, west side of **Columbus Avenue** between **63rd** and **64th Streets**

LINCOLN CENTER

West Side Story, the movie-musical about street gangs fighting over a vanishing neighborhood, is about a very real place and time. The area now occupied by Lincoln Center was once known as San Juan Hill, a densely built community of mostly Black, Hispanic, and Irish families living on what were essentially the northern fringes of Hell's Kitchen. The neighborhood got its name from the Black infantrymen (known as Buffalo Soldiers) who fought alongside Theodore Roosevelt

Lincoln Center (Opera House and Fountain)

at the Battle of San Juan Hill in Cuba in 1898. San Juan Hill encompassed some 20 blocks centered on 62nd Street at Amsterdam Avenue. In its early years, San Juan Hill was racially divided, with Black residents living west of Amsterdam Avenue and White residents east of it. Deadly race riots broke out regularly in the 1900s and youth gangs held sway over many streets.

In the 1910s and 20s, ever more Black residents of San Juan Hill moved north to Harlem. Their population vacuum was filled by newly arrived Caribbean migrants, creating the sort of Sharks–Jets tension depicted in *West Side Story*. In the 1940s, as part of a wave of so-called "urban renewal" projects across the city, the western half of San Juan Hill was razed, replaced by a public housing project called the Amsterdam Houses. A decade later, the city earmarked the remaining eastern half of the district for "slum clearance." In 1955, Fordham University announced its intention to build a new campus on part of the cleared site; shortly after, plans for a new performing arts center were unveiled by the city. Together, these two projects would eliminate what remained of San Juan Hill.

An estimated 7,000 families were pushed out of their homes to build Lincoln Center. The residents of San Juan Hill, many of whom had lived here for generations, were scattered to the wind. Virtually none of the new housing built in the area was set aside for residents displaced by the reconstruction. A 1957 report by NIH psychiatrist Dr Leonard Duhl criticized slum clearance as a cure-all for city ills. "We forget that to the people who live there, what we call slums is home. People find it hard to give up their homes. Contacts with familiar neighbors, chats through open windows, passing comments to the neighborhood grocer, cop or bartender, all are part of a normal and comfortable day."[188] San Juan Hill was gone by 1959, along with its estimated 20,000 residents.

In exchange for San Juan Hill's destruction, New York got a state-of-the-art performing arts complex which consolidated nearly a dozen schools, organizations, libraries, and other programs in one sprawling campus. After a decade of construction, Lincoln Center was largely complete by 1969. Its three main performing arts venues are arrayed around a grand plaza with a fountain at its center.

On the north side of the plaza is Philharmonic Hall (now David Geffen Hall), designed by Max Abramovitz. It was built to house the New York Philharmonic, which relocated from Carnegie Hall. On its opening in 1962, the hall's acoustics were found to be lacking and the interior was gut-renovated in 1976 in an attempt to fix the problem. In 2020, its interior was again completely rebuilt in an attempt to address lingering acoustical and logistical issues. It reopened in 2022 after the half-billion-dollar makeover to generally positive reviews.

On the south side of the plaza is the New York State Theater (now the David H Koch Theater), designed by Philip Johnson. Its original name was in honor of the State of New York, which provided funds for the building's construction as part of its support for the city's 1964 World's Fair. It was built to house the New York City Ballet, which relocated from New York City Center on the new venue's opening in 1964.

On the west side of the plaza is the Metropolitan Opera House, designed by Wallace K Harrison. It replaced the original

"Met" which opened on Broadway at 39th Street in 1883, playing a pivotal role in Society's evolution during the Gilded Age. Its opening capped an arduous four-decade process for the opera company, which had been trying to build a new, more modern home venue since before the 1920s. The Great Depression scuttled plans for it to relocate to the then-under-construction Rockefeller Center. Tentative plans for a new opera house to be built on Columbus Circle and the Upper East Side also fell flat.

When it finally opened at Lincoln Center in 1966, the opera house's design struck a starkly modern tone for one of the city's most traditional cultural organizations. The exterior, in keeping with the theme of its neighbors, is made of white travertine with soaring windows and promenades facing onto the plaza, welcoming onlookers to admire the glitz. Inside, white walls are set off by acres of deep red carpeting as crystal chandeliers burst overhead. Murals by Marc Chagall hang in the lobby, visible from the plaza, reinforcing Lincoln Center's stance as a place where the public and the arts are encouraged to intersect.

Aside from its three main venues, Lincoln Center is also home to Broadway's Vivian Beaumont Theater, designed by Eero Saarinen, as well as a bandshell, performing arts library, film center, and numerous recital halls, not to mention the Juilliard School, which relocated here from its original campus in Morningside Heights (page 264). In all, Lincoln Center provides a splendid one-stop-shop for all that's best in the world of New York's performing arts scene.

From **Lincoln Center**, walk north along **Broadway** to **72nd Street**

Along the way, note the exuberant facade of the Dorilton, a Parisian-style apartment tower at the northeast corner of 71st Street and Broadway. Designed by the firm of Janes & Leo, it was completed in 1902 as part of a wave of development along this stretch of Broadway in anticipation of the opening of the subway in 1904. Across from the Dorilton, in the traffic island just south of Verdi Square, stands one of the subway's only surviving headhouses from its initial opening in 1904. The small brick building, which is still in use today, is a lovely reminder of the subway system's humble origins.

Stop 2 → At **Verdi Square**

VERDI SQUARE

Verdi Square is a pleasant enough spot to sit and people-watch today. A steady stream of humanity flows through it, passing in and out of the subway pavilion, buying coffee from the kiosk, or sitting on the ample rows of seating. But it wasn't always such a lovely and innocuous spot. It was named Verdi Square in 1906 following the installation of a statue of the composer, a gift from the city's Italian community, but by the 1970s, it and the surrounding neighborhood had declined precipitously. It reached its nadir with the release of the 1971 film *The Panic in Needle Park*, which portrayed it as a center for the area's drug trade and use. The park and several surrounding buildings were cleaned up and landmarked over the following decades, transforming it into its present state through improved lighting, landscaping, and transit access.

From Verdi Square, it is easy to see several remarkable, landmarked buildings, including the Apple Bank building, which overlooks the park's northern edge. Opened as the Central Savings Bank in 1928, it was one of the last monumental bank buildings to be completed in New York prior to the stock market crash of 1929. Today, though it still houses a bank branch in its ground floor, much of the building has been repurposed as apartments.

THE ANSONIA

Across Broadway from the bank is the spectacular beaux-arts pile known as the Ansonia, which opened in 1903 as one of the largest apartment buildings in the world. Like the Dorilton, it was built as a luxury residential block meant to attract well-heeled residents uptown in anticipation of the subway's opening in 1904. It was designed by the French architect Paul EM Duboy, who was brought over for the project by developer William Earl Dodge Stokes. Heir to a copper and manufacturing fortune, Stokes was an ardent promoter of the Upper West Side's development, building dozens of townhouses and apartment towers up and down its length.

The Ansonia was Stokes's greatest project by far. Seventeen stories tall and capped by gleaming domes and finials, it would easily fit in on any avenue in Paris. "A rich, startling mass of scrolls, brackets, balconies and cornices, with leering satyrs over the doorways,"[189] the Ansonia offered a level of luxury previously unseen in New York. Aside from panoramic views of the city, Central Park, and the Hudson River, the building's interior boasted mosaic chandeliers, cafes and tea rooms, Turkish baths, a palatial ballroom, the world's largest indoor swimming pool, and a lobby fountain which was stocked with seals. It also originally kept a small farm on its roof, with chickens, cows, and a pig named Nanki-Poo. It was a world unto itself, and one of the architectural jewels of the city.

From its earliest days, the Ansonia attracted an eclectic population of artists, musicians, and celebrities, including Lily Pons, Arturo Toscanini, and Florenz Ziegfeld. Had it been built on the Upper East Side, it would likely have been one of the most storied locales of New York's late Gilded Age, vying with the Waldorf-Astoria, the Carlyle, and the Plaza. But because it was built on the west side, which was always a more diverse and creative crowd, its fate was scrappier and more obscure, one of a cluster of such luxury buildings along Broadway and Central Park West which would decline in later decades into a state of glamorous Bohemian decrepitude.

By 1968, the Ansonia's basement-level Turkish spa was operating as a gay nightclub and lounge called the Continental Baths, where in between trysts in the steam room, guests could catch musical acts like Bette Midler and Barry Manilow in the lounge (Bette's 1998 album *Bathhouse Betty* recalls these performances as the beginning of her illustrious career). The lobby seals are long gone, as are the rooftop farm and the subterranean sex club, but the Ansonia remains a symbol of the Upper West Side's long history and diverse personalities.

From **Verdi Square**, walk east along **72nd Street** toward **Central Park**

The Ansonia and Apple Bank Building

Verdi Square

Hardenbergh Townhouses (73rd Street)

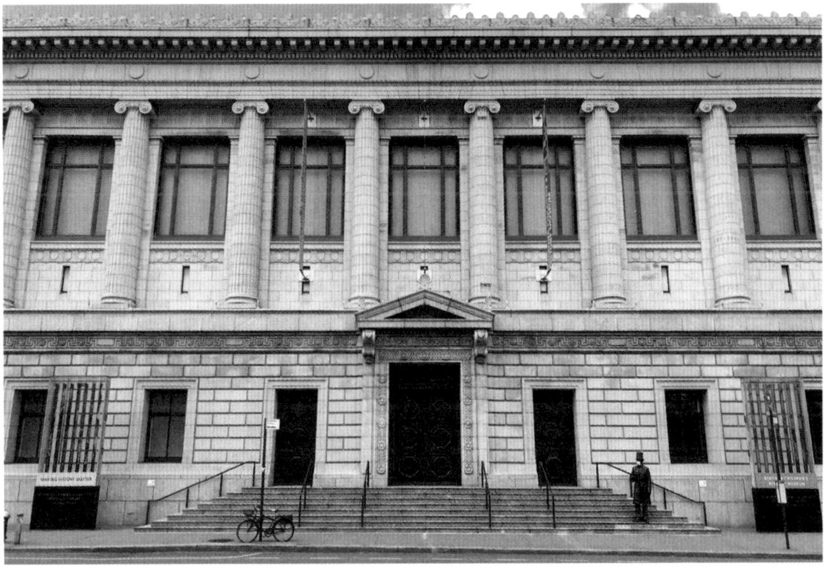

New-York Historical Society

The Dakota

Along the way, note the jumble of architectural styles and scales. Brownstone and limestone townhouses from the 1880s, most with storefronts inserted into their street levels, remain squeezed in between enormous apartment blocks from the turn of the 20th century and the building boom which accompanied the arrival of the subway in this area. An excellent place to see the flow of everyday life for the neighborhood's residents, 72nd Street is one of several main shopping streets on the Upper West Side.

At the corner of **72nd Street** and **Central Park West** stands one of the city's oldest and most storied apartment buildings

Stop 3 → The Dakota

THE DAKOTA

No apartment building in New York can compete with the Dakota. It is the oldest, the most famous, the most exclusive co-op in the city and possibly the world. When it was constructed in 1884, nothing else like it existed in the city, especially so far uptown. The Upper West Side in 1884 was only just beginning to develop, with vast empty tracts of land gaping between rows of newly built townhouses. An oft-repeated but ultimately untrue story supposes that the Dakota was named for its remote location, as far from the city as the distant Dakota Territory. What little construction was taking place in the area at that time was mostly speculative, seeking to capitalize on the recent arrival of an elevated train line on 9th Avenue.

The Dakota was designed by the architect Henry Hardenbergh, who went on to also design the 1907 Plaza Hotel, for Singer Sewing Machine Company co-founder Edward Clark. It was Clark who named the building, believing the names of the nation's new western states to have been "chosen with excellent taste."[190] For the project, Hardenbergh produced a hulking yellow-brick chalet, seven stories topped by a high-pitched many-windowed roof. In its 140 years of existence, the Dakota has stubbornly remained much the same as it ever was, growing only more "antique and aristocratic"[191] with age. Uniformed doormen still guard its 72nd Street entrance from a polished-brass vestibule flanked by enormous iron urns filled with seasonal plantings, all beneath real gas lanterns.

Like many Upper West Side apartment towers, the Dakota has long attracted a population of well-heeled creative types. Its residents have included everyone from Rosemary Clooney and Lauren Bacall to Judy Garland and Leonard Bernstein. But its most famous residents by far were John Lennon and Yoko Ono, who moved into the Dakota in 1973. Lennon was murdered in the 72nd Street entryway of the building on December 8, 1980, making it a popular tourist destination and point of pilgrimage for fans of him and the Beatles. Ono, now his widow, remained in the Dakota until 2023 when, at age 90, she retired to a farm in the Catskills. With her departure, an era ends at the Dakota, and as has been the case repeatedly over more than a century, another begins.

From the **Dakota**, walk north along **Central Park West** to **73rd Street** and turn left

With the notable exception of the Park Royal apartment building which was inserted midblock in the 1920s, most of the north side of 73rd, from No. 15 through to the five-story corner building at Columbus Avenue, was designed by Henry Hardenbergh and built on speculation for Edward Clark. The row, originally 27 houses in total, was completed by 1885 as part of Clark's heavy investment in the area, which included the neighboring Dakota. The houses not only echo the architectural ebullience of the Dakota but foreshadow the neighborhood's overall embrace of eclecticism in design, differentiating the Upper West Side streetscape from the far more staid Upper East Side.

From **73rd**, turn right onto **Columbus Avenue** and turn right again onto **74th Street**

Here, on the south side of the block, stands what was likely the last row of single-family townhouses built during the Upper West Side's building boom. This row was built in 1904 for heirs to Edward Clark's estate. By the time of their completion, the subway was open a short walk away and the age of modern apartment buildings had begun. In many ways, this row of tidy red-brick houses, which stand back-to-back with Clark and Hardenbergh's earlier row on 73rd Street, represents "the swan song of the upper-middle-class, urban row house."[192]

Walk east along **74th Street** to **Central Park West**. Turn north and head up to **77th Street**

Along the way, note the many impressive apartment towers which define the neighborhood's parkfront skyline: the Majestic at No. 115, the Langham at No. 135, the San Remo at No. 145, and the Kenilworth at No. 151.

Stop 4 → At No. 170 Central Park West

NEW-YORK HISTORICAL SOCIETY

The New-York Historical Society was formed in 1804, at a time when memories of the American Revolution were still fresh, "for the purpose of discovering, procuring, and preserving whatever may relate to the natural, civil, literary, and ecclesiastical history of the United States in general and of this state in particular."[193] More than two centuries later, it continues to fulfill that purpose, acting as one of the greatest repositories of historical documents and artifacts in the nation. After its founding, the Historical Society was a nomadic collection for 50 years, often stored in rented rooms around the city. In 1857, it moved into a purpose-built structure on 2nd Avenue at the southeast corner of 11th Street and remained there until it moved to its present home on Central Park West in 1908. The building was designed by York & Sawyer, an architectural firm best known for their formidable bank buildings, which were modeled after Florentine palazzi. Echoes of the same are easily observed in the Historical Society's treasure chest of a building.

Inside, in addition to a cafe and restaurant, the New-York Historical Society holds a peerless collection of rare documents and artifacts which are kept on constant rotational display. On any given day, visitors may view a piece of the equestrian statue of King George (page 11) which was destroyed by New Yorkers in 1776, paintings by Picasso and Keith Haring, or the world's largest collection of Tiffany lamps.

Just across **77th Street** from the New-York Historical Society

Stop 5 → In front of the original Victorian-Gothic entrance to the **American Museum of Natural History**

AMERICAN MUSEUM OF NATURAL HISTORY

The American Museum of Natural History was established in 1869 and first opened to the public inside the Central Park Arsenal building in 1871. The museum's rapidly growing collection soon outgrew the Arsenal and so the following year, it was granted permission to construct a new building in Manhattan Square, the 17-acre (7-hectare) parcel which it presently occupies under the name Roosevelt Park. Manhattan Square is the sole survivor of five such pocket parks which were drawn up on the city's 1811 street grid plan.

Hamilton Square (66th to 68th Streets, 3rd to 5th Avenues), Bloomingdale Square (53rd to 57th Streets, 8th to 9th Avenues), Harlem Square (117th to 121st Streets, 6th to 7th Avenues), and Observatory Place (89th to 94th Streets, 4th to 5th Avenues) were either never laid out or were removed soon after their establishment in favor of Central Park. But Manhattan Square endured, in part because it was originally conceived as a home for the city's "menagerie," a collection of live animals which would later evolve into the Central Park Zoo. Instead, the square was given over to the newly formed Natural History Museum and there, in 1874, President Ulysses S Grant laid the cornerstone for a grand new building which would provide untold generations of future New Yorkers access to a world-class collection of fossils, minerals, and specimens of insects, plants, and animals.

Today, the American Museum of Natural History's physical campus is a hodgepodge of various expansions and alterations built over the course of a century and a half. The south-facing 77th Street facade is the only portion built to the original master plan, designed by Calvert Vaux and Jacob Wrey Mould, who are better remembered for their masterful work in Central Park. That original plan envisioned a sprawling Victorian Gothic campus, with four identical facades on each side of the park, all crowned by a soaring central tower. An initial portion of this plan, now home to the North American and African mammals dioramas, was completed and opened to the public in 1877.

Vaux and Mould's Gothic plan was overhauled in 1897 by the firm of Cady, Berg & See, who retained its original footprint, but recast the building in the then-fashionable Romanesque Revival style. Their plan was carried out to great effect on the museum's extant 77th Street facade, which was completed in 1900. The museum's appearance was further altered in 1936 with the completion of a wholly new entrance facade on Central Park West. Dedicated as a memorial to President Theodore Roosevelt, who died in 1919, the new wing was designed primarily by John Russell Pope in the then-fashionable Roman Revival style.

These two facades, south and east, form the main body of the American Museum of Natural History as experienced by most visitors. Notable major expansions in later years include the new Rose Center for Earth and Space on the museum's north side, which opened in 2000 and includes the Hayden Planetarium, as well as the Gilder Center for Science, Education, and Innovation on the complex's west side, which opened in 2023 and vastly improved connectivity and circulation within the museum. Today, the American Museum of Natural History is among the most popular science museums on earth, with an estimated five million annual visitors.

After exploring the museum and surrounding parkland, walk west along **81st Street**

The buildings passed along West 81st Street are typical of much of the Upper West Side's architectural stock: a mix of late-19th-century townhouses, mostly built on speculation following the opening of a now-lost elevated train line along 9th Avenue, alongside later tenements, apartment blocks, and houses of worship. Of note is No. 143 West 81st, which is all but enveloped by an enormous wisteria vine which is one of the Upper West Side's most delightful local landmarks, particularly in springtime when its purple flowers burst into bloom.

At **Broadway**, turn left toward **80th Street**

Stop 6 → At **Zabar's** at another local landmark

ZABAR'S

The buildings now occupied by Zabar's were originally constructed in 1882 as tenements, but in 1920 received a stucco and half-timbering makeover which gave them their current Tudor-revival appearance. In 1941, one of the row's Broadway storefronts was rented to Louis and Lillian Zabar, who opened a small delicatessen. The Zabars both came to the United States in the 1920s as a result of the 1919 anti-Jewish pogroms in Ukraine, then a part of the Russian Empire. They married in 1927 and opened a market stall in 1934 before taking their permanent place on the Upper West Side seven years later.

Zabar's offered specialty foods, many of them catering to the area's burgeoning Jewish community, but many intended for a wider New York audience. Potato salad, coleslaw, and blintzes were in time supplemented by smoked fish, fresh-roasted coffee, and all manner of prepared and packaged foods. Louis Zabar died in 1950, but the business has been sustained by generations of Zabar descendants. Over time, the store was expanded to fill five storefronts, making it one of the largest grocers in the neighborhood. The Zabar family also owns a number of buildings in the area, but have made headlines for resisting redevelopment of their properties. "We're not interested in development," Louis and Lillian's son Saul Zabar told *The Times* in 2002. "The neighborhood shouldn't be overwhelmed by East Side-type buildings. It supported us, it gave to us, and we owe something back."[194]

Walk west from **Broadway** along **80th Street**

American Museum of Natural History

Zabar's and All Angels' Church

Sliced Houses

Riverside Park

ALL ANGELS' EPISCOPAL CHURCH

Just behind Zabar's stands the sole surviving building of All Angels' Episcopal Church. The history of this congregation is more fascinating than its edifice, which says a lot considering it was designed by Henry Hardenbergh, the architect behind the Dakota, the Plaza, and numerous other major New York City landmarks. But All Angels' is far older than its building, which was completed as the congregation's rectory in 1905, having been established in the 1830s to serve the majority-Black community of Seneca Village (page 201).

Seneca Village was condemned and demolished in the 1850s to build Central Park, but the wooden All Angels' Church was physically moved to a new plot of land at the southeast corner of 81st Street and West End Avenue. That original building was demolished and replaced with a new stone structure in 1890. That too was demolished in the 1970s when, in response to dwindling attendance, the church sold off much of its compound and moved into its 80th Street rectory. It remains one of the only physical ties to Seneca Village.

Continue west along **80th Street** to **Riverside Drive**. Turn right and walk north along **Riverside**

Stop 7 → At **83rd Street**

SLICED HOUSES

Riverside Drive is one of the showplaces of New York. Bucking Manhattan's otherwise rigid grid system, it follows a curvy, picturesque route up the island's west side. It began opening to development in 1880 as part of the larger Riverside Park project, which sought to polish the scruffy ridgeline above the Hudson River north of 72nd Street. The park was designed by Frederick Law Olmsted, the same visionary responsible for Central and Prospect Parks. Riverside Drive was envisioned not only as a pleasant driving route, but ultimately as a way to pull wealthy residents away from 5th and Madison Avenues, long the preferred domain of Gilded Age elites.

This optimistic vision of Riverside Drive as an unbroken chain of grand mansions eventually ran headlong into the social and economic realities of New York at the turn of the 20th century. Wealthy families were simply unwilling to move so far west, away from their east side strongholds. By the time meaningful development arrived on Riverside, New Yorkers had mostly shifted from single-family homes to highrise apartments. Townhouses and mansions remain a definite minority along Riverside Drive, overshadowed by their much larger, taller multi-family neighbors.

Some of the most remarkable houses left on Riverside Drive are Nos. 103–109 at the southeast corner of 83rd Street. This row was designed by prolific west side architect Clarence True and was constructed in 1899. The houses originally featured deeply embellished facades, with bay windows, stoops, and a massive round corner tower which gave them a collective picturesque appearance, like an Elizabethan palace on the Hudson. In 1903, however, a neighboring property owner sued the houses, alleging that they illegally blocked her view. Whether or not her views were actually infringed upon (she lived around the corner at No. 331 West 82nd Street), True's Riverside houses did indeed project far beyond their property lines.

Workers arrived at the Riverside Drive row in late 1910 and spent the next year carefully deconstructing the portions of the houses which overran their legal boundaries. Elements of the original Clarence True design were incorporated into the newly flattened facades, expertly masking the upheaval which forced their alteration. Knowing the story, however, passersby may easily notice the unusual flatness of these facades and the truncated roundness of the corner house's crenelated tower.

Enter **Riverside Park** from the gate between **83rd** and **84th Streets**

MOUNT TOM

You will be just north of the huge rocky outcropping located here, just inside the park walls, known as Mount Tom. It was here, atop this promontory, that Edgar Allan Poe sat admiring the view in the summers of 1843 and 1844 when he and his wife Virginia rented rooms at a nearby cottage, hoping the country air would help with her tuberculosis. Most notably, Poe likely wrote his masterpiece *The Raven* while staying at the cottage in 1844. He also gave the stone its name, in honor of Tom Brennan, the son of his Upper West Side hosts, Mary and Patrick Brennan.

Passing **Mount Tom**, follow the park path downhill to a **broad pedestrian boulevard**

This straightaway is among the most pleasant strolls in all of New York, with mature trees shading ample benches overlooking the Hudson far below. Take note of the giant metal grates embedded in the grassy lawns in the middle of the walkway. These exist because this portion of Riverside Park was built atop still-active railroad tracks, originally laid out for the Hudson River Railroad in 1849 and currently used by Amtrak.

For nearly a century, this rail right-of-way blocked residents of the Upper West Side from accessing the riverfront. In the 1930s, Robert Moses oversaw the so-called West Side Improvement project (page 115), which covered the tracks from 72nd to 123rd Streets near Grant's Tomb. This allowed for the expansion of Riverside Park and the construction of the Henry Hudson automobile parkway along the river.

Walk north through the park until reaching the dog park near **87th Street**. Here, turn right and follow the path uphill and upstairs

Stop 8 → At the plaza on **Riverside Drive** at **89th Street**

SOLDIERS' AND SAILORS' MONUMENT

The Soldiers' and Sailors' Monument is one of the jewels of Riverside Park, completed in 1902 as a memorial to the New York regiments who fought in the American Civil War. Plans for some sort of memorial in the city had circulated since the 1860s, but no serious action was taken until 1893 when funds were finally allocated and a board installed to oversee the project's execution. The original plan was to erect a monument at Grand Army Plaza at the entrance to Central Park at 59th Street and 5th Avenue (this location is instead occupied by the gilded equestrian statue of General Sherman, page 189).

Debate over the monument's appearance and location dragged on for years. A design competition was held in 1897 and the current site for the monument was chosen in 1899. The cornerstone was finally laid in a ceremony in late 1900 attended by Governor Theodore Roosevelt, and it was dedicated on Memorial Day in 1902. The monument is roughly 100 feet (30 meters) tall and features a slender marble drum surrounded by Corinthian columns surmounted by eagles and a band which reads "TO THE MEMORY OF THE BRAVE SOLDIERS AND SAILORS WHO SAVED THE UNION." Stone slabs which flank the plaza boast listed names of New York regiments, Union generals, and the battles in which they fought.

Walk north along **Riverside Drive** to **91st Street**. Turn right and walk east along this street to **Broadway**

Along the way, admire the great diversity of late-19th-century brownstone and limestone townhouses.

At **Broadway**, turn left and walk up to **92nd Street**. Turn right and walk east along **92nd Street** a short distance

Stop 9 → On the south side of the block between **No. 214 West 92nd Street (St James Court)** and **No. 206 (the Senate)**

MANHATTAN BEDROCK

If you peer through the metal gate between these two buildings, you'll see an immense slab of Manhattan bedrock, hidden inexplicably in the middle of the Upper West Side.

Incredibly, this is a largely forgotten remnant of the neighborhood's urbanization at the beginning of the 20th century. It marks the property line between two buildings and also marks the original path of the Bloomingdale Road, which was straightened and widened to become modern Broadway in the 1870s. St James Court was built at the southeast corner of Broadway and 92nd Street in 1900, and No. 206 was built next door several years later. That gap in their construction likely accounts for the rocky outcropping's survival, as neither building wanted to damage itself or its neighbor by blasting it away. Whatever the details, this slice of ancient bedrock hints at the Upper West Side's rapid and multi-layered development more than a century ago.

Return to **Broadway** and walk north to **95th Street**. Turn left and walk west

Stop 10 → At **No. 265 West 95th Street** at the little iron gate beneath a stone sign which reads **Pomander Walk**

POMANDER WALK

It shouldn't exist on the Upper West Side, this charming cluster of two- and three-story houses dressed up in stone, brick, and stucco like some small-town English high street. But Pomander Walk does exist, a quirk of the city's early-20th-century development.

Pomander Walk

Riverside Drive

Firemen's Memorial

Schinasi Mansion

It was constructed in 1922 with 20 houses, 10 on each side of a narrow, private walkway, and seven more facing 94th and 95th Streets. The houses are small, a fact made all the more apparent by the enormous modern highrises which loom over them today.

But Pomander Walk was likely never meant to survive into the 21st century. It was built as a sort of place-saver development for wealthy nightclub owner Thomas Healey. In 1920, he obtained a 200-year lease on this oddly shaped slice of land west of Broadway and announced his intention to build a 16-story hotel on the site. In the meantime, he built Pomander Walk, which he named after a popular English stage play which takes place on just such a quaint Georgian street. This little slice of England on the Upper West Side was much admired for its unusual design and inherent exclusivity. Whatever Healey had planned for the plot in the long term, he died in 1927 before carrying it out, and Pomander Walk has survived, rather miraculously, for more than a century.

After peeking through the gates to **Pomander Walk**, continue west to **Riverside Drive** and turn right

RIVERSIDE DRIVE

At 96th Street, note that Riverside actually becomes a viaduct, built in 1902, which soars over the street below. Here, the hilly topography of the Upper West Side is on full display. This steep ravine was once known as Strycker's Bay, one of the most notable inlets along Manhattan's western shoreline. The Hudson River once pushed inland here as far as present-day West End Avenue. Though the bay was long ago filled in to accommodate new train lines, highways, and parkland, the fact that 96th Street does not intersect Riverside Drive is a reminder of a wilder, more natural Manhattan.

On Riverside Drive, on the north side of 96th Street, stands a highly unusual apartment building bearing a raucous Mesoamerican design motif. This is the Cliff Dwelling, built in 1916 to designs by Herman Lee Meader. The architect took deft advantage of the building's oddly shallow lot, placing all habitable rooms along its Riverside Drive and 96th Street walls. He then clustered all the building's utilities, including elevators and stairwells, on the east side, out of view. For its exterior, Meader used extensive terracotta detailing which boasts a whole cacophony of Aztec, Mayan, and other Native American motifs. Meader had a love for Native American design, regularly traveling to Chichén Itzá and other sites on the Yucatán Peninsula. The style is eye-catching, especially coming from an era better known for its French-inflected architecture. Another, similar example of Meader's work can be found at No. 130 East 25th Street near Gramercy Park.

Passing the **Cliff Dwelling**, continue north along **Riverside Drive**

Stop 11 → At **100th Street**

FIREMEN'S MEMORIAL

The Firemen's Memorial on Riverside Drive is one of the most poignant monuments in New York. Dedicated in 1913, it commemorates the hundreds of firefighters killed in the line of duty since the city's establishment. New York suffered a number of catastrophic fires in the 18th and 19th centuries which ultimately led to the construction of the Croton Aqueduct in the 1830s and the passage of a succession of fire safety ordinances (wooden buildings were outlawed in 1866 and fire escapes were required on tenement buildings in 1867). Against this backdrop, New York established an official Fire Department for the city in 1865.

The memorial's origins can be traced back to 1908 when a deputy fire chief was killed while fighting a conflagration at No. 215 Canal Street. Charles Kruger, a beloved and long-serving member of the force, fell through the floor of the building into a cellar filled with 8 feet (2.5 meters) of water and no way out. Dragged down by his heavy gear, Kruger drowned before he could be pulled out. Within a week, a committee which included Andrew Carnegie, Isidor Straus, and Bishop Codman Potter was formed to raise funds for a memorial.

After initially choosing a site on the north side of Union Square (this raised the ire of firemen who didn't want such a sober memorial built in a plaza better known for political rallies), the current spot at the western end of 100th Street was acquired and work got underway. The memorial was designed by architect H Van Buren Magonigle, with much of the sculptural work executed by Attilio Piccirilli, both of whom also worked together on the *Maine* monument at Columbus Circle. It features an enormous bronze bas relief depiction of a horse-drawn engine racing to a fire flanked by marble figures representing *Duty* and *Sacrifice*. Carved into the eastern side are the words: "To the men of the Fire Department of the City of New York, who died at the call of duty, soldiers in a war that never ends, this memorial is dedicated by the people of a grateful city."

When the memorial was officially dedicated in 1913, more than 7,000 uniformed firemen attended, and the site has since hosted annual gatherings of the FDNY. It gained added poignancy following the attacks of September 11, 2001, in which 343 New York City firefighters were killed.

From the **Firemen's Memorial**, descend the red-brick stairs to lower **Riverside Drive** and cross to the park side of the street. Turn right and walk north

Enjoy the beauty of this stretch of Riverside, with its low stone wall, high tree canopy, and expansive views.

At **106th Street**, cross back to the city side of the street and ascend the stairs past the statue of Franz Sigel, the German-born military strategist who served as a Major General for the Union in the American Civil War. Turn right and walk a short distance south on **Riverside Drive**

Stop 12 → At the New York Buddhist Church at **No. 332**

A JAPANESE STATUE ON RIVERSIDE DRIVE

The statue that you see here is of Shinran, a Buddhist monk who died more than seven centuries ago, which was cast in Japan around 1930. It was first installed outside a temple near Hiroshima, about a mile from the epicenter of the nuclear blast which devastated that city in 1945. It survived the bomb, albeit with some discoloration to Shinran's robes, and was gifted to New York as a symbol of peace and serenity. It was installed here, in front of the New York Buddhist Church, in 1955. Funding was provided by Japanese businessman Seiichi Hirose, who said the gift of this statue was intended "to promote a spirit of 'no more Hiroshimas.'"[195] Perhaps ironically, or perhaps simply as an example of the historic prominence of the Upper West Side, the man credited with the invention of the atomic bomb, J Robert Oppenheimer, grew up just a short walk south of the Shinran statue, at No. 155 Riverside Drive.

The block of Riverside Drive between 105th and 106th Streets is one of its most picturesque. Extending north and south of the Shinran statue are seven grand, surprisingly intact mansions from the beginning of the 20th century and the waning days of single-family mansion dwelling on the Upper West Side. Residents of the row over the years included the actress Marion Davies (who was installed at No. 331 by her longtime partner, William Randolph Hearst, who lived nearby with his wife at No. 137), jazz legend Duke Ellington (who owned Nos. 333 and 334), pencil factory owner Lothar Faber (who lived at No. 337), and baking powder magnate Robert Benson Davis at No. 330.

Walk north along **Riverside Drive** to the corner of **107th Street**

Stop 13 → At **107th** and **Riverside**

SCHINASI MANSION AND ROERICH MUSEUM

A striking white-marble house stands on this corner, one of the last freestanding single-family mansions left in Manhattan. Morris Schinasi was born in 1855 into a Sephardic Jewish family of humble circumstances in the Ottoman Empire (modern Turkey). After immigrating to New York with his brother Solomon in 1890, he made a fortune in the tobacco industry, helping to popularize Turkish cigars, which were much stronger than what could otherwise be found on the American market. By 1907, Schinasi was wealthy enough to engage William B Tuthill, the architect behind Carnegie Hall, to build for him a splendid mansion on this ample piece of land on Riverside Drive at the corner of 107th Street. The house, which was completed in 1909, features walls made of white Vermont marble set off by the roof, which is covered in green terracotta tiles and copper finials. Schinasi died in 1928 and his family sold the house in 1930. Despite serving as a school and daycare for several decades, it re-entered private hands in 1979 and has since been lovingly restored.

Behind the Schinasi mansion, the townhouse at No. 319 West 107th Street houses the Nicholas Roerich Museum. Roerich was a Russian polymath who specialized in painting, writing, and philosophy. He and his wife Helena first visited New York in 1920 and returned frequently, settling in the city for several years. In 1929, patrons of Roerich commissioned the 27-story Master Building, a combination art museum and apartment tower at Nos. 310–312 Riverside Drive. That project fell into financial and legal troubles during the Great Depression, and the Roerich Museum was shuttered there in 1938. It was revived in the 1950s thanks to musician and Roerich acolyte Dudley Fosdick, who turned his own home on 107th Street into a center for the arts. When he died in 1957, the house was turned permanently into the Nicholas Roerich Museum, featuring hundreds of the artist's works on free public display.

From the **Schinasi Mansion** and **Roerich Museum**, walk east along **107th Street** to a small triangular greenspace wedged between **Broadway** and **West End Avenue**

STRAUS PARK

Isidor Straus was a German Jewish immigrant who moved to New York shortly after the American Civil War and made his fortune selling dry goods. In 1871, he married fellow immigrant Ida Blun and the couple went on to have six children. In 1884, the family purchased a wooden home and stables in Bloomingdale, then still quite a rural area, at what is now the northwest corner of 105th Street and Broadway. By all accounts, the Strauses were a happy, tight knit family and from their home they would have enjoyed fresh river breezes and picturesque drives down the city via the Bloomingdale Road. By the 1890s, Isidor held full or partial ownership of the department stores Abraham & Straus and RH Macy & Co., becoming one of the city's most prominent citizens.

Isidor and Ida Straus died in the sinking of the RMS *Titanic* on April 14, 1912. Their story quickly became legend as reports emerged that the couple had refused seats in lifeboats, Isidor because too many other women and children had yet to be rescued, and Ida because she wouldn't leave without Isidor. They were last seen on deck, "she clinging to his arm and patting it, smiling in the face of death,"[196] a loving and devoted couple to the end. A month after the sinking, the Straus children sold their parents' Bloomingdale home, which was soon demolished and replaced by the 13-story Cleburne Building which remains there today.

In 1915, on the anniversary of their deaths, a memorial fountain was unveiled in their honor. The granite pool and bench feature a bronze statue by the artist Augustus Lukeman which depicts a young woman enrobed, gazing pensively downward, a foot dangling toward the water. Into the bench behind her are carved the words "Lovely and pleasant were their lives and in their death they were not parted." Lovely and pleasant indeed is Straus Park today, a leafy respite from the busy streets around it. Though the fountain no longer flows, the memorial stands as a poignant tribute to two long-ago Upper West Side residents.

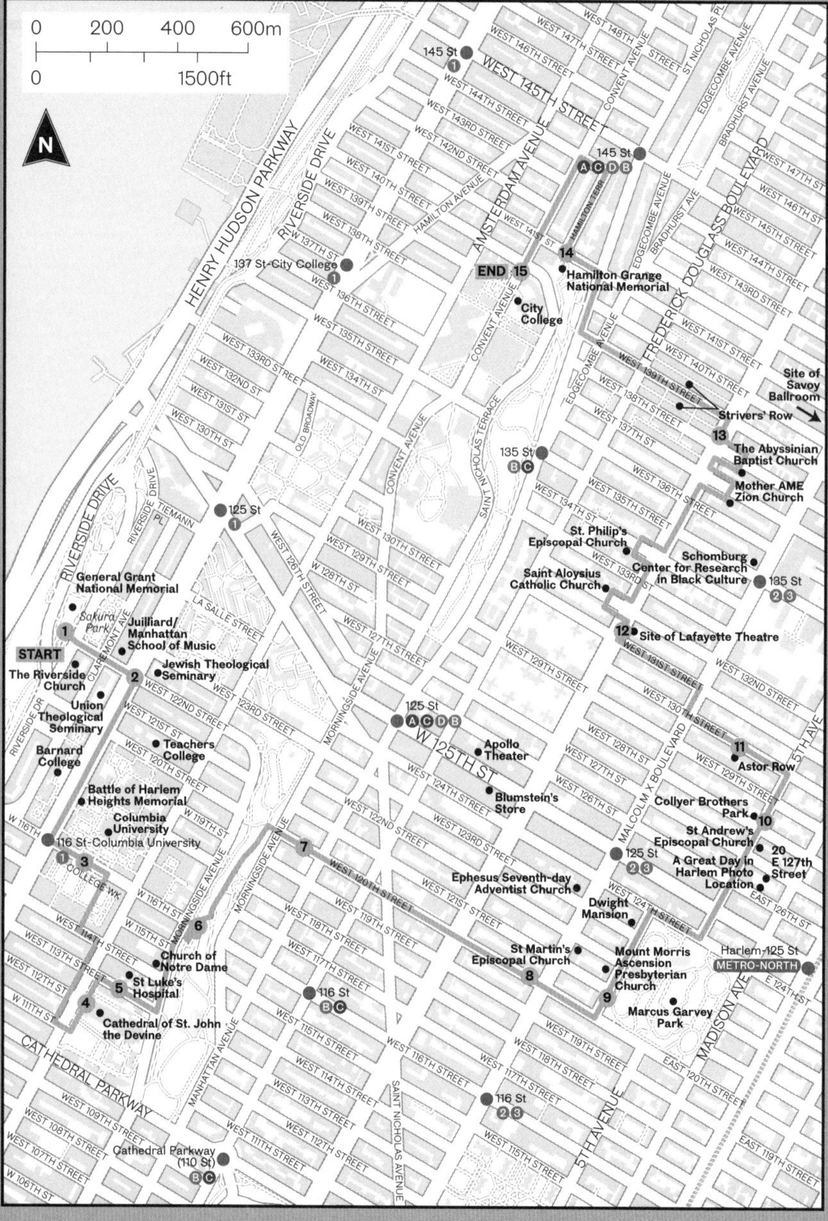

0 200 400 600m
0 1500ft
N
START
1
The Riverside Church
General Grant National Memorial
Sakura Park
Juilliard/ Manhattan School of Music
2
Jewish Theological Seminary
Union Theological Seminary
Barnard College
Teachers College
Battle of Harlem Heights Memorial
Columbia University
116 St-Columbia University
3
COLLEGE WK
4
Cathedral of St. John the Devine
5
St Luke's Hospital
6
Church of Notre Dame
7
8
St Martin's Episcopal Church
9
Mount Morris Ascension Presbyterian Church
Marcus Garvey Park
Dwight Mansion
Ephesus Seventh-day Adventist Church
10
Collyer Brothers Park
St Andrew's Episcopal Church
20 E 127th Street
A Great Day in Harlem Photo Location
11
Astor Row
12
Site of Lafayette Theatre
Saint Aloysius Catholic Church
St. Philip's Episcopal Church
Center for Research in Black Culture
Schomburg
13
The Abyssinian Baptist Church
Mother AME Zion Church
Strivers' Row
Site of Savoy Ballroom
14
Hamilton Grange National Memorial
END 15
City College
Apollo Theater
Blumstein's Store
125 St
145 St
137 St-City College
135 St
135 St
116 St
116 St
125 St
Cathedral Parkway (110 St)
Harlem-125 St
METRO-NORTH
HENRY HUDSON PARKWAY
RIVERSIDE DRIVE
AMSTERDAM AVENUE
CONVENT AVENUE
HAMILTON AVENUE
HAMILTON TERR
EDGECOMBE AVENUE
BRADHURST AVENUE
FREDERICK DOUGLASS BOULEVARD
MALCOLM X BOULEVARD
5TH AVENUE
5TH AVE
MADISON AVE
SAINT NICHOLAS AVENUE
SAINT NICHOLAS TERRACE
ST NICHOLAS PL
MORNINGSIDE AVENUE
MANHATTAN AVENUE
OLD BROADWAY
CLAREMONT AVE
RIVERSIDE DR
TIEMANN PL
LA SALLE STREET
CATHEDRAL PARKWAY
W 125TH ST
WEST 145TH STREET
WEST 126TH STREET

Harlem: more than any other neighborhood in New York, its name conjures an image and a feeling. For more than a century, it has been rightfully celebrated as the cultural nucleus of Black America, the beating heart of the Jazz Age and of the Renaissance which birthed a wholly new vision for the nation's future. Starting on the landmark-strewn highlands of Morningside Heights, this walk weaves through Harlem's four centuries of evolution. From Grant's Tomb and Columbia University to Strivers' Row and City College, it is a vast neighborhood encompassing all the multitudes of the great American experiment.

MORNINGSIDE HEIGHTS AND HARLEM

ROUTE STOPS

1. Grant's Tomb
2. Subway Viaduct
3. Columbia University
4. Cathedral of St John the Divine
5. St Luke's Hospital
6. Morningside Park
7. 120th Street
8. Mount Olivet Baptist Church
9. Marcus Garvey Park
10. Collyer Mansion
11. Astor Row
12. Lafayette Theatre
13. Strivers' Row
14. Hamilton Grange
15. City College

DISTANCE
4¾ miles (7.7 km)

TIME ALLOWED
3–4 hours

ROUTE No.

11

A CULTURAL CRUCIBLE

Harlem is a big place, home to more than 360,000 people, encompassing everything north of Central Park up to 155th Street, from river to river, and as far south as 96th Street on the east side. (There is debate as to whether or not Morningside Heights should be considered a part of Harlem, but for the purposes of this discussion, it is. In fact, its very name comes from the fact that when the sun rises over Harlem, the light hits the cliffs of Morningside first, making it literally the *morning-side* of Harlem.) Large as it is, Harlem can best be understood as a series of sub-neighborhoods, each with its own identity, architecture, and demographic makeup. In general, Harlem can be broken down into three regions: East, Central, and West.

Western Harlem, including Morningside Heights, Manhattanville, Hamilton Heights, and Sugar Hill, is defined by high ridges, part of a continuous outcropping which stretches up through Washington Heights, Inwood, and Riverdale into the Hudson Valley.

East Harlem, generally agreed to be the area lying north of 96th Street east of the Metro-North train viaduct on Park Avenue, was once a marshy river delta now defined by sloping lowlands.

Central Harlem occupies the vast flatlands in between, stretching from Central Park up to the Harlem River. It would be impossible to see and appreciate the vast multitudes of Harlem in one sojourn, so this walk is meant to serve as an introduction and jumping-off point for further exploration.

Start 1 → Grant's Tomb, 122nd Street at Riverside Drive

GRANT'S TOMB

Standing in the plaza in front of Grant's Tomb, it is easy to appreciate the unique character of Morningside Heights. It is an unusual place, rife with monumental architecture and world-class institutions. For most of its early history, Morningside remained disconnected from the rest of New York's growth and development. This was largely due to its elevated topography, with high ridges defining its boundary on three sides. It sits 100 feet (30 meters) above the Hudson River to the west, Manhattanville to the north, and the central Harlem plain to the east. This meant that for much of Morningside Heights' early history, it was an unusually isolated area, bypassed by all major roads and transit lines, left to dawdle in rural quietude even as urbanity consumed everything around it.

By the end of the 19th century, Morningside was among the last under-developed areas of Manhattan, and city leaders took note of its latent possibility. At the time, New York below Central Park had become an overcrowded jumble of busy streets and densely built tenement districts. During this era, Gilded Age New Yorkers wanted to prove that their city was as refined, cultured, and respectable as London or Paris. With lower Manhattan seemingly an irredeemably lost cause, Morningside Heights was viewed as the perfect spot to establish a new civic, academic, and ecclesiastical heart for the city. Its elevated location inspired comparisons to the Democratic ideals of Athens, with Morningside dubbed "The Acropolis of the New World."[197]

By 1930, more than a dozen major institutions had relocated to Morningside Heights, including the Teachers College, Barnard College, the Union Theological Seminary, the Jewish Theological Seminary, the Institute of Musical Art (later renamed Juilliard), St Luke's Hospital, and, perhaps most notably, Columbia University. The grandeur of the area was heightened by the completion of Riverside Park on its west side, Morningside Park on its east side, and the construction of the enormous Cathedral of St John the Divine on Amsterdam Avenue. But the neighborhood's identity as New York's Acropolis really began in 1885 when Morningside was selected as the burial site for Civil War hero and former United States President Ulysses S Grant.

Shortly before Grant died in July of 1885, he wrote: "There are three places from which I wish a choice of burial place to be made." It was widely expected that he would be entombed in glory in Washington, DC. Instead, his choices included West Point: "I would prefer this above others but for the fact that my wife could not be placed beside me there." His second choice was "Galena, or some other place in Illinois. Because from that State I received my first General's commission." Lastly, he suggested "New York. Because the people of that city befriended me in my need."[198]

To the nation's great surprise, the Grant family chose New York. West Point did not allow for the burial of women, and Julia wished to one day join her husband in eternal slumber. Galena, Illinois, was considered too remote for the American public to be able to pay their respects in great numbers. Meanwhile, Ulysses and Julia had grown fond of New York, whose citizens had welcomed them with open arms following the end of his presidency in 1877. Wealthy New Yorkers gifted the Grants a brownstone mansion on East 66th Street and endowed them with $250,000 to ensure their ease and comfort in later years. They were, for all intents and purposes, members of New York's Gilded Age Society (one of their granddaughters was, in fact, included in Ward McAllister's "official" list of *The 400* in 1892).

The tomb would be built on a high ridge at the northern end of Morningside Heights, affording sweeping views of the Hudson River from "a spot of rare natural beauty away from the noise and turmoil of the great and busy city."[199] Grant's body lay in state at City Hall until August 7 when it processed uptown. Tens of thousands crowded into City Hall Park to catch a final glimpse of the great soldier, and hundreds of thousands more lined the processional route up the length of Manhattan. It took another 12 years before Grant's mausoleum was dedicated, during which time he lay in repose within a temporary tomb designed by Jacob Wrey Mould, the

Englishman who designed the Crystal Palace for the 1853 World's Fair as well as Bethesda Terrace in Central Park. Sadly, this temporary tomb no longer exists.

Grant's permanent tomb was built to designs by John H Duncan, the architect behind numerous Gilded Age mansions as well as the great memorial arch in Brooklyn's Grand Army Plaza. Duncan modeled Grant's tomb after the Mausoleum at Halicarnassus, one of the Seven Wonders of the Ancient World. With an exterior of light-colored Maine granite, the tomb stands 150 feet (46 meters) tall. Inside, walls of granite and marble are surmounted by a great plasterwork dome. The Grants are entombed below the main floor, visible through a circular cutout, in sarcophagi carved from solid Wisconsin porphyry stone. Each weighs an estimated 10 tons.

Duncan's design for the monument was approved in 1890 and it was officially dedicated in April 1897, at which time the great General's body was moved from the temporary mausoleum nearby. Despite cold and blustery weather, an estimated one million people turned out for what was heralded as "Grant Day," with thousands of Civil War veterans (including many from the Confederacy) marching in formation and a eulogy delivered by President William McKinley.

The construction of Grant's Tomb on Morningside Heights signaled the start of this neighborhood's emergence as New York's "Acropolis." By the time Julia Grant died in 1902, the surrounding blocks boasted some of the nation's greatest architectural gems. Morningside was accessible from the city via Riverside Drive or the Boulevard (now Broadway), but lay far enough removed to feel like an island unto itself. Even as nearby Harlem and the surrounding area filled with speculative rowhouses and transit lines, Morningside remained a bastion of bucolic isolation. That all changed with the arrival in 1904 of the city's first subway line.

From **Grant's Tomb**, cross **Riverside Drive** and follow **122nd Street** downhill to **Broadway**

Along the way, admire the beauty of Sakura Park, so named for its rows of cherry trees, which transform the area into a fleeting wonderland of windblown petals each spring. Just south of the park stands Riverside Church, the tallest such building in North America at 392 feet (120 meters). It opened in 1930, built with funds provided by John D Rockefeller. Its bell tower houses the largest carillon on earth, with 74 tuned bells including a 20-ton bourdon bell (that which peals the lowest tone), the heaviest ever cast.

Just east of Sakura Park, at 122nd Street and Claremont Avenue, stands the Manhattan School of Music, founded in East Harlem in 1917. The school's buildings, however, were originally home to the Institute of Musical Art, which was renamed the Juilliard School following a substantial financial gift from philanthropist Augustus Juilliard. That school relocated to Lincoln Center in 1969, after which time its Morningside campus was taken over by the Manhattan School of Music.

Pass the school and cross the road

Stop 2 → On the sidewalk island in the middle of **Broadway** and **122nd**

SUBWAY VIADUCT

From the north side, look through the iron fence at a most unusual sight: a subway train emerging from the ground. Upper Manhattan is an undulating, topographically diverse place, with high, rocky ridges sliced through with deep ravines. The most notable of these ravines is Manhattan Valley, a wide, low delta which cuts diagonally from central Harlem to the Hudson River at Manhattanville. Here, the land drops away so dramatically that the subway line beneath Broadway is forced to emerge into broad daylight for half a mile, from 122nd Street to 135th. Prior to the subway's construction, however, this valley is part of what made Morningside Heights – and all of upland western Manhattan – so slow to develop. It was hard enough to navigate the rambling terrain between the city and these pastoral heights, but once one reached them, there was hardly any place to go but back from whence one came.

Manhattan Valley was conquered twice in rapid succession: first by the extension of Riverside Drive beyond Grant's Tomb via a grand elevated roadway which opened in 1901, and soon after by the completion of a parallel viaduct for the new Broadway subway line. "There is no handsomer arch in the city than the big one, with a 170-foot [50-meter] span, passing over the Manhattan Valley,"[200] gushed *The Sun* on the system's inauguration in October of 1904. Beyond its beauty, the new subway line opened the upper reaches of Manhattan to rapid development for the first time. Acre by acre, rural estates were carved into building lots, ancient wooden houses were cleared away, and urbanity consumed Morningside Heights along with everything north of it: Washington Heights, Inwood, and on into the Bronx.

Standing in the middle of Broadway today, watching the 1 Train slip into and out of its tunnels, the depth of Manhattan Valley is apparent. The roadbed vanishes downhill from here on either side of the train tracks, which vanish far off in the distance beneath 135th Street where the land rises once again to meet them. The 125th Street subway station sits fully 50 feet (15 meters) above street level, a novelty between its subterranean neighbors at 116th and 137th.

Before leaving the traffic island, take note of the imposing architecture of Morningside's two great religious schools: the gray Gothic fieldstone compound of Union Theological Seminary, looking every bit like a rural English abbey, sits catty-corner from the soaring red-brick tower of the Jewish Theological Seminary. Both are now affiliated with nearby Columbia University. Cross to the east side of Broadway and turn right to head south toward 116th Street. Along the way, be sure to observe the large bronze plaque embedded in the wall at the crest of the hill. This commemorates the Battle of Harlem Heights, a pivotal engagement during the American Revolution in which General George Washington successfully defended fortifications here in September of 1776.

Continue on to **116th Street**

Stop 3 → At the **116th Street** entrance to **Columbia University**

COLUMBIA UNIVERSITY

Columbia University was established as King's College by charter from King George II in 1754. The college, comprising eight students and one professor, first met in a schoolhouse on the grounds of Trinity Church on Broadway at the foot of Wall Street. Four years later, in 1758, the school relocated to its own proper campus just north of town, on land donated by Trinity Church as part of the 215-acre (87-hectare) estate granted to it by Queen Anne. That original campus occupied two city blocks just north of what is now the World Trade Center, bound by West Broadway and Church Street between Barclay and Murray Streets. In 1776, when New York was captured by British forces during the American Revolution, the college shuttered and its buildings were used by the occupying forces as a military hospital.

King's College, patriotically renamed Columbia College following the war's conclusion, at last resumed classes in 1784. By the turn of the 19th century, the school had grown rapidly and was in need of more space. In 1814, the state legislature gifted Columbia a tract of land in what is now Midtown which had been the Elgin Botanical Garden, expecting them to build a new campus there. Instead, Columbia turned the old garden into income-generating rental properties and in 1857 built a more modest uptown campus nearby on Madison Avenue between 49th and 50th Streets. Meant to be temporary, that new campus was used by Columbia for 40 years, during which time it rapidly evolved from a provincial college into a proper world-class university.

All the while, Columbia College banked its generous income from the Elgin Garden property, which encompassed everything along the west side of 5th Avenue between 47th and 51st Streets, land which became exponentially more valuable during the mid-19th century as the city's population pushed its way uptown. They used this income to purchase the Bloomingdale Insane Asylum on rural Morningside Heights in 1892. This new property was situated far north of the city center on a ridge with sweeping views of the Hudson River and Harlem Valley. There, they hired the architectural firm of McKim, Mead & White to design for them a monumental new campus which opened in 1897, the same year Grant's Tomb was dedicated, as part of Morningside's emergence as the city's "Acropolis."

Today, Columbia is among the most prestigious institutes of higher learning in the nation. Built as a veritable citadel of academia, it continues to define the culture and mold the identity of Morningside Heights. From outside the campus gates, note the forbidding nature of the school's external buildings. High stone walls, with windows hidden behind iron bars, give the impression of a fortress, an inward-facing cloister whose beauty is kept hidden from outside eyes. Keep in mind that, when Columbia moved to Morningside Heights, there was no subway running along Broadway. A journey to this campus would have been made with the promise of just such a sense of security, importance, and isolation. It was a place built to allow for a purity of study far from the madding crowds downtown. Despite more than a century of change, Columbia retains that special sense of isolated monumentality.

BARNARD COLLEGE

Across Broadway from Columbia stands one of its affiliate schools, the women-only Barnard College, which was established in 1889 in response to Columbia's refusal to admit women as students. In fact, Columbia College, the core school of Columbia University, did not officially admit women until 1983, more than a century after activists began agitating for their admission. Barnard opened amid a proliferation of such women's schools across the country, including Vassar in 1861, Wellesley in 1870, Smith College in 1875, and Bryn Mawr in 1883. The notion of allowing women to study alongside men was a hot-button issue at the end of the 19th century. Despite persistent support from Columbia's then-president Frederick Barnard, proposals to admit women to the school were vigorously opposed by its deans and "consistently thwarted by the trustees."[201]

Barnard College, named in honor of Columbia's recently deceased president, opened in 1889 at No. 343 Madison Avenue, just a few blocks south of Columbia's Midtown campus. The new school was lauded as "one of the city's features to be pointed at with pride."[202] They would not stay on Madison Avenue for long, however, as Barnard soon chose to follow Columbia in its relocation to Morningside Heights. The school purchased a plot of land on the west side of Broadway at 120th Street, just across from Columbia's new campus, and both schools opened there in 1897. "Students arriving at the new colleges discovered a largely undeveloped neighborhood of vacant lots and farm plots," explains historian Andrew S Dolkart, "with the grand new institutional structures contrasting dramatically with this semi-rural landscape."[203] Indeed, photos of the area from the 1890s show an almost dream-like landscape of great limestone domes and pinnacles rising above literal pastures and wooden shacks.

If possible, walk through Columbia via **116th Street**, which runs through the school's quad as a pedestrian pathway. Spend some time exploring its leafy nooks and artworks before exiting onto **Amsterdam Avenue** to head south toward **112th Street**

Stop 4 → In front of the awesome western facade of the **Cathedral of St John the Divine**

CATHEDRAL OF ST JOHN THE DIVINE

Construction began on the Cathedral of St John the Divine in 1892, and it remains incomplete more than a century later, earning it the nickname St John the *Unfinished*. What was intended to be a point of pride for New York and its Episcopal adherents has instead become an object lesson in hubris, misplaced optimism, and unmet expectations. From its inception at the end of the 19th century, the cathedral's progress has been stymied by infighting and controversy, all exacerbated by a chronic lack of funding.

When first proposed, the new cathedral was meant to be an Anglican response to the recent completion of the Catholic Cathedral of St Patrick on 5th Avenue (page 180), which topped out in 1888 as one of the greatest religious landmarks in the Western Hemisphere. Episcopalians, the American version of the Church of England, counted among their flock a solid majority of the nation's wealthiest and most powerful families. Even those who weren't born Episcopalian often converted, or at least attended Episcopal services, due to the church's social and cultural centrality. Congregations such as Trinity, Grace, St Thomas, and Ascension were some of the most vital and influential centers for Gilded Age public life, playing host to every major wedding, funeral, and baptism that mattered in the Society papers.

And so it was viewed as a kind of crisis when the city's Catholics, those often-impoverished Irish and Italian immigrant masses who filled Manhattan's teeming tenement blocks, built for themselves one of the grandest and loveliest church buildings ever erected on this side of the Atlantic. St Patrick's Cathedral instantly became a symbol of pride and optimism, anticipating a future in which Catholics dominated New York's public and political life. Episcopalians had nothing to compare, having long opted for smaller neighborhood chapels to meet their needs.

St John the Divine was meant to fill that void, providing a highly visible centerpiece for New York's Protestant population. It would be built on a prominent ridge at the southern end of Morningside Heights, on property purchased from the Leake & Watts Orphan Asylum (the red-brick Greek-revival building presently sidled up against the south side of the cathedral is the orphanage's former administrative building, completed in 1843, making it the oldest structure in the neighborhood). "No cathedral in any great city in the world," proclaimed Episcopal Bishop Henry Codman Potter, "has to-day a site which, for commanding dignity, will approach that which we have secured."[204]

Instead, St John the Divine was birthed in conflict. Every step of the cathedral's inception was marred by infighting and debate, starting with its design competition. Four designs were submitted in 1891, two of which were considered too unimaginative or too impractical. Of the remaining two designs, one by Potter & Robertson was ultimately rejected in part because one of the partners, William Appleton Potter, was the brother of Bishop Potter, who wished to avoid accusations of nepotism. In the end, to the satisfaction of almost nobody, only one design proposal was seriously considered: the Gothic-Byzantine compromise submitted by the firm of Heins & LaFarge.

George Lewis Heins and Christopher Grant LaFarge were by all accounts well respected and decidedly capable architects in their own rights. Their design for St John the Divine was a soaring pile of domes and barrel vaults, a sort of marriage between the Romanesque innovations of HH Richardson and the ancient Christian aesthetic of Istanbul's Hagia Sophia. What the architects confronted in the aftermath of their victory was a quagmire of disagreement which saw the project almost immediately stall for want of funds. The fickle sensibilities of New York's philanthropic class felt alienated by the opacity of the cathedral's design competition. As donations trickled in, the cathedral underwent a series of radical changes in design and orientation. Rather than face south, lofting its grand entry porticos over the city below, it was turned west, in accordance with Episcopal tradition, toward the claustrophobic side streets of Morningside Heights.

The cornerstone for St John the Divine was laid in December of 1892, but work was soon halted by the discovery of an unstable sandy layer in the bedrock below. The foundation wasn't completed until 1895. "By 1900, $2 million had been spent, but it seemed that little had been achieved."[205] Progress inched along for years, focused mainly on the crossing at the heart of the cathedral, made up of four colossal rough-cut stone arches which are still visible on the building's north and south facades. First, workers had to confront the daunting task of raising eight 54-foot (16-meter) granite columns, quarried in Maine, which had to be erected in the apse before the crossing could be built around them. Each column weighs an estimated 130 tons and is so tall that the hoists used to lift them upright had to be built using logs shipped in from the Pacific Northwest. All of this led to near-constant cost overruns.

The cathedral's crossing was finally enclosed by an enormous tile dome executed by Rafael Guastavino, Jr, in 1909. That dome, meant to be temporary, remains in place today and is one of the most striking features of the cathedral. With it, St John the Divine could at last be used for religious services. In 1911, just days after the partially built structure was consecrated, its trustees quietly replaced Heins and LaFarge as architects with Ralph Adams Cram, a move decried in the press as surprising if not unethical. This public-relations snafu did little to improve support for the project, which seemed increasingly unlikely to ever be finished.

With Cram in charge of design and construction, St John the Divine was reimagined as a more purely Gothic edifice, more in keeping with the fashion of the new century. Construction work began briefly in 1916 but was soon halted for another decade by World War I. Finally, in 1924, the cathedral began to take shape in earnest, with the baptistry, much of the nave, side chapels, and the enormous five-portal western facade constructed between then and 1941, when the whole project was rededicated. Much of the cathedral's modern appearance is thanks to this burst of industry. But just days after the rededication ceremony, the United States entered World War II, stymying any plans for another three decades.

Finally, in 1978, work began anew. A stoneyard was established on the cathedral's north side and there, local youths were invited to apprentice with master stonemasons who set about pushing the project closer to completion. Dozens of new statues as well as a portion of the southern bell tower were underway when a fire broke out inside the cathedral in December of 2001. Any funds earmarked for construction were thereafter diverted for repair and restoration. Today, the cathedral awaits completion at some future date. "Like the great Medieval cathedrals and churches of the world," insists its website FAQ section, "St. John the Divine will continue to be constructed over many centuries." Currently, priority is given to charitable outreach and to maintaining the structural integrity of the cathedral, much of which is now more than a century old.

Take time to explore St John the Divine from all angles. Visit the perplexing statue on Amsterdam Avenue at 111th Street, known as the *Peace Fountain* though it has no running water. Sculpted in 1985 by artist Greg Wyatt, it depicts the battle between good and evil. Michael the Archangel is portrayed having just slain Satan, whose head is held in the pincer of an enormous crab, which represents humanity's origins in the sea. If possible, also visit the small garden and grounds on the south side of the cathedral (security guards may not allow access if the Cathedral School is in session). A visit to the cathedral's interior is also highly recommended, if time allows.

Be sure to look closely at the many statues and carvings on and around the cathedral's main portals on Amsterdam Avenue. Try to find the pedestals which, in depicting the apocalypse, include a broken Brooklyn Bridge and the New York City skyline being destroyed by a tidal wave. The latter is particularly haunting, as it was sculpted prior to 2001 and includes the twin towers of the World Trade Center.

Before moving on it is worthwhile to pay a visit to the Hungarian Pastry Shop just across from the cathedral at No. 1030 Amsterdam Avenue. Open since 1961, it serves excellent coffee and pastries and is among the best opportunities (aside from the cathedral itself) for a restroom break before entering the residential blocks of Central Harlem.

Walk north past the cathedral to **113th Street** and turn right

Stop 5 → Midblock in front of the former **St Luke's Hospital**

113TH STREET AND ST LUKE'S HOSPITAL

Along 113th Street, blocking much of the cathedral's northern facade, stand a pair of shockingly modern 15-story residential towers which went up in 2016, much to the consternation of local residents. Called The Enclave, these towers exist as part of a 99-year land lease from the cathedral which provides a much-needed source of income for the unfinished landmark. Perhaps in another century, the towers might be removed and the cathedral might at last be finished. Only time will tell.

On the north side of 113th Street stands a gorgeous beaux-arts campus designed by Ernest Flagg which until 2013 served as home to St Luke's Hospital. Founded in what is now Midtown in 1858, St Luke's relocated to Morningside Heights in 1896 as part of the "Acropolis" movement. It later merged with Roosevelt Hospital in 1979, then with Beth Israel in 1997 and finally with Mt Sinai in 2013. That same year, the historic wing of the hospital on Morningside Heights was shuttered and reopened as luxury rental apartments in 2019.

Turn left to walk north along **Morningside Drive**

CHURCH OF NOTRE DAME

The Church of Notre Dame at 114th Street is worth a peek inside if it is open. Work on the church began in 1910 and dragged on for half a century before it was permanently discontinued. An intended surmounting dome was never completed, giving the church its unusually boxy profile. But inside, the church's altar is dedicated to St Bernadette, who reportedly saw a vision of Mary in a grotto. That grotto is replicated here, with rough gray stone filling the rear wall where typically one would find a formal reredos. It is a wholly unusual sensation, entering a church which feels more like a cave.

Continue northward toward **116th Street**

Cross to the east side of **Morningside Drive**

Stop 6 → On **116th Street** at the statue of **Carl Schurz** and take in the sweeping views over **Harlem**

THE DEVELOPMENT OF HARLEM

The view of Harlem from Morningside Heights at the 116th Street overlook is hard to beat. From here, the entirety of Harlem's low-slung cityscape spreads out below, a patchwork of grays, reds, and greens. On a clear day, the Bronx–Whitestone Bridge is visible way off in the distance. Such a vista is made possible by the surprising height disparity between Morningside above and Harlem below. It is easy from here to understand why the two neighborhoods developed so differently and on such varied timelines. While Morningside's high, rocky terrain stymied its development until the arrival of the subway in 1904, Harlem's flat expanse made it far more attractive for laying down transit lines, which attracted such rampant overdevelopment in the 19th century. Row upon row of tenements and townhouses were thrown up across Harlem between the 1870s and the start of the 20th century, making up the majority of its building stock to the present day.

Harlem wasn't always so densely developed. In pre-colonial times, its flat grassland was used as a hunting ground by the native people who lived in the area. Soon after the Dutch arrived in the 1620s, farms were carved into the landscape, taking advantage of the rich, flat earth. It was formally organized by Dutch Director-General Peter Stuyvesant in 1658, taking the name Nieuw Haarlem in honor of the village of Haarlem in the Netherlands. Centered along the Harlem River near what is now the intersection of 125th Street and 1st Avenue, Harlem's initial purpose was twofold: firstly, it placed Dutch settlers on the northern end of Manhattan Island, extending the colony's reach. Secondly, it made canaries out of those settlers, allowing them to absorb any attack from the mainland and warn New Amsterdam to the south. No such attack ever materialized; when the British came in 1664, they arrived by sea. Harlem remained a quiet, rural, rather isolated farming community for the next two centuries.

The isolation enjoyed by Harlem's earliest African and European residents came to an abrupt end in the 1870s with Harlem's formal consolidation as part of New York City and the arrival of elevated train lines along 2nd, 3rd, and 8th Avenues. Spewing smoke as they clattered over the fields and farms, these trains halved travel time between Harlem and City Hall to just 45 minutes, and with that, "the uptown area was drawn into the orbit of city life."[206] Harlem was soon flooded with new construction, its streets lined with fine homes and modern apartment buildings which boasted elevators and servants' quarters. Even its tenements, mostly clustered east of the train tracks in what is now East Harlem, were cleaner, brighter, and more comfortable than their dingy downtown counterparts. There were theaters, department stores, dance halls, social clubs, and even an opera house opened in 1889 by Oscar Hammerstein. "People generally took it for granted that Harlem would develop into an exclusive, stable, upper- and upper-middle-class community."[207]

Harlem did attract a steady stream of new residents, many of them drawn by the promise of better housing stock within commuting distance of Manhattan's business districts downtown. By 1890, roughly half of Harlem's population was either German (often Jewish) or Irish in origin, joined by a smaller Italian minority on the east side which would form the city's first so-called "Little Italy." In 1895, the city promised to build a new subway line through the middle of Harlem, leading to a massive speculative building boom along Madison, 5th, and Lenox Avenues, enough "to accommodate approximately 30,000 new settlers,"[208] according to a local trade journal. But the anticipated demand for so many new homes failed to immediately materialize.

Such rapid development in Harlem occurred at a time of breakneck growth all across the city, and uptown developers faced stiff competition from similar construction projects in Brooklyn, Queens, the Bronx, and the Upper East and West Sides. New Yorkers did not want for choice of new places to live, and development uptown proved to be overzealous. To make matters worse, the promised subway line did not open until 1904, leaving much of central Harlem's new development virtually inaccessible from downtown. Though Harlem's population did grow quickly during these heady decades, it was not enough to immediately fill the thousands of homes built for them. Many properties sat empty as the local real estate market threatened to collapse. "By 1905 financial institutions no longer made loans to Harlem speculators,"[209] and the neighborhood plunged into economic crisis.

Around this time, New York's Black population was on the move, thanks in part to the destruction of the west side Tenderloin district, long home to a sizable Black population, to build Penn Station and its railyards. Adding to this, the "Great Migration" saw thousands of Black migrants pour into New York at the turn of the 20th century, most of them coming from the American South and the Caribbean, in search of better jobs, housing, and prospects. What they found instead was a city largely shut off to them, which overcharged them for rent while refusing their access to most lucrative career paths. Many new arrivals came with little schooling, having been barred from educational attainment down South, exacerbating their struggle to succeed in New York.

And so, an uneasy marriage was made of New York's burgeoning Black population and Harlem's real estate speculators. Apartments were let at inflated costs to Black tenants who could least afford such prices but struggled to find welcome anywhere else. Speculative townhouses were subdivided, with half a dozen or more families living in each. And as Black residents moved in, many White residents moved out, in part because landlords knew they could make higher profits off Black tenants. "A certain class of buyers, whose only conscience was money," noted Black realty man John M Royall in 1914, began "placing colored people in property so that they might buy other parcels adjoining"[210] as their White tenants departed, allowing them to expand their profits with ever more overcharged Black tenants.

One of the more tragic results of this racial transformation was that Harlem became massively overcrowded, estimated to be at least twice as densely populated as any other neighborhood in New York by the 1920s. This density went hand in hand with increasingly entrenched poverty, crime, vice, poor health, and a housing stock which rapidly declined due to overuse and habitually deferred maintenance by its often White, often absentee owners. By the 1930s, as wider society turned a blind eye, Harlem suffered the highest rates of tuberculosis in the nation, along with "unusually high rates of infant and maternal mortality, juvenile delinquency, illegitimacy, dope addiction and all the other yardsticks of urban maladjustment."[211]

This is not to say that the era was all struggle and negativity, for out of this tumult emerged the Harlem Renaissance and Harlem's Jazz Age. It is in spite of generational racism and entrenched, quantifiable injustice that Harlem's Black population thrived culturally, spiritually, and artistically, cobbling together a wholly new definition of what it means to be Black in America. Black real estate speculators, such as Philip Payton and Hannah Elias, got rich from the neighborhood's demographic shift. And beyond metrics of disease and destitution, Harlem was among the first places in the world where such a diverse African-origin population came together in such close proximity. Unique musical, religious, and literary traditions from all across the globe melded together in Harlem, creating the basis for modern African-American culture. In Harlem, Black Americans emerged as a formidable political bloc, printing their own newspapers and broadsides, and setting the stage for the Civil Rights Movement of later decades.

MORNINGSIDE PARK

Understanding this piece of Harlem's history is vital to understanding the physical and psychological landscape of the neighborhood as it exists today. With this in mind, descend the stairs from the Carl Schurz memorial into Morningside Park. This park, long, skinny, and steep, is part of a chain of similar parks stretching north from Central Park's Great Hill through Morningside, St Nicholas, Jackie Robinson, and Highbridge Parks to the tip of Manhattan at Inwood. These ridges were protected from development in part thanks to the advocacy of former city parks commissioner Andrew Haswell Green, who helped to earmark them as future parkland back in the 1870s.

At the first landing of the grand granite staircase, turn left and continue downhill on and on until reaching a playground near ground level. Staying inside the park, turn left, and walk north along the path

Stop 7 → At **120th Street** where a small staircase on the right leads out to **Morningside Avenue**

BROWNSTONES

Walking across Harlem is a bit like examining the rings of a tree: each block has a different architectural flavor, a result of Harlem's growth at the end of the 19th century. With this in mind, follow 120th Street east into the heart of Central Harlem. On the north side between Morningside and Manhattan Avenues, there is a superb row of speculative brownstone houses, built for the sort of comfortably middle-class people moving to the area in the aftermath of the elevated train's arrival on nearby 8th Avenue in 1879.

These houses are typical of their era, with a raised basement, high stoop, and three floors above, all crowned by a pressed-tin cornice in an Italianate style. They were built for large multi-generational families who could afford live-in servants. Most had to be extensively retrofitted during the Harlem Renaissance as the neighborhood's newly arriving Black residents tended to be younger, poorer, and unattached. A dozen or more rental apartments were carved out of the interiors of these houses originally intended for a single family.

Continue walking east across **Manhattan Avenue**

Notice how the architectural quality and uniformity changes to include tenements and old warehouses, a symptom of this block's proximity to the crowds and commerce of nearby 8th Avenue (now Frederick Douglass Boulevard). Somewhat confusingly, the 9th Avenue elevated train ran along 8th Avenue here, a result of the area's topography, since 9th Avenue runs into the cliffs of Morningside Park at 110th Street. The now-vanished El had to swing east to 8th Avenue to continue its journey into Harlem.

The 9th Avenue elevated train ran through Harlem from 1879 until 1940, when it was replaced by the 8th Avenue subway lines below. Thanks to the elevated train's presence, the streetscape of Frederick Douglass Boulevard is dominated by tenements and commercial buildings rather than single-family townhouses. No one in the 19th century with the means to live in a single-family home would deign to live in the shadow of the noisy, messy elevated tracks.

One short block east of Frederick Douglass, St Nicholas Avenue cuts a diagonal across Harlem. Its unconventional path through otherwise-gridded upper Manhattan is because St Nicholas is a remnant of a much older Native American highway, once connected to the Bowery downtown, which has been all but erased from the map between Madison Square and Harlem. Humans have trod its path for millennia, a humbling notion.

Brownstone townhouses reappear just east of St Nicholas Avenue, close enough for their residents to commute downtown, but far enough away to not have to deal with the noise. Approaching Adam Clayton Powell, Jr Boulevard, the streetscape shifts again, this time to large elevator apartment buildings, looming six or more stories over the sidewalk. These date to the turn of the 20th century, as upper- and upper-middle-income families began preferring the thrift and convenience of apartment living to the expense and difficulty of maintaining a whole townhouse.

Adding a sense of grandeur to the Harlem streetscape, both 7th and 6th Avenues (officially known as Adam Clayton Powell Jr, Boulevard and Lenox Avenue/Malcolm X Boulevard, respectively) are luxuriously broad, boasting tree-lined medians and double-wide sidewalks. As the city grew northward downtown, both 6th and 7th Avenues dead-ended at 59th Street, Central Park's southern boundary. This allowed uptown developers to reimagine these streets above 110th Street as Parisian boulevards rather than the sort of crowded, claustrophobic thoroughfares they had become downtown.

Cross **Adam Clayton Powell** and continue east

The block of 120th Street between Adam Clayton and Malcolm X is one of the loveliest in Harlem. Its north side is an almost unbroken chain of speculative brownstones, built in the 1880s just as this chocolatey-hued sandstone was falling from favor in New York. The south side of the block, built slightly later, is dominated by light limestone and brick, newly fashionable in the wake of brownstone's exile. Blocks like this one are a treasure, capturing a highly specific window of time during a major inflection point for the city's architectural tastes: the end of the brownstone era and the beginning of all that came after.

Reach **Malcolm X Boulevard** (also called Lenox, Harlem's 6th Avenue)

Stop 8 → At **No. 201 Malcolm X Boulevard** at the northwest corner of **120th Street**

MOUNT OLIVET BAPTIST CHURCH AND TEMPLE ISRAEL

You'll see in front of you a mighty temple, now known as Mount Olivet Baptist Church, which imbues the whole block with a rigid dignity. Mount Olivet is one of countless gorgeous churches which litter the Harlem landscape. To walk these blocks on a Sunday morning is to be serenaded by any number of choirs, bands, and preachers lifting their voices in euphoric praise. Busloads of tourists come to gawk, their presence at gospel services an uncomfortable but fiscally necessary part of modern reality for many churches as attendance declines.

Mount Olivet was founded at the turn of the 20th century, on the cusp of Harlem's emergence as a majority-Black community which would birth the Renaissance for which it has become famous the world over. But like most churches in Harlem, the original congregation of Mount Olivet could not afford to build their own house of worship in those lean early years. Instead, they took savvy advantage of White Flight to repurpose an older building for their use. The mighty edifice which now houses Mount Olivet Baptist Church was built in 1907 as Temple Israel, a still-active Jewish congregation which was established in Harlem by German immigrants in 1873.

Temple Israel was incorporated as Congregation Yad b'Yad, which means Hand in Hand. It was the first Jewish synagogue in Harlem and, as such, it held a major place of importance at the center of the neighborhood's early Jewish life. Their grand limestone temple on Lenox Avenue was their first purpose-built home building and a major point of pride. As demographics shifted over the decades, Temple Israel moved twice more, first to the Upper West Side in 1920 and again to the Upper East Side in 1967, where it currently resides.

The congregation's departure from Harlem made room for Mount Olivet to repurpose the temple as their church. Look closely, however, and signs of the building's original purpose remain: nestled in the middle of the scrolls which top the four giant columns out front are Stars of David. The building, and many like it across the upper reaches of Manhattan, is a physical reminder of a time when Harlem and Washington Heights jointly formed the largest Jewish community in the Western Hemisphere. Today, they serve as living embodiments of the neighborhood's history and the enduring importance of faith in the lives of Harlemites.

Crossing to the east side of Malcolm X Boulevard, 120th Street turns into one of the

Grant's Tomb

120th Street near Malcolm X Boulevard

Mount Olivet Baptist Church

Columbia University, Lowe Library

Manhattan Avenue at 120th Street

Malcolm X Boulevard at 122nd Street

most splendid corridors in the city. These are some of the largest, finest, and most intact brownstone homes in New York and serve as reminders of the great wealth and optimism present here during the end of the 19th century. This block sits within a short walking distance of the bustling Metro-North Station at 125th Street, which was originally built to serve the Vanderbilt family's New York & Harlem Railroad. From that station, wealthy Harlemites could zip down to Grand Central in a matter of minutes, providing them with all the benefits of city life from the safe and comfortable distance of suburban uptown.

At the end of the block, the horizon opens up to reveal a verdant square

Stop 9 → At **Marcus Garvey Park**

MARCUS GARVEY PARK AND THE FIRE WATCHTOWER

Marcus Garvey Park is a 20-acre (8-hectare) square at the heart of central Harlem. It is dominated by a high, rocky promontory known as Mount Morris, so imposing that 5th Avenue actually terminates at 120th Street and resumes north of the park at 124th, the only interruption in its 7-mile (11-km) journey up from Washington Square. Mount Morris was originally known as Snake Hill, later renamed for the locally prominent Morris family. As one of the highest geographic points for miles around, Mount Morris is crowned by a cast-iron fire watchtower, completed in 1856. It was "staffed by watchmen who rang bells and used lamps and flags to alert firefighters"[212] on the ground.

At the time of the fire watchtower's construction, New York City was growing rapidly and fire was one of the chief impediments to its long-term success. It's why the city secured a permanent water supply via the Croton Aqueduct system in 1842 and why wooden construction was outlawed city-wide in 1866. Fire watchtowers like the one on Mount Morris were built on prominent points of high ground all across the island. Over time, however, technology made such towers obsolete and most were long ago torn down to make way for denser development. Only Harlem's survives today, spared by the fact that its promontory was turned into a park.

After a recent restoration, Harlem's fire watchtower looks today much the way it would have when first erected in 1856. Visitors who climb to the top are rewarded with sweeping views stretching as far afield as the Empire State Building to the south, Riverside Church to the west, and passing Metro-North trains to the east. From the ground, the tower is most easily viewed during winter when the trees are bare.

MOUNT MORRIS

The blocks around Mount Morris developed mostly in the 1880s, boasting some of the largest, most beautiful and heavily embellished brownstone houses found anywhere on Manhattan Island. There is a reason the area just west of the park was designated Harlem's first historic district in 1971. "The love and care lavished on these fine houses," reads its designation report, "bears witness to the pride of both their original owners and their present occupants."[213]

Remarkable for a city which has demolished so much of its built heritage in the name of profit and progress, these brownstone rows remain virtually unchanged from their original appearance during the heady years of New York's Gilded Age. In fact, there may be no better place in the borough to see in living color what sort of city the Astors and Vanderbilts might have experienced downtown.

The most notable of the many stunning houses along Mount Morris Park West is No. 31 at the northwest corner of 123rd Street. Unusual for Harlem, which is filled largely with rows of houses built on speculation, this Venetian-inspired home was custom-built in 1890 for wealthy businessman John Dwight. Along with his brother-in-law, Austin Church, Dwight had founded the chemical manufacturing firm Church & Dwight, most famous for its Arm & Hammer brand of baking soda. In the decades after Dwight's death in 1903, his Harlem home served variously as a medical practice, an arts center, and a synagogue (rust stains on the 123rd Street side hint at the fire escape which once marred its facade). It returned to private residential use in 2010, receiving a loving restoration.

In contrast with the largely preserved architectural landscape which surrounds it, Mount Morris Park underwent great change, particularly in the 1960s. In an effort to improve the park's appearance and utility, a swimming pool complex opened there in 1967. Two years later, an amphitheater was constructed on its western edge, a gift from legendary composer Richard Rodgers who spent part of his childhood living around the corner at No. 3 West 120th Street. Also in 1969, the park hosted the Harlem Cultural Festival, a months-long celebration known unofficially as "Black Woodstock," which featured a succession of weekly concerts and gatherings. Performers included Gladys Knight, Mahalia Jackson, Nina Simone, and BB King, and the whole event was immortalized by the 2021 film *Summer of Soul*, which won the Academy Award for Best Documentary.

As for Mount Morris Park, it is now known as Marcus Garvey Park. Jamaican-born Garvey is largely credited with bringing Black Nationalism to the United States in the early 20th century. He advocated for stronger spiritual, economic, and physical bonds with Africa in order to facilitate increased racial independence as well as Africa's redemption from colonialism. In 1919, Garvey founded the Universal Negro Improvement Association as well as the Black Star Line, a transatlantic shipping company meant to eventually ferry goods and passengers between Africa and the Americas. Convicted of mail fraud, he was deported in 1927 and died in London in 1940. Referred to, whether reverently or pejoratively, as "Negro Moses," Garvey remains a potent figure in the arc of the formation of a Black political consciousness. Mount Morris Park was officially renamed in his honor in 1973.

If time allows, it is worthwhile to wander the blocks west of Marcus Garvey Park, admiring the many architectural gems on display between the park and Lenox/Malcolm X. Of particular note are the many splendid religious buildings here. In addition to the aforementioned Mount Olivet Baptist Church (built in 1907 as Temple Israel), there is also St Martin's Episcopal Church (Nos. 230–236 Lenox Avenue, built in 1888), Mount Morris Ascension Presbyterian Church (Nos. 15–21 Mount Morris Park West, built in 1906 as

Malcolm X Boulevard at 122nd Street

Harlem Presbyterian), and Ephesus Seventh-Day Adventist Church (No. 267 Lenox Avenue, built in 1887 as the Reformed Low Dutch Church of Harlem).

Moving on past **Marcus Garvey Park**, rejoin **5th Avenue** at **124th Street** and walk north

Crossing **125th Street**, the main commercial corridor of Harlem, you may look right to see the Metro-North station built atop Park Avenue. Far to the left, you may catch a glimpse of the Apollo Theatre's iconic neon marquee several avenues away. For now, though, continue northward.

For lovers of jazz history, be sure to visit No. 17 East 126th Street, site of the iconic photo *A Great Day in Harlem*, taken on its stoop in 1958. One block north, lovers of literary history will want to visit No. 20 East 127th Street, home to Langston Hughes from 1947 until his death in 1967.

Continue northward along **5th Avenue**, past **St Andrew's Episcopal Church** (**No. 2067 5th Avenue**, built in 1873)

Stop 10 → At the northwest corner of **5th Avenue** and **128th Street**

COLLYER BROTHERS PARK

This small park at No. 2078 5th Avenue occupies the site of a long-demolished brownstone home, architecturally twinned to its extant neighbors at Nos. 2080–2084. On the morning of March 21, 1947, local police were mysteriously summoned to the address by a caller who claimed that there was a dead man inside. No. 2078 was the longtime home of reclusive brothers Homer and Langley Collyer, notorious as local eccentrics and shut-ins. When officers arrived, no one answered the door, forcing them to break in with an ax.

The Collyer brothers were descendants of an old and prominent New York family. Both attended Columbia University and were rumored to be fabulously wealthy. Homer, born in 1881, and Langley, born in 1883, moved into the large corner brownstone in 1909 with their parents, Dr Herman Collyer, and his wife Susie. Herman died in 1923 followed by Susie in 1929, leaving Homer and Langley alone. Over the years, even as the Harlem Renaissance swirled all around them, they receded from public life. Rarely seen in daylight, Langley purportedly wandered the city at night, dressed in decades-old clothing, searching for bargain food prices and collecting rubbish. They shut off their gas, electricity, and phone lines, and stopped opening their mail. "You can't imagine how free we feel,"[214] claimed Langley in a rare 1938 interview.

Homer went blind around 1940, becoming entirely dependent on his brother. Langley insisted Homer's sight would return, plying him with oranges and hoarding newspapers for him to read when it did. Rumors swirled about the Collyers: "some say its interior resembles an Arabian Night's dream of antique tapestries and other rarities; others say it's a rat-infested scene of filth and squalor."[215] Then in 1947, that phone call arrived, and police broke into the mysterious house. They found no treasure; instead the home was piled high with trash and broken antiques. Crude booby traps lined the few pathways through the refuse, threatening to drop heavy boxes on any trespassers.

A day into their search, police discovered Homer Collyer, seated in an old chair near a second-story window, dead for perhaps a month. As word spread about the macabre discovery, a crowd sometimes as large as 2,000 people gathered at the intersection to watch as police sifted through the home, room by room, dumping literally tons of detritus from its windows. Car parts, pianos, clocks, bicycles, generators, and thousands of books were emptied from the house as officers disassembled the many traps and tunnels assembled by the brothers inside.

All the while, Langley was missing. Calls poured in that he had been spotted wandering the streets of New York, or even eating dinner in Atlantic City, though he even failed to attend Homer's funeral on April 1. The mystery ended a week later, however, when police found Langley's rat-chewed body in the house, mere feet from the chair where Homer had died, buried beneath one of his own booby traps. As work on the house continued, dozens of Collyer "cousins" came out of the woodwork, trying to stake their claim on whatever treasures might be found. When it became clear that there was no gold hidden anywhere and, more disappointingly, that the brothers were actually in debt, these claims receded as quietly as they'd materialized. The Collyer house was emptied and demolished, too rotted for repair.

The small park which now occupies their lot was officially named in their honor in the 1990s, though not without pushback from locals who felt they were unworthy of such an honor. To this day, however, the Collyer name remains shorthand for a hoarding situation, with police and fire departments around the world calling them "Collyer Mansions."

Continue north past the **Collyer Park** to **130th Street** and turn left

Stop 11 → On **130th Street** between **5th Avenue** and **Malcolm X Boulevard**

ASTOR ROW

Here on the south side of 130th Street can be found one of the loveliest and most unexpected blocks in all of Harlem, or even in New York City. Its houses, all alike and in pairs, were built in the early 1880s as a speculative investment by William B Astor, Jr, grandson of John Jacob Astor and husband to the Gilded Age's Caroline Astor, better known as *The* Mrs Astor (page 211). The Astor dynasty got its start in the fur trade in the heady years after the American Revolution, but family patriarch John Jacob Astor saw future wealth in real estate investment. To that end, he bought cheap land all across Manhattan, trusting that it would pay future dividends.

Astor purchased these parcels on 130th Street in Harlem in 1844, just four years before his death. Afterward, the land passed to his son William, who held it until his death in 1875. It then passed to *his* son, William, Jr, who hired the architect Charles Buek to take advantage of Harlem's rising real estate prospects by filling the land with comfortable, attractive homes. In all, so-called Astor Row was built with 28 houses, all built between 1881 and 1883, with three stories of red brick with light-colored stone trim and delicate wooden porches set behind deep front gardens. Writer Claude McKay, in his 1928 *Home to Harlem*, called Astor Row "The Block Beautiful," with its "charming green lawns and quaint white-

Astor Row

139th Street near Edgecombe Avenue

Hamilton Grange

Convent Avenue at 143rd Street

fronted houses, it preserved the most Arcadian atmosphere in all New York."[216]

The houses of Astor Row remain a delightful departure from typical townhouse development of their era, a sign of what might have been had Harlem's speculative boom not forced its aggressive over-development in later years. The brownstone houses on the north side of the block, built just a few years later, are far more typical of the sorts of houses found elsewhere. The Astor family retained their Harlem houses until the 1920s. By then, the economic fortunes of upper Manhattan had begun to waver amid the neighborhood's racial transformation. Astor Row, long reserved only for White tenants, was sold off and followed the prevailing demographic trends. By 1925, it was almost entirely home to Black tenants.

Over the following years, Astor Row joined in Harlem's downward economic slide. By 1981, the year these houses were designated official New York City landmarks, most had been carved up into small, often single-room-occupancy, apartments. Many had lost their wooden porches, their brick facades slathered in paint. Beginning in 1992, an aggressive restoration project got underway, led by the private non-profit New York Landmarks Conservancy and funded in part by the charitable foundation of Vincent Astor, grandson of William Astor who built the row. This restoration brought "ignored, tumble-down"[217] Astor Row back to something like its original beauty. Sadly, in 2021, the home at No. 28 was demolished due to neglect. What will become of this glaring gap in an otherwise intact row remains to be seen.

Walk west past **Astor Row** to **Malcolm X Boulevard**. Turn right and then left again onto **131 St Street**. Walk the length of this block, dominated by unusually intact rows of speculative late-19th-century brownstone houses

Stop 12 → On the east side of **Adam Clayton Powell Jr Boulevard** between **131st** and **132nd Streets**

LAFAYETTE THEATRE

A bland and frankly uninspiring apartment building currently occupies the entire blockfront here at No. 2235 Adam Clayton Powell Jr Boulevard (Harlem's 7th Avenue). What's worse is that the building demolished to make room for it was among the most storied and historically important structures in the neighborhood. The Lafayette Theatre stood, in some form or another, for a century before falling prey to redevelopment. To understand the Lafayette and its place in Harlem history, it is important to have a clear mental image of what this place looked like when it was in its prime.

Harlem in the 1920s was a neighborhood pulsing with youth and energy. In the face of economic adversity and entrenched societal racism, its Renaissance was ascendant, on course to transform the oeuvre of American music, art, cuisine, literature, and politics. Harlem's staid brownstones and apartment blocks, built a generation earlier for White tenants, were crowded with a whole new generation of Black Harlemites, many of them transplants from the Deep South and Caribbean isles. It was one of the most intensely exciting places on earth.

In such a thrumming, energetic neighborhood, 7th Avenue was an outlet and escape. A wide, tree-lined boulevard, it came alive after dark with the glow of theater marquees and the clamor of nightlife spilling from its sidewalks. Arguably the most important theater in Harlem was the Lafayette, on 7th Avenue between 131st and 132nd Streets. When it opened in 1912, Black attendees were only allowed in the balcony. But as the Lafayette struggled to make money, it integrated in 1913, and was featuring all-Black theatrical troupes by 1915. Luminaries such as Bessie Smith, Ethel Waters, Moms Mabley, Leadbelly, Duke Ellington, Fletcher Henderson, Earl Hines, Stepin Fetchit, and others headlined there through the 1920s.

One of the most famous productions to be put on at the Lafayette was an all-Black production of Shakespeare's *Macbeth* staged in 1936 as part of the Works Project Administration's Negro Theatre Unit. It was directed by Orson Welles, then just 20 years old. Welles transferred the play from Scotland to a mythical West Indian island, its witches replaced by voodoo priestesses, raising eyebrows in the city's more originalist theatrical circles. But the enthusiasm of the cast, crew, and indeed the audience was enough to sufficiently silence any criticism. Opening night was a glittering triumph, with throngs of onlookers spilling out into the street beneath the neon-lit awning as a brass band played and press photographers jockeyed to capture the stream of celebrity attendees.

Outside the Lafayette Theatre stood Harlem's Wishing Tree. The details are hazy, but it seems to have been an elm tree, one of hundreds planted all along 7th Avenue, which happened to stand just outside the stage door of the Lafayette. By the 1920s, the tree was considered lucky: anyone taking the stage at the Lafayette, or wishing to land a job there, would stand in its shade and rub its bark for good fortune. Everyone from Paul Robeson to Bill "Bojangles" Robinson wished on the tree over the years.

The tree began to die, however, turning into a sad scraggly thing (if indeed it was an elm, it may have succumbed to Dutch Elm Disease which ravaged America's urban forests at this time) until city parks employees arrived on August 20, 1934. Axes in hand, they declared the Wishing Tree a hazard and felled it before a devastated crowd. But that wasn't the end of the Wishing Tree. Its stump was saved and preserved, slathered in epoxy and polish, and placed in the traffic median across from the theater. A new tree, renamed the Tree of Hope, was planted next to it, though it eventually died as well.

After World War II, Harlem's nightlife became a shadow of its former self. The Lafayette shuttered and in 1951 was sold and turned into a church. In 1990, over the cries of local historians and preservationists, its facade was jackhammered away "to make it look more like a church than a theater,"[218] according to its pastor. It was demolished entirely in 2013, replaced by the current apartment building which provided the church with space on its ground level. As for the stump? Miraculously, it survives. A section of it is now kept at the Apollo Theater on 125th Street, where it is still rubbed by theatrical hopefuls each night. It endures as a rare physical link to Harlem's Renaissance of a century ago.

Passing the site of the former **Lafayette Theatre**, walk north along **Adam Clayton Powell**. Along the way, if Harlem's ecclesiastical history is of interest, there are four tremendously important church buildings tucked away on either side of the avenue

FOUR CHURCHES

First, there is St Aloysius Catholic Church at No. 219 West 132nd Street, built in 1904 by William Renwick, nephew of James Renwick who designed Grace Church (page 143) and St Patrick's Cathedral (page 180). Its busy, eclectic polychrome facade "is based on Italian Gothic prototypes, not often seen as the source of stylistic inspiration for buildings in New York City."[219] It remains an eye-catching outlier among the area's more reserved architecture, a joy to behold.

Second, there is St Philip's Episcopal Church at No. 204 West 134th Street, built in 1911 by renowned architect Vertner Tandy. Born in Kentucky, Tandy studied at the Tuskegee Institute and Cornell University before becoming the first registered Black architect in New York State. Renowned as "Black America's richest church"[220] thanks to its vast real estate investments, St Philip's was established downtown in 1809 by Black congregants from Trinity Church (page 22) and St Paul's Chapel (page 29) who'd tired of the racism and segregation within these White-led institutions. They relocated to Harlem in 1911, one of the first major Black churches to do so. It remains the oldest Black Anglican congregation in New York and a powerful presence in Harlem's spiritual, social, and political realms.

Third, there is Mother AME Zion Church at No. 140 West 137th Street, built in 1925 to designs by Vertner Tandy's longtime associate George W Foster. Mother AME Zion is the oldest Black congregation in New York, tracing its history all the way to 1796, when it formed as an offshoot of the John Street Methodist Church. Over the ensuing decades, New York's Zion congregation planted the seeds for a whole conference of similar churches across the nation, all involved in abolition and social justice (luminaries including Harriet Tubman and Frederick Douglass counted themselves as Zion Conference members). Zion moved to Harlem in 1914 and has remained a guiding influence in the neighborhood ever since.

Fourth, one block north of Zion, is the Abyssinian Baptist Church at No. 132 West 138th Street. Built here in 1923, its congregation was founded in 1808, making it the second-oldest Black church in New York, second only to neighboring Mother AME Zion. Established as an offshoot of First Baptist, Abyssinian struggled to remain solvent for its first half-century before finding sure footing under the leadership of Reverend William Spellman between 1856 and 1885. Beginning in 1908, Abyssinian was led by Reverend Adam Clayton Powell, Sr, who oversaw its movement uptown to Harlem and growth to an estimated 10,000 congregants. His son, Adam Clayton Powell, Jr, became the first Black person elected to the United States Congress from New York, serving in that office from 1945 until 1971. Nationally prominent, Abyssinian retains its local focus, with a long list of social outreach programs and a renowned choir which draws tourists by the busload to this corner of Harlem.

Continue walking north along **Adam Clayton Powell**, the boulevard named for the aforementioned congressman

Stop 13 → At **138th Street**

STRIVERS' ROW

Manhattan is notorious for its lack of alleyways, an omission most obvious on hot summer days when the garbage bags pile up on sidewalks, offending the senses and harboring hordes of rats. New York's street grid was designed in 1811 without alleyways because they were seen as a waste of valuable space in a city whose primary function was the building of wealth. Imagine the acreage required to open up every single one of Manhattan's hundreds of streets, carving a minimum of 10 feet (3 meters) of roadbed through every block, all so we could have someplace to hide away our trash bins. It goes against the city's nature, for better or worse.

So it comes as a bit of a shock, having grown accustomed to Manhattan's aversion to alleyways, to stumble upon Harlem's Strivers' Row. These two blocks, comprising 160 houses on 138th and 139th Streets west of Adam Clayton Powell, were conceived by David H King, a successful builder and contractor who was drawn to Harlem during its 19th century real estate boom. He purchased this land from the neighboring Watt-Pinckney Estate and hired some of the age's most well-respected architects to assemble a speculative development unlike anything anywhere else in the city. Most notably, King ordered alleyways cut through the rear yards of the houses, hidden behind high iron gates, neatly obscuring all the necessary mess of urban life. Such gentility remains unmatched in the city to this day.

Strivers' Row encompasses two blocks but was designed by three architectural firms, each of which brought their particular flair to the project. The south side of 138th Street is the work of James Brown Lord, a man better known for his monumental commissions downtown, including the 1890 Delmonico's building at No. 56 Beaver Street (page 19) and the 1900 Appellate Division Courthouse at No. 33 East 25th Street. For the King houses, Lord was relatively restrained, designing a row of high-stooped brick houses with brownstone trim, "the embodiment of Victorian conformity."[221]

On the north side of 138th Street, Bruce Price and Clarence Luce were more ebullient in their design, one which is twinned a block over on the south side of 139th Street. As the centerpiece of Strivers' Row, the double block by Price and Luce gives personality to the whole endeavor. In place of dreary red brick and dark stone, they masterfully employed a creamy palette of pale yellow brick and off-white terracotta, with Greek-key motifs above spritely arched doorways, all set off by the graceful black ironwork of their double-height stoops and parlor-floor balconettes. Though stylistically unusual for New York, the rows by Price and Luce are timeless in their design, feeling fresh and inviting even after more than a century of wear and changing tastes.

Lastly, the north side of 139th Street was designed by Stanford White of McKim, Mead & White, a man as famous for his personal proclivities and eventual murder in 1906 atop Madison Square Garden (which he incidentally also designed) as he was for his talent as an architect. For his share of Strivers' Row, White deviated from his colleagues in that he omitted stoops altogether, foreshadowing a trend which would catch on a decade or more later. His houses are more inward-looking than those by Lord or Price

Strivers' Row (138th Street)

& Luce, only hinting at the warmth and comforts to be found inside. Made of dark rust-colored brick, they convey the look and feel of an Italian palazzo, a style introduced to New York by White in 1884 when he designed the brownstone Villard Houses at Nos. 451–457 Madison Avenue. He perfected the style in the mansion he designed in 1892 for James Hampden Robb at No. 23 Park Avenue, a building which survives today on Murray Hill (page 168).

In all, Strivers' Row is a triumph of 1890s good taste and refinement. Referred to as the "King Model Houses," the blocks were meant to serve as a blueprint for a better way forward all across the city, though they remained available only to White residents. Ultimately, the King houses got caught up in Harlem's real estate bubble and the whole project was foreclosed upon during the financial panic of 1893. Many units sat empty for nearly 30 years. Finally, in 1919, the houses opened to Black New Yorkers and quickly attracted some of the greatest luminaries of the era, including the aforementioned architect Vertner Tandy, who lived in one of the Stanford White houses at No. 211 West 139th Street. It was during this era that the King Model Houses became better known as Strivers' Row, indicating "the great desirability of living in this two-block area."[222]

Feel free to wander both blocks of **Strivers' Row** before walking west to **St Nicholas Avenue**. Turn right and walk to **141st Street**. Turn left and walk uphill along **141st**

Stop 14 → At **Hamilton Grange National Memorial**

HAMILTON GRANGE

Perched just inside the park is a yellow, wooden house with wide verandahs that was the final home of founding father Alexander Hamilton.

Alexander Hamilton was a consummate New Yorker. His identity was tied to the city ever since he arrived from the isle of Nevis in 1773. As most other American founding fathers retired to their respective dignified countryside estates, Hamilton and his family attempted to make a life downtown. But a yellow fever epidemic in 1793, which sickened both Alexander and his wife Eliza, sent them in search of an escape. They found it uptown, where they'd sail up the Hudson and spend the summer months hunting and fishing Harlem's forested expanses. They took half-ownership of a farmhouse here in 1798 and began planning for construction of their own estate.

Hamilton purchased 32 acres (13 hectares) in 1800 from Jacob Schieffelin and Samuel Bradhurst, encompassing everything from what's now 139th to 146th Streets between St Nicholas Terrace to Hamilton Place. It was convenient to downtown via the Bloomingdale Road (now Broadway) and had sweeping views over the island and river valley. The new Hamilton family home was completed in 1802, and named The Grange. It was designed to be the height of rural fashion and comfort for the era by the eminent John McComb, Jr, who also designed Gracie Mansion and New York's City Hall (page 30).

Of course, anyone who's seen the hit Broadway musical by Lin-Manuel Miranda knows that Alexander Hamilton didn't get to enjoy

The Grange for long. He died in Greenwich Village on July 12, 1804, following a duel with Aaron Burr in Weehawken, New Jersey. The Grange was sold by his family in 1813 and they moved downtown. The Hamilton home attracted the construction of some of the city's finest rowhouses along Convent Avenue and its side streets, built for New Yorkers willing to pay a premium to live within view of the great patriot's former home.

Over the years, The Grange aged and sagged. It was picked up and moved down the block in 1889 to serve as chapel and rectory for St Luke's Church, which remains standing today, albeit abandoned and worse for wear, at No. 435 West 141st Street. A statue of Hamilton remains in the churchyard as a reminder of its former presence there. The Grange remained sandwiched between the church and a neighboring apartment building until 2008, when it was picked up and moved again. This time, it was hoisted and dragged down the avenue and around the corner to nearby St Nicholas Park, where it was restored to something resembling its original Hamiltonian splendor. Here it remains, more than two centuries after its original occupant met his end, preserved for posterity and open to the public.

SUGAR HILL

Across from The Grange is a quiet little street called Hamilton Terrace. Walk north under its thick tree canopy, admiring the architectural beauty of this unlikely corner of Harlem. This whole area, nestled along the top of the ridge leading up to Washington Heights, has always been a highly coveted area. When Hamilton's house still stood nearby on Convent Avenue, builders flocked to construct fine rows of houses such as these on Hamilton Terrace to house those New Yorkers eager to live in the presence of patriotic greatness.

When Harlem's demographic majority shifted from White to Black in the early 20th century, these houses largely attracted the sort of wealthy, prominent Black buyers who could overcome the inherent racism baked into the city's real estate market. In short, the houses in this area remained intact, occupied by many of the nation's leading politicians, artists, musicians, actors, and athletes throughout the Renaissance and Jazz Age. Knowing this, Harlemites subjected to increasingly overcrowded conditions down in the central part of the neighborhood, looked up at this area with envy. They claimed that those people up there must be living the sweet life. And thus, the moniker Sugar Hill was born.

Follow **Hamilton Terrace** to its bend at **144th Street** and follow it west to **Convent Avenue**

Of note, the stunning conical-towered townhouse at No. 339 Convent was prominently featured in the 2001 classic film *The Royal Tenenbaums* by Wes Anderson.

Turn left onto **Convent Avenue**

Walk south past some of the loveliest homes in New York. With deep gardens and unusually eclectic facade embellishments, they are a treat for the senses.

Continue southward, across **141st Street**

Stop 15 → On **Convent Avenue** in the central quad of **City College**

CITY COLLEGE OF NEW YORK

The core campus of City College is a riot of Collegiate Gothic architecture. Wrought in dark gray schist and creamy terracotta, it boasts more than 1,000 grotesques and gargoyles, no two of which are alike. Hidden along the rooflines, doorways, and cornices are an army of tiny carved professors and owls, laborers with hammers and saws, and acrobats who seem to serve no narrative purpose other than to entertain passersby with their antics. The whole complex was designed by the renowned architect George B Post, who is perhaps most famous for his work on the New York Stock Exchange Building (page 22). For City College, he sought to convey the academic grandeur of Oxford or Cambridge, but perched atop a bluff overlooking the brownstone blocks of Harlem.

The City College of New York was established in 1847 as the Free Academy. True to its name, the school was tuition-free and open to all, including those who might not otherwise be admitted to most institutes of higher learning at the time: the poor, the immigrant, and the non-Christian people who made up such a large and rapidly growing percentage of the population. The school's first campus was a broad, spindly structure designed by James Renwick, Jr, at the southeast corner of 23rd Street and Lexington Avenue, just north of Gramercy Park. It remained there from 1849 until 1907, during that time building a reputation as one of the best colleges in the nation. It attracted many students and professors of outstanding academic merit and potential who could not gain admission or secure tenured positions at most other elite institutions. City College was sometimes called, not altogether pejoratively, "the poor man's Harvard."

Ground was broken on this new campus in 1903 and a grand dedication ceremony was held five years later. Over the ensuing decades, City College prided itself on educating generations of scholars, many of whom were the first in their families to achieve such heights of academia. To date, at least a dozen City College alumni have been awarded the Nobel Prize, by that metric placing it among the topmost tier of schools in the nation.

Today, City College retains its reputation for academic excellence and continues to educate scores of New York's brightest minds. This campus serves as the flagship for the City University of New York (CUNY), a sprawling association of more than two dozen schools enrolling more than a quarter-million students each year. Through it all, the hundreds of grotesques which adorn the school's walls, towers, and downspouts have kept silent vigil. They watch, grinning cheekily as the world continues to spin all around them. Here, on a bluff above Harlem, the past remains present.

City College

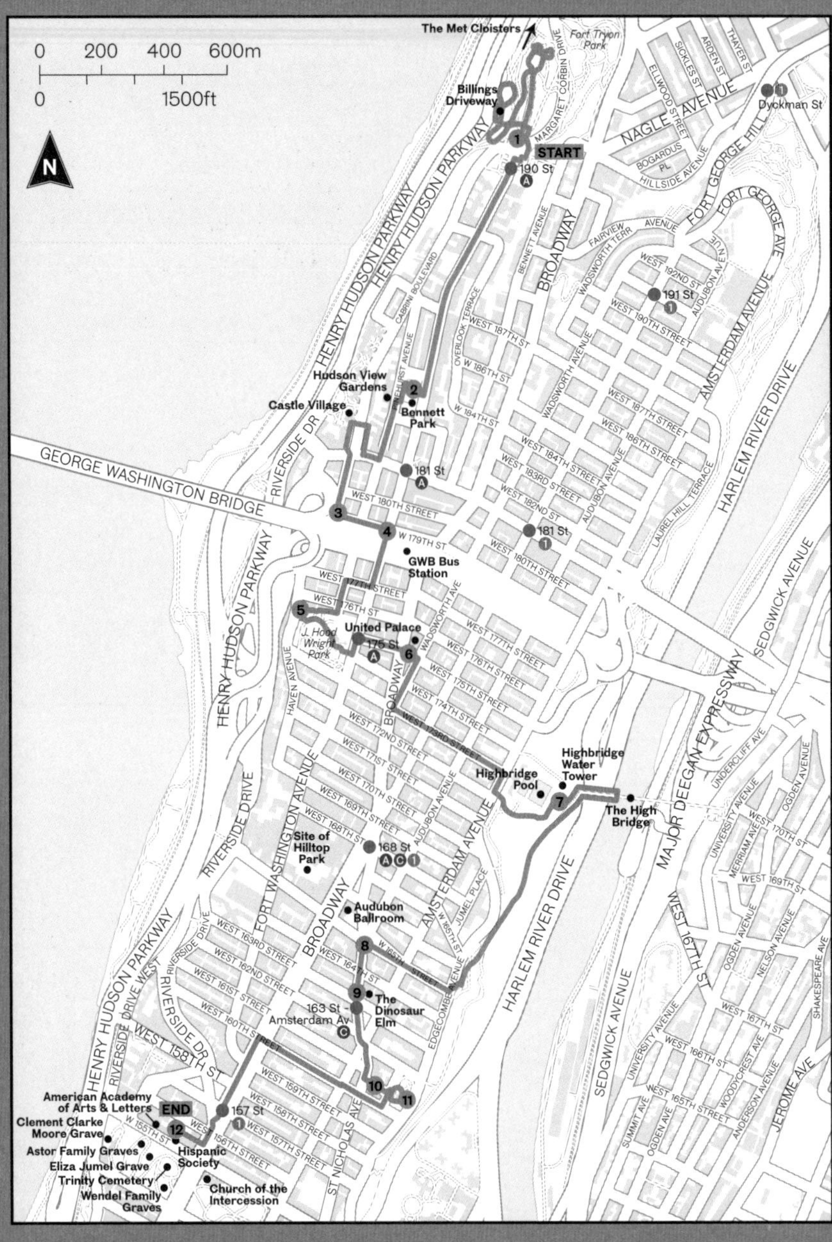

The Met Cloisters
Fort Tryon Park
Billings Driveway
START
190 St
Dyckman St
Hudson View Gardens
Bennett Park
Castle Village
181 St
George Washington Bridge
GWB Bus Station
United Palace
175 St
J. Hood Wright Park
Highbridge Water Tower
Highbridge Pool
The High Bridge
168 St
Site of Hilltop Park
Audubon Ballroom
The Dinosaur Elm
163 St - Amsterdam Av
157 St
END
American Academy of Arts & Letters
Clement Clarke Moore Grave
Astor Family Graves
Eliza Jumel Grave
Trinity Cemetery
Wendel Family Graves
Hispanic Society
Church of the Intercession
0 200 400 600m
0 1500ft
N

WASHINGTON HEIGHTS

Perched along the craggy ridgelines of Manhattan's most northerly reaches, Washington Heights is a neighborhood of intense diversity, home to the largest concentration of Spanish-speaking residents in Manhattan today. In some ways, Washington Heights sprang forth almost overnight with the arrival of the subway in 1904. But landmarks like the Morris-Jumel Mansion and the Met Cloisters freight the landscape with centuries of cultural and architectural history. Within the confines of this neighborhood's countless prewar apartment towers play out the daily lives of a quarter-million New Yorkers.

ROUTE STOPS

1. Fort Tryon Park at Margaret Corbin Plaza
2. Bennett Park
3. George Washington Bridge
4. GWB Bus Terminal
5. J Hood Wright Park
6. United Palace
7. High Bridge Park
8. McKenna Square
9. The Dinosaur Elm
10. Sylvan Terrace
11. Morris-Jumel Mansion
12. Audubon Terrace

DISTANCE
4¾ miles (7.75 km)

TIME ALLOWED
3 hours

ROUTE No.

12

THE TOP OF MANHATTAN

Washington Heights is a large and densely populated neighborhood which encompasses everything from 155th Street to 190th Street (or Dyckman Street depending on who you ask). To the south is Harlem and to the north lies Inwood and, beyond that, Marble Hill and the Bronx. Long considered a rural backwater of time-worn inns, farms, country houses, and battle sites, the landscape of Washington Heights exploded in the 20th century with the arrival of the subway. Suddenly, the city and its hundreds of thousands of residents were a short commute away from the leafy beauty of Manhattan's northernmost reaches.

Because Washington Heights developed seemingly all at once, most of its building stock today reflects its youthful post-subway heyday between the 1910s and 1930s. Its blocks are made up of mostly 6- to 10-story residential towers, peppered throughout with churches, schools, garages, and hospitals. Its apartments are generally large and comfortable, built for the sort of upwardly mobile New York families who made up its earliest demographic: those of German, Italian, Russian, Irish, and Jewish extraction who had worked their way out of the tenements and sought the trappings of the American middle class.

Over the past century, Washington Heights has continued to attract successive waves of New York's newest, most ambitious residents. Most notably, it has become home to the city's densest concentration of people of Caribbean heritage, chiefly hailing from the Dominican Republic and Puerto Rico, who bring with them their language, cuisine, music, and vibrant culture. Washington Heights remains one of the largest, most populous, and most historically fascinating parts of New York City.

Start 1 → The entrance to **Fort Tryon Park** on **Margaret Corbin Plaza**

FORT TRYON PARK

Fort Tryon Park is easily one of the most beautiful public spaces in all of Manhattan. Beloved by locals, it flies under the radar of the city's broader population largely thanks to its relative remoteness at the top of the island. Most New Yorkers' familiarity with Fort Tryon begins and ends with a visit to the Met Cloisters, but even a short stroll along the park's many-tiered walking paths reveals just what a special place it is.

Sitting atop a ridge once called Long Hill, Fort Tryon got its present name from the fortifications which were built here during the American Revolution. It was part of a sprawling defensive network on this ridge, built as part of the larger Fort Washington to the south (now Bennett Park) with Fort George on the neighboring ridge to the east (roughly at Audubon Avenue and 192nd Street), which were all lost by American forces in the Battle of Fort Washington, which was fought here on November 16, 1776. This was the final battle for control of Manhattan, and the Americans' surrender here meant New York City would be occupied by British forces for the duration of the war.

Despite the loss, one of the war's more notable acts of heroism occurred during the battle when nurse Margaret Cochran Corbin became the first known American woman to fight in active combat. Twenty-five-year-old Margaret was at Fort Washington alongside her husband, cannoneer John Corbin, who was killed during the onslaught. Having watched him countless times, Margaret took his place at the cannon, admirably firing the weapon until she, too, was hit by enemy fire. She was captured in the surrender of Fort Washington, but after the Revolution ended, in honor of her bravery, she became the first American woman to receive a military pension.

The triumphant British thereafter named this fort in honor of Lord William Tryon, the last British colonial governor of New York. Though most British place names were stripped away after the colonists' victory in 1783, the name Fort Tryon has stuck to this place for nearly a quarter of a millennium.

This land changed hands several times before it was purchased in 1901 by the wealthy horse aficionado Cornelius Kingsley Garrison Billings. CKG Billings was born at Saratoga Springs, New York, in 1861. Raised in Chicago, he graduated from college at age 17 and joined his father's natural gas company that same year. He rose through the ranks to become president at age 26 and retired from the business in 1901 at age 40. By this time, he was one of the nation's wealthiest men and was known as America's Horse King due to his showy success on the race course. It made sense then, when it was announced in late 1901 that Billings had purchased a collection of choice parcels at Manhattan's northern end and that he intended to build a mansion and stables there.

Attractively, Billings' new estate sat in close proximity to the newly opened Harlem Speedway, the best thoroughfare for carriage riding in the nation at the time. At first, he built only a lodge for himself, a sort of gentleman's retreat for when he ventured uptown to tend and race his horses. This initial structure, a lookout tower affording sweeping views over the entire Hudson Valley, inspired Billings to move uptown permanently. He enlisted architect Guy Lowell to expand the tower lodge into a proper mansion named Tryon Hall. Billings moved in, along with his family and 23 servants, in 1907.

The Billings home was filled with sumptuous antiques and expensive works of art. The rooms were decorated with the finest materials imported from Europe as well as the most modern American conveniences such as a bowling alley, swimming pool, and electric light switches in every room. The house centered on a two-story glass-roofed courtyard lined in French limestone, with a hand-painted canvas hung above to modulate the light. The dining and drawing rooms lined the ground floor's west side, taking advantage of the views. Bedrooms were upstairs, with servants' quarters above that. East of the house lay Billings' immense stables, with one wing for his collection of automobiles and a suite of apartments upstairs for his jockeys and stablehands.

But upper Manhattan was beginning to change at the turn of the 20th century. In 1901, the same year Billings purchased old Fort Tryon, an engineering marvel was nearing completion a few miles down the road: a great iron viaduct, 80 feet (24 meters) high that extended Riverside Drive across the valley at Manhattanville (modern 125th Street) which had long impeded the movement of people, horses, and automobiles up the island's west side. Beyond the viaduct, Riverside Drive was pushed all the way north to Boulevard Lafayette at 158th Street, providing an unbroken 10-mile (16-km) thoroughfare which soon rivaled the Harlem Speedway as the city's greatest driving course.

Enter **Fort Tryon Park** and follow the path to the left, down a short flight of stairs and then left again. Descend a longer flight of stairs which will take you down toward an enormous stone arcade, once the **Billings driveway**

But Billings faced a dilemma: though his new mansion stood directly above the new road, it was separated from the action below by 50-foot (15-meter) cliffs of jagged schist. Getting from his house to Riverside Drive required a circuitous drive downhill to Broadway, then up to Dyckman Street where he could finally gain access to Riverside. For a man of his stature, this was unacceptable. In late 1912, he hired the architectural firm of Buchman & Fox to design a driveway capable of carrying automobiles and carriages between his house and the roadway far below. Local legend states that Billings sent a neighbor's cow up the cliff to find the most natural route. That route, a series of hairpin switchbacks, would be impossible to navigate by car. So the architects devised a solution: rounded switchbacks whereby one of the curves swings out into open air before continuing its ascent. The open-air curve would be supported by an immense granite arcade which would also serve to create a sweeping lawn and balcony for the house.

Construction of the new driveway cost a staggering $250,000 and lasted the better part of a year, but gave Billings the grandest, most outlandish entrance of any home in the city. Entering via Billings' new bronze gates on Riverside Drive, visitors would have gaped at the stone arcade as their ascent slowly revealed ever more stunning views of the river and palisades before revealing the mansion itself at the top. Amazingly, just three years later, Billings tired of life uptown. He sold the estate, along with its spectacular driveway, to John D Rockefeller for $750,000.

Follow the **Billings driveway** through the stone arcade, following its S-curve uphill to the overlook atop the arches

John Davison Rockefeller, Jr, only son of the legendary billionaire oilman, purchased the Billings estate along with dozens of adjacent acres in late 1916, intending to donate it all to the city as parkland. He also purchased hundreds of acres of land on the New Jersey side of the Hudson River in order to preserve the view from Manhattan. Mayor John Purroy Mitchel was poised to accept the land-gift, but the outbreak of World War I pushed Rockefeller to try to convert the Billings Mansion into a hospital for wounded soldiers. This plan fell through, and just months later,

Mayor Mitchel died falling out of a plane in Louisiana. His successor was less keen on the idea of accepting so many acres of "unimproved" land for which the city would then be financially responsible.

Another major issue was the Billings Mansion itself: unable to find a use for it, Rockefeller wished to demolish it, but local architects objected. They suggested that it be used instead as a museum "for the preservation of relics associated with the history of the city and State."[223] But the city didn't want responsibility for a mansion, nor was it interested in a new municipal museum. Rockefeller's gift was rejected, and he was forced to wait, renting out the buildings in the meantime. Nearly a decade passed. In March 1926, smoke was seen pouring from the roof of the old Billings Mansion. The renting family fled, but firemen were unable to maintain enough water pressure to fight the flames. Within hours, Tryon Hall was destroyed.

With the Billings Mansion gone, it was no longer a sticking point for the city, which at last accepted it from Rockefeller as new public parkland. Designs were executed by Frederick Law Olmsted, Jr, son of the designer of Central Park, and work began in 1931 to transform the 100 acres (40 hectares) of lawns and forests into a garden playland for all New Yorkers. Rockefeller requested that the new park be named Forrest Hill Park,[224] declaring it distasteful and unpatriotic to name it for British Lord Tryon. But his protests went unheeded.

From the overlook, continue uphill through the heather garden and onto **Linden Terrace,** which provides sweeping views in all directions, including of the **Cloisters Museum** to the north.

THE CLOISTERS

Despite this, behind the scenes, Rockefeller was quietly working with the artist George Grey Barnard on another, even more ambitious project: a new museum for the new park.

George Grey Barnard was living with his family in the French countryside in 1904. While visiting a nearby farm, he noticed two sculpted figures outside their henhouse: remnants of an ancient chapel, long since destroyed, explained the farmer, and they helped the chickens to lay eggs. Barnard spent the next month negotiating with the farmer for the statues, ultimately buying them for 40 francs. Over the next decade, he acquired hundreds more medieval artifacts from across France, including an entire arcade from the Abbey of St Michel de Cuxa (the French Government objected to this leaving the country, and ultimately agreed to allow Barnard to take part of it while leaving the rest in place).

Barnard erected his treasures on his property on Fort Washington Avenue at the northeast corner of 190th Street, opening them to the public in 1914. The Cloisters instantly became a popular local landmark. But the high cost of maintaining the art as well as rising tax assessments were too much for Barnard; he was forced to put the whole collection up for sale in 1922.

Enter John D Rockefeller, Jr, who purchased the collection and donated it to the Metropolitan Museum of Art as a medieval outpost. In 1935, Rockefeller reached a deal with the Met and the city to build an immense new medieval museum inside the newly opened Fort Tryon Park. Construction lasted for three years, with the new museum opening on May 10, 1938. Robert Moses, Mayor LaGuardia, and Rockefeller were in attendance. But one man was conspicuously absent that day: George Grey Barnard, whose collections formed the nucleus of the Cloisters Museum. He died on April 24, just two weeks prior to its opening.

Today, Fort Tryon Park is the crown jewel of Washington Heights. Entering from Fort Washington Avenue, visitors can turn left and descend the stairs to the bottom of the cliff where they will encounter the surviving stone pillars from CKG Billings' estate entrance. From there, they are drawn uphill via the arcaded driveway he had built more than a century ago. Atop the cliff, at the end of the S-curve path, lies the park's heather garden. Originally laid out in 1935, it was fully rehabilitated in the 1980s and is a riot of color and texture in warmer months.

Just north of the heather garden stands Linden Terrace, a 20th-century homage to the fort which once stood nearby. The "architectonic"[225] terrace offers sweeping views of the Hudson River to the west, the Cloisters to the north, and the cityscape of Inwood and the Bronx to the east. In autumn, the stately linden trees for which the terrace is named, turn a brilliant yellow, but it is an enriching visit in any season.

Make your way out of **Fort Tryon Park**, where our walk began, and walk south along **Fort Washington Avenue.** Just south of **185th Street**, enter **Bennett Park**.

Stop 2 → Inside **Bennett Park**

BENNETT PARK

Bennett Park is the highest natural point on Manhattan Island and as such, was an obvious location for a defensive fortification during the American Revolution. This ridge, including what is now Fort Tryon Park, was the site of the final and most crushing defeat of American forces during the battle for control of Manhattan Island. Fort Washington's loss in 1776 meant the end of American control of New York City for the remainder of the war.

The land upon which Fort Washington stood was bought and sold several times over the following century as an increasing number of wealthy New Yorkers sought land uptown for country estates or simply as investment properties. In 1871 this ridge was purchased by James Gordon Bennett, prominent founder of the *New York Herald* newspaper. On his death the following year, the land and the newspaper passed to his son, James Gordon Bennett, Jr. The younger Bennett was a bit of an eccentric, known in social circles as much for his business acumen as for his knack for scandal. According to a 1962 biography, Bennett "spent an estimated $30 to $40 million as an internationally famous yachtsman, sportsman, womanizer, and boon companion of some of the more raffish members of the European aristocracy."[226]

It was Bennett who relocated the *New York Herald* to 35th Street in 1893, renaming the plaza in front of the headquarters building Herald Square in its honor. That building, long since demolished, was designed as a sumptuous Venetian palazzo, with a street-level pedestrian arcade which invited New Yorkers to linger and watch the *Herald*'s presses at work within. Along the roofline

Fort Tryon Park, Billings Overlook

Fort Tryon Park, Billings Arcade

Fort Washington Avenue

Hudson View Gardens

181st Street near Cabrini Boulevard

stood a bronze statue of the goddess Minerva standing above a bell and two ringers, nicknamed Stuff and Guff, who heralded the hour. Fanning out from them were nearly two dozen bronze owls, Mr Bennett's obsession, some with illuminated green glass eyes which blinked out at the city by night.

James Gordon Bennett, Jr, loved owls. He loved them so much that, in addition to the owls adorning the *Herald* Building on 35th Street, he "had owls on his stationery, owned live ones, wore owl-engraved cuff links and wanted to be buried in a 125-foot [38-meter], owl-shaped tomb set atop a 75-foot [23-meter] pedestal."[227] The tomb, sketched out by the architect Stanford White only weeks before his death in 1906, was to be built here on Bennett's Washington Heights property, the highest natural point in all of Manhattan.

Bennett's highly unusual mausoleum would have been visible for many miles around and was planned to be a major tourist attraction. He instructed the sculptor, Andrew O'Connor, that the owl should be made of glazed granite and should "*glower* 'quite ferociously.'"[228] The interior was to be hollow, allowing visitors to ascend via a grand circular stairway to the owl's eyes, "which were to be windows looking out over New York City."[229] Suspended from the owl's head, hanging from two great chains, would be Bennett's sarcophagus. Following Stanford White's murder in 1906 (page 157), Bennett's grand postmortem plans were never executed.

When Bennett died in 1918, his tract of land on Washington Heights was divided and sold off for the development of modern apartment buildings. The one exception was the roughly 2-acre (0.8-hectare) parcel where Fort Washington once stood. It was kept clear and was ultimately sold to the city as parkland in commemoration of the Revolutionary War battle which was fought there. But the new park's name would honor the Gilded Age playboy who had hoped to be entombed there: James Gordon Bennett, Jr.

HUDSON VIEW GARDENS

Behind Bennett Park, on the west side of Pinehurst Avenue, stands an unusual apartment complex called Hudson View Gardens. These charming Tudor-revival buildings were completed by 1925 and provided not just sweeping views of the Hudson River but also some of the first truly modern co-operative apartments on this northern stretch of Washington Heights. The man behind Hudson View Gardens was Charles Vincent Paterno. Born in Italy, Paterno came with his parents to New York as a child in the 1880s. Though he obtained a medical degree from Cornell University, he transitioned to real estate following the death of his father, a longtime developer, in 1899.

Charles and his brother Joseph prospered, taking advantage of the city's rapid growth and the expansion of its transit system to build apartment blocks all across the city. Charles was well-off enough by 1907 that he purchased this tract of land just north of 181st Street and just west of the Bennett property. Here, he built one of the most unusual houses in all of New York. Situated on a bluff 150 feet (46 meters) above the Hudson River, the so-called Paterno Castle quickly became one of the best-known landmarks of upper Manhattan. Built of marble blocks, it looked like something out of a fairy tale and boasted such luxuries as a Turkish bath, a swimming pool, and a mushroom cellar. To extend the house's lawn, Paterno constructed an immense stone retaining wall topped with a pergola-shaded promenade. The whole project dragged on until 1916 and cost an estimated $500,000 to build.

Exit **Bennett Park's** west side and walk south along **Pinehurst Avenue**, downstairs to **181st Street**. Turn right and then right again onto **Cabrini Boulevard.** Look for the large black gate on the left

By 1920, development had begun to encroach on Paterno's estate, including next door on the former Bennett property. Rather than fight progress, he chose to profit from it, building Hudson View Gardens as a citadel of middle-class comfort directly adjacent to his clifftop dwelling. Barely a decade later, in 1938, Paterno chose to demolish his marble castle. In its place, he built the five immense red-brick towers, which now line the west side of Cabrini, containing some 580 apartments. Fittingly named Castle Village, the towers remain some of the most sought-after residences in Washington Heights.

Though the castle is gone, the immense retaining wall remains on the west side of the complex, visible from the Henry Hudson Parkway (it partially collapsed in 2005 but has been repaired). But more than just the wall survives. Look closely at the pair of crenelated marble pillars and the impressive iron fencing here on Cabrini Boulevard. Upon closer inspection, there is a golden letter "P" atop the fence posts: Paterno. This otherwise unassuming fence and gateway is one of the last surviving remnants "of the period when [Washington Heights] was a suburban section of New York City."[230]

Follow **Cabrini Boulevard** south

Stop 3 → At the corner of **179th Street** and **Cabrini Boulevard**, overlooking the ramps of the **George Washington Bridge**

GEORGE WASHINGTON BRIDGE

Plans for a bridge to cross the Hudson River had circulated, with varying levels of feasibility, since the colonial era. Groundbreaking ceremonies were actually held in 1895 for a bridge connecting Hoboken, New Jersey, to 23rd Street in Manhattan. And grand plans for a massive car and rail bridge at 57th Street were circulated for decades. But neither project became reality. It was only in the 1920s that construction actually began on a trans-Hudson span, though it would rise miles north of any previous planned iteration. Eventually named the George Washington Bridge, it connects Fort Lee, New Jersey, to Manhattan at 179th Street, reigning as the longest bridge on earth from its completion in 1931 until it was surpassed by California's Golden Gate Bridge in 1937.

Beyond the superlatives, the construction of the George Washington Bridge meant the destruction of dozens of buildings which lay in the path of its Manhattan landing.[231] Washington Heights was in the midst of a building boom when the first shovels entered the ground for the great new bridge, and the area was thickly settled with six- and 10-story apartment blocks, theaters, and churches. Twenty buildings, some of them less than a decade old, were razed between 1925 and 1927. The destruction continued in the 1950s when 82 buildings housing 1,835 people were destroyed to make way for a tangle of new ramps to more easily funnel automobiles between the bridge and the newly built Trans-Manhattan and Cross-Bronx Expressways.[232] Washington Heights was irrevocably split in two.

Standing at the corner of 179th Street and Cabrini Boulevard today, where some 300,000 cars rumble past each day, it is easy to forget that it wasn't always this way. Prior to the bridge's construction, Cabrini, Pinehurst, and Haven all continued uninterrupted through the neighborhood, each lined with schools, churches, houses, theaters, and the same sort of sturdy prewar apartment blocks which define so much of the surrounding neighborhood to this day.

Walk east along **179th Street**

Stop 4 → At **Fort Washington Avenue** and the **George Washington Bridge Bus Terminal**

GWB BUS TERMINAL

Designed by Pier Luigi Nervi, the George Washington Bridge Bus Terminal opened in 1963 as an uptown answer to Midtown's Port Authority Bus Terminal. Though forbiddingly monolithic at street level, and unfortunate in the way it darkens this block of Fort Washington Avenue, the structure is a marvel of space age engineering. Windowed concrete wings, more delicate than concrete ought to appear, define its roofline and help to bathe the interior departure concourse in light. The legendary architecture critic Ada Louise Huxtable said of Nervi's work: "The clarity of its structure and the grace of its forms combine to give new meaning to the unfashionable word 'beauty.'"[233] This is Nervi's sole completed project in the United States, and it is an under-appreciated landmark.

Follow **Fort Washington Avenue** south to **176th Street.** Turn right and enter **J Hood Wright Park** via the dead end midblock on the left. Inside the park, ascend to the overlook terrace on the west side

Stop 5 → On the overlook terrace at the northwest corner of **J Hood Wright Park**

J HOOD WRIGHT PARK

This tidy neighborhood park was named for James Hood Wright, a Philadelphia-born banker, businessman, and investor. Following their 1881 wedding, Wright and his wife Mary purchased a rocky parcel of high ground on Washington Heights and built for themselves a comfortable stone house which they called "The Folly."[234] Though James died in 1894, Mary spent much of the rest of her life at their uptown estate. Not long after she died in 1924, the land was taken by the city and earmarked for conversion into a public park.

By this time, the area around the Wright estate had become thickly developed with large apartment buildings and a new school. "This section is becoming rapidly congested," wrote one reader to *The Times* in 1925. "The traffic on the streets is dangerous to the life and limb of the children, who, without a proper playground, must play in the streets."[235] But the new park didn't open for more than another decade, stalled in part by the Great Depression. Much of its current appearance is in fact the result of a WPA project which oversaw the construction of its playground, overlook terrace, and recreation building. Today, its overlook affords one of the greatest views of the George Washington Bridge available anywhere in the neighborhood.

Aside from the view, don't miss the unusual 36-foot (11-meter) metal object standing in the center of the platform. This sculptural work of art by Terry Fugate-Wilcox was installed in 1974. It comprises eight compressed layers of aluminum and magnesium which will, according to artistic-scientific plan, "combine over many years to blend into a darker, mottled surface,"[236] hence the name of the work, *3000 AD*. Ten centuries from now, this column will theoretically remain in place, albeit chemically altered into a wholly new alloy.

Exit the park to walk east along **175th Street** to **Broadway**

Stop 6 → In **Plaza de Las Americas** in front of the **United Palace** to **Broadway**

UNITED PALACE

On the morning of February 22, 1930, a column of 1,000 local boy scouts marched up Broadway from 170th to 175th Street to celebrate the flag-raising ceremony which heralded the opening of the city's newest and grandest movie palace: the Loew's 175th Street Theatre.[237] With more than 3,400 plush red seats, its interior was designed by Thomas W Lamb to be a gilded fantasy of light, color, and elaborate "Indo-Persian" fretwork[238]. This was the last to open of the five so-called "Wonder Theatres" with which Loew's sought to redefine the very meaning of cinematic luxury. In 1929, Loew's opened the Valencia in Jamaica, Queens; the Paradise in the Bronx; the Kings in Brooklyn; and the Jersey in Jersey City.

Barely a month after the Jersey opened, the stock market crashed, heralding the start of the Great Depression. The Loew's 175th Street in many ways marked the apex of a golden age of cinema construction in New York. The Depression gave way to World War II, followed by technological advances such as television and air conditioning which made giant movie theaters like this increasingly outmoded and obsolete. The Loew's 175th Street closed in 1969. The other Wonder Theatres likewise shuttered in the 1970s (the Valencia and the Kings) or were chopped up into multiplexes (the Paradise and the Jersey) before eventually closing as well.

Miraculously, despite decades of wear and abuse, all five Wonder Theatres remain standing today. The Jersey and the Kings now serve as entertainment venues; the Paradise and the Valencia are both currently in use as churches. As for the former 175th Street Theatre, it is a blend of both. Renamed the United Palace of Spiritual Arts, it hosts religious services as well as concerts, film screenings, and special events. It hosted the gala premiere of the movie *In the Heights* in 2021 as well as the Tony Awards in 2023.

From the **United Palace**, turn south onto **Wadsworth Avenue**

United Palace

Highbridge Park

The High Bridge and Water Tower

Amsterdam Avenue at 165th Street

Sylvan Terrace

St Nicholas Avenue at 163rd Street

HOUSES OF WORSHIP

At the corner of 174th Street, note the lovely spire of Fort Washington Presbyterian Church, designed by Thomas Hastings and completed in 1914. Working with longtime partner John Merven Carrère as the firm Carrère & Hastings, he also worked on such landmark commissions as the New York Public Library's main branch (page 173) and the Frick Collection (page 217). Washington Heights is littered with dozens of incredible houses of worship including synagogues, both formerly and currently active, as well as Christian churches of every denomination, reflecting the neighborhood's heritage as a bastion of cultural diversity.

From **Wadsworth Avenue**, turn left on **173rd Street** and walk east to where it dead-ends at **Amsterdam Avenue** in front of the Highbridge Recreation Center. Enter the park on the south side of the recreation center, following the path past the swimming pool

Stop 7 → Atop the staircase in the **plaza** overlooking the Harlem River and the Bronx below

HIGH BRIDGE

The High Bridge was completed in 1848, making it by far the oldest bridge in New York City. While other bridges were built to carry horses and carriages and, later, automobiles, buses, and trains, the High Bridge was built to carry something even more vital into the city: water. New York in the 1830s was a city desperate for a reliable water supply, whether to drink and cook without fear of disease or to fight the fires which too regularly devastated the city and its still mostly wooden building stock. If these existential problems couldn't be addressed, New York risked fizzling out altogether, squandering its many advantages which by then included the heavy flow of commerce through its harbor thanks to the newly opened Erie Canal upstate.

And so New York City acquired hundreds of acres of property along the Croton River in Westchester County. They dammed the river, created the Croton Reservoir, and then piped that water down to Manhattan via more than 40 miles (65 km) of Roman-style, gravity-powered aqueduct. The single biggest obstacle in the project's path was the deep chasm of the Harlem River valley which separates Manhattan from the mainland. The High Bridge carried the pipeline and the life-giving water across the valley atop its 16 stone arches, after which it continued its journey downtown to reservoirs and, ultimately, into people's homes and businesses.

As the Croton water system expanded over the years, a reservoir was built atop the bluff on the Manhattan side of the bridge to provide a constant supply of water to the rapidly growing population at the north end of the island. To help pump the water up the bluff and maintain water pressure throughout upper Manhattan, an ornate water tower was constructed in 1872. By the mid-20th century, the old water system was superseded by newer pipelines and superior technology. The reservoir was given to the city and rebuilt as a swimming pool in 1936, part of the Highbridge Recreation Center. The water tower likewise remains a major city landmark, looming high above the Harlem River Drive, though it ceased to pump water in 1949.

As for the High Bridge itself, five of its stone arches were removed in the 1920s, replaced by a single steel arch to allow for the easier flow of river traffic. It was officially removed from the city's water system in 1949, after more than a century in service. Despite this, it was a popular local landmark, and a vital pedestrian link between upper Manhattan and the southwest Bronx, until its closure in the 1960s. It reopened to great fanfare in 2015 following an extensive restoration.

To visit the bridge, descend the intimidating staircase near the water tower. After taking in the views up and down the Harlem River, rather than climb the stairs back up, follow the asphalt path south into the lush greenery of Highbridge Park.

Follow the asphalt path south through the park before exiting the park via the basketball courts at **165th Street** and walk west from **Edgecombe Avenue**

Stop 8 → At **McKenna Square** at **St Nicholas Avenue**

HILLTOP PARK

From McKenna Square it is possible to see the postmodernist block of New York-Presbyterian's Morgan Stanley Children's Hospital just to the west on Broadway. That building occupies the site of Hilltop Park, a long-lost stadium, constructed in 1903 for the city's American League baseball team. Due to the stadium's impressive location atop Washington Heights, with sweeping views of the Hudson and palisades, the team was nicknamed the Highlanders. The team's logo, largely finalized by the 1909 season, was an interlocked N and Y worn on their chests and caps. When they departed Hilltop Park for the nearby Polo Grounds in 1912, their new home sat at the bottom of a bluff near the banks of the Harlem River, making their nickname obsolete. They were instead referred to by their secondary moniker, a play on their American League affiliation: The Yankees.

Turn south onto **St Nicholas Avenue**, part of the ancient Native American Wickquasgeck Trail, which later European settlers called the Kingsbridge Road

Stop 9 → On **St Nicholas Avenue** at the northeast corner of **163rd Street**, where a massive tree stands in the middle of the sidewalk

DINOSAUR ELM

This stunning elm tree is so large that two adults working together would have difficulty wrapping their arms around its trunk. It is an English elm and is thought to be at least 300 years old, an astounding age for any tree in such an urban environment. It stands on the edge of St Nicholas Avenue, the most ancient of Manhattan's major thoroughfares, meaning the tree would have shadowed the paths of countless travelers and notables making their way to and from New York City since the 18th century. A common tale purports that it was under this elm tree that General George Washington stood to watch the smoke rising from New York as it burned following his defeat there in 1776. The tree is old enough, and Washington did spend a month living at the nearby Morris-Jumel Mansion in September and October of that year, so it is almost guaranteed that Washington would have at least passed the tree, making it a living link to the nation's turbulent earliest days.

Continue south along **St Nicholas Avenue**

Stop 10 → Between **161st** and **160th Streets**, turn left onto the small staircase in the stone wall and enter **Sylvan Terrace**

SYLVAN TERRACE

Every visit to Sylvan Terrace is a surprise and a delight: a row of 20 wood-frame rowhouses, 10 on each side of the street, built in 1882 by speculator James E Ray who sold them to middle-class laborers drawn uptown by this formerly rural area's newfound accessibility via elevated train. The street itself roughly traces the original path of the carriageway which connected the nearby Morris-Jumel Mansion to the Kingsbridge Road (modern St Nicholas Avenue). Longtime mansion owner Eliza Jumel died in 1865, sparking a decade-long fight among her relatives over her estate. So it wasn't until the 1880s that her vast acreage on Washington Heights was carved up and sold for development, including that of Sylvan Terrace and its charming wooden houses.

These homes changed little until after World War II, when many of them were renovated to modern sensibilities: their clapboard facades were stripped down, replaced by aluminum, stucco, and asphalt. By the 1970s, it was hard to tell they'd ever been a cohesive whole. That began to change in 1979, when a Federal grant allowed for the houses to be restored to their original appearance at no cost to residents. Work was completed in 1981, except for one holdout at No. 16: its owner, Thelma Walker, objected to the renovations, saying "before this project began, each of us had houses that were different and we never minded. I liked it much better because I don't think much of the building materials they use nowadays."[239] Her house was eventually restored, completing the reunification of the 1882 row, and transforming it into one of the city's cherished secret spots.

Follow **Sylvan Terrace** east to **Jumel Terrace** and the entrance to the **Morris-Jumel Mansion**

Stop 11 → On the grounds of the **Morris-Jumel Mansion**

MORRIS-JUMEL MANSION

At the eastern end of Sylvan Terrace lies the oldest home in all of Manhattan. It is a startlingly large and, in architectural terms, extraordinarily modern home for its age, boasting a double-height Palladian portico, false-stone quoining (blocks at the corner of a building), and an octagonal wing on its north side. Its scale and style reflects the wealth and worldliness of its original owner, British Colonel Roger Morris and his wife, Mary Philipse Morris. Built in 1765, it has survived everything from the American Revolutionary War to 20th-century urban redevelopment, and remains one of the only places on Washington Heights where one can truly imagine how the area might have looked and felt during centuries long past.

"A house has a character given to it by the people who live in it, who are the soul of the house" explained a 1916 profile of the house's history. "A character for honesty, for truthfulness, for culture, for distinction. It is courted or shunned by its neighbors as they approve or disapprove of the people who live in the house." The Morris-Jumel Mansion is indeed "an aristocrat among houses."[240]

The Morrises who built the mansion as their country retreat were loyalists who fled New York at the onset of the Revolution, abandoning the house to be used by George Washington as his headquarters from September 14 to October 20, 1776, during the Battle of Harlem Heights. The Morris home survived the war but was confiscated and sold off by New York State in 1783 due to the Morris family's loyalty to King George III. The property was thereafter badly neglected for a generation, used briefly as an inn before sitting in decayed splendor amid its once-manicured lawns.

On July 10, 1790, it was once revisited by a nostalgic George Washington, now in his splendor as the first President of the independent United States. He and members of his new cabinet journeyed up the island to visit the site of old Fort Washington before hosting a dinner party at the Morris house (by then "in the occupation of a common farmer,"[241] per Washington's diary entry). The guest list included Washington, Vice President John Adams and his wife Abigail, Secretary of State Thomas Jefferson, Secretary of the Treasury Alexander Hamilton and his wife Eliza, and Secretary of War Henry Knox and his wife Lucy.

The Morris home was purchased in 1810 and restored by wealthy merchant Stephen Jumel. French by birth, he and his family made their fortune in Haiti before fleeing on the eve of the island nation's Revolution, which began in 1791. While establishing himself in New York, Jumel became acquainted with a most enigmatic and mercurial figure: the young, beautiful, and mysterious Eliza Brown. (Though she went by several names in her youth, including Madame de la Croix, her real name was most likely Elizabeth Bowen, born into poverty in Providence, Rhode Island, and possibly the daughter of a prostitute.)

The pair were married in 1804, though an oft-repeated tale purports that Eliza feigned fatal illness to pressure Jumel into the union. Once wed, "the sick lady recovered so rapidly that she was up the next day laughing at her new husband."[242] The Jumels were largely ostracized from New York Society, which was still too tightly wound with Knickerbocker (page 139) stoicism to overlook Eliza's checkered past. They found warmer reception in France, where they claimed friendship with Paris's Napoleonic elite. Their fortunes waning, the Jumels returned to New York permanently in the 1820s.

Stephen Jumel died on May 22, 1832, from injuries suffered during a fall from a wagon while traveling the Kingsbridge Road. He is buried in the churchyard of St Patrick's Old Cathedral (page 57). The very next year, in the parlor of her Washington Heights mansion, Eliza married Aaron Burr, even then still notorious for his killing of Alexander Hamilton almost three decades prior. Their union was short-lived, as Eliza accused her new husband of misusing her fortune. They separated after just four months of marriage, and Eliza enlisted none other than Alexander Hamilton, Jr, as her divorce lawyer. Burr died alone in a Staten Island boarding house on September 14, 1836, the very day the divorce was to be finalized.

Morris-Jumel Mansion

Broadway at 160th Street

The next three decades of Eliza's life were perhaps her most colorful, as she settled into increasingly demented seclusion. After several years of failed attempts to finally work her way into Society's inner circles, she retreated to her uptown estate and the company of no one but her retinue of servants. According to neighborhood legend, she hired several dozen out-of-work laborers from the city and had them form a sort of home guard and marching band for her. They kept sentry at her gates and marched in review before her. Though the specific tales may have been exaggerated in later years, "all the old residents of Washington Heights who remember Madame Jumel, remember her company of soldiers and the brass band."[243]

By the end of Eliza's long life, her grand mansion, which had been so carefully restored during her first marriage to Stephen Jumel, "had grown shabby for want of repairs. The paint was dingy. The grounds were unkept; weeds and bushes grew rank along the paths."[244] She kept just two servants for the whole estate: one working inside the house and one to oversee the grounds. Passersby reported hardly a light or any sign of life within, with barely a wisp of smoke trickling from the chimneys. The few people allowed to visit her reported that "her dress was slovenly and unkempt except when she put on her ill-assorted finery to sit in state on her dais in the great drawing-room, to receive some real or imaginary guest."[245]

Eliza Jumel died at her home on July 16, 1865, at what is thought to be at least 90 years old. Though she attempted to leave much of her remaining fortune to charity, her will was overruled on the basis of her aged mental state. An ugly and protracted legal battle ensued, with claims made by a purported illegitimate son, George Washington Bowen of Rhode Island, against Nelson Chase, husband of Eliza's niece and former ward, Mary Jumel-Bowen, and his children, Eliza and William. The highly publicized case dragged on for 17 years, but in the end, the Chases were victorious. They sold the Morris-Jumel Mansion in 1887.

In 1903, just as the city's first subway line prepared to open and Washington Heights sat poised for modern redevelopment, the Morris-Jumel Mansion was purchased by the city for $235,000. For more than a century, it has been maintained as an historic house museum, its grounds overseen by the city Parks Department. Standing in its gardens, with glimpses of long-ranging views still possible between high-rise buildings, the mind is able to conjure images of long-ago New York: of oaken timbers being milled to build the house for the Morris family, still under colonial rule; of General George Washington plotting his next moves from the house's octagonal parlor, or of President Washington returning with his cabinet a decade later; of Madame Jumel filling her rooms with French furniture and grand exaggerations. The Morris-Jumel Mansion is a testament not just to the history of Washington Heights, but to the entire history of New York and, indeed, the nation.

Leaving the **Morris-Jumel Mansion**, walk west along **160th Street** to **Broadway**, then turn left and follow **Broadway**

Stop 12 → At **Broadway** and **156th Street** and the entrance to **Audubon Terrace**

AUDUBON TERRACE

John James Audubon lived a fascinating and adventure-filled life. Born in Haiti in 1785, he was taken to France as a young child and was raised there, near the western city of Nantes. He moved to the United States in 1803 and spent much of the next four decades traveling around the remote reaches of the country drawing its birds and other wildlife. His artwork was compiled in printed volumes collectively titled *The Birds of America*, which were sold on subscription around the world. His work was "a monumental undertaking of its kind and of its time;" "a revelation" which "made common birds known to common people."[246]

In 1841, Audubon purchased a vast stretch of wooded land in upper Manhattan which he named Minnie's Land after the family nickname for his wife, Lucy Bakewell Audubon. The Audubon estate comprised everything between modern 155th and 158th Streets, from Amsterdam Avenue to the Hudson River. It was by all accounts a beautifully bucolic property, thickly wooded and stitched with freshwater streams which attracted a whole menagerie of birds and other wildlife which Audubon thrilled in observing. Amid the ancient forest, the Audubons built a two-story house with deep porches and large windows which welcomed the outside world in. "A secluded country house not entirely adapted to the scenery, but simple and unpretentious in architecture."[247]

John James Audubon lived a decade at Minnie's Land, "a short yet sweet twilight to his adventurous career."[248] He died there on January 27, 1851, and was buried at Trinity Cemetery, just across 155th Street, where a large stone cross monument memorializes him to this day. In the years following his death, Lucy Audubon carved the estate into several large lots which were sold to keep the family solvent. By 1860, Minnie's Land was home to nearly a dozen households and was more commonly referred to as Audubon Park.

By the turn of the 20th century, Audubon Park was beginning to be enveloped by the rapidly expanding urbanity of New York City. Aided in large part by the 1901 arrival of Riverside Drive, which cut diagonally across the property, and the 1904 opening of the city's first subway line beneath Broadway, all of Washington Heights was ripe for development. Anticipating the area's rise, railroad heir Archer Huntington purchased the southern portion of Audubon Park, bounded by 155th and 156th Streets, from Broadway to Riverside Drive, in 1904. There, he enlisted his cousin, Charles Pratt Huntington, to design a palatial new cultural center, "among the first of its kind in the country."[249]

Archer Huntington's cultural center on Washington Heights, aptly named Audubon Terrace, was ultimately home to half a dozen institutions: the Hispanic Society Museum & Library, which contains Archer's vast collection of Spanish and Portuguese art and artifacts; the American Geographical Society; the Museum of the American Indian; the American Numismatic Society; and the American Academy and Institute of Arts & Letters.

ENDNOTES

1. "Washington Taking Leave of the Officers of his Army At Francis's Tavern [sic], Broad Street, New York, December 4th, 1783," Lithographed and Published by Nathaniel Currier, 1848. The Metropolitan Museum of Art, Bequest of Adele S. Colgate, 1962. Accession Number 63.550.436. https://www.metmuseum.org/art/collection/search/661045
2. Ada Louise Huxtable, "Fraunces Tavern Controversy," *New York Times*, June 6, 1965, Section X, Page 15, https://nyti.ms/3AogUDw.
3. "Two Historic Places," *New York Times*, March 10, 1901, Page 20 https://nyti.ms/3X5ad1M.
4. "The Restoration of Fraunces Tavern," *New York Times*, March 17, 1907, Page 11 https://nyti.ms/3AsVkxw.
5. "Street Plan of New Amsterdam and Colonial New York," Designation Report (New York, NY, Landmarks Preservation Commission, June 14, 1983). https://s-media.nyc.gov/agencies/lpc/lp/1235.pdf.
6. "Delmonico's Building," Designation Report (New York, NY, Landmarks Preservation Commission, February 13, 1996). https://s-media.nyc.gov/agencies/lpc/lp/1944.pdf
7. *Buttonwood Agreement*, New York, NY, May 17, 1792. Securities and Exchange Commission Historical Society. PDF File https://www.sechistorical.org/collection/papers/1790/1792_0517_NYSEButtonwood.pdf (accessed August 16, 2024).
8. "Immigrants in the Progressive Era," Library of Congress, https://www.loc.gov/classroom-materials/united-states-history-primary-source-timeline/progressive-era-to-new-era-1900-1929/immigrants-in-progressive-era/ (accessed August 16, 2024).
9. "Trinity's New Stained Glass Window," Trinity Wall Street, May 30, 2022, https://trinitywallstreet.org/videos/trinitys-new-stained-glass-window (accessed August 16, 2024).
10. "Sixty-four New Skyscrapers Now Building," *New-York Tribune*, March 22, 1903, Part II, Page 1. *Chronicling America: Historic American Newspapers*. Lib. of Congress. https://chroniclingamerica.loc.gov/lccn/sn83030214/1903-03-22/ed-1/seq-17/.
11. "Equitable Building," Designation Report (New York, NY, Landmarks Preservation Commission, June 25, 1996), https://s-media.nyc.gov/agencies/lpc/lp/1935.pdf.
12. "Architects Back New City Zoning," *New York Times,* September 9, 1960, 60, https://nyti.ms/4dM1uY8.
13. "Greatest Banking House in the World, Planned for New York Federal Reserve Bank, to Occupy Nearly Whole Block in Financial District," *New-York Tribune*, November 16, 1919, Part II, 12. *Chronicling America: Historic American Newspapers*. Lib. of Congress, https://chroniclingamerica.loc.gov/lccn/sn83030214/1919-11-16/ed-1/seq-36/.
14. Christopher Gray, "Streetscapes/The Federal Reserve Bank of New York: Mix of Limestone and Sandstone, in Florentine Style," *New York Times*, November 11, 2001, Section 11, Page 7, https://nyti.ms/3yHN3Fo.
15. "Gold Vault," Federal Reserve Bank of New York, https://www.newyorkfed.org/aboutthefed/goldvault.html (accessed August 16, 2024).
16. David W. Dunlap, "Polished Marble and Sacramental Scuffs," *New York Times*, August 25, 2002, Section 11, Page 1, https://nyti.ms/3SSyypn.
17. Jeffrey I. Richman, *Brooklyn's Green-Wood Cemetery, New York's Buried Treasure* (Green-Wood Cemetery, 1998). "Notable Residents, .LINK.
18. Francis W. Maerschalck and G Duyckinck. *A plan of the city of New York from an actual survey, anno Domini, MDCC,LV.* (New York Printed, ingraved for, and sold by G Duyckinck, 1755) Map. https://www.loc.gov/item/73691802/ (accessed August 16, 2024).
19. Paul Goldberger, *The City Observed: New York, A Guide to the Architecture of Manhattan* (Random House, 1979).
20. Christopher Gray, "Streetscapes/25 to 41 Harrison Street: A Historic Renovation Improving With Age," *New York Times*, November 4, 2001, Section 11, Page 2, https://nyti.ms/46TtHK7.
21. "Tribeca West Historic District," Designation Report (New York, NY, Landmarks Preservation Commission May 1991), https://s-media.nyc.gov/agencies/lpc/lp/1713.pdf.
22. Eric Homberger, *Mrs. Astor's New York: Money and Social Power in a Gilded Age* (Yale University Press, 2002), Page 82.
23. "Arnold & Constable's Opening," *New York Times*, April 4, 1872, Page 5, https://nyti.ms/3AsctHM.
24. Aaron Shkuda, *The Lofts of SoHo: Gentrification, Art, and Industry in New York, 1950–1980* (The University of Chicago Press, 2016), Page 72.
25. "E. V. Haughwout Building, 488–492 Broadway," Designation Report (New York, NY, Landmarks Preservation Commission, November 23, 1965), https://s-media.nyc.gov/agencies/lpc/lp/0017.pdf.
26. "E. V. Haughwout Building," Landmarks Preservation Commission.
27. "E. V. Haughwout Building," Landmarks Preservation Commission.
28. Charles G. Bennett, "Moses Rebuffed on Expressway," *New York Times*, February 11, 1966, Page 43, https://nyti.ms/3X6en9T.
29. Christopher Gray, "Streetscapes/The Haughwout Building: Restoring a Richly Sculpted Venetian Palace," *New York Times*, January 1, 1995, Section 9, Page 5. https://nyti.ms/4ctj6GX.
30. Robert D. McFadden, "SoHo Gift to Wall St.: A 3 1/2-Ton Bull," *New York Times*, December 16, 1989, Page 31, https://nyti.ms/3WNcTzS.
31. "SoHo-Cast Iron Historic District," Designation Report (New York, NY, Landmarks Preservation Commission, August 14, 1973), https://s-media.nyc.gov/agencies/lpc/lp/0768.pdf.
32. Shkuda, *The Lofts of SoHo*, Page 37.
33. Roberta Smith, "Donald Judd, 65, Painter, Sculptor and Designer," *New York Times*, February 14, 1994, Page B8, https://nyti.ms/3X7N7b9.
34. Holland Cotter, "SoHo, Steadfast Bastion for Alternative Works," *New York Times*, April 21, 2011, https://www.nytimes.com/2011/04/22/arts/design/galleries-in-soho.html.
35. William Patton, "A Violent Past Still Haunts SoHo," *Villager*, September 11, 1975, Page 16. NYS Historic Newspapers, https://nyshistoricnewspapers.org/?a=d&d=tv19750911-01.1.1&e=-------en-20--1--txt-txIN-spring+AND+sands-------New+York--.
36. "Gay Activists Alliance Firehouse (Formerly Engine Company No. 13)", Designation Report (New York, NY, Landmarks Preservation Commission, June 18, 2019), https://s-media.nyc.gov/agencies/lpc/lp/2632.pdf.

37. "Gay Activists Alliance Firehouse," Landmarks Preservation Commission.
38. "Gay Activists Alliance Firehouse," Landmarks Preservation Commission.
39. Christopher Gray, "Streetscapes/139 Greene Street: The Longest-Running Restoration in New York City," *New York Times*, November 19, 1989, Section 10, Page 10, https://nyti.ms/3M82z0p.
40. The Gentleman's Companion, New York City in 1870, reproduced by *New York Times,* PDF accessed August 16, 2024. https://int.nyt.com/data/int-shared/nytdocs/docs/563/563.pdf.
41. Ada Louise Huxtable, "What's in a Wall?," *New York Times Magazine*, February 29, 1976, Pages 52–53, https://nyti.ms/4fL9JFw.
42. David W. Dunlap, "Saving Richard Haas's SoHo Mural, Chipped Away by Time and Vandals," *New York Times*, November 11, 2015, https://www.nytimes.com/2015/11/12/nyregion/saving-richard-haass-soho-mural-chipped-away-by-time-and-vandals.html.
43. George Dugam, "Old St. Patrick's Is Rededicated," *New York Times*, May 22, 1972, Page 38, https://nyti.ms/3AAWiYt.
44. Eric Ferrara, *The Bowery: A History of Grit, Graft and Grandeur* (The History Press, 2011), Page 16.
45. "Leaders of the Nation Laud Alfred E. Smith as a Truly Great American," *New York Times*, October 5, 1944, Page 12, https://nyti.ms/3YN2FSJ.
46. "To Remember 'Al' Smith," *New York Times*, December 30, 1944, Page 10, https://nyti.ms/4cBVYX6.
47. Hasia Diner, *Lower East Side Memories: A Jewish Place in America* (Princeton University Press, 2000), Page 19.
48. Christopher Gray, "Streetscapes/Eldridge Street Synagogue: A Prayer-Filled Time Capsule From the 1880s," *New York Times*, May 19, 1996, Section 9, Page 7, https://nyti.ms/3MatwAG.
49. Ronald Sanders, *The Lower East Side: A Guide to its Jewish Past in 99 New Photographs* (Dover Publications, Inc., 1979), Page 5.
50. "Anshe Slonim Synagogue (Originally Anshe Chesed Synagogue), 172–176 Norfolk Street," Designation Report (New York, NY, Landmarks Preservation Commission, February 10, 1987), https://s-media.nyc.gov/agencies/lpc/lp/1440.pdf.
51. "F.Y.I.: Lenin and a Crazy Clock," *New York Times*, July 27, 1997, Section 13, Page 2, https://nyti.ms/3X7wc8o.
52. "Aldermen Name Park For Roosevelt's Mother," *New York Times*, March 14, 1934, Page 21, https://nyti.ms/4cspfTU.
53. Diner, *Lower East Side Memories*, Page 47.
54. "East Village/Lower East Side Historic District," Designation Report (New York, NY, Landmarks Preservation Commission October 9, 2012), https://s-media.nyc.gov/agencies/lpc/lp/2491.pdf.
55. "Horror in East River," *New-York Tribune*, June 16, 1904, Page 1, *Chronicling America: Historic American Newspapers*. Lib. of Congress, https://chroniclingamerica.loc.gov/lccn/sn83030214/1904-06-16/ed-1/seq-1/.
56. Ada Calhoun, *St. Mark's is Dead: The Many Lives of America's Hippest Street* (WW Norton & Company, 2016), XV.
57. Sylvan Fox, "Historic St. Mark's in the Bowery Robbed Again," *New York Times*, February 6, 1969, Page 18 https://nyti.ms/3WPUmTr.
58. Charles Lockwood, *Manhattan Moves Uptown: An Illustrated History* (Dover Publications, Inc., 1976), 60.
59. "Brown Building Originally Asch Building)," Designation Report (New York, NY, Landmarks Preservation Commission, March 25, 2003). https://s-media.nyc.gov/agencies/lpc/lp/2128.pdf
60. Elizabeth McCracken, "Out of the Fire: A narrow escape from a deadly inferno shaped a long life," *New York Times*, December 30, 2001, "The Lives They Lived," Pages 19–20. https://nyti.ms/3WR2ymJ.
61. "141 Men and Girls Die in Waist Factory Fire," *New York Times*, March 26, 1911, Page 1, https://nyti.ms/3XYsrSa
62. Douglas Martin, "Rose Friedman, Last Survivor of Triangle Fire, Dies at 107," *New York Times*, February 17, 2001, Page B8, https://nyti.ms/3Z62vpV.
63. Edmund T. Delaney, *New York's Greenwich Village* (Barre Publishers, 1968), Page 123.
64. Edmund T Delaney and Charles Lockwood, *Greenwich Village: A Photographic Guide* (Dover Publications, Inc., 1976), Page 36.
65. "Julius' Bar Building," Designation Report (New York, NY Landmarks Preservation Commission, December 6, 2022), https://s-media.nyc.gov/agencies/lpc/lp/2663.pdf.
66. David M.Halbfinger, "For a Bar Not Used to Dancing Around Issues, Dancing Is Now the Issue," *New York Times*, July 29, 1997, Page B5, https://nyti.ms/3SQt8ei.
67. Jerry Lisker, "Homo Nest Raided, Queen Bees Are Stinging Mad," *New York Daily News*, July 6, 1969. Stonewall Forever, The Stonewall Riots Collection, https://stonewallforever.org/monument/homo-nest-raided-queen-bees-are-stinging-mad-from-new-york-daily-news-july-6-1969/ (accessed August 16, 2024).
68. Lacey Fosburgh, "Thousands of Homosexuals Hold A Protest Rally in Central Park," *New York Times*, June 29, 1970, Page 1, https://nyti.ms/4dhdVv3.
69. Fosburgh, "Thousands," https://nyti.ms/4dhdVv3.
70. Halbfinger, "Dancing," https://nyti.ms/3M7YnOd.
71. "The Realty Market: Old Greenwich Presents Mass of Ruins Along Subway and Seventh Avenue Work," *New York Times*, August 2, 1914, Section X, Page 13, https://nyti.ms/3yH4Ix0.
72. "The Snake Pit," from a Gay Activists Alliance Flyer, March 1970, NYCLGBTSites.org, https://www.nyclgbtsites.org/site/the-snake-pit/ (accessed August 16, 2024).
73. Fred W. McDarrah and Patrick J. McDarrah, *The Greenwich Village Guide* (A Capella Books, 1992), Page 86.
74. Andrew Dolkhart, *The Row House Reborn* (The Johns Hopkins University Press, 2009), Page 155.
75. "Cemetery Made a Public Park," *The Urn: A Monthly Journal Devoted to the Interests of Cremation*, June 25, 1894. Pages 8–9. Google Books (accessed August 16, 2024) https://www.google.com/books/edition/The_Urn/o9AsAAAAYAAJ?hl=en&gbpv=0
76. "Move to Condemn 11th Ave. Tracks," *New York Times*, September 24, 1907, Page 5, https://nyti.ms/4cxXycg.
77. R. L. Duffus, "Era of New Splendor Opens for West Side," *New York Times*, July 14, 1929, Section XX, Page 3, https://nyti.ms/4fLnnlV.
78. Mervyn Rothstein, "From Its Cookies Glory To Warehouse to Offices," *New York Times*, April 8, 1998, Page B6, https://nyti.ms/3SWfZ3E.
79. "Up Broadway to the Shopping District," *New York Times*, January 1, 1899, Illustrated Magazine Supplement, Page 2, https://nyti.ms/4fVyxdV.
80. "Big Store Thrown Open," *New York Times*, September 13, 1896, Page 16, https://nyti.ms/3AFMa0B.

81. Christopher Gray, "Streetscapes/401 West 21st Street: The Home of the Man Who Planned Chelsea," *New York Times*, October 20, 1996, Section 9, Page 4, https://nyti.ms/4fVeNXS.
82. "Washington Mews to Become a Latin Quarter," *New York Times*, December 19, 1915, Section 4 Page 8. https://nyti.ms/3YbACvy
83. "John Jacob Astor," *New-York Tribune*, March 30, 1848, Page 2, *Chronicling America: Historic American Newspapers*. Lib. of Congress, https://chroniclingamerica.loc.gov/lccn/sn83030213/1848-03-30/ed-1/seq-2/.
84. H. I. Brock, "Father of Good Father Knickerbocker," *New York Times*, April 2, 1933, Section 6, Page 12, https://nyti.ms/4dPoB3R.
85. H. M. Ranney (Firm), "Account of the terrific and fatal riot at the New-York Astor Place Opera House, on the night of May 10th, 1849," from the Columbia University Library Archive Page 6, https://dlc.library.columbia.edu/durst/cul:hdr7sqv9t6 (accessed August 21, 2024).
86. "Vision," About Cooper Union, accessed October 6, 2024, https://cooper.edu/about
87. "The Presidential Campaign: Another Republican on the Stump," *New York Herald*, February 28, 1865, Page 2. Chronicling America: Historic American Newspapers. Lib. of Congress. https://www.loc.gov/item/sn83030313/1860-02-28/ed-1/
88. Eric Homberger, *Mrs. Astor's New York: Money and Social Power in a Gilded Age* (Yale University Press, 2002), Page 137.
89. Eric Homberger, *Mrs. Astor's New York: Money and Social Power in a Gilded Age* (Yale University Press, 2002), Page 137.
90. "An Hour in the Astor Library," *New York Daily Tribune*, March 25, 1856, Page 2. Chronicling America: Historic American Newspapers. Lib. of Congress. https://chroniclingamerica.loc.gov/lccn/sn83030213/1856-03-24/ed-1/seq-5/
91. New York City alderman John Pettigrew, letter on the matter dated March 11, 1845, from the archive of the Center for Brooklyn History.
92. Eric Homberger, *Mrs. Astor's New York: Money and Social Power in a Gilded Age* (Yale University Press, 2002), Page 235.
93. Elizabeth Drexel Lehr, *King Lehr and the Gilded Age* (JB Lippincott Company, 1935), Page 15.
94. "Mrs. Stuyvesant Fish Has Come to be Known as New York's Best-Dressed Woman," *St. Louis Republic*, July 13, 1902, Magazine Section Page 8, *Chronicling America: Historic American Newspapers*. Lib. of Congress, https://chroniclingamerica.loc.gov/lccn/sn84020274/1902-07-13/ed-1/seq-44/.
95. William Winter, *Life and Art of Edwin Booth* (MacMillan and Company, 1894), Page 61, a letter from Booth to Rev. Samuel Osgood, March 7, 1863.
96. Winter, Life and Art of Edwin Booth, Pages 94–95.
97. Winter, Life and Art of Edwin Booth, Page 209.
98. *Artistic Houses*, Volume 2 Part 1 (D Appleton and Company, 1884), Page 61, PDF File from Archive.org https://ia600506.us.archive.org/12/items/Artistichouses2/Artistichouses2.pdf (accessed August 20, 2024).
99. TILDEN v. GREEN et al, 28 N.E. 880, 130 N.Y. 29 (Court of Appeals of New York, Second Division, 1891).
100. "Building Stones," *New York Times*, November 16, 1854, Page 2, https://nyti.ms/3TY2MYk
101. "The First Brownstone Front," *New York Times*, January 15, 1926, Page 20, https://nyti.ms/47Uyg7q
102. "Building Stones," Page 2.
103. James C. Young, "Brownstone Age is Coming to a Close," *New York Times*, January 10, 1926, Section 4, Page 11, https://nyti.ms/4dOQU2y.
104. Robert A. M. Stern, Gregory Gilmartin and John Massengale, *New York 1900* (Rizzoli International Publications, Inc., 1983), Page 15.
105. "Evelyn Nesbit, 82, Dies in California," *New York Times*, January 19, 1967, Page 1 and 31, https://nyti.ms/4dQqc9D.
106. Wayne Craven, *Gilded Mansions: Grand Architecture and High Society* (WW Norton & Company, 2009), Page 34.
107. Alfred Hoyt Granger, *Charles Follen McKim: A Study of His Life and Work* (Houghton Mifflin Company, 1913), Page 47.
108. "Mr. Morgan's Great Library," *New York Times*, December 4, 1908, Page 1, https://nyti.ms/2YVysAT.
109. "Full Text of the Will of J. Pierpont Morgan," *New York Times*, April 20, 1913, https://nyti.ms/3SXhv5q.
110. "(Former) James Hampden and Cornelia Van Rensselaer Robb House, 23 Park Avenue," Designation Report (New York, NY, Landmarks Preservation Commission, November 17, 1998). https://s-media.nyc.gov/agencies/lpc/lp/2026.pdf.
111. "James F.D. Lanier Residence, 123 East 35th Street," Designation Report (New York, NY, Landmarks Preservation Commission, September 11, 1979), https://s-media.nyc.gov/agencies/lpc/lp/1048.pdf.
112. "Idaho's Monte Cristo," *New York Sun*, October 28, 1894, Section 2, Page 7, *Chronicling America: Historic American Newspapers*. Lib. of Congress, https://chroniclingamerica.loc.gov/lccn/sn83030272/1894-10-28/ed-1/seq-19/.
113. "Idaho's Monte Cristo," *New York Sun*.
114. Wayne Craven, *Gilded Mansions: Grand Architecture and High Society* (WW Norton & Company, 2009), Page 354.
115. Gene Cohn, NEA Service Write, "What Will Become of Huge 150 Million Wendel Fortune?," *Brownsville Herald* via NEA Service, August 9, 1930, Page 2, *Chronicling America: Historic American Newspapers*. Lib. of Congress, https://chroniclingamerica.loc.gov/lccn/sn86063730/1930-08-09/ed-1/seq-2/.
116. Richard Barry, "The Passing of the 'Recluse of Fifth Avenue,'" *New York Times*, December 6, 1914, Section 6, Page 9, https://nyti.ms/4fSuCi8.
117. "Ella Wendel Rests in Vault With Kin," *New York Times*, March 16, 1931, Page 12, https://nyti.ms/4dwCDHY.
118. "Public Library Plans," *New-York Tribune*, December 5, 1897, Part 2, Page 3, *Chronicling America: Historic American Newspapers*. Lib. of Congress. https://chroniclingamerica.loc.gov/lccn/sn83030214/1897-12-05/ed-1/seq-13/.
119. "Vanderbilt's Latest Claims to Fame," *New York Times*, November 17, 1871, Page 4, https://nyti.ms/3yN2Se5.
120. "Grand Central Terminal Interior," Designation Report (New York, NY, Landmarks Preservation Commission, September 23, 1980), https://s-media.nyc.gov/agencies/lpc/lp/1099.pdf.
121. "Grand Central: Its Heart Belongs to Dada," *New York Times*, June 23, 1968, Section 4, Page 10, https://nyti.ms/3WY3tBA.
122. Diane Henry, "Jackie Onassis Fights for Cause," *New York Times*, January 31, 1975, Page 37, https://nyti.ms/3WYnRCG.

123. "Vanderbilts Spend Millions for Self-Protection," *New York Times*, May 1, 1904, Part 2, Page 1, https://nyti.ms/4g84gcf.
124. Meyer Berger, "About New York," *New York Times*, January 16, 1957, Page 27, https://nyti.ms/3MfY5Vy.
125. "Vanderbilt Home Being Torn Down," *New York Times*, September 18, 1947, Page 27, https://nyti.ms/4cwcebP.
126. Sara Cedar Miller, *Before Central Park* (Columbia University Press, 2020), Page 340.
127. Four-Footed Philistines," *New York Times*, October 17, 1885, Page 8, https://nyti.ms/3U0xm3I
128. Central Park in 1871," *New York Times*, June 5, 1921, Section 6 Page 11, https://nyti.ms/4eRXtBV
129. Sara Cedar Miller, *Central Park, An American Masterpiece* (Harry N. Abrams, Inc., Publishers, in association with the Central Park Conservancy, 2003), Page 56.
130. "Art Matters: Miss Emma Stebbins—The Bethesda Fountain at Central Park," *New York Herald*, May 17, 1873, Page 8, *Chronicling America: Historic American Newspapers*. Lib. of Congress. https://chroniclingamerica.loc.gov/lccn/sn83030313/1873-05-17/ed-1/seq-8/.
131. "The Bethesda Fountain," *New York Times*, June 1, 1873, Page 5, https://nyti.ms/3Xexcal.
132. "Overlooked No More: Emma Stebbins, Who Sculpted an Angel of New York," *New York Times*, May 29, 2019, https://www.nytimes.com/2019/05/29/obituaries/emma-stebbins-overlooked.html (accessed August 21, 2024).
133. Clarence C. Cook, *A Description of the New York Central Park* (FJ Huntington & Co., 1869. Washington Mews Books, an imprint of New York York University Press, Reprinted 2017.), Page 116.
134. Cook, *A Description of the New York Central Park*, Page 107.
135. Sara Cedar Miller, Central Park, An American Masterpiece, Page 116.
136. "Charles B. Stover Found Dead in Bed," *New York Times*, April 26, 1929, Page 25, https://nyti.ms/3Az6H7e.
137. "Central Park's Shakespeare Garden May Go," *New York Times*, April 2, 1916, Magazine Section Page 10, https://nyti.ms/4dPzh2l.
138. Meyer Berger, "About New York," *New York Times*, July 25, 1956, Page 32, https://nyti.ms/3yCOvsV.
139. Elizabeth Barlow Rogers, *Saving Central Park, A History and A Memoir* (Alfred A. Knopf, 2018), Page 234.
140. Mervyn Rothstein, "Joseph Papp, A Force in the Theater for 4 Decades, Is Dead at 70," *New York Times*, November 1, 1991, Page A1 and D19, https://nyti.ms/3YPNZSZ.
141. Peter Salwen, *Upper West Side Story: A History and Guide* (Abbeville Press Publishers, 1989), Page 47.
142. John Kifner, "Central Park Honor for Jacqueline Onasses," *New York Times*, July 23, 1994, Page 23, https://nyti.ms/3ZY3AQQ
143. "Historical Notes: Quality," *TIME Magazine*, January 19, 1953, https://time.com/archive/6885530/historical-notes-quality/ (accessed August 30, 2024).
144. "A Wedding Amid Flowers," *New York Times*, November 19, 1884, Page 5, https://nyti.ms/4cPcsuV.
145. "Mrs. Astor's Life and Long Leadership of Society," *New York Times*, November 1, 1908, Magazine Section Page 3, https://nyti.ms/3AG7282.
146. "One By One the Avenue's Landmarks Go," *New York Times*, February 21, 1926, Magazine Section Page 4, https://nyti.ms/4dLZTC2.
147. U.S. Census [June 1, 1900], New York, New York, Borough of Manhattan; ED 783, sh. 2; lines 35–50. From Ancestry.com (accessed August 30, 2024).
148. "Sara Delano Roosevelt Memorial House, 47-49 East 65th Street," Designation Report (New York, NY, Landmarks Preservation Commission, September 25, 1973). https://s-media.nyc.gov/agencies/lpc/lp/0702.pdf.
149. "Sara Delano Roosevelt Memorial House," Landmarks Preservation Commission.
150. "Seventh Regiment Armory Interior," Designation Report (New York, NY, Landmarks Preservation Commission, July 19, 1994). https://s-media.nyc.gov/agencies/lpc/lp/1884.pdf.
151. "The Seventh's New Home," *New York Times*, April 10, 1880, Page 8, https://nyti.ms/4g4sleo.
152. "The Seventh's New Home," *New York Times*.
153. "Hunter Dedicates 16-Story Building," *New York Times*, October 9, 1940, Page 27, https://nyti.ms/4cUxYyA.
154. Christopher Gray, "Streetscapes/69th Street and Park Avenue: Inside the Union Club, Jaws Drop," *New York Times*, February 11, 2007, https://nytimes.com/2007/02/11/realestate/11scap.html (accessed August 30, 2024).
155. Christopher Gray, "Union Club," *New York Times*.
156. "Union Club Forced Off 5th Av. By Trade," *New York Times*, June 20, 1927, Page 1, https://nyti.ms/3AMwhWw.
157. "Union Club's New $850,000 Home In Choice Private House Centre," *New York Times*, August 23, 1931, Section 11, Page 2, https://nyti.ms/4dZNbz4.
158. Thomas W. Ennis, "2 Park Ave. Landmarks Saved From Razing," *New York Times*, January 6, 1965, Page 1, https://nyti.ms/3X9Swxd.
159. "Miracle on 68th Street," *New York Times*, January 8, 1965, Page 28, https://nyti.ms/3WQP5uP.
160. Thomas W. Ennis, "Landmarks Bill Signed by Mayor," *New York Times*, April 20, 1965, Page 28, https://nyti.ms/4dJlH0y.
161. "Sculpture for the Hunt Memorial," *New-York Tribune*, January 6, 1901, Illustrated Supplement Page 6, *Chronicling America: Historic American Newspapers*. Lib. of Congress. https://chroniclingamerica.loc.gov/lccn/sn83030214/1901-01-06/ed-1/seq-42/.
162. Linda Greenhouse, "'Mean Guy' Thieves Get Central Park's Ugly Duck," *New York Times*, Page 78, https://nyti.ms/4dpKJ5b.
163. "A $5,000,000 Home for Henry C. Frick," *New York Times*, Page 4, https://nyti.ms/3yPFlne.
164. "Art's Most Princely Patron," *Washington Herald*, Page 32, *Chronicling America: Historic American Newspapers*. Lib. of Congress, August 15, 1973, https://chroniclingamerica.loc.gov/lccn/sn83045433/1915-04-11/ed-1/seq-32/.
165. "Death Reunites Waldos Who Had Been Years Apart," *New York Evening World*, May 28, 1914, Page 4, *Chronicling America: Historic American Newspapers*. Lib. of Congress. https://chroniclingamerica.loc.gov/lccn/sn83030193/1914-05-28/ed-1/seq-4/.
166. "Death Reunites Waldos," *New York Evening World*.
167. "R. Waldo's Mother Dies After Stroke," *New York Sun*, May 28, 1914, Page 11, *Chronicling America: Historic American Newspapers*. Lib. of Congress, https://chroniclingamerica.loc.gov/lccn/sn83030272/1914-05-28/ed-1/seq-11/.
168. "Gertrude Rhinelander Waldo Mansion, 867 Madison Avenue," Designation Report (New York, NY, Landmarks Preservation Commission, July 13, 1976), https://s-media.nyc.gov/agencies/lpc/lp/0927.pdf.

169. FRIENDS of the Upper East Side Historic Districts, *Shaped by Immigrants: A History of Yorkville* (Martin Printing, 2018), Page 5.
170. "175 East 73rd Street Building," Designation Report (New York, NY, Landmarks Preservation Commission, May 13, 1980), https://s-media.nyc.gov/agencies/lpc/lp/1064.pdf.
171. David Garrard Lowe, *Stanford White's New York* (Doubleday, 1992), Page 243.
172. "Pulitzer Mansion Leased to be Razed," *New York Times*, April 14, 1930, Page 15, https://nyti.ms/4fQHMfl.
173. "Upper East Side Historic District, Volume 1," Designation Report (New York, NY, Landmarks Preservation Commission, 1981), Page 809, https://s-media.nyc.gov/agencies/lpc/lp/1051.pdf.
174. "St. Jean Baptiste Church, 1067-1071 Lexington Avenue," Designation Report (New York, NY, Landmarks Preservation Commision, November 19, 1969), https://s-media.nyc.gov/agencies/lpc/lp/0420.pdf.
175. "The New York Society Library, 53 East 79th Street," Designation Report (New York, NY, Landmarks Preservation Commission, February 15, 1967), https://s-media.nyc.gov/agencies/lpc/lp/0427.pdf.
176. David Garrard Lowe, *Stanford White's New York* (Doubleday, 1992), Page 251.
177. Lowe, *Stanford White's New York*, Page 255.
178. "New York University Institute of Fine Arts (Formerly James B. Duke Mansion)," Designation Report (New York, NY, Landmarks Preservation Commission, September 15, 1970), https://s-media.nyc.gov/agencies/lpc/lp/0668.pdf.
179. "Jas. Buchanan Duke, Tobacco King, 68, Dies of Pneumonia," *New York Times*, October 11, 1925, Page 1, https://nyti.ms/3WVwv50.
180. Ada Louise Huxtable, "The 'Pathetic Fallacy' Or Wishful Thinking at Work," *New York Times*, February 11, 1979, Section 2, Page 29, https://nyti.ms/4dWfO00.
181. "Metropolitan Museum Historic District," Designation Report (New York, NY, Landmarks Preservation Commission, 1977), Page 92, https://s-media.nyc.gov/agencies/lpc/lp/0955.pdf.
182. Morrison H. Heckscher, "An Edifice for Art," In *Making The Met: 1870–2020*, ed. Andrea Bayer with Laura D Corey (The Metropolitan Museum of Art, New York; Distributed by Yale University Press, 2020), Page 18.
183. Roberta Smith, "A Museum Finds Small is Beautiful," *New York Times*, November 16, 2001, Page E29, https://nyti.ms/3T36Kyn.
184. Ada Louise Huxtable, "That Museum: Wright or Wrong?," *New York Times*, October 25, 1959, *New York Times Magazine*, Page 16, https://nyti.ms/3Z0tpiH.
185. "The Cooper Union Museum," *New York Times*, September 26, 1897, *New York Times Illustrated Magazine,* Page 11, https://nyti.ms/3ALtPiK.
186. Heather Ewing, *Life of a Mansion: The Story of Cooper Hewitt, Smithsonian Design Museum* (Cooper Hewitt, Smithsonian Design Museum, 2014), Pages 21–22.
187. "56 East 93rd Street House (Formerly William Goadby Loew House)," Designation Report (New York, NY, Landmarks Preservation Commission, March 14, 1972). https://s-media.nyc.gov/agencies/lpc/lp/0437.pdf.
188. Lawrence E. Davies, "Slum Clearance Is Criticized For Cutting Emotional Roots," *New York Times*, December 4, 1957, Page 41, https://nyti.ms/4g4FxW4.
189. Peter Salwen, *Upper West Side Story: A History and Guide* (Abbeville Press Publishers, 1989), Page 136.
190. Christopher Gray, "Streetscapes/The Dakota: The Elusive Mystery of Its Name," *New York Times*, August 15, 1993, Section 10, Page 7, https://nyti.ms/4cR0lxk.
191. Nan Robertson, "The Fabulous Dakota Remains Symbol of Elegant Apartment Living Here," *New York Times*, September 7, 1959, Page 18, https://nyti.ms/3Xaoqtl.
192. Salwen, *Upper West Side Story*, Page 71.
193. "A Chair, A Flagstaff, A Woman and A Row," *New-York Tribune*, February 4, 1917, Part V, Page 1, *Chronicling America: Historic American Newspapers*. Lib. of Congress. https://chroniclingamerica.loc.gov/lccn/sn83030214/1917-02-04/ed-1/seq-37/.
194. Christopher Gray, "Streetscapes/Zabar's, Broadway Between 80th and 81st Street: As Its Horizons Widened, It Never Left Home," *New York Times*, November 10, 2002, Section 11, Page 9, https://nyti.ms/4dGVksp.
195. "Buddhist Statue Here," *New York Times*, September 12, 1955, Page 18, https://nyti.ms/3T9Zilo.
196. "Mr. And Mrs. Isidor Straus," *New York Times*, April 22, 1912, Page 10, https://nyti.ms/3T9LUgQ.
197. Andrew S. Dolkart, *Morningside Heights: A History of its Architecture & Development* (Columbia University Press, 1998), Page 1.
198. [No Title], *New York Times*, April 25, 1897, Sunday Magazine Supplement Page 2, https://nyti.ms/3TcQevW.
199. "Making Ready the Tomb," *New York Times*, July 29, 1885, Page 1, https://nyti.ms/4e8Yp4k.
200. "The Finest Subway in the World Opens This Week," *New York Sun*, October 23, 1904, Second Section Page 8, *Chronicling America: Historic American Newspapers*. Lib. of Congress, https://chroniclingamerica.loc.gov/lccn/sn83030272/1904-10-23/ed-1/seq-24/.
201. Dolkart, *Morningside Heights*, Page 204.
202. "College Girls At Work," *New York Times*, December 14, 1890, Page 13, https://nyti.ms/3MvVozq.
203. Dolkart, *Morningside Heights*, Pages 154-155.
204. George Hodges, *Henry Codman Potter, Seventh Bishop of New York* (The MacMillan Company, 1915), Pages 206–207.
205. Christopher Gray, "Streetscapes/The Cathedral of St John the Divine, Amsterdam Avenue Between 110th and 113th Streets: Much-Changed Century-Old Vision, Still Unfinished," *New York Times*, July 28, 2002, Section 11 Page 7, https://nyti.ms/3z4fvBC.
206. Jeffrey S. Gurock, *When Harlem Was Jewish 1870–1930* (Columbia University Press, 1979), Pages 14–15.
207. Gilbert Osofsky, *Harlem: The Making of a Ghetto* (Harper & Row, 1963), Page 77.
208. Gurock, *When Harlem Was Jewish*, Pages 31–32.
209. Osofsky, *Harlem: The Making of a Ghetto*, Page 91.
210. Jervis Anderson, "Harlem I: The Story of a Refuge," *The New Yorker*, June 21, 1981, https://www.newyorker.com/magazine/1981/06/29/harlem-i-the-journey-uptown (accessed September 2, 2024).
211. Osofsky, *Harlem: The Making of a Ghetto*, Page 153.
212. Jonathan Gill, *Harlem: The Four Hundred Year History from Dutch Village to Capital of Black America* (Grove Press, 2011), Page 94.
213. "Mount Morris Park Historic District," Designation Report (New York, NY, Landmarks Preservation Commission, November 3, 1971), https://s-media.nyc.gov/agencies/lpc/lp/0452.pdf.

214. Christopher Gray, "Streetscapes/128th St and 5th Ave, Former Site of the Harlem House Where the Collyer Brothers Kept All That Stuff: Wondering Whether A Park Should Keep Its Name," *New York Times*, June 23, 2002, Section 11, Page 7, https://nyti.ms/47dRZ1x.
215. "Harlem Agog as Hermits' Home Faces Opening by Court Order," *Washington Evening Star*, August 5, 1942, Page B6, *Chronicling America: Historic American Newspapers*. Lib. of Congress. https://chroniclingamerica.loc.gov/lccn/sn83045462/1942-08-05/ed-1/seq-31/.
216. Claude McKay, *Home to Harlem* (Harper & Brothers, 1928).
217. Christopher Gray, "Streetscapes/Astor Row on West 130th: In Harlem, Restoration of Rowhouses at Mid-Stage," *New York Times*, October 9, 1994, Section 9, Page 7, https://nyti.ms/4cPapqz.
218. Christopher Gray, "Streetscapes/Harlem's Lafayette Theater: Jackhammering the Past," *New York Times*, November 11, 1990, Section 10, Page 6, https://nyti.ms/4gkMWRk.
219. "St Aloysius Roman Catholic Church, 209–217 West 132nd Street," Designation Report (New York, NY, Landmarks Preservation Commission, January 30, 2007). https://s-media.nyc.gov/agencies/lpc/lp/2164.pdf.
220. Michael Henry Adams, *Harlem Lost and Found: An Architectural and Social History*, 1765–1915, (The Monacelli Press, 2002), Page 210.
221. Adams, *Harlem Lost and Found*, Page 112.
222. "St Nicholas Historic District," Designation Report (New York, NY, Landmarks Preservation Commission), March 16, 1967, https://s-media.nyc.gov/agencies/lpc/lp/0322.pdf.
223. "Rockefeller's Gift Unit of Bigger Park," *New York Times*, January 7, 1917, Page 8, https://nyti.ms/4cVSiPU.
224. "Rockefeller Dislikes Tryon As Name for Park He Donated," *New York Times*, September 11, 1930, Page 27, https://nyti.ms/47s2qPv.
225. "Fort Tryon Park," Designation Report (New York, NY, Landmarks Preservation Commission, September 20, 1983), https://s-media.nyc.gov/agencies/lpc/lp/1417.pdf.
226. Richard O'Connor, *The Scandalous Mr. Bennett* (Doubleday, 1962), Page 9.
227. Alex Vadukul, "With a Bird's Eye View of Herald Square, Seeing All but Noticed by Few," *New York Times*, November 1, 2013, https://www.nytimes.com/2013/11/02/nyregion/with-a-birds-eye-view-of-herald-square-seeing-all-but-noticed-by-few.html.
228. O'Connor, *The Scandalous Mr. Bennett*, Page 226.
229. "Unfinished Tomb of James Gordon Bennett," *New York Times*, May 26, 1918, Magazine Section Page 5, https://nyti.ms/3Zb89ag.
230. "Paterno Castle to be Demolished," *New York Times*, August 7, 1938, Section 11, Page 1, https://nyti.ms/4gaLnVL.
231. "Land for the New Hudson River Bridge Approaches to Cost Over $10000,000," *New York Times*, April 20, 1930, Section 11, Page 14, https://nyti.ms/3AOCt08.
232. Bernard Stengren, "Houses Giving Way for Roads To George Washington Bridge," *New York Times*, September 24, 1958, Page 35, https://nyti.ms/3XtJmwS.
233. Ada Louise Huxtable, *Masters of World Architecture: Pier Luigi Nervi* (George Braziller, Inc, 1960), Page 9.
234. "Mrs J Hood Wright Dies," *New York Times*, August 1, 1924, Page 11, https://nyti.ms/3MuL0rK.
235. "A Park on Washington Heights," *New York Times*, April 3, 1925, Page 18, https://nyti.ms/3AX6avS.
236. Jill Gerston, "Park Gets 36-Foot 'Silver Wafer,'" *New York Times*, November 16, 1974, Page 35, https://nyti.ms/4dDzqGB.
237. "New Loew Theatre Opens," *New York Times*, February 23, 1930, Page 29, https://nyti.ms/3X8cND3.
238. "United Palace (Formerly Loew's 175th Street Theatre)," Designation Report (New York, NY, Landmarks Preservation Commission, December 13, 2015). https://s-media.nyc.gov/agencies/lpc/lp/0656.pdf
239. George W. Goodman, "Historic Homes in Harlem Restored," *New York Times*, February 27, 1983, Section 8, Page 6, https://nyti.ms/3Xwb9wl.
240. William Henry Shelton, *The Jumel Mansion* (The Riverside Press, 1916), Page 223.
241. "Diary entry: 10 July 1790," *The Diaries of George Washington*, vol. 6, *1 January 1790–13 December 1799*, ed. Donald Jackson and Dorothy Twohig. Charlottesville: University Press of Virginia, 1979, Pages 92–94, https://founders.archives.gov/documents/Washington/01-06-02-0001-0007-0010.
242. Shelton, *The Jumel Mansion*, Page 151.
243. Shelton, *The Jumel Mansion*, Page 181.
244. Shelton, *The Jumel Mansion*, Page 186.
245. Shelton, *The Jumel Mansion*, Page 188.
246. John Kieran, "A Book That Opened A New Window," *New York Times*, June 19, 1938, Section 7, Page 10, https://nyti.ms/3z7i99J.
247. Reginald Pelham Bolton, *Washington Heights Manhattan: Its Eventful Past* (Dyckman Institute, 1924), Page 111.
248. Bolton, *Washington Heights*, Page 112.
249. "Audubon Terrace Historic District," Designation Report (New York, NY, Landmarks Preservation Commission, January 9, 1979), https://s-media.nyc.gov/agencies/lpc/lp/1001.pdf.

ABOUT THE AUTHOR

Keith Taillon is a New York City historian whose research focuses primarily on the development of Manhattan in the 19th and early 20th centuries. He holds degrees in History and Urban Planning, and it is this academic background which informs his work and writing. In 2020, Keith walked every street of Manhattan, from the Battery to Marble Hill, and chronicled his journey on his Instagram account @ keithyorkcity. His walks, taken during the depths of the COVID-19 pandemic, attracted a devoted audience as well as profiles in Condé Nast Traveler, The Times of London, The New Yorker, and elsewhere. In 2021, Keith began offering historic walking tours of Manhattan and, through them, he has helped thousands of people to better understand its history. He has since been invited to be a guest lecturer at institutions across the city, including the Metropolitan Club, the Harvard Club, the Montauk Club, the National Arts Club, and the Cooper-Hewitt, Smithsonian Design Museum. Born in Plattsburgh, New York, he was an Air Force kid who was raised in Abilene, Texas. He moved to Manhattan in 2010 and now lives in Harlem with his partner, Clinton, and their cat, Rosie.

ACKNOWLEDGEMENTS

The seed which would evolve into this book was planted many years ago. To write a book, to see my words on printed page, has been a dream of mine as long as I can remember. It is a uniquely sweet thrill to see it come true. To thank everyone responsible for this book's completion would be to thank everyone in my life who's fostered, encouraged, or otherwise welcomed my love of history, buildings, and cities. To the public school system of Abilene, Texas, whose gifted and talented programs allowed me to research and write about our town's forgotten landmarks; to the faculty and staff of the Urban Planning graduate program at Hunter College, who taught me to write and research more professionally while thinking more broadly about the way cities function; to the vast network of authors, historians, professors, tour guides, podcasters, and bloggers whose work every day broadens my understanding of New York: thank you. Many of my most beloved sources of information are featured prominently in my endnotes, but I must specifically express gratitude for the existence of so many massive, often free archives which make my work so much easier: the Digital Collections of the New York Public Library, the Chronicling America project at the Library of Congress, the digital archive of the New York Times, and the diverse collections of the New York Society Library. I'd also be remiss if I didn't thank the people who took a chance on me and my work over the years: Will O'Connor, who gave me my first writing gig in 2019; Marc Tio, whose profile of me in 2020 helped bring my work to a wider audience; Carl Raymond, who's repeatedly welcomed me onto his brilliant podcast; Harriet Griffey, who connected me with the talented, patient folks at Hardie Grant and Quadrille who helped cobble my scribbles into cohesion. I remain endlessly grateful to everyone who's attended one of my lectures, joined me on one of my tours, shared my work with their friends and family, or otherwise supported me when none of my successes seemed assured or even likely. Thank you to my family, my original support system and lifelong cheerleaders. Most of all, though, thank you to my partner, Clinton, without whose support, love, and patience, none of this would be possible.

Quadrille, Penguin Random House UK,
One Embassy Gardens, 8 Viaduct Gardens,
London SW11 7BW

Quadrille Publishing Limited is part of the Penguin Random House group of companies whose addresses can be found at global. penguinrandomhouse.com

Published by Quadrille in 2025

www.penguin.co.uk

A CIP catalogue record for this book is available from the British Library

ISBN 978-1-78488-970-8
10 9 8 7 6 5 4 3 2

Publishing Director: Kate Pollard
Assistant Editor: Phoebe Bath
Designer: Stuart Hardie
Cartographer: Leanne Kelman
Copy-editor: Wendy Hobson
Proofreader: Vicki Vrint
Production Manager: Sabeena Atchia

Colour reproduction by p2d

Printed in China by C&C Offset Printing Co., Ltd.

The authorised representative in the EEA is Penguin Random House Ireland, Morrison Chambers, 32 Nassau Street, Dublin D02 YH68.

Penguin Random House is committed to a sustainable future for our business, our readers and our planet. This book is made from Forest Stewardship Council® certified paper.